Drought and Man

The 1972 Case History

Volume 1: **Nature Pleads Not Guilty**

Other IFIAS Publications

GARCIA, R. V.
Drought and Man
Volume 2: The Constant Catastrophe: Malnutrition, Famines and the Drought
Volume 3: Case Studies

KING, A.
The State of the Planet

KING, A. and HEDEN, C-G.
Social Innovations for Development
A Symposium in the IFIAS Ulriksdals Seminar Series

NOTICE TO READERS

If your library is not already a standing/continuation order customer to this series, may we recommend that you place a standing/continuation order to receive all new volumes immediately on publication. Should you find that these volumes no longer serve your needs, your order can be cancelled at any time without notice.

A Related Journal

WORLD DEVELOPMENT
The Multidisciplinary International Journal devoted to the Study and Promotion of World Development
Free specimen copy available on request.

Drought and Man

The 1972 Case History

Volume 1: Nature Pleads Not Guilty

by
Rolando V. Garcia

with a section on climatic variability
by
J. Smagorinsky

and special contributions from
M. Ellman
H. Gambarotta
S. Ruttenberg
J. Siotis
*Prepared at The Graduate Institute for
International Studies, Geneva, 1976-1979*

PERGAMON PRESS

OXFORD · NEW YORK · TORONTO · SYDNEY · PARIS · FRANKFURT

U.K.	Pergamon Press Ltd., Headington Hill Hall, Oxford OX3 0BW, England
U.S.A.	Pergamon Press Inc., Maxwell House, Fairview Park, Elmsford, New York 10523, U.S.A.
CANADA	Pergamon Press Canada Ltd., Suite 104, 150 Consumers Rd., Willowdale, Ontario M2J 1P9, Canada
AUSTRALIA	Pergamon Press (Aust.) Pty. Ltd., P.O. Box 544, Potts Point, N.S.W. 2011, Australia
FRANCE	Pergamon Press SARL, 24 rue des Ecoles, 75240 Paris, Cedex 05, France
FEDERAL REPUBLIC OF GERMANY	Pergamon Press GmbH, 6242 Kronberg-Taunus, Hammerweg 6, Federal Republic of Germany

First edition 1981

British Library Cataloguing in Publication Data

Garcia, Rolando V
Drought and man
Vol. 1: Nature pleads not guilty
1. Famines
2. Droughts
I. Title
II. International Federation of Institutes for
   Advanced Study
361.5'5'09047   HC79.F3   80-41115

ISBN 0-08-025823-9

Printed in Great Britain by A. Wheaton & Co. Ltd., Exeter

Foreword

In the late 1960s drought visited the Sahel region of Africa, which borders the Sahara Desert on the south and separates it from the Savannah farther to the south. The drought was not exceptionally severe compared to some that struck earlier in the century. However, it triggered a catastrophic train of events that brought the stark tragedy of famine to millions at its climax in 1972, a year also characterized by drought in India, the USSR, Australia and elsewhere.

This volume, "Nature Pleads Not Guilty", seeks to interpret the drought and the causes of the human anguish that followed in the Sahel and elsewhere. The Sahel drought riveted the attention of Africa and the world on the plight of the world's poor and exploited people when visited by climate anomalies, and particularly by sustained failures in normal rainfall. Oppressed by a marginal condition of life, malnourished as the normal state of affairs, at the bottom of an exploitative social system, the poor of the Sahel were excessively vulnerable to the catastrophe that drought triggered. This exceptional instance of human disaster made the world both aware and alarmed. From Africa to Europe, America, the Soviet Union and elsewhere people responded to the distress signals. Emergency aid came to the victims, sometimes effective and sometimes not; deep political repercussions resulted; developed and developing countries established new policies and attitudes; books and articles poured forth, while the rains did not. This volume examines in depth The 1972 Case History, in its full global context.

The International Federation of Institutes for Advanced Study (IFIAS) and the Aspen Institute for Humanistic Studies (Aspen) responded to seek a deeper analysis of the causes of the disasters that culminated in 1972. In this year widespread and rather anamalously severe droughts struck not only in already parched African Sahel, but in many other important agricultural regions of the world. The result of the effort of IFIAS and Aspen is a provocative 38-month study conducted by Rolando A. Garcia and a distinguished team of collaborators. The many products of the study are documented in this volume and two sequel volumes.

In May 1974, 2 years after the drought of 1972 had galvanized world reactions, IFIAS and Aspen organized a seminar at the University of Bonn to establish priorities for studies that examine the impact of climate anomalies on man. *Drought and Man—The 1972 Case,* was identified as a top priority research need. From the discussions at Bonn also developed a recommended style of transnational and transdisciplinary research.

As emphasized at the Bonn workshop, the studies should probe deeply into the social, political, economic and ethical implications of the climate anomaly. The studies should be the independent product of distinguished scientists and scholars, unfettered by preconceptions of IFIAS, Aspen or the project's financial sponsors. The studies should not avoid controversial areas or unpopular findings. The role of

Aspen, IFIAS and the sponsors was perceived as assuring that the resources for the work were available, that the work was done responsibly and on schedule, and that the findings reached public attention. It was made clear in the planning meetings that the findings, when finally adduced by the study authors, would be the sole responsibility of the study authors, and will not necessarily reflect the views of IFIAS, Aspen or the organizations that funded the study.

In February 1975 IFIAS and Aspen sponsored a specific 4-day international workshop to improve and refine the project design. This was held at the Aspen Institute in Berlin with participants from nine countries, including the USSR. The workshop presented numerous recommendations for the study author, not yet at that time identified. This workshop again emphasized that the commissioned study should be the independent product of the study author and his team. It should not fear stating unpalatable conclusions or identifying mistakes of maladministration of measures intended to alleviate the adversity of the 1972 climate events. Such criticism, the workshop emphasized, would be of constructive value. The workshop also recommended creating a steering committee to assist in selection of a study author, and to monitor later progress. The workshop initiated the process that led to the felicitous choice of Professor Rolando A. Garcia to head the study.

The findings of Garcia and his colleagues are important, novel and in some instances controversial. Garcia and his colleagues assert that many of the assumptions underlying the responses of the more developed countries to the drought are faulty. At stake, they claim, is the whole future development process and the role of science and technology transfer in development. Nothing short of a total structural change in the underlying practices that comprise the "normal" for today's society will reduce the developing world's vulnerability to climate adversity as a trigger of socio-economic instability and frequent catastrophe. If the authors are right, vast alterations of development strategies are desperately important to the rich and the poor of the world, and to capitalist and socialist socio-political systems alike. A return to normal, as after the Sahel drought, cannot be a return to the precarious and miserable condition that prevailed before the drought, if we are to avoid repeated future collapses or to learn any lessons from the past disasters.

It is a pleasure for the authors of this Foreword to recommend close and mindful attention to the study and a critical assessment of its conclusions and recommendations. If the assertions of the Garcia study promote disagreement, let the disagreements be fully debated, and if necessary, let additional viewpoints be adduced; if the analyses are found to be valid, let them form the basis for resolute constructive action.

WALTER ORR ROBERTS
IFIAS Climate Project Director
Aspen Institute for Humanistic Studies
Boulder, Colorado

SVEN EVTEEV
Assistant Executive Director
Programme Bureau
UNEP, Nairobi

Acknowledgement

To be in charge of an IFIAS project has been a unique experience in many respects. The association with a large number of distinguished researchers around the world was a continuous source of challenging problems, inspiring ideas and original knowledge. I cannot do justice to all of them. The "list of collaborators" includes only the names of those who sent written contributions or participated in at least one of the workshops organized by the project. The final responsibility for what is said in the present volume is, however, entirely mine, except for the various signed papers included as annexes to several chapters.

It should be emphasized that my judgements may not be shared by all collaborators. Although I sometimes do contradict what has been said, in writing, by some contributors, I am grateful to them because they pushed my analysis into deeper grounds.

IFIAS provided a working frame entirely free from pressures or constraints. There were no commitments other than serving the objectives of the project, and no submission to principles other than those involved in a truly scientific enterprise.

A strong support from IFIAS officers was present whenever it was needed. It was remarkable at some crucial moments, in particular when it became clear that the project would not develop as it had been expected at the outset: a few months after the project began, the research took a direction that departed from the type of work that was envisaged and outlined at the briefing sessions. Moreover, a number of conclusions began to emerge touching highly sensitive political issues. Some of them were very controversial. I did not hesitate to take clean-cut positions whenever the analysis indicated that they were based on solid grounds. Such positions were sometimes of such a nature that one could assume that they might not be liked by some of the sponsoring institutions who provided financing for the project, not even by IFIAS members. This in no way influenced the attitude of IFIAS officers.

I want to express my profound gratitude to an Institution that was able to create and preserve such an atmosphere of complete intellectual freedom.

ROLANDO GARCIA

Contents

List of Contributors to the Drought and Man Project

Carlos ABALO
Solomon AYALEW
Debabar BANERJI
Moises BEHAR
José Maria BENGOA
Pierre BONTE
Michael J. ELLMAN
José Carlos ESCUDERO
Gilbert ETIENNE
Santiago FUNES
Jorge GADANO
Hector GAMBAROTTA
J. DIAZ GARCES
Enriqueta GARCIA
Alicia GILLONE
C. A. GONZALEZ GARLAND
Raul H. GREEN
Daniel R. GROSS
Bärbel INHELDER
Peter KIANGI

Elsa LOPEZ
Oscar MAGGIOLO
G. MARTINS DIAS
Adolfo MASCARENHAS
Pedro MOSINO
Edison NUNES
Richard ODINGO
Laban OGALLO
A. ONATE VILLARREAL
E. ORTIZ CRUZ
Jean PALUTIKOF
P. R. PISHAROTY
Juan Carlos PORTANTIERO
Stanley RUTTENBERG
Fabrizio SABELLI
P. SHARMA
Jean SIOTIS
Joseph SMAGORINSKY
Pierre SPITZ
Benedict STAVIS

Other Participants

Julius ADEM
Michel BAUMER
Jean-Pierre GONTARD
J. GONZALEZ M.
Shinichi ICHIMURA
Robert KATES

Raul LIVAS VERA
James McQUIGG
Nancy MIKESELL
G. PATINO
Aloune SALL
V. SUBRAMANIAN

General Introduction

Climate has been held responsible for the rise and decay of civilizations. More recently, modern civilization has been held responsible for fundamental climatic changes in the remote past are overwhelming although the "why" and the "how" remain unanswered. Evidences for climatic changes in our century are far from conclusive, and the predictions for the future no more than conjectures.

The fact that the life of a given society depends very much on climate is generally accepted. The nature and the scope of this dependency is little known and widely misunderstood. There is a tendency to consider both climate itself and the climatic fluctuations as a *given*. Society is thus conceived as a passive receptor of the "impact" of climate with only limited possibilities of "adapting" itself to a climatic variability. The conceptual unidirectionality of the climate-society relationship prevails even among those who seriously take into consideration the man-induced climatic changes they predict for the future. For the "impact" of society on climate is in this case only indirect through, for instance, some changes in the composition of the atmosphere. At each stage of this changing composition the climate of a geographical area would be well determined, and here again the direct impact of climate on the particular society concerned is taken to be one-way.

The bias in the interpretation of the climate-society relationship has a multiple origin. There is, in the first place, a long tradition that tends to blame nature for many of the misfortunes of mankind. This tendency is so strong that causal chains are often turned upside down: effects are taken as causes and vice versa. The responsibility is thus allocated to the wrong actors.

There is, in addition, an intrinsic difficulty in the subject that makes it hard to interpret or even to detect the interaction process. The root of the problem can be found, as is so often the case in the history of science, in a wrong formulation of the questions to be asked. The most dramatic advances in the history of human thought came about not as a consequence of the discovery of new answers for old problems but as a result of the discovery of new questions for old problems. This process almost invariably led to a relativization of the concepts that had been accepted until then as possessing some sort of absolute character. In some cases the stroke of a genius was necessary to put it straight. Mankind had to wait for Einstein to find out that to be "simultaneous" or "successive" were not absolute properties of two events but a "fact" that only had a meaning with reference to a specific observer. And quantum mechanics went still deeper in introducing the observer and the observing instruments into the very definition of the concepts that were supposed to describe the "objective" properties of the physical world.

We had found a striking similarity between this evolution of modern physics and the problems we were confronted with when IFIAS asked us to investigate the "impact" of the extended droughts, *circa* 1972, on the society, at the national, regional and international levels. The difference was that we did not need to wait for an Einstein who would put some order in the conceptual framework. On the one hand, there were already a number of ecologists, agriculturalists and social scientists quite aware of the complexity of the interrelations between climate and society. To our surprise, however, we found no systematic treatment of these problems and no *mis au point* of any adequate methodology to deal with them. On the other hand, the fact that most studies we came across in this field were in need of a complete reformulation became fairly obvious as soon as we started asking some unorthodox questions.

Let us first clarify why we think that the climate-society relationship is generally ill-defined. We stated above that "there is a tendency to consider climate and climatic fluctuations as a *given*", and that "society is thus conceived as a passive receptor of the 'impact' of climate". In verbal discussions on these matters we have found readiness to accept this criticism, but for the wrong reasons. The usual answer is: "of course, we must take into consideration that society in turn modifies the climate". This may be true, but we do not mean only that. We refuse to consider society as a passive receptor of climatic "impact", not—or not only—because society may in turn influence the climate, but because climatic phenomena are only meaningful with reference to a certain society. In other words (and here we find the similarity with physics we referred to above), they are not absolute concepts describing a physical reality which is independent of man's actions. They are relative terms which—most of times implicitly—assume a certain kind of human activity.

A few simple examples may illustrate this notion. Droughts and floods are always associated with a "normal" distribution of rainfall levels of rivers and lakes, etc., on a certain territory. The curves of average precipitation or of river flow are, of course, determined by purely physical phenomena. But the definition of "drought" or "flood", with reference to those curves, is not. Spitz, in one of his contributions to this project,[1] provides a crystal-clear example:

> "A river in spate, up to certain level curves, is considered to be normal and it is used rationally for the production of flood plain crops, of which Egypt provides the best-known example. The spate becomes destructive when it exceeds certain curves, and it is then called flooding. Below other curves, again, an insufficient spate is identified with a drought situation."

Likewise, drought can only be defined with reference to a certain productive system. This fact is concealed when a drought situation is defined with reference to an average water supply for the region. For one forgets in this case that the departure from average beyond which there is a declared drought situation is a figure dictated by the type of production that is *expected* in that area.

It is therefore necessary to sharply distinguish between "water deficiency" and "drought". We shall take the view, in this Report, that *drought is the social perception of a water deficiency with reference to a normal condition socially defined*.

So far we have only considered what we may call the effects of the normal variability of climatic conditions. This variability is so ingrained in the production systems that we tend to ignore this close association and to speak of each situation as if it were only determined by physical phenomena. The true intermixed nature of

[1] "Drought, aridity and society", Introduction to Part Four of Volume 3.

each situation becomes apparent when we study the evolution of some territories that have undergone important changes is their agro-systems throughout the historical periods.

And yet we could say that once the characteristics of an agro-system over a certain territory are fixed (kinds of crops, type of technology being applied), then a drought situation may be exclusively defined in terms of hydrometeorological variables. Because then, and only then, can a relationship be established between water deficiency and output of production. However, this is true only up to a certain point. The interrelations between climate and the productive systems become much more complex in the case of pronounced anomalies in some hydrometeorological parameters leading to the so-called "natural disasters" or "natural catastrophes". In this case the relationship between water deficiency and output of production does not suffice to explain the catastrophe. For natural disasters are not physical phenomena. They are a social phenomenon induced by physical events. One of the main objectives of this Report is to show that this is so.

The above remarks may help to explain our approach to the problem as well as the very structure of the Report.

IFIAS' proposal to study in detail what happened to world climate in the early 1970s (particularly in 1972) was motivated by a serious preoccupation for social, economic and political events that resulted in much human suffering in various parts of the world and in a world food crisis. The problems were supposed to be the effects of climatic anomalies (droughts) occurring simultaneously in several continents.

A few months after the beginning of the Project an entirely different picture began to emerge. We became gradually convinced that the role of the drought in that period was much smaller than was assumed; that the nature of the link between the droughts and the social events referred to above was far from a simple cause-effect relationship; that, in some cases, the references to the drought in order to explain certain events was not at all justified; that, in other cases, the drought was just a trigger of events that would have occurred, sooner or later, without a climatic perturbation. From there on the main job was to find enough confirmatory evidences in favour or against this working hypothesis.

In order to accomplish this task it was necessary to count on the understanding, the expertise and the willingness to work of a large number of scholars around the world. We were very fortunate in obtaining such a collaboration. Research groups and individuals, sponsored by the "Drought and Man" Project, started working in a large number of universities and research institutes along similar lines of thought. They were established in Kenya, Tanzania, Senegal, Ethiopia, India, Mexico, Venezuela, Brazil, as well as in France, Switzerland and the United States. We wanted primarily to have a view of the problems from inside the countries, as expressed by those who not only knew but who also had lived through these problems. We also wanted the judgement of experienced and sympathetic outsiders. Several workshops were held in various countries in order to discuss local problems and to develop a common understanding with local researchers. In the mid-term international workshop held in Geneva (September 1977) thirty-six participants attended the discussions. The outcome of the work of so many national, regional and international research groups and individuals has been channelled through forty special papers written for the Project, most of them included under the signature of their authors, in the three volumes of this Report. A number of them are outstanding original contributions to their field. Other are compilations and critical analyses of valuable information. The four papers selected for inclusion in this first Volume refer to quite general problems directly related to the main subjects of this Report. The papers dealing with specific case studies are to be found in Volumes 2 and 3.

The present volume is intended as a comprehensive presentation in an integrated way, of what we consider to be the most relevant material that may support, clarify or illustrate the main theses put forward in our Report. We have made use of only a fraction of the information we and our collaborators have accumulated. If some of our statements appear not to be sufficiently well founded in the text they should not be considered to be the result of superficial opinions or sloganistic empty talk. We have convinced ourselves before drafting the text that no single assertion (unless explicitly expressed as a conjecture) has been made without having sufficient confirmatory evidence for it.

Part One

The Social Dimensions of Drought

Introduction

1. Climate and Man

Throughout the ages, meteorological phenomena have occupied a central place in the preoccupations of mankind. In no other field has man felt himself so constantly and intensively at the mercy of "natural forces" and so defenceless against events affecting his daily life, often with tragic consequences. Droughts, floods, freezes, and other climatic disasters inimical to life, have always been regarded as inevitable. There was nothing else to do but to endure them. We still mostly endure them, but we are learning to organize our activities to reduce catastrophic impacts.

Perhaps because of its inescapable nature, the climate has also become one of the major discussion topics of the contemporary world, often used as an "explanation" of situations which cannot otherwise be easy to explain. It is altogether too easy to fix blame for the ills suffered by a large proportion of mankind, first of all on a fluctuation of climate, and then on the other three contemporary "horsemen of the Apocalypse": the *population explosion, environmental pollution* and the *desertification* of soils. The *climate* is the fourth fatal factor usually invoked. Some would brandish these four "horsemen of the Apocalypse" as spectres haunting the path of Man, threatening to drag him into an abyss from which there is no return. Their thesis is that the uncontrollable and violent "natural forces" together with the excessive human urge to reproduce, serve to hasten the day when an inescapable destiny of poverty and death is reached.

We already have a foretaste of this gloomy and apparently inevitable future in the set of phenomena described in the preface to this report, which are usually given as a "sample" of what will happen in the not too distant future. The epicentre of these phenomena was situated in the Sahel. This vast region in Africa was afflicted by a fatal famine, at the beginning of the present decade. The dramatic nature of this famine shook the world. No one could remain indifferent to the moving press accounts and the pathetic photographs of suffering. A feeling of collective shame and a swelling public opinion began to demand that an explanation be given of the reasons for such a misfortune: Why could it not have been foreseen and prevented?

The "four horsemen" were invoked. There is no doubt that climate, or more exactly a climatic fluctuation, was one of the factors directly responsible: starting in 1968, there was a prolonged drought in the Sahel, spreading to East Africa by 1973. But there have been other similar droughts in the past and their consequences have not been so dramatic. Why was this one so serious? The explanation was provided by adding the three other apocalyptic figures: destruction of the natural environment; the soil depleted by an excessive number of animals, the "over grazing" of which accelerated desertification; and, of course, the unfailing demographic pressure. There are many reports, books and official publications produced by well-known researchers and published by authoritative institutions explaining the causes of the 1972 Sahelian disaster along these lines: Nature, with her immutable laws, and

Man, the "sinner" (e.g. wanton destruction of his own environment, and instable reproducer). We shall adduce considerable evidence that this is a very incomplete depiction.

We ascribe the incompleteness of this depiction to a willingness to take authoritative figures on food and population, for example, at face value, and to a willingness to reason along linear lines of interpretation until a conclusion is reached that seems in accordance with common sense. We use the term "inductive-generalization" to describe this type of interpretation, as discussed in more detail shortly. Our criticism of it is that the interpreter is tempted to stop the analysis and interpretation too short. We believe that further, wider, deeper analysis is necessary. We believe that human structures (societal, political, economical) must be examined, and their interactions studied in order to reveal the actual forces at play. It is this set of forces, perhaps triggered by a physical disaster, that determines in the end what will be the effects on man and his structures.

In the next few sections of this introduction we will attempt to persuade the reader why we ourselves rejected the inductive-generalization interpretation and examined the human structural elements that shaped the 1972 situation.

2. Man and His Environment

Man is a sentient, observing and wondering member of the animal kingdom. The evolution of Man's adaptation, use and occasional misuse of his natural environment, and the evolution of his thinking processes (development of explanations and conceptual frameworks in which these explanations serve purposes) is a fascinating study, quite beyond the scope and intent of this project. However, these two evolutionary processes are somewhat germane to our study and its methodology, and we point out some of their features. We do not by any means intend to imply any specific relationships between these two evolutions, that is the province of other studies. Suffice it to say that the former seems to always have preceded the latter, by a considerable pace.

In his early evolutionary stages, Man or his evolutionary ancestors lived in the natural environment rather passively, much the same as did his ancestral relatives. True, he soon learned the use of tools, but evidently so did his simian contemporaries. He also learned that groups could accomplish more than a simple multitude of individuals, and he began to evolve social structures. So did other animals, or at least we may infer as much from observations of contemporary behaviour of their evolved descendants.

As a food-gatherer and hunter, Man also learned that some materials that at first glance seem unlikely candidates as food, could indeed be used so, sometimes by transformations such as in cooking. At a critical moment, Man also discovered that some plant materials could be raised under his control, and stored for use later. As these discoveries were developed further, and as primitive agriculture evolved into a well-organized activity, it became apparent that only some fraction of the total population was needed for the business of raising food. Time became available to some of the population to pursue other activities—arts, crafts, building of common facilities (storage areas, water-control projects, monuments), increased exploration of the environment and discoveries, for example, of how to extract metals to make better tools. Social organizations were invented and thrived, power structures were invented and developed. Very quickly, populations became structured, and élites played special roles.

3. Conceptual Frameworks of Understanding

Turning now to the evolution of understanding and development of conceptual frameworks, Man not only wonders about his surroundings and how they work, it seems that he is driven to "explain" their nature and workings. We discern three levels of such explanation.

In the first, Man ascribes natural happenings to the plans or whims of the Gods. Man has a relationship with his Gods, they having invented the world, its contents and its workings, and then placed Man in it to function. To thrive, Man observed a proper relationship to the Gods; to do otherwise caused Man and his works to suffer.

A natural calamity, such as a flood, drought, volcanic eruption, plague, occurs because Man is guilty of some transgression against the rules of order and the Gods' needs, i.e. Man sins. The characteristic of this level of explanation is that it is direct and focused. A man, or a tribe, sins; the wrath is directed quickly and is focused on the perpetrator. Expiation removes the effect. Further expiation and observance of ritual prevents its occurrence. For convenience in our discussion, we shall call this a *first level* interpretation (animistic) of how nature works.

Later, the personal Gods became replaced in some societies by a less personal and more general, all-wise God or Spirit, one who not only made the world and put Man in it, but made the physical laws by which the world functions. The idea becomes developed that laws can be discerned and understood, even expressed mathematically, and thereby used to explain and predict. The notion emerged of "Nature" as being a set of physical laws, at first divinely given and then as properties of the physical world itself.[2] While it remained true that "sin" could be rewarded with punishment—plagues, droughts, etc.—it also evolved that sometimes a disaster could be ascribed merely to the unfathomable workings of Nature, as a "natural" event. Thus, guilt need not be associated with the event as related to a cause. However, it still is a fact that we use the term "act of God" to assign the blame for an insurance loss caused by flood, earthquake, lightening, etc. Nevertheless, it was seen that the actions of humans, as an aggregate in an organized society, became part of a physical-human causality chain. The reasoning is still direct—there are linear relationships that prevail. Mathematically, we have the notion of dependent and independent variables: A causes B, which in turn causes C. It is possible to isolate an element in this structure and discuss how a change in the element causes something else to change, the originating element remaining unchanged itself. In societal-nature relationships, the effects are generally felt in largest part by those who perform the acts that are inharmonious with the laws of nature—those who increase their numbers beyond local capabilities of supply, or items of trade, run out of food. Those who overgraze a range lose their herds from eventual lack of food for them. It may have been true in the past that some essentially closed societies did respond in such linear ways to their own doings. There is also good evidence that, left to range over sufficient land, such societies also evolved very complex and highly evolved social and managerial mechanisms to exist comfortably enough even in areas of marginal climatic conditions, such as in the Sahel (cf. Chapter 8).

For convenience we term this linearized man-nature relationship a *second-level* mode of interpreting causal chains and predicting consequences. As discussed later in this volume, most aspects of the 1972 situation can be explained only partially, if at all, by this second-level type of linear reasoning, that is just an example of generalizing from a few facts. We may therefore also call this kind of interpretation the inductive-generalization approach.

We prefer to look more widely into human-nature relationships to describe and understand the recent events as typified by the 1972 case-study of this project. We believe that there are many societal, political and economic factors that must be included along with the physical factors to provide adequate insight into the evolution of events in which physical factors certainly do play a role. But we are not satisfied that the physical factors are the driving mechanisms. They may be powerful triggering events, but the real driving forces are societal. It is their nature that determines what will happen, where, and to whom. Moreover, events that "cause" things to happen are themselves modified by the happenings. We will find that we will not be able to isolate completely physical or human factors and write simple equations governing their evolution from point A to point B as a change in an independent variable C. The kind of relationships that are in operation here include as fundamental elements the political, economic and cultural structures of society. We shall invariably turn to structural interpretations of the events of the 1972 period and their precursors in order to reveal what we believe to be the essential mechanisms at work. We term this approach a *third-level* structural interpretation.

4. Approach Used in this Study: A Conceptual Framework

In this study we had access to the same basic data base as other investigators. However, we regarded that data from different viewpoints and we reached different conclusions. As a first step, we became familiar with the methods, arguments and conclusions of much of the published work on these matters, and we were struck by what we thought were biases in their analyses; biases perhaps, not in the sense that information was used incompletely or was intentionally distorted to bolster preconceived notions, but biases stemming from failure to take analysis far enough to unravel the many complex interrelationships underlying the problems. There was a failure to uncover incipient conditions that, in our view, preconditioned the human societies to make them more susceptible to the natural perturbations.

We must admit here to our own preconception: we were unsatisfied with the conventional wisdom referred to earlier in this Introduction. We made an assumption that the data base held more information than had been extracted heretofor. We were impelled to look much deeper into the extant information, to follow clues to wider sets of information, and to develop a conceptual framework within which a wide variety of interrelated data could be analysed.

As a result, we believe that we have satisfied ourselves that the arguments comprising the conventional wisdom are not successful in elucidating the basic nature of some of the problems and in revealing the dynamics of the interrelating forces at play.

Our study has led to conclusions which are essentially different from the "Apocalyptic" model. The differences are fundamental, and concern three basic factors: (i) we differ in the identification of the *facts* on the basis of which the situation is described; (ii) we differ in the determination of the *causal chains* on the basis of which an attempt is made to explain the "causes of the present situation"; (iii) lastly, we do not share the same "conceptual frame" within which facts are detected, causes analysed and phenomena explained.

Let us start with the first question. Since this report deals extensively with information usually labelled as "fact", we digress at this point to discuss some basic philosophy that we consider essential to our approach and methods. Just what is a "fact"?

THE NOTION OF FACTS

Knowing does not start by registering and processing the raw information provided by man sensory system. It is not the case that sensation is simply registered and *then* processed. When we see a yellow object, as a particular object that is yellow, it means much more than perceiving an optical pattern and detecting some wavelength of the light coming from it. It means that we have included our perception in a class, together with other objects already classified as yellow, and that a distinction has been made with reference to non-yellow objects. For a child, it also means that he is able to recognize a certain optical pattern as being an object; and this only happens after the child has already a sufficiently advanced experience is playing with objects.

For a scientist, when he sees a yellow line in his spectrometer, he "sees" sodium; and this means that he has incorporated his optical sensation into a highly sophisticated theoretical and experimental framework.

Thus, the "reading" of what is given in experience requires cognitive instruments able to assimilate the data, in the same way as the intake of food by a living organism requires a biological structure able to assimilate it. Any "observable" assumes much more than a simple recording of something "given" in the perceptive field. From this point of view it is useful to introduce a distinction between an "observable" and a "fact". Both imply a certain interpretation of the raw data given in the experience. But the former is localized in space and time, whereas a "fact" (whether it refers to a property, to an action or to a more complete event) requires a much larger context. Still in a more obvious way than in the case of an observable, a fact is not the object of direct perception. It is assimilated by means of a pre-existing conceptual frame. Perceiving a withered branch as such, and not merely as an optical pattern, implies having a previous knowledge of a living branch and realizing that it may dry up owing to lack of water.

In a social process the facts, as such, are even more difficult to identify. Very often, what is called a social fact is a single movie frame, as it were, chosen from a complex time sequence of actual conditions. Sociologists refer to this as a "cutting", i.e. a transverse cut from a complex continuum. It is clearly difficult to reconstruct from this single frame or transverse cut the "plot" (or in our case the history of relationships) that determines the place of the abstracted element in the whole. We can imagine many possible "plots"; without additional information we cannot eliminate the inappropriate ones. This process of selection, in order to *abstract* certain elements, leads to obscuring or minimizing the role of the relationship between what is being abstracted and what is left aside. This in turn, can invalidate many interpretations. There are two ways in which a set of data drawn from an "observable" situation can lead to wrong information or an interpretation that cannot stand a validity test.

PSEUDO-FACTS

Contemporary philosophy made an important contribution to the theory of knowledge when it was able to show that some of the classic problems to which various schools of thought devoted much attention were in fact pseudo-problems.[3]

That is, some of the questions philosophers tried to solve were not in fact meaningful questions; and some of the statements made, although quite correct from the grammatical point of view, were not statements at all from the point of view of the meaning. They were pseudo-questions and pseudo-statements.

We may apply the same type of analysis, *mutatis mutandis,* when we refer to facts. We have already indicated that facts are not *given,* but they are rather an interpretation of data provided by the experience. They are built on the basis of "observables" included in a larger contrast. It follows that if the context is a wrong one, the interpretation of the observables will *distort* the reality it intends to depict. The data, on the basis of which the "fact" was built, are there, but the meaning attributed to them is false or misleading. The assumed "fact" will not depict, strictly speaking, anything that has the right to be considered a valid description of reality.

PARTIAL FACTS

Naturally, even if the appropriate context is used, an incomplete set of data inferred from the observable allows only a partial depiction, thus a "partial fact". Partial facts, since they provide an insufficient description of a complex situation, can lead to failure to recognize many of the fundamental factors involved. This, in turn, leads to the termination of analyses before arriving at deeply rooted causal relationships.

It is not always obvious that a depiction is incomplete. How do we identify a fact as "partial"? Often it is only by going through an iteration in the process of interpretation. We may then realize that some aspects of the original situation we try to explain are missing; we may discover that the inferred depiction is not in accordance with other observables or other inferences.

We come now to the second step in our questionning. Any explanation assumes the possibility of establishing *causal relationships* between facts, i.e. in this case, giving an acceptable reply to the question: "What were the causes of the famines in the Sahel in 1972/3?"

CAUSE AND EFFECT

The concept of "cause" plays such an essential role in all studies on the impact of natural phenomena on society, that it will be necessary to pause for a moment on this matter. Let us take an extremely simple and frequently occurring example taken from the daily press. A car being driven at excessive speed on a slippery surface is unable to brake in time at a pedestrian crossing and runs over one of the pedestrians.

The direct physical cause is the excessive speed brought about by a human cause: the carelessness of the driver. What would we think of the judge who would close the case by holding the slippery surface responsible?

Another similar example of a causal chain, but with a different "explanation", could be taken from a not uncommon occurrence during spells of cold weather which affect some cities in winter. Newspapers, besides containing photographs of traffic jams or of warmly clad children playing in the snow, may contain reports like this "One old person died last night as a result of the cold weather". The old person was probably destitute, possibly ill, without adequate clothing who almost certainly died in the street because of having nowhere to take shelter. To say that the person died "because of the cold" is equivalent to, although less obvious than, asserting that the pedestrian in the last example was run over "because of the slippery road". Stopping the causal chain at some particular point of the process of tracing a given event back to its source entails an arbitrary judgement and sometimes a conscious decision.

Yet in many circumstances in which thousands of persons perish or millions are subjected to terrible suffering, the reports on the "facts" and their causes usually do not go any further than in the analogies given above. Are there not unnumerable authorized medical reports "certifying" deaths of large numbers of children caused by measles or dysentery? And yet it is known, and frequently emphasized in this Report, that in actual fact it is a question of underfed children at the mercy of any infection. But for those who design systems of recording causes of death, malnutrition is not the "basic cause of death" and therefore should not even be mentioned on the death certificate (cf. Chapter 3 below). It is one thing to hold a virus responsible, but a totally different matter to place the responsibility on an economic and social system. One again, the killer is not the driver but the low coefficient of friction of the road surface!

In 1973 thousands of children died in the Sahel. What was the cause? Epidemics. And the cause of the epidemics? Malnutrition due to the widespread famine which resulted in the death of a large proportion of the inhabitants. And the cause of the famine? A very prolonged drought which lasted several years. At this point, most investigations stop, it being contended that an explanation of the phenomenon has been found, in having determined the "natural cause". And here, the word "natural" is used in its two accepted meanings: first, as something produced by "nature"; secondly, naturally (logically) arising from the circumstances of the case. In investigations conditioned by the logic of what we have called interpretations of the second level (simple inductive-generalizations) the aim was thus to discover the natural phenomenon—in this case the climate—which might originally be responsible for the disaster, and also to show that in fact it was "natural" (in the sense of being logical,) that such-and-such a cause produced such-and-such an effect. The case is then closed: the children in the Sahel died because of the drought!

But is so happens that in 1976 there was also a drought in Great Britain. We believe that nobody would have thought it "natural" for thousands of British children to die *because of the drought.* The loss of even a few dozen children would have been nothing less than a scandal.

The fact that the massive death of children in Sahel is accepted as natural, when it is attributed to a "cause" which would be unacceptable if the event had occurred in some other part of the world, and the fact that the investigation of the causes of the massive death is stopped when it arrives at identifying a "natural" cause such as the drought, certainly do not constitute *methodological* errors. Nor does it strictly follow that it is a question of *error*. The investigators who stop at this point do so because they are operating in a conceptual framework that has not advanced to consider the human-societal structures involved, i.e. to interpretations of the third level.

We insist that this is not a methodological error. Methodology is merely a tool for the process of investigation, the content of which arises in actual fact from what we may call, in the philosophical sense, an *epistemic frame,* or, in its political sense, *ideological frame.* It is on the bases of these frames that the questions to be answered should be formulated. They will consequently determine the scope and limitations of the study, as well as the validity and acceptability of the explanations obtained. In the absence of the rigorous proofs of the logico-mathematical disciplines, and in view of the impossibility of carrying out an *experimentum-crucis* when there are alternative hypotheses, the social investigator reaches his conclusions and decides on recommendations in ways which implicitly reflect his own conceptual framework. The social science have to use a methodology which makes it necessary to work with a set of partial inductions, of abstractions based on an uncontrolled historical experience, of inferences from unverifiable premises. As a last resort, the only possible "connecting rod" is a certain scheme for society, a given concept of man and of the world, a *Weltanschauung.*

It is from this position that we disagree with the explanations which consider the climate to be "directly and solely responsible" for a series of situations which affect both the social conditions in extensive areas of the world, and the world economic situation. We do not set out to deny that a severe drought could produce—and in certain cases it really does produce—the dramatic effects such as those attributed to the "1972 case". We are not unaware that food prices fluctuate with variations in world production and the pressure of the market. We know that when the international price of a product increases appreciably, importing countries with limited resources may find themselves deprived of foodstuffs. However, even accepting the existence of each of these causal links, we question the validity of an *explanation* built up on such terms alone. Put in the form of a diagram, the "explanations" we have mentioned would lead to a linear process as shown on the following page.

The studies which we undertook in developing the project on "Drought and Man" provide sufficient empirical evidence to enable us to confirm our thesis that the causal chain, shown diagrammatically above is not valid. As we shall show in Chapter 2, it includes facts which were mutually independent or which had a very slight interaction. Moreover, some of the most significant facts are disregarded. A structural analysis (i.e. a "third-level interpretation") leads us to a quite different interpretation.

We know that this assertion and the conceptual frame on the basis of which we make it confronts us with a difficult challenge. By means of a partial theme of limited scope, through a modest investigation restricted to a spatial-temporal and economic boundary of minimal dimensions, we endeavour to penetrate to the root of some problems of vital importance for a wide sector of mankind, from a different point of view from that usually adopted. It is a task as ambitious as it is risky. However, we believe that our work will succeed in providing acceptable explanations

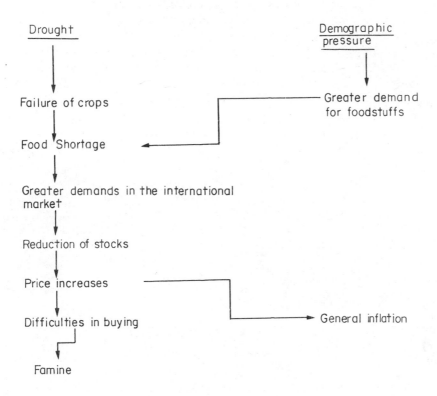

Diagram 1.

for the set of problems posed by the project within the epistemic frame we have selected. And, what is more important, we think that we can show that these problems *can* be avoided. This obviously supposes that it can be asserted that there are solutions for them.

CHAPTER 1

Facts, Pseudo-facts and Misleading Causal Links in the 1972 Case History

Famine is the central feature and the principal scourge of the apocalyptic vision of the world of the future to which we alluded in the Introduction. In this conception the four contemporary apocalyptic horsemen ride an earth that is increasingly unable to produce the minimum of food necessary for its population, which itself is increasing in an explosive manner. Exhausted soil, devastated by the action of man and by vagaries of a climate deteriorating under man's influence, completes the picture and makes the gloomy prophesy inevitable. Those who paint this dark picture for the destiny of generations to come usually do not limit themselves to formulating a prediction. Their analysis amounts also to a diagnosis of the present world, the evils of which are presented as symptoms and a forewarning of the tragic path which will be followed in the future. Various facts are invoked as phenomena that demonstrate the trend of events and make it possible to infer the cause of the evils.

In examining this viewpoint critically it is necessary to distinguish clearly between two groups of problems of a very different nature, which it would be wrong—and risky—to confuse. In the first place, we are faced with the elaboration of a *forecast,* i.e. an estimate of the way in which the physical and social conditions (and their interrelationships) will probably evolve on our planet during the next generations. In the second place, this is supplemented by an analysis of the conditions in the contemporary world, both at the present time and in the recent past. This *diagnosis* of the present gives to the proponents of this view an indication of the problems which could arise and cause a crisis in the medium term.

Acceptance of the forecast as an assertion, with a far from negligible probability of being realized, in no way implies acceptance of the diagnosis. By making this distinction, we are able to agree with certain aspects of the forecast (although with considerable reservations): things may very well get even worse before they can get better. But we shall attempt to show that the diagnosis is incomplete and misleading, that it belongs to what we call, in the Introduction, the "second level of interpretation", and that only a "third-level interpretation", based on structural considerations, will provide a more correct perspective. We therefore reject the validity of the above diagnosis as an adequate analysis of the actual conditions.

It is evident that analysis of the second kind (i.e. the analysis corresponding to the second level of interpretation within the framework explained in the Introduction) is centred on the problem of food production, a subject which appears as the essential question in most of the studies dealing with the universal famine that is supposed to threaten the future of our species. We shall devote this chapter to an analysis of that problem, starting with certain assertions expressed in publications, assertions which have contributed in a decisive manner to forming public opinion on the subject. A major starting-point for many analyses with which we differ are the reports of the UN World Food Conference, 1974. In fact, when the Project began, we started there too. We soon became unsatisfied with the analysis contained in the most important working document presented to the Conference and approved by it.[2] We doubted that a careful analysis of the food production and trade statistics inevitably led to the conclusion that a "food crisis" as central to the concern of the World Food Conference existed in actuality. This chapter contains our arguments why we considered many contemporary analyses inadequate and misleading.

The *Report on Climate and Food,* published by the United States Academy of Sciences (Washington, DC, 1976), opens with this assertion:

"World food reserves are now no more than sufficient to compensate for a single year's bad harvest that may result from natural fluctuations of weather and climate."

and on page 3 we read the following:

"In 1972, a year when the climate was particularly unfavorable for food production, millions of people starved throughout the world."

At a wider, popular level, the book by Lester Brown and Erik Eckholm (*By Bread Alone*) opens with a similar assertion:

"In the early seventies the soaring demand for food, spurred by both continuing population growth and rising affluence, has began to outrun the productive capacity of the world's farmers and fishermen. The result has been declining food reserves, sky-rocketing food prices and intense competition among countries for available food supplies. Fundamental changes in the world food situation have left government institutions and individuals everywhere unprepared and vulnerable."

Some other quotations, selected from a wide literature with the same trend, show the similarity of the arguments used by a wide variety of authors. It will suffice to transcribe two more examples:

". . . the impact of the bad weather of 1972 was serious to a degree that was out of proportion to the reduction in total world food production. The climatic anomalies were felt in regions that upset the pattern of purchase of wheat from the United States and Canada. The stability of the world cereal trade price structure was shaken, and the consumer felt the impact in the form of higher prices for the bread and grain-fed meat."

(The Rockefeller Foundation: "Climate change, food production and interstate conflict", a Bellagio Conference, 1975).

"Events during and following 1972 show that North Americans are highly susceptible to unusual weather occurrences on the seas and in other lands. The degree of this interdependence (between climatic variability and resources-food) was clearly demonstrated in 1972. That year the climate was generally favorable in the cereal producing areas of North America providing good crops. But over much of the world disastrous globe girdling zones of drought and excessive moisture greatly stressed many nations. (. . .) The result was regional famine, a scramble for available grain reserves, market speculations and widespread inflation.''

(G. A. McKay and T. Allsopp: ''Global interdependence and the climate of 1972'', July 1976.)

The picture of the problem which emerges from these quotations, and which we shall call ''the *official* version of the 1972 food crisis'' (since they stem from the governmental UN World Food Conference), leads directly to formulating distorted causal chains of the second level to which we have referred in the Introduction. As a result of such incomplete causal analysis and some spurious relationships, one is led to identifying as causes of certain phenomena factors which were only concomitant with them, or have only influenced their development in a secondary manner. In other cases, effects are taken as causes, and vice versa. In order to demonstrate this, we shall consider in this first chapter the facts that are adduced as being at the origin of the 1972 crisis. We leave to the next chapter a presentation of what, in our view, was the actual situation, bringing into the analysis the various structural elements and dynamics we believe are necessary to understand the situation.

Our contention will be that each one of the statements asserted in the ''official version'' to be a fact represents the actual situation quite imperfectly and that therefore the official version distorts reality in the same way as a glass with impurities and deformations distorts the shapes of the objects behind it. They are *partial facts* or *pseudo-facts* in the sense explained in the Introduction. They either provide an insufficient description of a far more complex situation or introduce a distortion of it which misleads the inferences to be drawn. We shall call them ''P-facts'', the ''P'' standing either for ''partial'' or ''pseudo''.

The following list contains those ''P-facts'' which, in our opinion, are the most significant.

P-Fact I:

''The food crisis began in 1972, when the worldwide output of cereals declined sharply for the first time in over 20 years.''

(Timothy M. Laur: ''The world food problem and the role of climate'', *Trans.Am.Geoph.Union*, April 1976.)

''The present world food crisis, originating from a combination of longer term problems and temporary set-backs, suddenly emerged in a pronounced form in 1972. In that year the output of food in the world declined for the first time in more than 20 years. In particular, world output of cereals (wheat, coarse grains and rice) fell by a large amount—33 million tons. World production of cereals, presently totalling about 1,200 million tons, had to increase on an average by about 25 million tons each year to meet the rising world demand. The sudden drop in the 1972 production created, therefore, a heavy deficit at the time when the North American countries were engaged in supply-management programmes to bring down their large surpluses. Also, this was the first time in recent decades that adverse weather affected production in several sub-continents simultaneously—USSR, China, India, Australia, Sahelian Africa and South-East Asia.''

(FAO: "Assessment of the world food situation. Present and future." Main Working Document presented to the World Food Conference, 1974.)

P-Fact II:

"The Soviet Union imported an exceptionally large amount of grain in 1972/73 and in 1973/74 the developing countries increased their grain imports. These purchases quickly depleted the reduced stocks of the major exporting countries, especially those of the United States which had held the largest quantity."

(US Department of Agriculture: "The world food situation and the outlook until 1985")

"As a result, the wheat stocks of the main wheat exporting countries fell from 49 million tons in 1971-72 to 29 million tons in 1972-73 and are expected to be even lower in the current year. Stocks in many importing countries were also sharply reduced. Coarse grain stocks fell similarly and rice reserves were virtually exhausted. Although in 1973 harvests were reasonably good, the increase in production in the market economy countries was insufficient to prevent a further fall in exporters' stocks. Production recovered in most developing countries, with the main exception of the Sahelian Zone countries where a major international emergency operation was necessary to avert widespread starvation."

(FAO: *op. cit.* Continuation of paragraph quoted above.)

P-Fact III:

"The world is now in a highly vulnerable position. In 1973 and 1974, world reserve capabilities in relation to consumption needs fell far below any previous level in the post-war era, to the equivalent of only twenty-six days worth of world consumption."

(L. Brown and E. Eckholm: *By Bread Alone,* page 57).

P-Fact IV:

"No one could have foreseen the failure of the Russian wheat crop in 1972. As a result, between 1971 and 1972 American wheat exports almost doubled."

(Earl O. Heady: "The agriculture of the US", *Scientific American,* September 1976).

P-Fact V:

"Between late 1972 and early 1974, international food prices escalated rapidly in response to the growing excess of world demand over available supplies and the decline of world food reserves. Wheat and rice prices tripled, and soybean prices more than doubled."

(L. Brown and E. Eckholm: *op. cit.,* page 62).

P-Fact I

Taking as a starting-point the FAO figures for world production of food grains, Fig. 1.1, we find that indeed in 1972 there was a drop in absolute production of about 2.2%. We propose analysis of the drop as follows.

Starting with 1965, there was an impressing increase in production. Two record peaks occurred in 1971 and 1973. Instead of focusing attention on 1972 as a disaster,

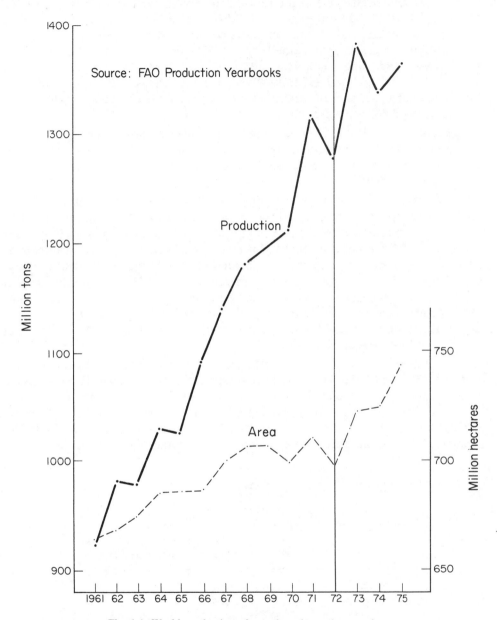

Fig. 1.1. World production of cereals and area harvested.

we could well ask, what was the reason for the great production of 1971? First of all, to consider as a crisis a drop back of 2.2% in cereal production in the year following an abnormally good year is a distortion of logic. Overall, substantial gains were being made in food production, gains that were outstripping population growth. The production in 1972 was 5.7% higher than the average production in the period 1965-70. To give perspective to the food-population picture, it was one conclusion of the UN World Food Conference (1974) that a yearly world increase of 25 million tons on the average, and at that time, was necessary to meet rising food demand. The absolute increase in production between 1970 and 1971 was 102.7 million tons, and between 1972 and 1973 98.4 million (FAO-PY-72, 74, 75). Including the decrease between 1971 and 1972, the 3-year average increase was 54.4 million tons per year, double the amount indicated by FAO as needed to compensate for the greater demand for consumption.

The report of the World Food Conference and many authors cite world food production and world food reserves relating to the "crisis" of 1972. We assert that the analyses in the above two paragraphs, based on FAO world figures, do not justify the "crisis" designation.

The drop in production in 1972, against a healthy upward trend in prior and succeeding years, poses another question. How much of the 1972 decrease could be ascribed to conditions other than "climate"? Faced with the surpluses of 1971, for example, the USA production for 1972 was curtailed by reducing planted acreage by 10%. This reduced storage costs and also allowed some of the lower fertility land to be fallowed; this was sound economic-agricultural policy. The reserve capability of this fallowed acreage may be estimated to be the equivalent to about 26 million tons. This production would have reduced the 1972 wrinkle in Fig. 1.1 by about two-thirds. L. Brown estimates that the equivalent in grain of all the cultivable land not used in the USA was 78 million tons.

To present a few more details of interest, in Table 1.1 the wheat production is given for 1971 and 1972. The US-USSR grain deal in 1972/3 is widely considered a major factor in the "food crisis". Let us see what the figures show when we remove these two powers from the analysis. We find a world *increase* of 4.17% in 1972 over 1971. Wheat prices rose substantially, but perhaps not as a direct result of the 1971-2 change in production. This matter is elaborated in detail in Chapter 2.

TABLE 1.1
Production of wheat
(millions of tons)

Region	1971	1972	Percentage change from preceding year
World total	353.9	347.9	- 1.70
US	44.0	42.0	- 4.55
North America	58.4	56.6	- 3.08
USSR	98.8	86.0	-12.96
US and USSR	142.8	128.0	-10.36
Developing countries	71.2	79.0	+ 10.96
World total less US and USSR	211.1	219.9	+ 4.17

Source: *FAO Production Yearbook 1973*, pp. 44-45

We believe that the figures in Table 1.1 show that it is unreliable and misleading to use world production figures as a springboard for such alarms as "World food crisis in 1972". Moreover, the relationships between the large-scale droughts in 1972 (actually starting in West Africa in 1968), the world food situation and the extreme plight of many peoples are not revealed in the world production figures. The plight of peoples and severe suffering was real enough, even though the global food crisis may have been only illusionary. In the face of adequate food supplies (on a world basis), peoples suffered famine. Why? We must look far deeper than into mere food *production.* We must look at those structural elements of society that, in the face of apparent plenitude of food, work to make the food unavailable in sufficient amounts to many segments of society in many areas. That is, we must undertake structural analyses, third-level interpretations, as discussed in the Introduction. We do that later in this volume and we elaborate on the methodology in Chapter 6.

P-Fact II

As we have already agreed, this assertion is also put into a context which endeavours to provide an explanation of the mechanism which set off the "food crisis" which started in 1972.

It is clear that an attempt is made here to present a sequence as if it were a causal chain: as a result of the fall in world food production (*P-Fact I*), the Soviet Union and the developing countries purchased large quantities of grain, which led to a depletion of stocks and the exceptional price increase of grain and "other foodstuffs". We not only question the linear causal connection between the various facts, we also question each of the specific assertions which are put together in P-Fact II as stated above.

We leave to P-Fact V discussion of the role of purchases by the Soviet Union. We find no substantive evidence for influences in the world market of actions by a group of countries having a limited participation in the world's grain trade, as we shall demonstrate below.

First, let us consider the grain market during the period concerned. The figures normally used are those giving total imports. Thus the record figure of 157.7 million tons is given as the total world imports of cereals in 1973 (FAO: *Trade Yearbook, 1975*, p. 119) and is compared with the 131.4 million in 1972. The analysis which serves as the basis of the report of the US Department of Agriculture, from which we took the above-mentioned quotation, covers six cereals: wheat, maize, oats, barley, rye and sorghum. In Table 1.2 the report gives net exports and imports of these grains.

Table 1.2 shows clearly the impact produced by the enormous increase in the amount bought by the Soviet Union, when the figure jumped from 1.3 million tons in 1971-2 to 19.6 million tons in the period 1972-3. These figures do not merely reflect production problems experienced by the Soviet Union due to drought during that period. There were other factors, both political and economic, that need to be taken into account. We shall deal with this in detail with reference to P-Fact V below.

TABLE 1.2
World net grain exports and imports

Country	1969/70-1971/2 average	1971/2	1972/3	1973/4
	million metric tons			
Developed countries	31.9	41.9	62.4	58.4
United States	39.8	42.8	73.1	72.5
Canada	14.8	18.3	18.8	13.1
Australia & New Zealand	10.6	10.8	5.8	9.9
South Africa	2.5	3.7	.4	4.0
EC-9	-16.6	-14.0	-13.4	-13.0
Other West Europe	- 4.8	- 4.3	- 5.3	- 8.9
Japan	-14.4	-15.4	-17.0	-19.2
Central plan countries	- 6.8	-13.0	-32.2	-15.9
East Europe	- 7.6	- 9.2	- 8.0	- 4.8
USSR	3.9	- 1.3	-19.6	- 4.4
PRC	- 3.1	2.5	- 4.6	- 6.7
Developing countries	-19.1	-26.9	-23.2	-30.3
North Africa & Middle East	- 9.2	-11.9	- 8.1	-14.9
South Asia	- 5.7	- 5.4	- 4.5	- 7.0
Southeast Asia	3.2	3.3	1.2	2.5
East Asia	- 8.4	- 9.2	-10.4	-10.2
Latin America	3.2	- 2.0	—	.7
Central Africa	- 1.9	- 2.0	- 2.0	- 2.1
East Africa	- .3	.3	.6	.7
Other	- .2	- .2	- .3	- .3
World total exports	107.6	111.2	141.8	151.0

Source: This table is a reproduction of Table 3 on page 4 of the US Department of Agriculture Publication *The World Food Situation and the Outlook until 1985*—
negative values indicate net imports.

As regards the increase in grain imports by the developing countries (market economy), the table we have just considered enables us to make two comments which are very obvious from the numbers themselves:

(a) The most notable increase in the imports of those countries occurred *before* the critical period 1972-3; in actual fact, net imports *decreased* at that time. It may easily be seen that the increase in 1973-4 with respect to 1971-2 is less than the "jump" which exists between the average for 1969-71 and the period 1971-2 itself. This relative dip in the rising curve for grain purchase by developing countries makes untenable the explanation that the increased demand from those countries was any major factor in the exceptional increase in prices that started in 1972. The group developing countries had already increased its imports—and more sharply—without having any effect on the market and obviously without being pushed by the scarcities created by the 1972 drought.

(b) Even if we limit ourselves to analysing the increase in these imports in the period 1973-4 with respect to the previous period, the argument is also unacceptable. Another glance at Table 1.2 will show that the only appreciable increase occurred in North Africa and the Middle East, with 6.8 million tons and in southern Asia with 2.5 million. The first region was not affected by droughts in 1972 nor did it have any problems in production. As regards southern Asia, the country which had a decisive influence on the increase is India. This country, for apparently political reasons, had bought practically no grain in 1972. When it reverted the next year to the usual quantity of imports, this produced the greater part of the relative increase of the region. It does not seem mandatory to invoke climatic anomalies here.

These facts, which spring to view in the figures contained in Table 1.2, do not support the assertion that the developing countries used the world market to compensate for the deficit, let alone that this was produced by the drought. The causal sequence implied in the report of the US Department of Agriculture has no sound basis in our opinion, in the comparative figures of the world grain market.

We also feel that the figures of the table are inadequate to make a complete analysis of the problem. Such is not our aim, for the moment. The subject is extremely complex, and we are only considering here those elements which provide the basis for our dissatisfaction with the logic behind the explanations of "P-Fact II" and its context, in the alleged causal relationship which would lead to understanding the reasons for the "1972 food crisis".

We should not examine in isolation the increases in imports that took place after 1972. The wider context is that the curve for total world grain imports shows a continuous upwards progression except during the period 1966-9 and in 1974, i.e. an increase in the level of imports is the normal and predictable trend of the market. From this point of view it is interesting to compare the curve for quantities of imports with the curve showing values in dollars. Figure 1.2 gives both curves and to complete the analysis we have added the variations in export price indices. We have computed similar curves for the major cereal-exporting countries and added the variations of the reserves (stocks) whenever available. The curves show some significant differences which are not germane to this analysis. The essential outcome of this analysis was that it would be very difficult to try to maintain that the variations in prices bear any relation to demand, or to stocks or to a combination of both. There is no possible explanation in terms of "elasticity" of prices which would account for the uniformity of the curve for unit values between 1960 and 1972 or the discontinuity after that year. The argument based on the increase in the cost of energy used in the process of production is, likewise, untenable, since the increase in the price of the raw materials for energy started only later, in October 1973.

We believe, and shall discuss further below, that the graphs show fairly clearly a fundamental change in the *structure of the grain trade*. They also show an anomaly in the variation of prices which in no way fits in with the "law of supply and demand", which evidently was repealed for that period, other forces having come into play. We shall deal with this question specifically in Chapter 2, but at this stage of the analysis we shall confine ourselves to showing that the presumed deficit in food production in the developing countries has no significant effect on the curve for world exports.

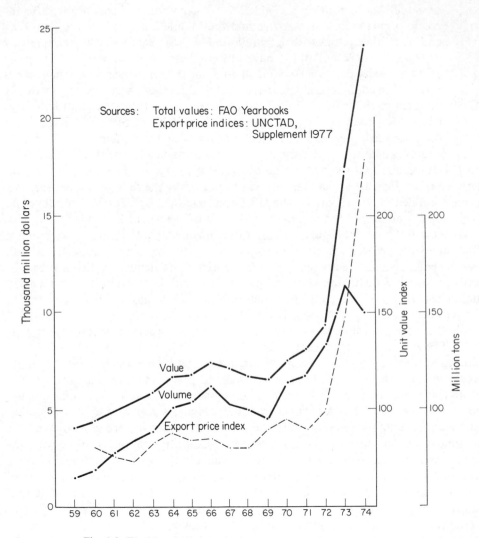

Fig. 1.2. World grain imports and export price indices (1972 = 100).

It is evident that the world grain trade is a market in which the economically developed countries or areas dominate: North America, Western Europe, Japan and the Soviet Union. To these we must now add the developing countries that are members of OPEC, due to their enormous financial wealth.

In recent economic history, the largest importer of cereals has been Japan, exceeded only slightly by the Soviet Union in 1973. Let us look at Table 1.3 which shows net imports and comparing the figures for non-American developed countries with two basic areas in developing countries, during the significant period from 1971 to 1974.

TABLE 1.3
Net imports of cereals—1971-4
(in million tons)

Country or Region	1971	1972	1973	1974	Total period
Japan	14.0	16.0	18.0	19.3	67.3
United Kingdom	9.0	8.4	7.4	7.3	32.1
Italy	6.5	6.6	7.8	7.4	28.4
Fed. Rep. of Germany	6.8	6.6	6.0	5.2	24.6
USSR	-5.6	11.0	18.6	-0.6	23.4
Africa (developing countries)	4.7	4.5	5.7	6.3	21.2
Latin America	-4.0	2.6	2.1	1.0	1.7

Source: FAO Trade Yearbook, 1975.
Note: negative signs indicate net export.

Once again, the figures are clear and define the situation: in 1973 and 1974, all the developing countries in Africa together imported less cereals than Italy, the United Kingdom or the Federal Republic of Germany taken separately. Indeed they imported *less than a third* of the quantity imported by Japan. Latin America, which was an exporter until 1972, imported 2.6 million tons in 1972 (against 48.3 tons for the developed countries included in the table). Latin America imports even decreased to a minimum of 1.0 million tons in 1973/4. It is evident that, although in the "critical year" of 1972 this region changed from being a small exporter of grain to being an even smaller importer, this change cannot be considered as important when compared with the total figures for the world market, as regards prices, stock and supply-demand.

There remain the Sahelian countries. What, then, were the total net imports of cereals for the six Sahelian countries for the entire period of the drought which lasted from 1968 to 1973? (see Table 1.4).

TABLE 1.4
Total imports of cereals of the six Sahelian countries
(in million tons)

1968	1969	1970	1971	1972	1973	1974
0.3	0.4	0.3	0.5	0.5	0.7	0.8

Source: FAO Trade Yearbooks, 1970, 1974 and 1975.

The figures are, undoubtedly, low. Even making some allowance for that, we claim that they are not *statistically* significant in terms of world trade. The world import-export figures illustrate our point. In 1973, according to official figures,[3] the total world exports of grain were 164.49 million tons, whereas imports totalled 157.65. The difference (6.84 million tons) is ten times greater than the imports of grain by the Sahelian countries the same year. It is not a question of an isolated error which occurred in the tables for 1973. If we add up all the FAO figures for exports between 1960 and 1970, and then do the same for imports, the difference between the two totals for the decade amounts to 22,132 million tons. It is certainly not difficult to explain the mystery of these persistent discrepancies when one realizes that the figures for exports are systematically larger than the figures for imports. But this is not the proper place to enter into such an analysis. If we use this example in the present context, it is simply to be able to show that the imports of cereals by the Sahelian countries were quite insignificant on a statistical basis. It also shows that the *net* variations of imports of grain for the developing countries in 1972 and 1973 are of the same magnitude as the discrepancies contained in official statistics. But, of course, people do not consume statistics as food. Our only point here is to illustrate that the world trade fluctuations, even if they affect many large regions, did not reach directly into the much smaller and more isolated populations of the Sahel to deprive them of food.

So far, we have analyzed the subject using total figures for the international grain trade, but let us look now at the trade in each type of grain for further evidence of change in the nature of the grain market. The two major cereal markets are those of wheat and maize. In these markets are concentrated 72% of the total operations of world cereal trade. It is in these two markets that large variation occurs of the total value of exports of both cereals, and also the values per unit volume. The structure of each market is quite different. Let us look, first of all, at maize imports during the period 1971-6 (Table 1.5).

TABLE 1.5
Total imports of maize
(in millions of tons)

	1971	1972	1973	1974	1975	1976
World	30.8	38	47	49.2	51.8	62.1
Western Europe	19.6	20.2	22.6	24.3	25.3	26.8
USSR	0.9	41	5.4	3.4	5.5	11.4
Japan	5.0	6.1	7.8	7.9	7.5	8.4
Developing countries	2.6	3.1	4.8	5.8	7.2	6.2

Source: *FAO Trade Yearbook 1975* and *1976*.

If we consider net imports, the situation of developing countries is seen in a different light, as Table 1.6 shows.

TABLE 1.6
Net imports of maize
(in millions of tons)

	1971	1972	1973	1974	1975	1976
Western Europe	14.3	15.6	17.0	18.3	19.6	20.9
USSR	0.8	3.9	5.0	2.6	5.5	11.2
Japan	5.0	6.1	7.8	7.9	7.5	8.4
Developing countries	-7.7	-3.0	-1.5	-3.7	-0.4	-0.9

Source: FAO, *op. cit.*
Note: negative values indicate net exports.

The figures show clearly that the developing countries as a whole have always been *net exporters* of maize. Obviously it cannot be these countries which cause any "crisis" in the international market. However, it is of interest to analyse the progressive decrease in exports which took place, starting in 1971. This variation is very marked in Latin America and more particularly in three countries: Argentina, Brazil and Mexico. Let us look in Table 1.7 at the figures for each of these countries.

TABLE 1.7
Net exports and imports of maize
(in million tons)

	1971	1972	1973	1974	1975	1976
Argentina	-6.1	-3.0	-4	-5.5	-3.9	-3.1
Brazil	-1.3	-0.2	-0.4	1.1	1.1	-1.4
Mexico	-0.3	-0.2	1.1	1.3	2.6	0.9

Source: FAO, *op. cit.*
Note: negative values indicate net exports.

The picture presented by the wheat market is quite different, inasmuch as the developing countries are net importers of this cereal, in considerable quantities. (Table 1.8).

The increase in imports shown for Latin America during the 3-year period 1972-4 must mainly be attributed to Brazil and Chile. We must also take into account an unusual purchase by Argentina in 1973 of 422,000 tons. In this year the country reached a record figure for exports of 3 million tons and the imports only covered heavy export commitments. The political reasons for the increase in imports by Chile are quite clear. It should be remembered that US had cut off food supplies to Allende's government but provided 450,000 tons to his successor, General Pinochet, a few months after his *coup d'état*. The reasons for a similar increase in Brazil are less directly political.

As regards Africa, it was the countries in the North and in the Middle East which imported more, in spite of the fact that 1972 was a record year for production and, although not as high as in 1973, was still higher than in 1971.

TABLE 1.8
Imports of wheat
(in million tons)

	1970	1971	1972	1973	1974	1975	1976
World total	54.9	57.6	61	76.7	66.4	73.4	70.6
Europe	18.2	19.4	18.1	18.0	16.9	16.3	18.6
Japan	4.7	4.9	5.1	5.4	5.4	5.7	5.8
USSR	2.2	2.7	8.5	15.6	3.1	9.6	7.2
Developing countries	22.5	25.5	22.7	30.0	32.6	36.5	34.8
Latin America	5.7	6.3	7.0	8.7	8.6	7.2	9.1
Africa	2.9	3.5	3.7	4.6	4.6	6.3	5.4

Source: FAO, *op. cit.*

In order to complete this brief analysis of the increase in imports of the developing countries during the period in question, it remains to consider Asia and the particular case of India. A strange fact stands out, namely, that a minimum in the imports in this country occurred in the "critical" year of 1972. In the following year India had recourse to a loan of 1.8 million tons to compensate for its deficit from 1972. For this loan India did not turn to the major Western exporters but to the USSR. We can discern political and economic motivations or forces here but not climatic.[4]

In the tables for wheat imports we thus find a situation which is very different from that normally shown by the analysis of the "food crisis". A tendency for an increase in the wheat imports of developing countries is clearly seen. This increase is not linked to any particular climate phenomenon, nor, as we shall see further on, to demographic factors having a decisive effect on this tendency. We believe that the fundamental cause is the *change in agricultural policy,* particularly by the United States. We shall deal with this subject in Chapter 2.

Summing up this rather lengthy discussion of P-Fact II, we would point out the following conclusions:

1. The Soviet Union made large grain purchases in 1973, but in themselves these were not the main driving force in the rise of food prices. Here, we must leave this as an assertion. We elaborate our argument under P-Fact V.

2. We find no support in the FAO figures, for all grains or for individual grains, for the assertion that purchases from developing countries exerted any significant pressure on the world market and thereby on prices.

3. We do find evidences of changes in the structures of world grain trade as accountable influences on prices.

4. We find no support for the assertion that these factors and dynamics of the world markets played direct roles in the sufferings in the Sahel, the condition that prompted initiation of this study project.

5. We do find some evidences of political-economic and governmental policies as important influences, in support of our belief that the diagnoses of the world situation in the period must include social, economic and political structural elements in order to reveal the forces and dynamics at work, e.g. we must adopt the level-3 structural analyses described in the Introduction.

P-Fact III

The general context is which this assertion is made is to be found in another contribution to the subject by L. Brown himself, "World population trends: signs of hope, signs of stress", World-Watch Paper 8 1976):

"The recent hand-to-mouth situation contrasts sharply with the relative security of the fifties and sixties. Then, food reserves more then offset crop shortfalls. Then, the price of grain was comparatively stable, access to exportable supplies was assured, and the United States always stood ready to intervene whenever famine threatened. But now, during the seventies, the depletion of world food stocks has weakened both the capacity and the will of the international community to respond to food shortages."

The foregoing assertion is dramatic, but we venture to cast doubts on whether it is applicable or even true. In actual fact, an analysis of the evolution of the *stocks* and a study of the *policies* which led to an adjustment of reserves make it difficult to justify the assertion made by Brown. Let us first examine on what basis "P-Fact III" is asserted. We start by noting that the greatest reserves of cereals in the world are held by the United States. In 1961-2 this country held 76% of the total grain stock of the market economy countries: 116 million tons. The rest, 37 million, was divided between Argentina, Australia, Canada, France, India and Japan. From then onwards, stocks in the United States continuously declined, falling to 58.2 million in 1967-8. Even this represented 58% of the total reserves of the market economy countries. The North American stock rose again the following year, but again fell in 1970-71 (54.5 million). Stocks again went up in 1971-2 to 73.4 million, but then started to fall sharply reaching an absolute minimum of 27 million tons in 1974-5 (42% of the total of countries mentioned).

We again refer to L. Brown, who illustrated this situation in Table 1.9 (*op. cit.*, page 60).

The striking title of Table 1.9[5] and also the figures it contains ensured for it a wide distribution. "World grain reserves only enough for 30 days' consumption." No one could avoid the alarm contained in this phrase and it would be difficult to think of a better way of spreading the feeling that there is a "world food crisis". At the same time, the notion that *food security* depended on such world grain reserves was quickly adopted in the language used by the international agencies. Thus, the then Director-General of FAO in his report on "The State of Food Supplies and Agriculture in 1974" says:

"For the third consecutive year the world food and agricultural situation must be viewed with grave concern. During much of 1974 there were high hopes that this year would bring the bountiful harvests so badly needed for the world to begin to emerge from the food crisis that started with the widespread bad

TABLE 1.9
Index of World Food Security, 1961-74
(millions metric tons)

Year	Reserve stocks of grain	Grain equivalent of idled US cropland	Total reserves	Reserves as days of annual grain consumption
1961	154	68	222	95
1962	131	81	212	88
1963	125	70	195	77
1964	128	70	198	77
1965	113	71	184	69
1966	99	79	178	66
1967	100	51	151	55
1968	116	61	177	62
1969	136	73	209	69
1970	146	71	217	69
1971	120	41	161	51
1972	131	78	209	66
1973	106	24	130	40
1974[a]	90	0	90	26

weather and poor crops of 1972. Although there was a substantial recovery in production in 1973, very large harvests were needed in 1974 if a beginning was to be made in returning to any reasonable degree of security in world food supplies."

To what kind of "security" do L. Brown and the Director of FAO refer? Apparently, and from what is implied from the context of the expression "food security", the reserves are aimed at protecting those countries which might suffer from a shortage of food. It is clearly suggested by their arguments that if stocks fall to very low levels, an intangible "international community" would not be able (nor have "the will" as L. Brown suggests) to "provide relief" to countries falling a victim to famine. It is also explained that the United States is not "always prepared to take action, anywhere that there is the threat of famine" and consequently the only solution is to maintain reserves at reasonable levels.

However, it was not necessary to wait many years before the same sources made assertions flagrantly contradicting those on which we have just commented. In the FAO document "Rapport et perspectives sur les produits, 1976-1977" we find the following statement:

"World carryover stocks of wheat and coarse grains (excluding those held in the USSR and China), which FAO estimated at 146 million tons at the end of 1976/77 marketing years, could thus rise by a further 20-30 million tons by the end of the 1977/78 season, and exert downward pressure on grain prices throughout 1977 and well into 1978. Should world stocks expand to levels forecast, an adjustment in production policies, particularly in the main exporting countries, will be required in 1978 if a situation of serious over-supply is to be avoided."

This paragraph shows clearly the true role of reserves: to serve mainly as a price regulator. We know that we are not clearing up any mystery and it was certainly not necessary to read an FAO report to find out about it. But what we wish to emphasize here is the philosophical and practical discrepancy from one FAO document to another in dealing with the subject of the world food production and stocks. In certain documents dealing with the economic situation, such as the one we have considered, this body adopts a language in which it is recognized that the world food market—like that for cars, shoes or perfumes—does actually operate on the basis of purchase-sale of commodities with the maximum possible profit. In these documents the argument of the "world food security" is irrelevant.

The idea of linking the reserves of the major exporters of cereals with world food security does not appear in the analyses of many economists who deal with the policies to be developed in the matter of reserves. Thus, for example, Fred H. Sanderson, in his article entitled "The great food fumble" (AAAS Report, *op. cit.*) deals in a very precise way with this subject without at any time mentioning grain reserves as a guarantee of "world food security". That concept appears to have no place in his line of thought, which is clearly representative of the official point of view of the United States Government (Mr. Sanderson was Director of the Office for Food Policy and member of the Planning Committee of the State Department). Let us look at a paragraph of this article:

> "The experience of the years of 1963 to 1967 and 1972 to 1975 suggests that an even larger reserve, of more than 80 million tons, over and above privately held working stocks, would have been required to keep real grain prices reasonably stable during the latter period."

Once again the volume of reserves is related to price stability. This, and nothing else, is what preoccupies the decision-makers in the matter of reserves, and their specialized consultants.

We may ask: Why this feverish preoccupation to avoid the destabilization of prices? Sanderson recognized that exports of cereals and soya beans in 1974 brought in about 16,000 million dollars for the US. This figure represents 22% of the total earnings of the United States in exports during that year. The author is, of course, aware that through these earnings in food exports the United States resolved, at least temporarily, its serious trade balance problems by selling grain. Fred Sanderson explains three powerful reasons for it being highly desirable that the price of grain should maintain its stability:

(a) "Higher food costs are locked into the wage and price structure of the nonagricultural sectors, which is flexible only upward. Any subsequent decline of grain prices will have only minor effects on retail food prices (60 per cent of which are accounted for by processing and marketing costs) and even smaller effects on the cost-of-living index. The rise in the level of nonagricultural prices, in turn, will cause a permanent increase in agricultural production costs as farmers have come to depend rather heavily on inputs purchased from the nonagricultural sector. This 'ratchet effect' of commodity booms—their tendency to give a permanent boost to the inflationary spiral—provides an important justification for efforts to stabilize supplies and prices of primary commodities."

(b) "It is true that current shortages and the resulting high prices were helpful in swelling our export proceeds for these commodities; in the long run, however, excessive instability of supplies and prices would be likely to stimulate protectionist tendencies abroad."

(c) "Last, but not least, the United States shares with other countries a concern about averting famine abroad. When grain supplies are short and prices are high, the flow of food aid tends to dry up. Domestic needs and commercial exports take precedence over the pressing needs of countries unable to pay cash. Where funds have been set aside to finance food aid, the may buy less than half the quantities programmed before prices went up. Thus the quantities of grain shipped by the United States on concessional terms dropped to a 20-year low in fiscal year 1974."

This last paragraph, (c), is the only one which is in any way linked to the so-called "food security", although Sanderson certainly did not use that expression. In fact, in the precise language of the author, the link is indirect and in practice is even more tenuous. One way of showing this is to compare the periods of "crisis" in the stocks with the corresponding world food *situation.* We start with a quotation from the book edited by D. Gale Johnson and John A.Schnittker (*US agriculture in a world context,* page 11): "In the 1960s and to the present time, carry-over policy was set by executive determination rather than by legislative action. The Secretary of Agriculture saw in 1961 that surplus carry-overs of wheat, coarse grains, cotton, and dairy products were so burdensome to the Treasury and the future of US farm policy that they had to be reduced. The programme changes described earlier in this paper were designed to limit production of various crops so that carry-overs could be systematically reduced."

In the year mentioned of 1961, the Department of Agriculture had published the *World Food Budget, 1962 and 1966,* Foreign Agricultural Economic Report 4 (October 1961), containing cries of alarm concerning malnutrition in the world. Thomas T. Poleman, in his paper on "World food: A perspective" (AAAS Report, *op. cit.*), makes the following comment in this connection: "Three years later the USDA repeated the exercise. The map on the cover of the second report, World Food Budget, 1970 (8), revealed few new diet-deficit countries. But it is difficult not to believe than an important political angle had been discovered. Exaggeration of the extent of hunger in the developing world was clearly good politics for the USDA, faced as it was at this time with increasingly bothersome surpluses. Sales of gifts to the LDC's under Public Law 480 could postpone the day of more stringent controls or lower prices (or both) to American farmers."

We shall not elaborate on this subject of the expediency of Public Law 480 and the political functional character of "assistance" with food. For the time being, we only wish to point out the role played by both, as a "regulator" of reserves, in serving the *domestic policy* of the United States. We shall see later on that they also played a part in establishing international policy.

In conclusion we may summarize our view as follows. We cannot use figures to show the unfounded implication of this P-fact, that a main purpose of agriculture is to provide world security. Of course, food is a fundamental requirement for life. There is a demand for it, since quite a few peope do not grow their own. Therefore it is a marketable commodity, subject to the market forces of all commodities. Agriculture is a business and those who engage in it must make a profit. There is nothing wrong, conspiratorial or immoral about this within the general philosophy of market economies. Therefore, we must take a rational view of agriculture, not as an abstraction having to do primarily with humanitarian aspects, but as a practical business that must maintain an appropriate balance between forces: supply, demand, production costs, distribution aspects and relations to other large commodities in trade. The fact that inventories are held, and are useful, makes their secondary use as emergency food stocks, in a full market economy, possible. This is fortunate, but we must be careful not to push humanitarian values too far. The inventories are also subject to a more powerful force: their cost-benefit ratio. Further detailed discussion will be found in the paper by Siotis, included in this volume as an Annex to Chapter 5.

P-Fact IV

Once again, the assertion contained in this statement is strengthened by the conceptual context to which it pertains, and which may be summarized in the following quotation from L. Brown ("The politics and responsibility of the North American breadbasket", World Watch Paper 2):

"The Soviet decision to offset crop shortfalls with massive imports rather than via the more traditional method of belt-tightening by customers is the most destabilizing single factor in the world food economy today, one which is enormously costly to consumers everywhere. The instability derives not so much from the scale of Soviet grain imports as from their unpredictable and secretive nature."

We structure the point of view of those who support P-Fact IV into five "steps" or successive assertions which lead from the failure of Soviet crops to the shortage and increase in price of wheat throughout the world:

(a) The Soviet Union was faced with serious endemic agricultural problems due to climatic conditions and institutional inefficiency (in L. Brown's own words: "Where political expediency joins hands with agricultural inefficiency", *op. cit.*).

(b) The food situation in the Soviet Union became critical in 1972 due to severe climatic conditions which caused the wheat crop to fail (lack of snow in winter 1971 and lack of rain in spring 1972).

(c) In order to avoid a food shortage (or not have to "tighten their belts" in the vivid language of L. Brown (also used in the Flanigan Report, cf. Chapter 2 below)) the Soviets found themselves forced to buy enormous quantities of grain.

(d) This situation took the Western world by surprise, particularly the United States. Nevertheless that country agreed to sell.

(e) Consumers throughout the world suffered as a result of the depletion of reserves, and this in turn led to a rapid rise in prices.

The abundant information which is now available enables us to carry out an analysis of the food situation in the USSR in 1972 and also of the background to her trade agreements with the United States. These analyses contradict each of the five points made and show that the assertion contained in "P-Fact IV" is untenable. In order to reach this conclusion we used the basic document prepared for the IFIAS Project by Michael Ellman and included as an Annex to this chapter. We also made use of a paper by Carlos Gonzalez Garland ("Agreements on the sale of grain in 1972 in the context of US-USSR relations")[6] Other works on the subject include the detailed analysis on Soviet agriculture by the US CIA.

From a study of these data and documents, we conclude that:

(a) It is certain that the Soviet Union faced difficulties in agriculture, resulting from her geographical situation and the nature of her soils. But it is also certain that these adverse conditions only caused sporadic fluctuations in a steadily and appreciably rising production curve.

(b) The drought in 1972 in the USSR was much less severe than that in 1975, and the latter did not have the disastrous consequences which would be inferred from "P-Fact IV".

(c) There was no food shortage that year in the Soviet Union, nor had their been, even though there had been no grain imports. The relationship put forward between massive buying and the option to "tighten their belts" did not exist.

(d) The secrecy of the negotiations, which "surprised the western world" was beneficial both for the United States and the Soviet Union. For the United States, this operation took place at an exceptional time when a change in the structure of external trade, based on massive selling of cereals in accordance with the recommendations of the Williams Committee, had already set in.

(e) It was the decision to adopt this change in the policy of North American external trade which was to have an effect on the shortage of reserves and the increase in prices, whatever the selling channels used to dispose of the surplus.

Now let us look at some of the data and figures to confirm what we just said. In the first place, the impression of a "disaster" conjured up from reading the texts quoted in connection with "P-Fact IV" and its context is not in agreement with the actual figures contained in the tables for production. In the aforementioned CIA report on Soviet agriculture,[7] the chapter relating to production opens with an assertion similar to that quoted from L. Brown, attributing to the USSR limited productivity due to the environment, and also "managerial inefficiencies, and levels of applied technology lower than those in Western Europe and the United States". However, the report continues with a statement which is fundamental for evaluating P-Fact IV: "Average crop production in 1969-73 was 36 percent above the average production in 1961-65, and well ahead of the 15 percent population growth during the same period."

The Soviet Union is the principal producer in the world of wheat, barley, oats and rye (in addition to sunflower seeds, potatoes and beet). The largest production of grain is that of wheat, which was also the predominant grain bought in 1972-3. Many of those analysing the "food crisis" place special emphasis on the failure of the wheat crop in the USSR in 1972. But the figures far from support their assertions. The aforementioned CIA report says the following about this cereal: "The long-range trend of Soviet wheat production has been upward. The New Lands programme of the 1950's added significantly to the productive grain-growing area; since then, continuing improvements in yield, based primarily on new varieties and more fertilizer, have maintained the upward trend in production despite fluctuations in sown area. But the variability of weather in the USSR is so great that the difference in output between bad years and good years is still enormous.''

The curve for production contained in that report makes this concept sufficiently clear, but perhaps belittles the epithet "enormous" (Fig. 1.3).

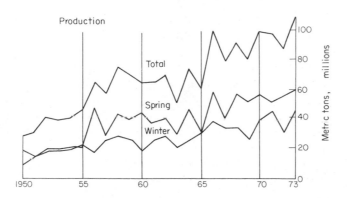

Fig. 1.3. Wheat production in the USSR.

The variability, which is mainly due to climatic fluctuations, is clearly seen in the curve. But the curve also shows clearly the progressive increase in production. The minimum in 1972 only appears important *with respect to the record years* of 1966, 1970 or 1973. The words "failure" or "disaster" do not appear to be justified.

But there is an even more significant aspect. If the total grain production in the 1970s is considered, the variations in grain production shown in Table A4 of Ellman's paper (see Annex to this chapter) makes it evident that the terrible drought of 1975 caused more serious ravages in grain production than the drought in 1972. In fact, with reference to 1973, which was the year of maximum production, the total production of cereals in 1972 was 24.4% less, whereas the decrease in 1975 was 37%. However, from the point of view of imports the two cases are very similar as shown by Table A.1 in Ellman's paper.

Two circumstances are found here which do not agree with the inductive generalization reasoning used to support "P-Fact IV". The first of these is that, evidently, the massive buying in 1975-6 did not have the catastrophic effect on the world market that is attributed to the buying in 1972-3, in spite of being of the same order of magnitude in tonnage (but considerably greater in dollars). The second is that, in spite of the fact that the loss of Soviet crops was much greater in 1975 than in 1972, the amount imported in 1975 was slightly less in total, that of wheat having been considerably less.

It is appropriate to analyse both of these circumstances separately. With regard to the first, we have already seen in examining "P-Fact IV" that the cause of the spectacular increases in the prices of cereals after 1972 was not the so-called law of supply and demand, nor the decrease in the level of reserves. Further on, the analysis of "P-Fact V" will lead us to specify the deep-rooted causes of these variations in price. However, it is appropriate now to consider an important aspect of this problem, in order to see in its proper perspective—the largest *buying operation in the history of world trade*—and to discover its actual effect on the "food crisis". The obvious question is, why did the USSR decide to resort to importing and, again, why did she import in such large quantities? We shall see, presently, how this gigantic buying operation was co-ordinated and carried out.

At the time when the droughts in 1972 diminished grain production, planning in the Soviet Union was at a stage which depended on a continuous expansion of meat production. The CIA document which we have already mentioned describes the situation in the following way (page 5). "The 1965 Brezhnev agricultural programme to provide more meat and other quality foods stimulated the domestic demand for grain as livestock feed, while the use of grain for food hardly changed. By 1969-70, grain input had fallen behind the increased demand, making necessary deep inroads into government reserves. The massive grain imports of 1972 were essential to maintain the livestock goals."

This statement is clear and is confirmed by the figures for meat production in the USSR given by Ellman. They show that in spite of the decrease in Soviet agricultural production in 1972 and 1975 meat production maintained high levels in the following years, with the exception of pork and possibly mutton. Ellman himself gives an explanation which, in our view, is very relevant:

> "In 1931 when there was a bad harvest, the USSR was a net *exporter* of grain to pay for machinery imports, despite shortages of basic cereals for human consumption. In 1963 when there was a bad harvest the USSR imported grain partly to ensure that there would be an adequate feed for the greatly expanded livestock population. In the 1970s when there were bad harvests the USSR imported grain to ensure that the animals would be fed so that the human population would have enough meat (as is done by West European countries). This change in policy over the years reflects the success of the Government's industrialization policy and its increasing attention to populate welfare, i.e. its increasing short term consumer orientation."

This review of the Soviet attitude at moments of agricultural crises during the last 40 years is far from being in agreement with the explanation given by L. Brown, in whose view the Russians formerly "tightened their belts" but now import cereals. But the necessity of not reducing cattle production does not entirely explain the impressive and massive buying of grain by the USSR in 1972. An indication of the real reasons is to be found in the question above from the CIA report, which mentioned the growing pressure on government reserves of cereals which in turn arose from Brezhnev's programme for the development of livestock rearing, i.e. that the USSR bought in order to compensate for the loss of crops, as much as to replace the depleted reserves.

Let us continue with the opinion of the CIA: "More than half of these imports consisted of wheat, apparently intended to replace the domestic wheat fed to livestock because of its poor milling quality. Wheat was also a better buy on the world market than corn or other feedgrains."[8]

It is certainly only necessary to study the way in which the operation was carried out to see that it was a paying proposition for the USSR. It has now been possible to reconstruct the developments in the negotiations for this enormous buying operation, which had repercussions on the international market, due to the fact that much of the information which was then "secret" has ceased to be so with the passage of time.

Within the framework of our project, Gonzalez Garland has traced these sources of information and placed the data obtained in their proper historical setting and in such a way as to render the entire process intelligible. It may be mentioned that much has already been written on this subject, although in general it is of a controversial nature; for this study more help was derived from personal communications giving an account of the experience of the individual concerned in parts of the process. From an analysis of this information, in its entirety, it is possible to reconstruct the causes and circumstances of that historical buying and selling operation, as follows:

(a) As is stated in the work by Gonzalez Garland: "beyond all reasonable doubt, the 1972 agreements on cereals, renewed in 1975, between the Soviet Union and the United States form part of the policy of *détente* or peaceful co-existence."

(b) The Soviet-North American agreement was, then, the result of an understanding, from which both parties expected to derive considerable benefits. For the United States, it meant a unique opportunity to get rid of excessive and costly reserves, to stabilize the balance of payments and stimulate domestic production by being able to lift subsidies and restrictions, putting into practice the recommendations of the Williams commission (cf. Chapter 2 below).

For the USSR it represented buying on advantageous terms, at low price and with a large credit, which enabled her to maintain plans for domestic consumption, meeting commitments with other countries (particularly in the Socialist area) not reducing reserves and, moreover, getting rid of dollars which were in the process of devaluation.

(c) There can be no doubt that the Soviet buying in 1972 took place in the greatest of secrecy. But there are uncertainties as regards who possessed the information and for whom it was secret. This subject appears to be beyond the scope of this work, were it not for the fact that it is closely linked to the problem of prices in the international market and, consequently, to one of our basic theories concerning the "food crisis". The information now available suggests the following course of developments as being that which provides the most plausible explanation.

(i) In 1972, a month or two before the harvest, the USSR already had a prediction, which proved to be correct, concerning the impact of the drought on grain production. At that time, the USSR sent *several* missions to negotiate independently and separately with the major exporting companies of the American continent. The missions were unaware of what they were doing in aggregated form.

(ii) It suited the USSR to keep the operation secret, in order to avoid publicity which, in view of the large scale of the buying, might have caused a sudden increase in prices. The operation was a success inasmuch as agreements were signed with *each* company individually at the low prices prevailing in the market at that time. And, as C. Gonzalez Garland has pointed out, this doubtless also influenced the scale of the buying. The favourable prices may have influenced the Soviets to buy more than they had contemplated.

(iii) The agreements with the companies could not have been signed without government approval. What was perhaps not appreciated beforehand by the US agencies that had to give their approval was the scale of the buying, in view of the points (i) and (ii) above. But it does seem very probable that there would have been any secret in this report for the US officials. Those who state this fact (e.g. Robbins in *The American food scandal*) relate it to corruption of the officials acting in the interests of the agricultural exporting companies. It is beyond the scope of this study to express any opinion as to whether this is so or not. For our purpose, what is important is that, even if this had been so, what was involved was an *official policy of the United States* which *necessitated* selling on a massive scale in view of the New Economic Policy of the Nixon Administration, and which used these sales agreements, their effects on stocks, their effects on producers and their effects on future buyers, to modify substantially the rules of the game in the international grain market. In fact, it seems to us that it mainly was a matter of good business on both sides.

Summarizing, on both sides, both from the point of view of the USSR and the USA, the general process of this now-famous sale of grain, greatly exceeds in importance, by its sheer magnitude, any other considerations which might arise in connection with the supposed "failure" of Soviet crops in 1972 and which occur in the analyses of those who support "P-Fact IV".

P-Fact V

This assertion, which implies that the 1972 drought caused a sudden rise in international food prices, was, as we have seen, generally accepted in many circles concerned with the subject, to the point that even such important reports as that of the World Food Conference (1974) accepted it without hesitation as a working hypothesis. In some instances, however, the argument appears to be tempered by the inclusion of other factors. This happened, for example, in the report of the US Department of Agriculture—ERS (*The world food situation*), which states on page 3 that: "The 1972 shortfall in world food production, the upsurge in food inputs, and the drawdown in stocks, along with inflation, rapid economic growth, and monetary adjustments, produced a dramatic increase in the prices of virtually all agricultural commodities (Table 4). The most severe impact was on the major food grains—wheat and rice."

This description, although it recognizes other causes which contributed to the impact of the drought on the increase in prices, still gives first place to the consequences of climatic factors. However, we are of the view that the increase in prices was not due to the decreased production, nor to the reduction of stocks. These situations were not the result of a climatic phenomenon that affected the market "naturally" through the law of "supply and demand". We think that we have also made it clear that it is an unjustifiable extrapolation to generalize assertions which are only valid for the *cereals* market, extending them to the entire *food* market.

The general increase in prices is repeatedly given as the most important consequence of the 1972 drought at the global level. Many authors of considerable prestige use this argument to illustrate both the vulnerability of the population of the world to natural phenomena, and the *interdependence* which would appear to characterize international relations in our times. The behaviour of food prices in the international market during the period starting in 1972 requires wider and more thorough consideration. In principle, simply by looking at the annual average price indices it can be seen that the increase of cereals forms part of a general rise of basic products, which is described as a "commodity boom".

Table 1.10, taken from UNCTAD, reflects this. It is therein pointed out that 1973 was the year with the largest "jumps" in prices and this gave it the distinction of being broken down into 3-monthly periods at the end of the table, in order to give the reader a better understanding of the phenomenon. A careful study of the figures makes it impossible to continue to maintain that it was the massive and "unex pected" selling of cereals which started the commodity boom.

TABLE 1.10
Average prices of certain primary products in the free market
(in dollars per ton)

Commodity	Wheat	Maize	Rice	Sugar	Wool	Sisal
1970	55	73	143	81	1962	156
1971	62	71	130	99	1786	180
1972	70	75	150	160	2976	246
1973	138	119	297	209	6989	535
1974	181	159	542	655	4916	1079
1975	151	154	363	450	3858	694
1976	134	139	254	255	3990	505
1973 I	102	96	195	200	7253	409
II	104	112	239	204	7253	451
III	160	137	344	202	7114	570
IV	186	132	409	231	6305	710

Commodity	Tea	Beef	Bananas	Copper	Lead	Zinc	Tin
1970	1093	1304	144	1415	304	296	3675
1971	1054	1346	140	1082	253	310	3503
1972	1051	1480	136	1071	302	378	3765
1973	1059	2011	145	1781	429	845	4813
1974	1393	1582	172	2058	593	1240	8190
1975	1382	1327	218	1235	417	746	6869
1976	1537	1581	215	1401	446	711	7584
1973 I	1061	1852	140	1289	344	428	4046
II	1075	1834	155	1629	403	573	4393
III	995	2226	147	2015	451	909	4993
IV	1104	2132	139	2189	519	1471	5819

The magnitude and distribution of the price variations shown in these tables indicate very clearly that these variations are reacting to a phenomenon of large proportions, which could not be merely a sudden change in the cereals market. Two situations which stand out clearly from the figures support our argument. In the first place, the prices of wool and certain minerals increased before the prices of cereals, and in some cases to a greater extent. On the other hand, not all agricultural products were subject to such increases. These two facts are enough to give rise to suspicions as regards the simple explanation which gives the drought as the cause of the increase in prices.

It is evident that this commodity boom arose in a situation of crisis involving, to a greater or less extent, all market economy countries. And so we must emphasize once again what we have insistently said throughout this report: those who have attempted to explain a supposed "food crisis" at the beginning of the 1970s on the basis of "*P-Facts*" such as we are analysing, have done no more than reverse the causal relationships, attributing the role of *cause* to what is only a manifestation or outward appearance of the process, and consequently an *effect* of it. We assert that it is the international economic crisis which produced the commodity boom, and not vice versa, although it does not mean that the relationship has been linear. It seems obvious to us that the various factors involved in the crisis interact with each other and mutually modify each other. What is of importance to point out is that the roots of the process should not be sought in climatic disasters, nor in a sudden increase in demand. They should rather be sought in the critical problems of the world economic system, the international monetary system and of the balance of payments of the developed countries. These problems arose before the commodity boom and before the 1972 drought.

This is not to say that there is a simple explanation, since there were many diverse factors which converged at that time to upset the balance of the situation as explained in Gambarotta's contribution (see Annex to Chapter 2).

SUMMARY AND FURTHER COMMENTS

In this chapter we have taken some examples of what we believe to be faulty conclusions or assertions based on inductive-generalized reasoning, level-2 interpretations, as discussed in the Introduction. We examined these assertions and the supporting evidence from the conceptual framework of linearized or serial causal chains and were dissatisfied that the "facts" supported the theses. We found many instances of necessity to look wider and deeper into related matters, along the lines of the level 3, or structural, reasoning that we advocated in the Introduction. These so-called (by us) P-Facts have been intended mainly to demonstrate the traps of maintaining a rigidly linear or serial conceptual framework. To generalize now (and we use the term "generalize" advisedly in view of our earlier remarks), we may point out a few salient features of the comparative analyses we have examined and undertaken.

First, using the same figures from FAO and other sources that we consider official and as complete and accurate as we believe that circumstances allow, we have been able to draw some conclusions quite different from those that have been derived by others, and which have played important roles in assessments and development of policies, such as those stemming from the UN World Food Conference, 1974. In physics, we never make only two measurements, for if they differ we cannot *a priori* distinguish which is right, or even if both are right. Here, the fact that we can draw a quite different conclusion than others have from the same data suggests in itself a problem. We devote further discussion to adduce additional agreements using a structural framework to reveal what we believe to be the main matters that deserve further study.

Second, in spite of the fact that we take as a matter of faith that the figures quoted here are reliable, we question their accuracy or representativeness. By reliable, we accept that they were compiled in good faith, that the governmental agencies that supplied them to FAO did so in good faith and honestly, and that the figures used by other authors, all of whom have scholarly reputations, are also "reliable" from a human point of view. However, under the discussion of P-Fact II, we point out discrepancies in large-scale figures that swamped any attempt to analyse small amounts of grain traded, produced, or lacking in malnourished of famine-ridden areas. We conclude that great care must be taken in the analysis of these figures. Accurate arithmetic itself does not reveal the real facts.[9]

To give another example of this problem, we reproduce here figures in Table 1.11 taken from FAO yearly handbooks. The yearly book gives production figures for a preceding 5-year period, with a lag of 2 years. For example, the figure for 1973 as given in the 1975 publication will have some errors. That is understandable. One will expect that the 1973 figures given in the 1976 yearbook may differ. Let us look into the table for an example that illustrates the danger of making a case from such figures above.

TABLE 1.11
*Indices of regional food and agriculture production for Africa
as reported in FAO publications*

Reference	1969	1970	1971	1972	1973	1974	1975
(1)	117	119	122	124	119		
(2)		121	124	124	121	127	
(3)			122	121	118	124	124

(1) *The State of Food and Agriculture 1974,* FAO, Rome, 1975, Table 1.2.
(2) *The State of Food and Agriculture 1975,* FAO, Rome, 1976, Table 1.2.
(3) *The State of Food and Agriculture 1976,* FAO, Rome, 1977, Table 1.3.

The 1971-2 change in production was specified in the 1975 yearbook as an increase of 2 index points. In 1976 the change was zero. In 1977 the change had become a decrease of 1 index point. We can see that an analyst can choose three interpretations, depending on which yearbook is consulted. No blame can be ascribed to FAO; they use the figures they obtain from the countries. What are the most reliable figures? How can we make a reliable analysis? This problem is pointed out to future analysts as one class of problem deserving detailed study.

Third, we feel that analysis of the world food situation mainly on the basis of grain is incomplete and therefore could be misleading. Of course, grains are an important ingredient of the human food complex. We see two areas of difficulty. One is that in many areas of the world, not completely insignificant even on the global scale, much grain and other food is grown and consumed locally, and never enters into the FAO compilations. Another possible error in reasoning to choose the grain as the primary food stock and reserve is that in times of need people subsist for long times on cassava, bananas, local non-cultivated foods, and also live by eating their animals. Thus, the "food security" projections based on "number of days of average per-capita consumption of reserve grain stocks" is probably a very conservative lower bound. In a real food crisis, other foods will be pressed into service. It is likely that grain suitable for direct human use would no longer be fed to animals, that the animals will be eaten, and that finally the grain no longer fed to animals will be eaten by humans. We do not advocate at all that by these means there is always adequate resiliency in the total food system. We urge that a more comprehensive analysis be made of the complex question of *total* food security.

Notes

1. We are grateful to Raul Green for his contribution to this and the following chapter. During the period of his association with the project he carried out an extended study of the international food production and trade. We are making use of only a fraction of the large number of tables and diagrams he compiled. Our supporting material for these chapters is therefore much stronger than the limited examples we provide as confirmatory evidences for our assertions. The idea of devoting a whole volume to this fascinating problem had to be abandoned owing to purely material reasons. Green's contribution was not confined to statistical work. Our discussions on the substance of these two chapters helped us to clarify our own thinking.

2. "Assessment of the world food situation. Present and future."

3. FAO *Trade Yearbooks*.

4. It must be borne in mind that in this period, during the India-Pakistan war, US sympathies were tilted towards Pakistan.

5. It seems that the expression "world food security" was first used by A. Boerma, Director-General of FAO in a meeting.

6. Available in mimeograph form, in Spanish. Not included among the contributions incorporated into the three volumes of this Report owing to the length of the text and difficulties in the translation.

7. *USSR Agriculture Atlas*. Central Intelligence Agency, December 1974.

8. We assume that the CIA refers here to the effect of the 1972 drought not only on the quantity but also on the quality of wheat produced.

9. We know, for example, that if we subtract one from the other two nearly equal large numbers, each of which having some small error (of about the same magnitude as the difference), then the difference will be statistically meaningless.

ANNEX

1972-3 Soviet Grain Imports and the Weather[1]

by Michael Ellman

(1) During the 1970s the USSR was a substantial grain importer, as Table A.1. shows.

TABLE A.1
Soviet grain imports, gross[a]
(millions of tons)

1970	1971	1972	1973	1974	1975	1976
2.2	3.5	15.5	23.9	7.1	15.9	20.6

Notes: (a) These figures exclude Soviet grain exports.
Sources: *Vneshnyaya torgovlya SSSR za 1970 god* (Moscow, 1971), p. 44,
Vneshnyaya torgovlya SSSR za 1971 god (Moscow, 1972), p. 46,
Vneshnyaya torgovlya SSSR za 1973 god (Moscow, 1974), p. 46,
Vneshnyaya torgovlya SSSR za 1974 god (Moscow, 1975), p. 49,
Vneshnyaya torgovlya SSSR v 1975 g (Moscow, 1976), p. 45,
Vneshnyaya torgovlya SSSR v 1976 g (Moscow, 1977), p. 42.

(2) During the 1970s the USSR was also a substantial grain exporter, as Table A.2 shows.

TABLE A.2
Soviet grain exports, gross
(millions of tons)

	1970	1971	1972	1973	1974	1975	1976
Total	5.7	8.6	4.6	4.9	7.0	3.6	1.5
of which to							
Poland	1.1	2.1	1.2	1.1	1.9	1.0	0.3
GDR	1.6	1.9	1.1	1.0	1.4	0.7	0.2
Czechoslovakia	1.4	1.5	1.1	1.1	0.7	0.6	0.1
Cuba	0.5	0.6	0.6	0.5	0.6	0.5	0.5
Korean People's Democratic Republic	0.2	0.2	0.2	0.2	0.2	0.2	0.2
UAR/Egypt	0.2	0.0	0.0	0.0	0.0	0.0	0.0
Chile	0.0	0.1	0.0	0.1	0.0	0.0	0.0
Others	0.7	2.2	0.4	0.9	2.2	0.6	0.2

Sources: *Vneshnyaya torgovlya SSSR za 1970 god* (Moscow, 1971), pp. 84-85,
Vneshnyaya torgovlya SSSR za 1971 god (Moscow, 1972), p. 85,
Vneshnyaya torgovlya SSSR za 1973 god (Moscow, 1974), pp. 87 and 313,
Vneshnyaya torgovlya SSSR za 1974 god (Moscow, 1975), p.89,
Vneshnyaya torgovlya SSSR v 1975 g (Moscow, 1976), p. 85,
Vneshnyaya torgovlya SSSR v 1976 g (Moscow, 1977), p. 77.

(3) Comparing tables A.1 and A.2, it can be seen that in the 7 years 1970-76, which included two bad harvests (1972 and 1975), the USSR was a net grain exporter in two, a substantial net grain importer in four, and in approximate grain trade balance in one. The tables also show that the main Soviet grain imports in this period were in two pairs of years (1972-3 and 1975-6). In each case they were a response to a poor harvest in the first of the years in the pair (1972 and 1975).[2] Table A.2 also makes it clear that Soviet grain exports go mainly to five countries, i.e. Poland, GDR, Czechoslovakia, Cuba and the Korean PDR.

It may be wondered why the USSR exports grain in years in which it is a net importer. The reasons appear to be as follows. First, the five chief recipients of Soviet grain exports are all countries with whom the USSR has close political links. To reduce exports to them might have undesirable political consequences. Secondly, because of the USSR's reserves of gold and foreign exchange, and its high credit rating, it is much easier for the USSR to finance grain imports than it is for countries such as Cuba and the Korean PDR. Thirdly, the chief recipients of Soviet grain exports receive it under long-term trade agreements. These can not normally be abrogated.

(4) Coinciding with the big Soviet net grain imports of 1972 and 1973 was a massive rise in world grain prices. This is often blamed on Soviet buying. It should be noted, however, that the internal factors determining world grain prices are current demand, current supply *and stocks*. A major factor in explaining the jump in world grain prices in 1972-3 was the (successful) policy of the chief exporting countries in reducing stocks (so as to save them financing costs and avoid depressing the world market).[3] The importance of this can be seen from the contrasting experiences of 1965-6 and 1972-3. In 1965-6 world stocks of wheat and coarse grains were reduced by some 35 million tons, or 25%, because of a poor harvest in the USSR and a threatened famine in India. In 1972-3 stocks fell by some 44 million tons, or almost 30%, mainly because of unusually large imports by the Soviet Union. The observable effect on prices and world trade in the first instance was negligible. In the second, however, prices rose dramatically and normal patterns of world trade were threatened with disruption. An important factor in these different outcomes was the state of world grain stocks. World grain stocks at the *beginning* of the 1972-3 agricultural shock were not much larger than at the *end* of the 1965-6 shock.[4] This reduction in stocks was the result of government policies of reducing the acreage sown to grain pursued in North America in the intervening years.

In addition, part of the explanation of the rise in world grain prices in 1972-3 was clearly external to the grain trade (because it coincided with a spectacular boom in virtually all commodity prices) and was caused by factors effecting the world economy as a whole in that period. Such factors include, simultaneous expansionary policies in a number of industrial countries leading to a sharp increase in world effective demand and the collapse of the capitalist world monetary system. When the external factors were not present, a big increase in Soviet grain imports (as in 1975-6 and 1977-8) was not associated with a jump in world grain prices.

(5) The big Soviet net grain imports of 1972, 1973, 1975 and 1976 largely reflected bad weather in two years (1972 and 1975) combined with certain Soviet Government policies (see below). As far as the weather is concerned, most of the major grain-producing areas in the USSR suffer from marginal climatic conditions. This is a commonplace of economic geographies of the USSR. Furthermore, because of complex meteorological factors[5] the weather in the USSR and particularly in the major agricultural production areas fluctuates substantially from year to year and significantly more than in other major world agricultural production areas. The extent of these fluctuations in annual average temperature and rainfall levels is still considerable even when they have been smoothed by means of applying a 5-year moving average. To illustrate the magnitude of these fluctuations, some data on weather oscillations in the USSR is set out in Figs. A.1 and A.2.

Figure A.1 shows the sharp year to year fluctuations in precipitation experienced by the USSR and its chief grain-growing regions. Figure A.2 shows the sharp temperature fluctuations experienced by the USSR and its chief grain-growing regions, and compares them with the Northern hemisphere as a whole. It can be seen that temperature fluctuations are much greater for the USSR as a whole, and especially for the central part of the European territory of the USSR, than for the Northern hemisphere as a whole.

This combination of marginal conditions and sharp weather fluctuations ensures that Soviet grain output fluctuates sharply from year to year in accordance with changes in the weather.

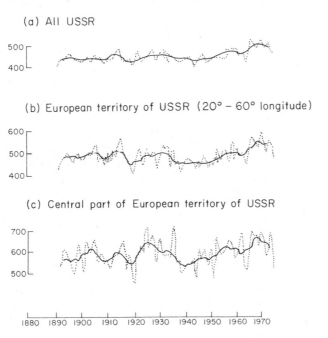

(a) All USSR

(b) European territory of USSR (20° – 60° longitude)

(c) Central part of European territory of USSR

Fig. A.1. Average annual and 5-yearly monthly precipitation for selected regions (mm of rain).

(6) The impact of the weather in Russia on the size of the harvest was already known long before the collectivization of Russian agriculture. Well-known studies are those by Fortunatov (1893), Brounov (from the late 1890s), Chetverikov (1920s) and Oboukhov (1920s). Before 1914 Russia was internationally recognized as being a pioneer in developing "the first comprehensive approach to the weather crop problem which extended over a large geographical area".[6]

Until very recently, however, very little attention was paid, either in the USSR or the West, to the use of weather data to explain fluctuations in Soviet harvests since 1929 (when the collectivization of agriculture was initiated). The reasons for this are quite simple. In the USSR, for many years the orthodox view was that under socialism the advantages of socialism would vastly outweigh "mere" natural conditions. "There are no fortresses that Bolsheviks cannot storm" was a well-known Stalinist slogan. Hence bad harvests were blamed not on weather but on "wreckers", "kulak saboteurs", etc.[7] Rather than admit that agriculture was not doing well and analysing the causes of this, the Soviet Government started publishing spurious output statistics (so-called biological yield) and relying on quacks (such as Lysenko).

(a) Northern Hemisphere

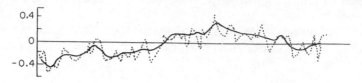

(b) All USSR

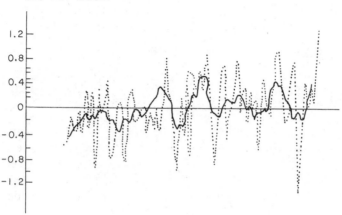

(c) European territory of USSR (20°–60° longitude)

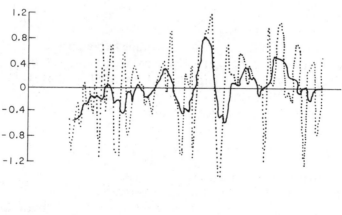

1880 1890 1900 1910 1920 1930 1940 1950 1960 1970

Fig. A.2. Average annual and 5-year anomalies in average monthly air temperature for selected regions (mm of rain).

(d) Central part of European territory of USSR

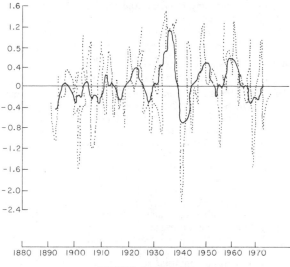

TABLE A.2 (cont.)

In the West, little attention was paid to the effects of the weather on Soviet harvests since this interpretation conflicted with propaganda needs. If each poor harvest showed "the failure of socialist agriculture" why bother about the effects of the weather? It is noteworthy that the United States Central Intelligence Agency has recently published a report in which the weather is used to explain away much of the *success* of Soviet agriculture in recent years.[8]

(7) Soviet grain output statistics in the third quarter of the twentieth century are characterized by two things. First, a strong upward trend. Second, very sharp year-to-year fluctuations. The first of these phenomena appears to be caused by a huge increase in modern inputs (e.g. chemical fertilizers and machinery), an increase in the sown area, and an improvement in the economic position of the farmers (whose real incomes have increased enormously in this period). The second is mainly caused by the weather. Some data on the trend and on fluctuations is set out in Tables A.3 and A.4.

Table A.3 shows clearly the high trend rate of growth of Soviet grain output over this 25-year period. This impressive achievement is not confined to grain, but applies to other types of agricultural production as well.

Table A.4 shows clearly the sharp year-to-year fluctuations, caused by the weather, to which Soviet agriculture is prone. In the bad year of 1972 bunker output was 7% less than in the previous year and 24% less than in the exceptionally good following year. In the other bad year of 1975, bunker output was 28% less than in the previous year. It should be noted that the drop in Soviet bunker grain output in 1972 was quite small in percentage terms. It was much less than that of 1975, and also less than that of 1967, 1965, 1963, 1959, 1957, 1953 and 1951.

Soviet agriculture in the third quarter of the twentieth century was a successful agriculture. According to US specialists,[9] in the quarter century 1951-75, total output grew at not less than 3.4% p.a. The population in this period grew at only 1.4% p.a., so that *per capita* output grew at *ca.* 2% p.a. This was a very satisfactory perfor-

TABLE A.3
The trend in Soviet grain output
(5-year averages, bunker output in millions of tons[a])

	1951-5	1956-60	1961-5	1966-70	1971-5
USSR grain output	88.5	121.5	130.3	167.6	181.6

Notes: (a) These statistics are not comparable with those for many other countries. The published Soviet statistics refer to "bunker" output. Most other countries (but not China prior to 1960 and possibly not China since 1960—see R. P. Sinha, "Chinese agriculture: A quantitative look", *Journal of Development Studies,* vol. 11, p. 204) measure "barn" output. The former exceeds the latter because it includes some moisture content of the grain; thrash and dirt admixtures; and losses during transport, handling and preliminary storage. The average relationship between bunker output and barn output is not known. Scattered evidence suggests that an average deduction of 20% from bunker output may give a rough estimate of the barn output (see K. E. Wädekin, "Soviet harvest losses and estimated barn yield of grain in 1975", *Radio Liberty Research Bulletin,* April 21, 1976). It is barn output that measures the output of useful grain.
    Whether measuring in bunker output distorts the trend, does not appear to be known.

Source: *Narodnoe khozyaistvo SSSR v 1975 g* (Moscow, 1976), pp. 310-311.

TABLE A.4
Fluctuations in Soviet grain output[a]
(annual bunker output, millions of tons)

	1970	1971	1972	1973	1974	1975	1976
USSR grain output	186.8	181.2	168.2	222.5	195.7	140.1	223.8

Notes: (a) Professor Wädekin has suggested (in correspondence with the author) that the percentage of losses tends to increase in years of very good harvests and to decrease with poor harvests. This is because of the shortage of harvesters and the protracted period of harvesting when the harvest is very good. If correct, this means that measuring bunker output rather than barn output magnifies the year-to-year fluctuations of Soviet grain output.

Sources: *Narodnoe khozyaistvo SSSR v 1975 g* (Moscow, 1976), p. 311, *SSSR v tsifrakh v 1976 godu* (Moscow, 1977), p. 120.

mance, and one much better than that of many other countries. For example, although there is considerable uncertainty about both population and output data for China, a well-known US specialist on the Chinese economy has estimated that there was probably no appreciable rise in *per capita* agricultural product in that country in the whole period since the foundation of the People's Republic.[10] Besides this *quantitative* improvement, there was also a *qualitative* improvement, with a significant increase in the output of high-quality products. Considered historically, the most important achievement of post-Stalin Soviet agricultural policy has been to eliminate famines in the USSR. Famines were endemic in Tsarist Russia. The USSR has experienced four famines, in 1921-2, 1932-4, 1941-3 and 1946-7. As a result of the progress of the Soviet economy since the end of the Great Patriotic War, it seems entirely likely that the famine of 1946-7 will be the last famine ever in Russia/USSR (save only in the wake of nuclear war). This is an achievement of fundamental importance in a country traditionally prone to famines.

Nevertheless, Soviet agriculture in the third quarter of the twentieth century suffered from four problems. First, its very low initial level (largely resulting from the policies pursued in the previous quarter century). Second, the fact that it was a high-cost agriculture, requiring massive inputs of land, labour and investment. Third, output, especially of grain, fluctuated sharply from year to year due to weather conditions. Fourth, the investment, labour and price policies pursued in the processing and distribution sector were not favourable to the general availability of good quality food.

(8) Bad harvests are a *necessary* condition for the USSR to enter the world grain market as a major importer. They are not, however, *sufficient.* In order to explain the Soviet imports it is necessary to consider also the policies of the Soviet Government with respect to international trade and grain use.

As far as international trade is concerned, it is well known that the USSR seeks a rapid expansion of it. It naturally wishes, however, to trade on favourable terms. Obviously one reason for the big grain imports of 1972 and 1973 in response to the modest decline in output in 1972 was the very favourable terms (with respect both to price and to credit) at which the USSR was able to buy grain. The author has no knowledge of the reasons for this state of affairs, so advantageous for the USSR. It is outside the scope of this paper to speculate on the causes of these favourable terms (e.g. the advantages of the state monopoly of foreign trade, the ignorance of US traders and of the US Government, desire to promote *détente,* purchase of conciliatory policy in Vietnam, desire of Republican Administration to benefit US farmers, etc). It is sufficient to note that the quantity of grain bought was undoubtedly influenced by the favourable terms on which it was available.

In the period 1965-75 the Soviet Government pursued a policy of rapidly expanding the output of meat. Some data is given in Table A.5.

TABLE A.5
Meat production in the USSR
(millions of tons)[a]

	1940	1965	1970	1971	1972	1973	1974	1975	1976
Total	1.5	5.2	7.1	8.2	8.7	8.3	9.4	9.9	8.4
of which									
Beef and veal	0.9	2.4	3.5	3.7	3.9	3.9	4.4	4.5	4.4
Mutton	0.2	0.4	0.4	0.4	0.4	0.4	0.4	0.4	0.4
Pork	0.4	1.8	2.2	2.9	3.2	2.8	3.1	3.3	2.1
Poultry	0.1	0.2	0.4	0.4	0.5	0.5	0.6	0.7	0.7
Other kinds of meat and category 1 offal	0.1	0.5	0.7	0.8	0.8	0.8	0.8	0.9	0.8

Note: (a) Columns may not add to totals because of rounding.
Source: *Narodnoe khozyaistvo SSSR v 1975 g* Moscow, 1976), p. 299.
Narodnoe khozyaistvo SSSR za 60 let (Moscow, 1977), p. 259.

Table A.5 clearly shows the rapid increase in meat output (especially poultry—largely reared by intensive methods) in recent years in the USSR. The result of this is that when the harvest fails, if the meat output increase policy is not to be jeopardized, substantial grain imports (or stock reductions) are necessary so as to provide feed for the animals. The data for 1973 and 1976 show that, even with massive grain imports, a poor harvest in one year normally leads to a fall in meat output (mainly pork) in the following year as a result of fodder shortages.

In 1931 when there was a bad harvest, the USSR was a net *exporter* of grain to pay for machinery imports, despite shortages of basic cereals for human consumption. In 1963 when there was a bad harvest the USSR imported grain partly to ensure that there would be an adequate supply of basic cereals for the human population and partly to ensure adequate feed for the greatly expanded livestock population. In the 1970s when there were bad harvests the USSR imported grain to ensure that the animals would be fed so that the human population would have enough meat (as is done by West European countries). This change in policy over the years reflects the success of the Government's industrialization policy and its increasing attention to popular welfare, i.e. its increasing short-term consumer orientation. This is manifested not only by its foreign-trade policy but also by its investment policy. Since the mid-1960s the USSR has been investing in agriculture on an enormous scale. Hence, although it is common in the West to criticize the USSR for its big grain imports of 1972 and 1973 (either because it indicates an inefficient agricultural system or because it disrupted the world economy) one might just as well praise the USSR for devoting much more attention in the 1970s than previously to the immediate living standards of the population.

The reader may well ask why the Soviet Government adopted this policy of increasing meat output. Is it not aware of the currently fashionable doctrine that animals are an extremely inefficient way of converting cereals to protein and that a more cereal-based diet throughout the world would be more in the interests of the world economy? In the USSR the pro-meat policy is explained with reference to the scientific norms for the consumption of various food products. (The method of norms is the basic method of consumption planning in the USSR). Some data on these norms is set out in Table A.6.

Table A.6 shows clearly the logic of the meat output expansion of the late 1960s and early 1970s. In 1970, whereas the actual Soviet consumption of bread was 124% of the norm, and of potatoes 134%, that of meat and meat products was only 59%. Hence the policy of improving the diet by reducing the share in it of bread and potatoes and expanding that of meat (and also other livestock products such as milk and eggs).

Where do these norms come from? In the Soviet literature they are treated as "scientific" norms derived from the findings of nutritional science. (They are compiled by the Academy of Medical Sciences.) It is obvious, however, that a major role is played by the international demonstration effect.

(9) Conclusion. The causal chain running from bad crop weather in the USSR in 1972, leading to a bad harvest in the USSR in 1972, leading to big Soviet grain imports in 1972 and 1973, leading to an explosion in world grain prices in 1972/3 is a weak one and overlaid with other factors.

First, the fall in world grain stock levels (resulting from the policy of the grain-exporting countries) and factors external to the grain trade (the world boom and the collapse of the Bretton Woods monetary system) played an important part in raising

TABLE A.6
Actual and normative food consumption in the USSR
(kilograms/head/year)

Food	Norm	1970 actual	1970 as % of norm
Bread (in terms of flour), groats, macaroni products	120	149	124
Potatoes	97	130	134
Vegetables and melons	146	83	57
Sugar	37	39	106
Vegetable oil and margarine	7	7	93
Meat and meat products	82	48	59
Fish and fish products	18	15	85
Milk and milk products	434	307	71
Eggs	17	9	53

Note: The figures have been rounded. This explains some minor discrepancies.
Source: P. Weitzman, "Soviet long term consumption planning: distribution according to rational need", *Soviet Studies,* July 1974.

world grain prices.

Second, poor weather was only one, and not the main, cause of the big Soviet grain imports of 1972 and 1973. In 1972 the weather in the USSR *was* unusual. In the European part of the USSR it was hot and dry, and in the Asiatic part of the USSR (especially Kazakhstan and Siberia) cool and wet.[11] Nevertheless, the weather was not so bad from an agricultural point of view. Measured by the percentage fall in grain output compared to the previous year,[12] the weather in the USSR was much better in 1972 than in 1975, and better than in 1967, 1965, 1963, 1959, 1953 and 1951. This finding is confirmed by direct measurement of the weather, which indicates that in 1969-74, and especially in 1970-73, Soviet weather was particularly *favourable* for grain production.[13] This favourable weather appears to have been just one aspect of a climatic fluctuation effecting the entire Northern hemisphere in this period. Other aspects were the Sahelian drought and failures of the Indian monsoon. Non-weather factors influencing Soviet grain imports in 1972 and 1973 were the very favourable terms on which the grain was available and the policy of the Soviet Government of building up livestock numbers in order to improve the people's diet.

This case study suggests the following hypothesis about the effect of climatic change on human society. While climatic change clearly has important effects on human society, the main factors effecting the development of human society at the present time are not external (such as weather) but internal (e.g. economic, social and political).[14]

Amsterdam University
March 1978

Notes

1. The problem, and the way to approach it, were suggested to me by Dr. R. Garcia, Senior Study Author of the "Drought and Man" Study. I am grateful to the participants in the September 1977 IFIAS Workshop for helpful comment and additional material; to Erik Dirksen for research

assistance; to Professor K. E. Wädekin for helpful criticism and to Mr. S. Wheatcroft for permission to use some of his work on the effect of climate on Soviet grain output.

2. It seems likely that this pattern will be repeated in 1977-8.

3. This has been widely noted. For example, Kaldor has written that "Many people are also convinced that if the United States had shown greater readiness to carry stocks of grain (instead of trying by all means to eliminate its huge surpluses by giving away wheat under PL 480 provisions and by reducing output through acreage restrictions) the sharp rise in food prices following upon the large grain purchases by the USSR, which unhinged the stability of the world price level far more than anything else, could have been avoided." (N. Kaldor, "Inflation and recession in the world economy," *Economic Journal,* December 1976, p. 713).

4. P. H. Trezise, *Rebuilding Grain Reserves* (Brookings Institution, Washington, DC, 1976), p. 1.

5. Basically this appears to be the combination of a highly continental weather pattern, with the occasional blocking in the seasonal paths of cyclones, which together occasionally produce the well-known *sukhovei,* dry hot east winds which blow from Central Asia across the Volga, North Caucusus and the Ukraine.

6. F. H. Sanderson, *Methods of Crop Forecasting* (Harvard, 1954), p. 188. The material in this paragraph, and some of the preceding material, is taken from S. Wheatcroft, "Work in progress on the reappraisal of the efficiency of Soviet agricultural production in the 1920s and 1930s," paper presented to the conference on "Soviet Economic Development in the 1930s" at Birmingham University in May 1977. I am grateful to Mr. Wheatcroft for permission to use this material. Mr Wheatcroft's work on Soviet inter-war grain statistics, and the effect on Soviet harvest outcomes of the weather, is a major contribution to the understanding of Soviet economic statistics and of Soviet economic history.

7. The widespread view (energetically propagated by the Soviet writer Sholokhov) that the fall in Soviet livestock numbers in the First Five Year Plan was entirely due to kulak sabotage appears to be a political myth. It neglects the role of the decline in available animal feed in this period.

8. *USSR: The Impact of Recent Climate Change on Grain Production,* Research Aid (CIA, Washington, DC, 1976).

9. J. R. Millar, "The prospects for Soviet agriculture", *Problems of Communism,* May-June 1977.

10. A. Eckstein, *China's Economic Revolution* (Cambridge, 1977), p. 212.

11. A. L. Katz, *The Unusual Summer of 1972* (translation by L. A. Hutchinson of book published by Gidrometizdat, Leningrad, 1973).

12. This is only an indirect way of measuring the weather, and may seem rather arbitrary. It should be noted, however, that so-called "direct" methods involve weighting different kinds of weather factor (e.g. precipitation, wind and temperature) over different regions and different months. Furthermore, it is not so arbitrary, given that it is the weather-induced fluctuations in grain output that we are interested in.

13. *USSR: The Impact of Recent Climate Change on Grain Production,* Research Aid (CIA, Washington, DC, 1976), *passim.*

14. Similarly, A. K. Sen has shown that the Bengal famine of 1943 was not primarily caused by a weather-induced failure of production, but by economic and social factors effecting demand and distribution. (A. K. Sen, "Starvation and exchange entitlements: a general approach and its application to the great Bengal famine," *Cambridge Journal of Economics,* vol. 1, no. 1, March 1977.) In the same vein, Dando has argued that in the millenium 971-1970 Russian famines were predominantly man-made, not natural, disasters. (W. A. Dando, "Man-made famines", *Ecology of Food and Nutrition,* vol. 4, pp. 219-34, 1976.)

CHAPTER 2

An Alternative View on the 1972 "Food Crisis"

1. Preliminary Remarks

A climate particularly unfavourable for food production (droughts hitting several continents), a soaring demand for food spurred by continuous population growth and rising affluence, have been the alleged reasons for the food crisis that began in 1972 and which resulted in food reserves declining and food prices sky-rocketing.

A large number of facts are currently referred to in support of such an allegation, and masses of data are provided to substantiate them. These facts are then arranged in sequences having the appearance of causal chains: unusual demands for food are the effect of crop failures and demographic pressures; these demands are the cause of increasing imports; these, in turn, are the cause of declining food reserves the effect of which is sky-rocketing prices, etc. We contend that each individual assertion in this chain is only a partial fact or a pseudo-fact, i.e. it is either an insufficient or a distorted description accounting for a particular situation which was far more complex than is assumed in these causal chains. We have called them "P-facts". We object to the inclusion of P-facts and to the omission of what we consider to be "objective" facts in these causal chains.

Some of the basic data supporting our claim are given in the preceding chapter. But so far we have put the emphasis of our analysis on the disproof of the current explanation of the 1972 food crisis. The main questions have remained unanswered: Was there indeed a food crisis during the period 1972-4? If so, what were its characteristics? How did it originate? How was it related to the 1972 worldwide drought?

Some of the answers have already been hinted at. Now it is time to elaborate them. In order to do this, we shall first make a distinction between two categories of problems, corresponding to two sets of events which are lumped together in current explanations of the 1972 crisis, but which, in our view, belong to two entirely different realms: the events related to the profound changes which took place on the international food market in the early seventies, and the events associated with the drought affecting several regions of the world at about the same period. Our thesis is that both sets of events were originally independent of each other, that the former started earlier and still lasts, and that the latter interacted afterwards with it. If this thesis is accepted—and we shall adduce evidence in its favour—then the interplay between natural phenomena, the people who died of starvation and the food traders will be seen in another perspective.

This means that we shall not start with the drought, nor with the crop failures, nor

51

with the appalling description of the Sahelian famines. In this chapter we shall only consider their alleged effects at the international level, in so far as is necessary, to disprove it. We shall come to those subjects at a later stage and then we shall deal with the real effects of the drought and the mechanism of action.

Before entering into a discussion of the main subject of this chapter, it seems desirable to make a few remarks in order to avoid misunderstandings with reference to our position. We have critisized in rather strong terms, both in the Introduction and in Chapter 1, the readiness of many authors to resort to apocalyptic-type explanations for the suffering and misery of large sectors of the world population. We must therefore emphasize that we are not falling, as a reaction, into what is called the "conspiracy-model". Certainly, when we reject the idea that natural disasters or other unplanned catastrophic events are the fundamental reasons for extended malnutrition in the world, this automatically implies that the causes are to be found in the actions of human beings. Nevertheless, it does not imply that whatever happened was planned by groups of people, or by institutions, or by governments, to be as it was. The number of variables at play, nationally and internationally, is so high, and their interactions are so strong, that carefully planned situations easily get out of control. We have devoted a full chapter to showing how only a structural analysis may clarify the combined effect of those interactions. What we maintain is that certain measures implemented by strong economic or political powers (governments, private corporations or whatever) do start socio-economic processes which have a dynamics of their own and which interact with natural processes in a very strong way. Sometimes the whole system will evolve in a manner which makes the processes irreversible or only reversible at a very high cost to the countries or the societies involved. Their whole socio-economic structure will then determine the future evolution, as much or even more than the initial actions (cf. Chapter 6).

2. Diagnosis of the Food Crisis

The thesis we shall attempt to prove in this chapter is that the 1972 food crisis had its origin in fundamental changes in the structure of the world food trade induced by some aspects of the economic crisis of market economies, the 1972 drought being only an aggravating short-term factor. We therefore need to make a brief survey of the international food market to single out those characteristics which will trigger off a crisis. In order to do that we shall be obliged to go over part of the material already referred to in Chapter 1, although in a somewhat different way.

A first quick glimpse of the structure of the international food market can be obtained by reference to a very simple table showing the origin and destination of food in the trade among the two large economic country groupings of market economies: developed market economies and developing market economies. Table 2.1 exhibits the appropriate data for some selected years in the period 1960-75.

The first striking feature of this table is the relatively low weight of developing countries in the total world food imports. Some simple comparisons may help to grasp the full significance of this fact. In the critical 1972-5 period, the total food imports of *all* developing countries were only 51% of the food imports of the European Economic Community; the food imports of Latin America only 50% of the food imports of the US; and the amount of food imported by Africa was only 57%

TABLE 2.1
Food exports of market economies
(Current value in thousand million dollars)

Exports from	Developed market economies	Developing market economies	Years
	8.39	2.92	1960
	13.05	3.40	1965
Developed market economies	18.75	4.54	1970
	21.33	5.03	1971
	26.46	5.65	1972
	37.33	8.92	1973
	42.12	13.18	1974
	47.27	14.50	1975
	6.32	1.54	1960
	7.39	1.95	1965
Developing market economies	9.84	2.08	1970
	9.74	2.38	1971
	11.42	2.82	1972
	15.11	3.87	1973
	18.26	6.09	1974
	18.04	6.92	1975

Source: United Nations, *Yearbook of International Trade Statistics 1976*, Volume 1, Trade by country, Special Table C, pp. 72-73.

TABLE 2.2
A comparison of food imports by selected countries and economic country grouping
(in million dollars)

	1970	1971	1972	1973	1974	1975	1972-75 Total	b/a
(a) European Economic Community	19,040	21,130	25,910	35,880	41,810	45,290	148,890	
								51%
(b) Developing market economies	8230	9140	10,130	15,540	24,110	25,930	75,710	
(a) US	5980	6330	7360	9270	10,720	9700	37,050	
								50%
(b) Latin America	2080	2310	2690	3950	5880	5910	18,430	
(a) UK	4500	4740	5310	6710	8230	9330	29,580	
								57%
(b) Africa	1780	1980	2150	3200	5420	6100	16,870	

Source: Basic data taken from UNCTAD, *Handbook of International Trade and Development 1976 and Supplement 1977.*

of UK food imports (see Table 2.2).

If we now turn to net exports and imports, we find some even more striking features. In the first place, the *developing* countries have always been net *exporters* of food, whereas the *developed* countries are net *importers*. Table 2.3 shows that this continued to be true even during the years of the food crisis. During the whole period 1970-75, the *net exports* of the developing countries with market economies amounted to 42,030 million dollars, whereas the *net imports* of developed countries reached the value of 32,420 million dollars. Moreover, in 1973, the famous year preceding the World Food Conference, and supposedly the year which would show the impact of the 1972 drought on international trade, the developing countries reached all time maximum values of food exports.

TABLE 2.3
A comparison of net food exports and imports for selected countries and economic country groupings
(in million dollars)

	1970	1971	1972	1973	1974	1975	1970-72	1973-75
Developing market economies	6340	5590	7220	8220	7420	7240	19,150	22,880
Developed market economies	-6080	-5480	-6390	-5720	-5810	-2910	-17,950	-14,470
Developing America	5080	4770	5880	7930	9310	10,800	15,730	28,040
US	830	760	1360	7310	9750	11,170	2950	28,230
Developing Africa	1790	1330	1630	1720	700	-260	4750	2160
UK	-3240	-3280	-3630	-4510	-5650	-6100	-10,150	16,260

Source: Basic data taken from UNCTAD, *Handbook of International Trade and Development 1976* and *Supplement* 1977.

One must therefore be very cautious in making general statements about *interdependency* in the trade relations between the major economic groups of countries. If there is any general conclusion to be drawn from Table 2.3, it is only in the sense of a strong *dependency* of developed countries with respect to developing countries, not vice versa.

Let us focus the analysis on the years 1971 and 1974, that is, the years immediately before and immediately after the critical 1972-3 period when, according to the official version, the food crisis began.

In 1974, in the depth of the food crisis, the developed countries (market economies) were *net importers* of food, amounting to 6.460 million dollars (obtained from Table 2.4A as the difference between 73,200 million of total imports and 66,740 million of total exports). The *net exports* of developing countries amounted to 7350 million dollars (similarly obtained from Table 2.4A as the difference between 31,460 million of exports and 24,110 million of imports). The developed countries exported to the developing countries an amount equal to 30.7% of their exports to other developed countries. The developing countries exported to other developing countries an amount equal to 30.9% of their exports to the developed countries. Altogether, the developing countries received 22.5% of all food exports in the world, whereas the developed countries received 68.4%. The difference (9.1%) went to socialist countries.

TABLE 2.4
*Food trade structure and population distribution
by economic country groupings*
1974
(in million dollars)

A. *Food trade structure*

Origin	Developed market economies	Developing markets economies	Centrally planned economies	Total
Developed market economies	48,500	14,880	3360	66,740
Developing market economies	21,530	6660	3270	31,460
Centrally planned economies	3170	2570	3150	8890
Total	73,200	24,110	9780	107,090

B. *Food trade structure compared with population distribution*

	Distribution of total food imports	Value of net food exports	Population distribution
Developed market economies	68%	-6460	19%
Developing market economies	22%	7350	49%
Centrally planned economies	9%	- 890	32%

Source: UNCTAD, *Handbook of International Trade and Development Supplement 1977*
FAO, *Production Yearbook 1975*
Note: the negative numbers indicate net *imports.*

The disparity in the distribution of total food imports and net food exports between developed and developing countries becomes more striking when it is compared with the population distribution (Table 2.4B). The developed countries with less than 20% of the world population received 68% of all food exports; the developing countries with half of the world population received 23% of food exports. And this was the year of the United Nations World Food Conference when the FAO proclaimed that the developing countries were experiencing a most serious crisis just because they did not produce enough food to catch up with their population growth under the pressure of environmental stresses. Perhaps what was really meant was that the developing countries could not keep up with the draining away of food towards the developed countries. If this is what was meant, it is undoubtedly true, although many factors other than population growth and climatic stresses were responsible for this situation.

There are, however, some important features of the *net* trade structure, as represented in Table 2.3, which are essential elements in our analysis. By far the largest variations in the table correspond to US exports. From 1971 to 1974 the net US food exports were multiplied by *thirteen*. It is undoubtedly to this jump that Lester Brown and Eckholm refer when they speak of "the degree of the world's dependence on one region—North America—for exportable food supplies", or they point out that "the United States has achieved a unique position as a supplier of food to the rest of the world". Table 2.3 shows that only *after* the dramatic increase in 1973 did the US export (*net*) *as much as* Latin America, whereas in the 1970-72 period US exports were less than one-fifth of the Latin American net exports.

A careful reading of the same table also brings out some other important points. The 3-year period 1972-4 shows a striking uniformity in the *values* of the net imports of developed countries and the net exports of developing countries, in spite of the large price variations which were characteristic of this period. However, US net exports increased by a factor of 7.2. These discrepancies show only that in analyzing the world food trade structure no analysis could be conclusive if it were restricted to the *country composition* only, without taking into account the *product composition* of the trade. When the latter is brought into the picture, it is easily seen that in spite of the continuous increase in the amount they export, the constancy of export value of developing countries means a deterioration of the exchange relations for them: they are selling at relatively lower prices and buying at relatively higher prices.

This fact is usually masked by the way in which the tables of food statistics are "read", that is, by the features of tables which are singled out and the conclusions drawn from such features. As an example, let us go back to Table 2.1; it shows that as already pointed out, throughout the period of crisis the food exports of developing countries still exceeded by far the food trade in the reverse direction. But the progression of trade in each direction is not the same: the value of the latter increased at a much faster rate than the value of the former. This may be more clearly grasped if we plot the figures. Figure 2.1 shows the curves we obtain. From 1972 to 1975 the food exports from the developing to developed market economies increased by 58%, whereas the reverse trade increased by 156%.

From these last figures one may be tempted to jump to the conclusion that the demands for food by developing countries are becoming much larger than the demands for food of developed countries. In fact, an analysis of the 1972 food crisis does imply this conclusion which we consider to be a blunder, for the argument is entirely fallacious. Table 2.1 may be read in another way: from 1972 to 1975 the developed countries increased their food exports by 37,500 million dollars. Of this amount, 23,300 million, i.e. 65.3%, corresponds to the increase of trade with other developed countries, whereas the increase for the developing countries is only 10,200 million, i.e.28.6%. Likewise, the developing countries increased their own exports of food by 15,900 million dollars, out of which 49.7% correspond to developed

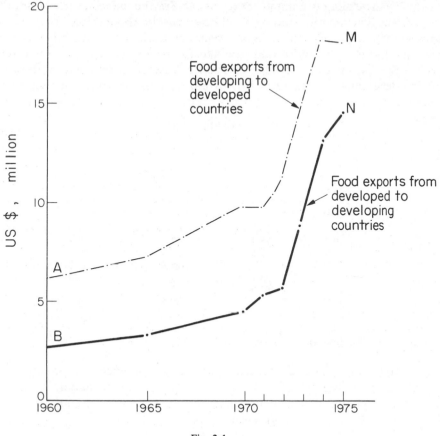

Fig. 2.1

countries and only 29% to other developing market economies. In other words, the fact that the two curves in Figure 2.1 become relatively closer has not changed the broad characteristics of the world situation concerning food trade. The developed countries still absorb about two-thirds of all food imports.

The two interpretations of Table 2.1 are obviously quite legitimate. We do not claim that the second is acceptable and the first is not. What we claim is that *both* interpretations are necessary to obtain a correct diagnosis of the situation, as each leads to different but complementary conclusions. As already mentioned, the latter shows that the country composition of the trade has not undergone much change. This being so, the former interpretation can only imply the product and price composition of the trade did change and it happened in such a way that the developing countries were seriously affected.

The reason why the "official view" has not reached this conclusion is, we believe, twofold. In the first place, tables like 2.1 are interpreted only in the first way, the second way being ignored. Secondly, most analyses do not refer to *food* trade, but to *cereals* trade, and the latter has quite a different structure. In fact most of the features of the world food trade we have described above are usually hidden is some well-known analyses of food crisis which are restricted to the international trade of *cereals.* We have already pointed out (cf. P-fact III) the fallacious use of cereal trade figures to depict the crisis and we shall now consider this subject in greater detail.

Those for whom the production of cereals and the international market of cereals are synonymous with food production and food trade may present some very impressive figures. Figures like those in Table 2.5 are often exhibited to show the increasing dependency of the rest of the world with respect to the developed market economies.

TABLE 2.5
Net exports of cereals
(in million tons)

Year	Developed market economies	Developing market economies	Socialist countries
1970	25.6	-14.6	- 8.4
1971	25.8	-17.9	- 7.3
1972	49.5	-20.0	-26.2
1973	67.8	-28.8	-32.2
1974	44.1	-29.8	-16.0
1975	62.0	-37.7	-24.7
1976	63.0	-30.6	-34.8

Note: negative figures represent net imports.
Source: FAO Trade Yearbooks 1975 and *1976.*

The above "facts" are just partial descriptions of a much more complex reality. By using the methodology of Chapter 1, we could include them among the P-facts. In order to show this we shall consider one by one each of the arguments which may be invoked to bestow on cereals such a predominant role.

(a) THE ARGUMENT OF THE VOLUME OF TRADE

A few comparative figures will dispose of this argument. They are:

(i) In the 1971-4 period, the trade in products of animal origin was 26% greater than the trade in cereals (see Table 2.6).

TABLE 2.6
Trade cereals compared with products of animal origin*
(in million dollars)

	1971	1972	1973	1974	1971-74
Products of animal origin	14,151	17,847	23,855	24,365	80,218
Cereals	9348	10,065	17,461	26,903	63,777

Note: * Include items 00, 01, 02 and 03 of the SITC.
Source: FAO Trade Yearbook 1975

(ii) Wheat is undoubtedly the main element in the international cereals trade. The value of the trade in wheat is, however, 42% *lower* than the trade in livestock and meat (items 00 and 01). The figures are as in Table 2.7.

TABLE 2.7
Value of wheat imports as compared with livestock and meat imports
(in million dollars)

	1971	1972	1973	1974	1971-74
Livestock and meat	7294	9636	13,236	11,797	41,963
Wheat	4298	4614	8173	12,541	29,626

Source: FAO Trade Yearbook 1975.

(iii) The second cereal in importance in world trade is maize. The total trade in 1971-4 is 29% *lower* than the trade in fishery products.

(iv) The value of the trade of only two fruits, bananas and oranges, is equivalent to 87% of the total trade of rice. The figures for the 1971-4 period are 7514 and 8592 million dollars, respectively.
(*Source: FAO Trade Yearbook 1975.*)

(b) THE ARGUMENT OF THE AMOUNT OF CULTIVATED LAND

The most frequently used argument to show the dominant role of cereals in food production is the total extension of cereal crops which cover the largest percentage of the total cultivated land. This argument should be handled with care. FAO tables on land use and on cereals production give the following figures which provide the adequate context to evaluate the role of cereals (year 1975):

Permanent pastures	3046 million ha
Arable land and land under permanent crops	1506 million ha
Cereals (area harvested)	743 million ha

This means that cereals were harvested in 1975 from 14% of the land usable for *food* production. To this we should add the food produced by oceans, rivers and lakes. No comparable area can be indicated, but the importance of the production can be roughly estimated by reference to the remark already made that the total trade of fishery products exceeds the corn trade. Even so, the role of cereals becomes overestimated unless we take into account relative yields of each product. The following figures show how misleading it is only to compare areas (Table 2.8).

TABLE 2.8
Yields of various foods (1974)

Tomato	19,752	kg/ha
Banana	12,719	kg/ha
Potatoes	13,491	kg/ha
Grapes	6167	kg/ha
Cereals	1834	kg/ha

Source: FAO Yearbook 1976

A similar picture is obtained if the production is expressed in dollar value per ha (Table 2.9).

TABLE 2.9

Tomato	8218	dollars per ha
Grapes	2240	dollars per ha
Banana	2234	dollars per ha
Potatoes	1708	dollars per ha
Cereals	330	dollars per ha

These tables clearly show that it is not fair to compare the "importance" of crops on the basis of the figures for cultivated area.

(c) THE STRUCTURE OF TRADE, THE ONLY VALID ARGUMENT

Since neither the total value of world trade nor the amount of cultivated land can explain the overwhelming importance given to cereals, we have to look elsewhere for the reasons. Perhaps we can find them by noticing that cereals are the *only item where the developed countries are net exporters,* whereas they are net importers in *all other* items, as shown in Table 2.10.

TABLE 2.10
Net food exports of OECD countries to developing countries
(in million dollars)

	1971	1974
Total	-7016	-7400
Live animals	-60	95
Meat	-714	-636
Dairy produce and eggs		
Fish and fishing products	-499	-1318
Cereals	1158	6492
Fruit and vegetables	-2012	-2838
Sugar	-1289	-3938
Coffee, tea and cocoa	-3819	-6096
Feeding stuff	-568	-606
Miscellaneous		

Note: negative figures represent net imports.
Source: OECD, *Trade by Commodities, 1971 and 1974.*

Let us now turn to prices. Table 2.11 shows the unit value indices (1970 = 100) and their variations. Thus, by comparing Tables 2.1 and 2.10, one can see that a considerable part of the decreasing difference between both directions of trade is taken care of by the deterioration of the export prices of food products from developed countries. For instance, according to Table 2.11, the *value* of the food exports from developed countries exceeded the value of their food imports by 100%, but in 1974 the difference was reduced to 39%; a correction for relative variations of unit value index would increase the latter figure to nearly 60%.

We arrive now at one of the central problems posed to the "Drought and Man" Project. We have already dismissed and generally accepted view that the sky-rocketing of cereal prices after 1972 was triggered by the depletion of stocks owing to the excess demand provoked by extended droughts and crop failures around the world. It remains to provide an alternative explanation. Gambarotta's paper, included as an Annex to the present Chapter, is the most satisfactory answer we have obtained. When we asked Gambarotta to undertake this study, we had only some general hypotheses and a strong conviction that the explanation we were seeking ought to be found in the complex structural problems of the contemporary economic crisis. We are glad that this IFIAS Project has originated a provocative and original contribution to a difficult subject. With Gambarotta's diagnosis, the role of the 1972 droughts within the international food market is reduced from the level of a cause to the more modest dimension of a second-order aggravating factor in a crisis having much deeper roots in the international economic order.

TABLE 2.11
Food exports of market economies
(Unit value index: 1970 = 100)

Exports from	Exports to		Years
	Developed market economies	Developing market economies	
Developed market economies	82	94	1960
	92	98	1965
	100	100	1970
	106	105	1971
	118	119	1972
	156	167	1973
	176	232	1974
	190	238	1975
Developing market economies	88	85	1960
	93	94	1965
	100	100	1970
	100	100	1971
	109	108	1972
	137	140	1973
	206	200	1974
	194	195	1975

Source: United Nations, *Yearbook of International Trade Statistics 1976,* Volume 1, Trade by country, Special Table C, pp. 74-75.

3. Etiology of the Food Crisis

The analysis of the international food trade structure and its evolution in the last 20 years makes it evident that, whatever the explanation may be, there was a fundamental change in the 1972/3 period. We endeavoured to describe this change. We shall now try to interpret it and to disclaim that the 1972 drought was responsible for generating it. In a certain sense, both things go together. By showing that some key events, which were presented as the alleged effects of the drought, were in fact the result of economic and political *decisions* taken before the drought appeared as a worldwide natural disaster, the disclaimer will be achieved and, at the same time. the basis for an alternative explanation will be provided. This notwithstanding, there is a great difference in the conclusions we arrive at: whereas the disclaimer will be conclusive, the alternative interpretation may not be quite as conclusive. We believe however that the presumptive evidence is overwhelming.

The key element in the alternative explanation is the set of measures adopted in the USA by the Nixon Administration, which introduced fundamental changes in international economic policy. This requires a brief historical introduction. The events recalled are recorded in two official US documents, the origin of which we shall first indicate.

On May 21, 1970, President Nixon appointed a "Commission on International Trade and Investment Policy" with Albert L. Williams as chairman. The Commission submitted its report, dated "July 1971", under the title "United States International Economic Policy in an Interdependent World", which is known as "The Williams Report". The views and recommendations of the Commission generated important measures taken by President Nixon, as well as concrete proposals to Congress for changes in legislation related to international trade policy. The background and the aims of these fundamental changes in US foreign policy are explained in the "International Report of the President" transmitted by Nixon to Congress in March 1973. The text of the President's report consisted of "The Annual Report of the Council on International Economic Policy" submitted by its Executive Director, Peter M. Flanigan. We shall refer to the latter document as "The Flanagan Report", but in view of the way it was transmitted to the Congress we also regard it as the President's adopted policy.

Let us first consider the Williams Report. The Commission which prepared this report was asked "to examine the principal problems in the field of US foreign trade and investment, and to produce recommendation designed to meet the challenges of the changing world economy during the present decade". The report starts by pointing out that "there are unmistakable signs in the United States of a developing crisis of confidence" in the existing multilateral trade and payments system. The following points are indicated as reflecting the crisis:

> "—mounting pressures in the United States for import restrictions as foreign-made textiles, clothing, shoes, steel, electronic products, and automobiles penetrate our market;
> —growing demands for retaliation against foreign measures which place American agricultural and other products at a disadvantage in markets abroad;
> —a growing concern in this country that the United States has not received full value for the tariff concessions made over the years because foreign countries have found other ways, besides tariffs, of impeding our access to their markets;
> —labor's contention that our corporations, through their operations abroad, are "exporting jobs" by giving away the competitive advantage in the United States should derive from its superior technology and efficiency;
> —a sense of frustration with our persistent balance-of-payments deficit and a feeling that other countries are not doing their fair share in making the international monetary system work;

—an increasing concern that the foreign economic policy of our government has given insufficient weight to our economic interests and too much weight to our economic interests and too much weight to our foreign political relations; that is still influenced by a 'Marshall Plan psychology' appropriate to an earlier period.''

The "crisis of confidence" can be traced back to two major developments: the increased pressure of imports on the US market and the fact that the US "ability to capitalize on (its) comparative advantages has been impeded by foreign barriers to (its) exports".

The report is quite explicit in singling out the two main sources of these problems: the European Community and Japan. There is a reminder that the USA—who "emerged, alone among the major industrial countries, with its production capacity and technological base not only intact, but strongly strengthened"—had "assumed primary responsibility for the economic viability and defense of the non-Communist world". The Marshall Plan, launched "to help Western Europe to get back on its feet", as well as the assistance provided to the economic recovery of Japan and the encouragement given to the European Economic Community, are mentioned as examples of "the overseas responsibilities the United States has assumed as the major power of the non-Communist world". Changes in the international setting, the Report claims, call for a "new realism" in the approach to these problems:

"Today, the United States still accounts for 40% of the production of the non-Communist world; but the European Community and Japan have become major centers of economic power and strong competitors in world markets. Western Europe and Japan have been slow to assume the responsibilities that come with power and strength.''

A serious criticism of this group of countries is of particular importance for our subject:

"The European Community's protectionist common agricultural policy has damaged some of our major agricultural exports; and its preferential links with other countries in the Mediterranean and Africa also have adversely affected our trade.
    —Japan has maintained many formal and informal import restrictions at the same time that it has greatly increased its exports to the United States. While Japan's spectacular increases in productivity were an essential condition of this export expansion, the latter has been stimulated by government measures and business practices not employed elsewhere nor contemplated in GATT. European restrictions on imports from Japan have contributed to increasing the flow of Japanese exports to our market.''

The main conclusion of the Williams Report is that "the United States must give high priority to new and intensified long-term efforts to export expansion". To this effect it is recommended that "a new comprehensive export-expansion program for the 1970s" should include:

—international efforts to reduce foreign tariff and non-tariff barriers;
—international efforts to limit the use of indirect export subsidies;

—intensified efforts to ensure that the US technological lead is maintained;

—thorough review and change wherever possible of all US policies, rules and regulations which serve to impede exports;

—expanded government promotional efforts and informational services to stimulate interest in the profit opportunities of export markets;

—a government framework that ensures US export interest a greater voice in the formulation of foreign and domestic economic policy.

Agricultural products are given a very special role within this export-expansion programme: "Endowed with plentiful good land and highly efficient technology and organization, we have a productive capacity far in excess of our domestic needs. Only on the basis of large and growing exports can we use our resources efficiently and thereby exploit our comparative advantages in agriculture" (page 141). The report expresses, however, the frustration of not being able to make full use of these potentialities.

To change this situation the report strongly recommends that the US should take the lead in developing "a new approach to the problem of agricultural trade", the basic question being "what strategy should the United States employ in order to obtain major, meaningful reductions in the barriers to agricultural trade". The main problem they have to face is the fact that the US foreign customers from farm products are not the principal suppliers of agricultural imports. The implications are clearly indicated: "Because of this three-cornered trade situation negotiations limited to agriculture are not likely to bring useful results. While Japanese and European Community farmers could not benefit greatly from increased access to US markets." The expression we have underlined may be linked with an implicit "warning": "Failure to obtain policy changes that permit significant liberalization of agricultural trade endangers the continuation of expansive trade policies in non-agricultural products" (pp. 142-3; the "non" is underlined in the original text).

The position of the Williams Report concerning the pressing need for expanding the agricultural exports is crystal clear. Not only the agricultural exports significantly affect its trade balance and thus its balance of payments, but also "exports are of critical importance to US farmers". The Report explains in detail why this is so and concludes: "In summary, the economic health of US agriculture is likely to become increasingly dependent on world markets. Furthermore, we have the capacity to export more if foreign markets are opened to us. We believe that our national interest demands agricultural trade policies that will permit and promote expansion of both US exports and imports of agricultural products, while meeting income objectives for farmers" (pp. 154-5). The word "both", which is underlined in the original text, is very important for our analysis. Its meaning becomes explicit on p. 243 where it is specifically recommended: "that the United States adopt policies which will expand both our exports and imports of agricultural commodities by shifting our farm resources toward products in which we have a competitive advantage, and away from goods in which we are non-competitive".

Time and time again the report insists on making use of "competitive advantages", and as far as agricultural products are concerned it spells out where they lie. In this connection it is indicated that "because of natural resource conditions and efficient organization, it is likely that the United States will have an enduring comparative advantage in field crops and especially soybeans and feedgrains". This contrasts with expected "increasingly weak competitive positions for products such as sugar, manufactured dairy produce, and some fruit and vegetables". The reason is given explicitly: "These products are in general more labour intensive and include crops for which US natural resources offer lesser advantages. Given access to markets abroad, the LDCs with their abundance of labour will become increasingly competitive in more labour-intensive products as they gain access to improved seeds, fertilizers, and other inputs, and as they are able to improve their marketing systems."

The Report also points out that out of the total US agricultural imports amounting to 5500 million dollars in 1970, there were about 2000 million dollars worth of "non-competitive products" such as banana and coffee, whereas "the remaining 3500 million were supplementary products, of which the two categories of sugar and 'beef and veal' each accounted for about 20% of the total in value terms".

The report makes it quite clear that it is on the basis of these differences that the whole structure of the US agricultural trade has to be reshaped. In order to achieve this goal a number of measures are suggested by the Commission in addition to those already mentioned for the "comprehensive new export-expansion program for the 1970s", such as the following ones:

(a) "Increased emphasis should be given by the Department of Commerce to encouraging the development of export trading companies. These companies could serve as selling agents for groups of US producers who individually are unable to mount significant export marketing efforts."

(b) "Given the increasing complexities of international business, (the Commission) believe(s) these services must be provided by specialists with intimate knowledge of markets and products." "(The Commission) believe(s) that (US) commercial services must be given greater status and importance. Accordingly, (the Commission) recommend(s) that (US) overseas commercial services be staffed by individuals expert in commercial activities and willing to devote their careers to such work."

There is evidence that the implementation of these recommendations to increase US exports would lead to a concentration of efforts in domains as sensitive as food consumption, which has characteristics very much related to culture patterns in many countries of the world. The importance of inducing such changes is recognized in the Williams Report. The following remark is very revealing in this respect: "Gains in consumer income worldwide that lead to increased consumption of animal products should be especially advantageous to the United States as the prime supplier of *feed ingredients*. The large gains in our agricultural exports to Japan have been the direct results of shifts in Japanese consumption patterns toward animal products and away from traditional staple foods such as rice" (*op. cit.*, p. 151).

The Williams Report is dated "July 1971". What happened after its submission to the President? The subsequent story is told in the Flanigan Report. Its initial statements and the dates referred to therein already show that the Williams Report started a profound policy change in the US. It was this change, and not the drought, which was the most decisive factor in the "food crisis" of the early seventies. Here is the text:

"With the bold initiatives announced by President Nixon on the evening of 15 August 1971, the post-war economic era came to a close, and a new age began. It is an age in which the United States no longer holds overwhelming dominance in the world economy, and in which the growing interdependency of nations can produce both increasing friction and unprecedented potential for abundance. That age is still only beginning. As a start towards realizing its full promise, the United States in 1972 and early 1973 made clear its determination to bring about basic reforms in the world's monetary and trading patterns to fit the realities of our time. Further major initiatives will be taken in 1973, both in international negotiations and in seeking legislation to make those negotiations more fruitful."

The Flanigan Report provides details about the background of "the bold initiatives" taken by President Nixon to overcome the US "immediate difficulties" and "to set the stage for fundamental reforms of the world's economic system". In the first place, reference is made to the dollar devaluation, which took place in December 1971 and February and March 1973, as the "international currency rate realignments" which "have strengthened . . . (the US) competitive position". The figure showing the variations of the effective rate of exchange of the US dollars in the late sixties and early seventies contains the following note: "Since 1970 the dollar has declined 12% in relation to other currencies taken as a group. However, the average incorporates a much greater depreciation against the EC and Japan, whereas most other countries have maintained their previous rates against the dollar. US products, therefore, will be more competitive with those of the EC and Japan in all markets." The Report points out that these "currency rates realignments" would not suffice for the intended purposes unless new international arrangements for the conduct of trade were also established. The reason is explicitly mentioned: ". . . the European Community and Japan have devices for the protection of their agricultural products which fully offset the effect of any currency depreciation, at a cost to their consumers and to our farms." This situation is declared to be "intolerable": "Barriers against our agricultural and high technology goods, where we have a competitive edge, are particularly frustrating" . . . "When the present framework was devised, the United States was still able to tolerate restrictive practices by others because of its economic pre-eminence. As has been stated repeatedly by many US spokesmen, this happy condition no longer persists."

What was the effect of these changes in US trade policies? It is easy to show that the product composition of the US food exports underwent structural changes which were quite in line with the analyses and recommendations of the Williams Report. Table 2.12 is very revealing in this respect: between 1971 and 1974 the net exports of cereals were multiplied by four and the exports of feeding stuff multiplied by three; the net imports of sugar were multiplied by three. On the other hand, dairy-produce went from positive to negative values. As for fruit and vegetables, the figures are difficult to analyse due to the heterogeneous composition of this item (with marked changes in "competitive advantage") and because they are very much distorted by a considerable amount of re-exporting.

The net result of these difference was spectacular. The changes are clearly reflected in the overall export and import of structure of the USA. In 1970 food items amounted to 16% of the total value of all exports; this figure increased to 23% in 1973. Conversely, food imports were 16% of all imports in 1970 and they went down to 13.7% in 1973 and 10.8% in 1975.

TABLE 2.12
US net food exports
(in million dollars)

	1960	1965	1970	1971	1972	1973	1974	1975
0. Total	-329	541	-1018	-1166	-705	3916	4604	6978
0.0 Live animals	-43	-81	-94	-72	-95	-43	19	-2
0.1 Meat	-197	-265	840	-859	-970	-1227	-963	-613
0.2 Dairy products and eggs	90	144	38	98	26	-230	-261	-43
0.3 Fish and fishing products	-279	-419	-700	-765	-1071	-1149	-1304	-1087
0.4 Cereals	1688	2597	2526	2376	3414	8389	10159	11463
0.5 Fruit and vegetables	90	9	-151	-134	-111	-20	133	286
0.6 Sugar	-530	-462	-780	-819	-907	-1029	-2373	-1917
0.7 Coffee, tea, cocoa	-1271	-1285	-1571	-1580	-1595	-2092	-2226	-2235
0.8 Feeding stuff	48	223	420	473	499	1191	1214	911
0.9 Miscellaneous	76	81	135	116	107	127	205	217

Source: OECD, *Trade by Commodities (Years 1960, 1965, 1970 to 1975)*.
Note: the negative numbers indicate net *imports*.

The evolution of food trade (FAO items o) between 1970 and 1975 was as shown in Table 2.13 (in million dollars).

TABLE 2.13

	1970	1971	1972	1973	1974	1975
Imports	4537	4606	5100	6599	7862	7173
Exports	4316	4450	5605	11,811	13,992	15,367
Difference	-221	-156	505	5212	6130	8194

Source: *FAO Trade Yearbook 1976*, p. 321.

We could still think that the 1972 drought played a major role in the sharp increase in the value of US food exports between 1972 and 1975. It did play a role, but the drought was neither the starting-point of the process nor the dominant factor of the process when it further developed. Two quite independent factors may be taken as confirmatory evidence for this assertion:

(a) We may admit that Soviet imports of feed grains and wheat were at least partially due to the drought, although the analysis of P-Fact V in Chapter 1 has shown that the reasons for the agreement were not that simple. But they could only account for about 40% of the increase of US exports in the 1972/3 period. The following comment provides an accurate evaluation of the situation: "In terms of their dollar value, US food exports to both Japan and the EEC countries increased by more than the amount of the grain sale to the Soviet Union. Furthermore, while the Soviet sharply curtailed grain imports in the two years following the 1972 sales, US and world grain exports remained high as a result of increased demand elsewhere" (cf. *US Food and Agricultural Policy in the World Economy,* Congress of the US Congressional Budget Office, Washington, DC, April 26, 1976, page 28).

A comparison between USSR and Japan imports of grain is quite revealing (Table 2.14).

TABLE 2.14
Grain imports
(in million dollars)

	1970	1971	1972	1973	1974	1975
USSR		277	955	1607	827	2856
Japan		1063	1050	1935	3327	3117

(b) The Williams Report stresses the need to take advantage of the competitive position of the US in the world market in agricultural and high-technology goods. With reference to high technology, the Commission points out that: US Government support for research and development today is concentrated in military fields having only modest civilian fallout." Guided by these remarks, we have taken the figures for US exports in both agricultural products and military equipment and plotted the curves showing their variations in the same diagram (Fig. 2.2). The striking similarity between the two curves

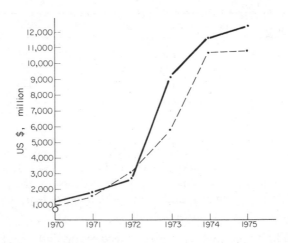

Fig. 2.2. US Agricultural exports and military sales.

makes it difficult to think that drought or any other natural catastrophe could be the common cause of the sudden "jump" in 1972/3. Neither do we ignore the fact that national catastrophes and subsequent scarcities produce social unrest which in turn leads to military actions. Ethiopia and Chad may serve as two examples, different as they may be. However, the changes in the exports under the Foreign Military Sales Programme can hardly be conceived as being induced by drought. On the other hand, they fit quite well into the changing patterns in commodity exports which were the result of Nixon's New Economic Policy.

ANNEX 2

An Integrated Approach Towards World Recession and Inflation in the Present Decade

by Hector Gambarotta

Introduction

This essay is a contribution to the IFIAS *Drought and Man Project:* the director of this project asked for a study of the current world economic situation from the beginning of the 1970s, the period of a disastrous drought of worldwide proportions. An investigation into the causes of world inflation was of major importance, in view of certain analyses which propose a strong cause-effect relationship between these disastrous climatic conditions and the worldwide acceleration in the rise of prices.

The paragraphs which follow will attempt to demonstrate that inflation in the 1970s is not a phenomenon directly caused by a specific event—such as a climatic disaster—but is, rather, a symptom of a much deeper and more complex problem, in turn related to the form which world accumulation has taken since the Second World War.

World recession and inflation which have appeared simultaneously in the 1970s is indeed a new phenomenon, which, as Robinson (1978) has pointed out, cannot be entirely explained by current economic theory and thus, in the world of Kaldor (1976), it presents a real challenge to economists.

I do not mean to take up this challenge here. An *explanation* of the current crisis would imply, in some sense, the construction of a new theoretical paradigm, adopting the terms of the theory-reality relationship outlined by Kuhn (1962).

I intend here only to describe the present crisis, to compare it with the preceding period of expansion and to attempt to isolate those trends and developments which have characterized worldwide accumulation during the last 30 years, in order to place the present *stagflation* phenomenon in some sort of general framework.

The unit of analysis in this study will be the world economic system. This approach involves a set of assumptions, developed by Salant (1977) in his "supranational" view of inflation, on the degree of integration in the world economy. Nevertheless, in my opinion, this approach to the problem does not restrict the scope of this study any more than would the more conventional approach, based on national economies.

The world "crisis" is used in this study in a comparative sense: what we recognize today as a crisis, appears so because we expected the previously 'normal' evolution of the world economy in the preceding stage, to continue.

This study will begin by describing the phases of expansion in the world economy during the post-war era; I will then outline those conflicts which emerged during that period and which, I argue, are the key elements for the understanding of the evolution of the world economic system during the 1970s; finally, I will proceed to a discussion of the main manifestation of the crisis.

I. The Post War Economy

The period between the end of the Second World War and the end of the 1960s was one of remarkable economic expansion, the major characteristics of which were imposed by the nature of the international agreements which regulated economic relations on the world market. Although these treaties permitted growth, they also generated and exacerbated conflicts which eventually proved an obstacle to its continuation.

(i) THE MAIN FEATURES OF WORLD ACCUMULATION

The institutional system, set up after the crisis years of the 1930s and strengthened towards the end of the Second World War, after the Bretton Woods agreement, served as an appropriate framework for the dynamic and unprecedented development of world accumulation.

On the whole, the world economy reached levels of sustained growth which contrasted with its erratic development in previous decades. Nevertheless, expansion took place more rapidly in the advanced countries, which had a faster *per capita* growth than the Third World—thus widening the gap between rich and poor countries. Table A.1 shows average growth rates for the period.[1]

TABLE A.1
Annual average growth rate of per capita real gross domestic product at market prices
(in per cent)

	1950-60	1960-70
Developed market		
Economy countries	2.8	4.1
United States	1.5	3.5
Japan	6.9	9.3
Europe	4.0	3.9
France	2.4	4.4
Italy	4.9	4.6
United Kingdom	2.4	2.5
West Germany	6.6	3.8
Developing Countries		
and territories	2.4	2.6

Source: UNCTAD (1976)

European reconstruction proved, in the first instance, to be the most important factor in world accumulation—witness the growth rate of Federal Germany. This was soon to be followed by the rapid expansion of the United States' and Japanese economies.

This allocation of resources was obviously determined by geopolitical factors, given the post-war European situation. The concentration of investment in Western Europe brought about a wave of expansion, which in turn accelerated the growth of international trade—given the economic structure of these countries, which lacked sufficient natural resources and needed large quantities of capital to reactivate their industries. The peculiarly characteristic point about this process is that the fastest growth in trade took place between advanced countries—Table A.2 shows, firstly, the accelerated growth in the exports of these countries, and secondly, the importance of trade between themselves.

TABLE A.2
A. *Annual average growth rates of international trade*
(in per cent)

	Exports		Imports	
	1950-60	1960-70	1950-60	1960-70
Developed market Economy countries:	7.0	10.0	6.5	10.2
United States	5.1	7.7	4.9	11.3
Japan	15.9	17.5	12.1	14.4
Europe	8.1	10.1	7.0	9.8
France	6.4	9.8	5.7	11.7
Italy	10.5	13.0	9.1	11.0
United Kingdom	4.8	6.3	3.7	6.0
West Germany	16.6	11.1	13.3	10.7
Developed countries and territories	3.0	6.9	4.1	6.3

B. *Share of world trade of selected countries and regions*
(in per cent)

Exports		Imports			
		EEC	USA	Japan	Total
EEC	1955-59	7.0	3.0	0.1	10.1
	1960-64	12.0	2.6	0.3	14.9
USA	1955-59	1.5	—	0.6	2.1
	1960-64	2.1	—	0.6	2.7
Japan	1955-59	0.1	0.9	—	1.0
	1960-64	0.2	1.2	—	1.4
Total	1955-59	8.6	3.9	0.7	14.2
	1960-64	14.3	3.8	0.9	19.0

Source: UNCTAD (1976)

TABLE A.2 (*cont.*)

	1950	1951	1952	1953	1954	1955
I. Source of funds	4226	5054	3995	4211	4899	5036
(a) Merchandise trade balance	1122	3067	2611	1437	2576	2897
(b) Investment income (net)	1460	1720	1675	1732	2112	2297
(c) Transactions in US official reserve assets (net)(*)	1758	-33	-415	1256	480	182
(d) Other	-114	300	124	-214	-269	-340
II. Use of funds	-4102	-5408	-4492	-4431	-4959	-5407
(e) Military transactions (net)	-567	-1270	-2054	-2423	-2460	-2701
(f) Capital flows (net)	491	-623	93	423	-219	-208
(g) US Government grants (excl. military)	-3484	-3035	-1960	-1837	-1647	-1901
(h) Other transfers and remittances	-533	-480	-571	-644	-633	-597
III. Error and omissions	-124	354	497	220	60	371

*Negative values (—) represent increments in US official reserve assets.
Source: US Department of Commerce Survey of current business, October 1972 (pages 26 and 27), June 1975 (pages 26, 27, 30 and 31).

I need only point out here that trade between eight developed countries—the six original members of the EEC, the US and Japan—reached 19% of world trade on average during the period 1964-9, to show just how concentrated was their share in international trade.

The rapid increase in trade (measured in value) between advanced countries in international markets was not only the result of a greater volume of exchange, but also reflected a tendency, in the long run, for the price of manufactured goods to rise with respect to the price of primary commodities.

This process of expansion in advanced economies, which heightened their degree of interdependence, was headed by the United States, a country which emerged from the war as the obviously dominating element in the world economic system, given its solvent financial situation, acquired through extensive accumulation of international assets in previous years.

This position allowed the United States to set up the dollar as the key currency in the international payments system which, in the short term, appeared as both stable and fluid. The agreement of the advanced countries on a regulatory international monetary system allowed them to sidestep conflicts which had earlier blocked the way to common economic growth.

The accelerated accumulation on a world scale led to a growing concentration of capital, largely in the hands of transnational corporations which, in this period, rapidly assumed an ever-increasing control over the production and circulation of goods and services.[2]

One cannot, of course, assert that during this period economic activity was entirely uninfluenced by temporary disturbances—the most significant being the so-called Korean boom; but, on the whole, price increases were held at reasonable levels and growth in production was sustained at relatively high rates.

(ii) CONFLICTS WHICH AROSE DURING THE EXPANSION

The process of expansion, which has been briefly described, obscures the growth in conflict which occurred on different levels and which demonstrates that the very nature of expansion was self-contradictory, given that it contained the seeds of its own destruction.

However, it is not sufficient to point out that the dynamics of accumulation are characterized by contradictory forces which render it unstable. One must single out the specific contradictions which arose during this period, together with their degree of importance, if one is to analyse the particular characteristics of the process.[3] I will therefore go on to describe the principal conflicts which occurred during this period of expansion and to study the trends which they gave rise to, as an essential step towards the analysis of the present crisis.[4]

(a) The struggle centred on income distribution in advanced countries

The extensive control acquired by transnational corporations over the production and circulation of commodities, together with the growing influence of the unions in determining nominal wages—within a framework of increased state intervention, in an attempt to regulate both the level of employment and income distribution—have drastically altered the basis of exchange in advanced countries, creating what might be called an institutionalized price and wages structure.

Using the approach of Balogh (1975), it can be stated that the central problem which arises in advanced countries evolves from the concentration of power in the hands of large corporations and the unions, allowing them to manipulate, to a very great extent, the level of wages and prices according to their immediate goals.

Various studies have pointed to the existence of "administered" prices in many areas of production. Sylos-Labini (1974) suggests that, in the short run, industrial prices are flexible with respect to costs, but rigid with respect to fluctuations in demand. Maynard and Van Ryckehem (1976) stress that the control of supply by big business introduces rigidities in price formation which makes firms reluctant to reduce prices even in extreme circumstances. This practice of the corporations limits markets competition in advanced countries and acts as an inflationary element because of the rigidities introduced by the oligopolistic determination of prices.

As for the unions, their attitude introduces another element of inflexibility—their continual opposition to reduction in nominal wage levels. Bienefeld (1977) considers this behaviour to be the key to understanding incomes in the developed countries: he stresses the fact that adjustment mechanisms in their economies do not conform to theoretical models which dominate economic thought on the distribution of income.

Given the nature of price determination and the level of trade union demands, wage levels are established, in the expression of Kaldor (1976), "by what the employer can afford to pay (without compromising his competitive position) and not by what he *needs* to pay, in order to obtain the necessary work force".[5]

In these circumstances, both prices and salaries are primarily determined by complex negotiations and confrontations; *power* relations appear to be the dominating factor in supply and demand and they subordinate all other market characteristics.

As the market in developed countries tends to become more oligopolistic—in industrial goods as well as in labour—internal price structures are inclined to diverge, reflecting different grades of imperfection in the market and different levels of conflict between large corporations and the unions. The fragmentation of markets, which is basically a result of product differentiations, in itself stimulated by monopolistic competition, increases the dependence of prices and wages on the decisions of an ever-decreasing number of units.

These characteristics limit the effectiveness of economic policy in the form of fiscal and monetary measures, and they give rise to a growing reliance on the so-called incomes policy, in which the state appears as the mediator between both parties, in an attempt to achieve agreement between those institutions involved in negotiations.

The most important consequence of an institutionalized price and wage structure is that competition as such is no longer the most important element in the exchange process. The way incomes are determined gives rise to a chronic inflationary situation in the advanced countries—the level of which will, in turn, depend primarily on the degree of conflict between large corporations and the unions, given the role of the state as mediator.[6]

This period is therefore an institutionalizing phase, which makes both the working of the economic system more inflexible and the process of income distribution more complex in advanced countries.

(b) The fight for hegemony in the world market

The need to expand production stimulates competition between the advanced countries, which is revealed in their conflicts in world economic relations. Although this need is a permanent characteristic of capitalist expansion, it takes on a particular expression in the post-war years, as a result of the confrontation that progressively developed between the United States and the other advanced countries.

The international situation in the years immediately following the Second World War was primarily influenced by the need to avoid the crises which characterized the interwar years: fear of chaos allowed the United States to impose a set of rules on international economic relations, which permitted growth in *all* advanced economies, while ensuring its dominance over the system as a whole.[7]

As is stressed by Horsefield (1969), one of the main objectives of the international monetary regulations established by the end of the 1940s was to avoid a confrontation between the advanced countries, by preventing a "war" of unilateral devaluations. In this way, the new system simply conserved the *status quo* in international economic relations and thus strengthened the United States' already dominant position.

Within the framework of strict regulations in the international market, the United States launched a strategy of world domination. An analysis of this country's balance of payments from the beginning of the 1950s would show how the United States proceeded to organize the world economic system.[8]

Diagram A shows how the United States "marshalled" its relationship with other countries, through the use of its large reserves and taking advantage of its current trade surpluses, as well as using its investment incomes from abroad—Table A.3 supplies the detailed statistical data.

The strategy of control over the world economic system was implemented by the injection into the world market of a flow of funds subject to strict conditions. Funds were directed towards military expenditure, government grants (linked primarily to

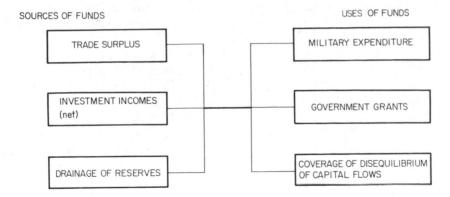

Diagram A. Operation of US external accounts.

food programmes) and long-term investment abroad, financed through the drainage of reserves, trade surpluses and investment incomes from abroad.[9]

Military expenditure was directed mainly towards Western Europe giving security to the expansion of American capital in those countries.[10] Food programmes helped to smooth activity in the United States' agricultural sector, while stabilizing the political situation in some Third World countries. Long-term investment abroad flowed all over the world but mainly concentrated in Western Europe which was embarking on a formidable project of "reconstruction".

These developments were made possible by the extremely advantageous position of the United States by the end of the 1940s. Its trade surpluses were a direct consequence of its technological superiority. The reconstruction of those countries most badly affected by the war, generated a demand for machinery and equipment which only the United States could supply. Its comfortable position as regards reserves was a result of an explicit decision to accumulate international assets, which had been taken years earlier, in order to preserve its own financial situation during the great depression.

Let us concentrate for a moment on the operation of the US external accounts.

The *heterodox* arrangement of the US balance of payments' data presented in Table A.3 demonstrated that the real dilemma of US international policy is to evaluate the *economic* risk of losing foreigners' confidence in the dollar against the *political* risk of reducing military expenditure and government aid. This is so because, as will become clear later on, the behaviour of other advanced countries tends to reduce the US trade surplus and the practices of American corporations lead to a desequilibrium in capital flows, thus necessitating a drainage of reserves to balance the accounts.

The constraints imposed by the behaviour of other advanced countries and American private corporations on the objectives of US foreign policy create a situation where it becomes contradictory for the United States to maintain a healthy balance of payments' position while at the same time consolidating its political domination through the expansion of military expenditure and government grants.

With these considerations in mind, let us proceed with the analysis of the conflict between advanced countries.

TABLE A.3.
US international transactions
(millions of dollars)

1956	1957	1958	1959	1960	1961	1962	1963	1964	1965	1966	1967	1968	1969	1970	1971	1972	1973	1974
6064	9577	7783	4150	8972	8765	9055	8611	10,837	10,484	8054	7659	3882	3162	9665	5722	-1567	6703	4297
4753	6271	3462	1148	4892	5571	4521	5224	6801	4951	3817	3800	635	607	2603	-2268	-6409	955	-5528
2494	2588	2584	2726	2287	2938	3311	3326	3936	4169	3597	3906	4004	3627	3521	4703	4321	5179	10,121
-869	-1165	2292	1035	2145	606	1533	377	171	1222	568	52	-880	-1187	3344	3065	742	209	-1434
-314	-117	-555	-759	-352	-350	-310	-316	-71	142	72	-99	123	115	197	222	-221	360	1138
-6454	-8589	-8144	-4410	-7911	-7733	-7890	-8204	-9883	-9978	-8629	-7470	-4328	-1669	-9198	3975	3453	4267	9131
-2788	-2841	-3135	-2805	-2753	-2596	-2448	-2304	-2133	-2122	-2935	-3226	-3143	-3328	-3355	-2893	-3621	-2317	-2158
-1733	-1616	-1633	-1672	-1855	-1916	-1917	-1888	-1808	-1910	-1805	-1709	-1649	-1736	-2043	-2173	-1938		-5461
-1243	-3403	-2648	843	-2858	-2623	-2814	-3158	-4981	-5015	-2777	-1136	1747	4635	-2586	10,511	10,853	1891	209
-690	-729	-745	-815	-628	-659	-712	-825	-881	-1033	-1007	-1303	-1223	-1327	-1512	-1600	1606	-1903	-1721
390	1012	361	260	-1060	-1032	-1165	-406	-954	-506	575	-189	446	-1492	-476	-9698	-1884	-2436	4834

Certainly the United States could have used these advantages—derived from its technological and financial superiority—in different ways, but the decision to use them primarily to control the international situation was the result of a determined policy, influenced by geopolitical factors in view of the political challenge presented by the Soviet Union. Despite its short-term benefits, this decision presented a wide range of difficulties in the long run.

The limitations of the post-war international economic order soon became clear. Keynes (1946) pointed to its transitional nature; referring to it, he wrote: "Here is an attempt to use what we have learnt from modern experience and modern analysis, not to defeat but to implement the wisdom of Adam Smith."[11] Nevertheless, the development of international economic relations showed no tendency towards liberalizing control regulations; indeed, the opposite was the case—there was a systematic growth in those bodies which sought to exercise even closer control, and the United States continued with the policies it outlined in the mid-1940s. The rationale of US policies becomes clear as long as it is considered as an attempt to reactivate effective demand through the use of its financial capabilities. As A. Hansen (1945) pointed out it was necessary to make use of those capabilities since, although the advantageous balance of payments position allowed the United States to increase employment—through its clearly multiplying effects—"to continue such a surplus paid in gold, is indeed a confession that we have failed to solve our problems".[12]

The manipulation of the United States' external accounts gives rise to the question of the *dollar shortage* in the world economy,[13] which became a major issue among the advanced countries in the 1950s. The discussion on the degree of the *dollar shortage* was centred on the control of international monetary flows and resulted from the rest of the world—or more precisely the advanced countries—demanding that the United States allow them the chance to direct accumulation in accordance with their own needs for expansion.

These disputes expressed themselves in the negotiations between the United States and other advanced countries. A disagreement arose on the trading front because of the growing level of tariff barriers: the United States made continued attempts to induce a reduction in tariffs in other countries, so as to stimulate its own exports and allow American private firms to operate freely on foreign markets. The rest of the world resisted on across-the-board reduction in tariffs, so as to guarantee a satisfactory level of activity in their own economies.

In the monetary sphere, the creation of the eurodollar market demonstrated the need for both the advanced countries and American firms operating abroad, to increase their liquidity beyond the limits imposed by financial authorities in the United States.[14]

Towards the end of the 1950s, the international situation began to demonstrate obvious signs of instability. Triffin (1960) made the point that:

> "The United States gold losses of 1958 are beginning to create some concern about the continued deterioration in the country's net reserve position. . . . Such a movement could not continue indefinitely without ultimately undermining foreigners' confidence in the dollar as a safe medium for reserve accumulation".[15]

The persistence of the strategy of the United States—in the terms depicted in Diagram A—led to a weakening of its reserves, while the other advanced countries showed inverse trends. The question therefore arises as to whether the United States by the beginning of the 1960s can continue to dominate the world economy: whether it can maintain the dollar as the international means of payments and consequently, whether it can go on controlling world accumulation.

As Salant *et al.* (1963) point out, this was not a purely monetary question: it was rather a problem of power relationships between advanced nations, based, in the last analysis, on the possibility of finding an agreement about the distribution of accumulation between them.

Towards the end of the 1960s, it became clear that the way in which international economic relations were still moving threatened the hegemony of the United States. It was becoming increasingly obvious that the structure chosen to accelerate accumulation throughout the developed world in this post-war period was on the verge of collapse.

The most obvious result of changes in the world economic situation was the weakening of the United States' external position. Its trade balances began to show ever-decreasing surpluses, while those of Western Europe and Japan began to look healthier. Table A.4 summarizes the trends in the trade balance positions of the United States, Japan and Federal Germany and shows the radical changes which took place between the beginning of the 1950s and the end of the 1960s.

TABLE A.4
Trade balance (fob-cif)
(billion dollars)

	United States	Japan	West Germany
1960	4.2	-0.5	1.3
1961	5.4	-1.6	1.8
1962	3.9	-0.7	1.0
1963	4.8	-1.2	1.6
1964	6.3	-1.2	1.6
1965	4.3	0.3	0.4
1966	2.7	0.3	2.1
1967	2.9	-1.2	4.3
1968	-0.7	0.0	4.6
1969	-0.3	1.0	4.1
1970	0.5	0.4	4.4
1971	-4.4	5.7	4.7
1972	-9.1	5.1	6.3
1973	-2.3	-1.3	12.7
1974	-9.5	-6.5	19.7
1975	4.3	-2.1	15.3

Source: IMF

As a result, more pressures developed on the dollar, as doubts grew about its capacity to continue as the international means of payments. These problems, centred on financial questions, obscure an accumulation problem for the developed world as a whole. The growing need for Western Europe and Japan to expand in world markets clashed with the limits imposed on this expansion by the United States' need to control the world economic situation.

(c) The disputes on investment resources allocation

Capitalist accumulation, accomplished mainly by transnational corporations which operate on a world scale, present individual countries with a dilemma centred on the possibility of conducting "national" policies capable of achieving full employment and adequate income distribution.

The concentration and consequent transnationalization of capital generates a crisis of control in the management of the economy in advanced countries; the quest for full employment and a "reasonable" distribution of income—goals claimed by *every* government in the advanced countries—is undertaken in the shadow of transnational capital: states find themselves subject to restrictions not previously experienced.

The growing importance of these transnational corporations increases the uncertainty inherent in the accumulation process in each country: it allows monetary and fiscal policies—which have been traditionally used to regulate the economic cycle in post-war capitalist countries—even less room for manoeuvre. This occurs because of an increasingly integrated world economy which offers a wide range of investment alternatives: transnational corporations evaluate these considering their *aggregated* profitability without being concerned with the situation of any country in particular.[16]

Expanding manufacturing activities outside the advanced countries—controlled primarily by transnational corporations—not only results from the need to reduce costs (mainly from labour) but also from the possibility of opening up otherwise inaccessible markets.[17] The growth of the industrial sector outside the advanced countries[18] even when it can guarantee a flow of surplus into the advanced countries through the remittance of profits is, however, essentially detrimental to their accumulation process, because it limits the possibilities of employment creation.

In their study of the relations between transnational corporations and nation states, Hymer and Rowthorn (1970) point to the beginning of a transitional period, in which the transnational corporations will challenge the 'weak' nation states for control over world accumulation. This confrontation does not rule out the possibility of alliances between individual states and corporations—as Murray (1975) has outlined—given government support in expanding capital on a worldwide scale; it does, however, suggest a tendency towards progressive divergence of interests.

The investment policy of the transnational corporations is not always in harmony with the need for accumulation in each advanced country: indeed, in certain cases, its policy is clearly at odds with that propounded by the nation states.[19] Paradoxically enough, Keynesian internal policies and international agreements between the advanced countries, undertaken to solve problems of growth, are often jeopardized by the behaviour of private corporations.

(d) The controversy on the level of commodity prices on the world market

Although growth in the Third World is insufficient to close the gap between rich and poor countries, it is generally enough to encourage new social forces to emerge within each separate country.

Since these forces are linked, directly or indirectly, with growing production activities, they can impose economic policies which influence social structure and increase their potential control over the productive process: it must be admitted, however, that they can never entirely dominate the internal process of accumulation.

These emerging forces in Third World societies have resulted primarily through industrial expansion; this was in turn caused by the need to substitute imports—either in response to acute external constraints, such as those generated by the Second World War, or through the expansion of international capital.

These social forces acquire a potential influence over world accumulation in two ways—the appropriation of the sources of production, and control over the prices of these commodities which Third World countries trade on the world market. Certainly, the degree of influence which a Third World country can wield will depend on the nature of the market of each product:[20] but what is significant for this analysis is that industrialization in the Third World introduces new factors in international economic relations.

It is capitalist development in the Third World which promotes the emergence of demands for improved commodity prices in the international market. Increasingly, growing manufacturing activities change the nature of the relations of production in the Third World.

They become more and more capitalistic in character, tending therefore to displace traditional forms of social organization on which relations of dependency had been based.

The superexploitation to which direct producers in the Third World were subject,[21] takes place in a society which compels its labour force to exist on a purely subsistence level. As these pre-existing forms of production are gradually displaced by capitalist methods, exploitation is confined within a well-defined set of boundaries. That is to say, it is governed by the laws of capitalist accumulation.

In this way, the very expansion of capital in the Third World decreases the possibilities for increasing exploitation—through those methods which originally led to its consolidation and then presses for better commodity prices in order to preserve the rate of profits, otherwise reduced by the impossibility of further cost reductions.

These remarks about the ability of certain Third World countries to reverse unfavourable trends in their terms of trade—which were persistently adverse throughout the 1950s and 1960s, as Table A.5 shows—do not imply that one can disregard the concept of dependency: rather, one must place it in a dialectic context—it must be assumed to be a process contradictory in itself which can be overcome, in economic terms, when capitalist accumulation on a world scale allows it.[22]

By the end of the 1960s, political factors which emerged worldwide—mainly after the end of the Vietnam War—together with the strengthening of capitalist type social forces in the Third World, led to a progressive change in the nature of international relations, creating a framework in which Third World demands were more likely to be met by adopting a more aggressive role in commodity markets.

(e) World political confrontation

The overwhelming importance of the world market in the process of capitalist accumulation implies that any element which influences its development and which is subject to other laws constitutes an obstacle for its own expansion.

TABLE A.5
Terms of trade of primary commodities
(index number 1963 = 100)

1950	121	1960	102
1951	126	1961	100
1952	116	1962	98
1953	116	1963	100
1954	117	1964	102
1955	115	1965	98
1956	110	1966	97
1957	111	1967	95
1958	108	1968	93
1959	105	1969	93

Source: UNCTAD

The increasing influence of the Soviet Union and other socialist countries in determining the nature of international relations on the political as well as on the economic front deflects the course of capitalist accumulation. Priority in the investment of resources is given to those areas in which the influence of socialist countries is stronger—as happened in Western Europe in the immediate post-war period.

The structure of industrial production is also affected by the capitalist/socialist conflict—witness the importance given to the manufacture of armaments, which is one of the most important sustaining elements of effective demand in advanced countries.[23]

On the other hand, those countries whose accumulation strategy is not capitalist, inhibit the development of transnational capital, because they restrict its potential field of activity. Although the number of investments made by transnational corporations in the socialist block has increased, they are far from being significant. As Wilczynski (1975) points out, except for Yugoslavia, "it must be realized that the inflow of investment capital from capitalist countries is more important in its aspects of curiosity than in volume".[24] On the whole, these investments are accepted because of the need for "know-how" on the part of those countries where transnational corporations are admitted.

Despite the limited development of transnational corporations in socialist countries, their potential expansion is disputed by different fractions of capital; particularly noteworthy is the advance made by corporations based in Western Europe.

As far as international trade is concerned, the integration of the socialist block within the world economic order, which has been proposed by the advanced countries, has not yet reached any significant proportions. Indeed, the socialist block only account for 2% of world trade—a figure which has remained unchanged throughout the post-war period.[25]

The shrinking in world markets and the need to take strictly political factors into account when allocating resources, bring the capitalist world up against restrictions to accumulation not experienced on a comparable scale prior to the Second World War.

II. The Present Crisis

So far, this study has dealt with those trends and conflicts which have arisen in the world economic system up till the end of the 1960s. The next section will attempt to demonstrate how, in the present decade, these conflicts interact in such a way as to produce stagnation in output together with sustained rises in world prices.

(i) THE INTERACTION OF THE MAJOR CONFLICTS

Diagram B shows the main conflicts which have arisen in the world economy during the post-war period and which have already been analysed. They can be summarized as follows:

—The confrontation between unions and the large corporations in the advanced countries, centred on income distribution which arises from the nature of the mode of production and which produces an institutionalized price structure.

—The clash between advanced countries in world markets which derives from their need for expansion and is expressed in terms of tighter control over international economic relations.

—The contradiction between the interests of transnational capital and individual states as a result of the acceleration in the concentration of capital and which takes the form of a dispute on the geographical allocation of investment resources.

—The controversy between advanced countries and the Third World on the price level of basic commodities, resulting from the evolution of the international division of labour and shown in alterations in relative prices in world markets.

—The tension between advanced countries and the socialist block created by their differing objectives and manifested in their political and economic relations.

There are therefore, five major areas where conflicts tend to arise: the establishment of macroeconomic policies in the advanced countries; the regulation of international economic relations; the geographical allocation of accumulation resources; the working of the international commodity markets; East-West relations.

These conflicts themselves can be defined as follows:

conflicts which led to the imposition of a negotiated international economic order after the war

—the struggle centred on income distribution in advanced countries,
—the fight for hegemony in the world market;

conflicts which influenced the nature of the international economic order imposed after the war

—the confrontation between advanced countries and the socialist block;

conflicts which emerged as a consequence of the international economic order imposed after the war

—the dispute between transnational corporations and national states on accumulation resources' allocation,

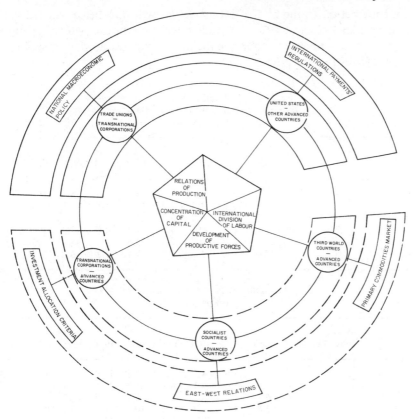

Diagram B. Main conflicts in the world economy.

—the controversy between advanced countries and the Third World over the price level of basic commodities.

The first set of conflicts can be identified as *crisis-provoking* conflicts, which are related to the essence of capitalist production and its historical expression.[26] The remaining two sets can be defined as *character-determining* conflicts—that is, those which affect the outcome of the crisis; they are historical developments whose relevance became apparent in the post-war period.

In his analysis of the post-war economy, Dobb (1963) emphasizes the importance of the consolidation of the socialist block and the emergence of new nation states in the Third World: he describes them as events which "future historians will in retrospect (probably) see . . . as the outstanding landmarks of the mid-twentieth-century watershed between historical epochs".[27] That is, they are developments which radically alter the structure of international relations and influence the character of world negotiations.

Crisis-provoking conflicts reached a critical point by the end of the 1960s: the upsurge in worker militancy in Western Europe and the international financial disorder are signs of the beginning of a difficult stage for capitalist accumulation.

Symptoms of recession appear clearly from about 1970—see Table A.6. Industrial production falls in the United States, and in the following year there is already a significant contraction in the rate of industrial growth in other advanced nations. Production rises in 1972 and 1973, but falls once more in the two following years and from that point is unable to continue the line of expansion which it had pursued during the previous two decades.

TABLE A.6
A. *Industrial production. Annual rate of growth*
(in per cent)

	Average 1960-69	1968	1969	1970	1971	1972	1973	1974	1975	1976	1977	Averag 1970-7
United States	5.9	5.8	4.6	- 3.6	2.0	8.8	8.5	-0.4	-8.8	10.2	5.6	3.5
Japan	13.4	15.2	15.8	13.8	2.7	7.3	15.6	-3.8	-10.6	11.0	4.1	3.4
France	6.1	2.4	11.7	5.3	6.0	5.7	7.1	2.5	-7.3	8.8	1.6	3.4
Italy	7.2	5.8	3.6	6.5	-0.1	4.4	9.7	4.0	-8.9	11.6	0.0	2.8
United Kingdom	2.9	6.7	3.1	1.0	0.0	2.0	8.8	-1.8	-5.4	1.0	1.9	0.9
West Germany	5.7	9.2	13.3	6.4	1.0	5.0	7.1	-1.2	-6.2	7.3	3.0	2.2

B. *Consumer prices. Annual rate of growth*
(in per cent)

	Average 1960-69	1968	1969	1970	1971	1972	1973	1974	1975	1976	1977	Avera 1970-7
United States	2.4	4.2	5.4	5.9	4.3	3.3	6.2	12.4	10.8	7.5	8.0	7.2
Japan	6.5	5.4	5.2	7.6	6.1	4.5	11.7	24.5	18.0	8.8	8.2	11.2
France	3.9	4.6	6.4	5.3	5.3	6.1	6.6	13.7	11.7	9.1	10.4	8.5
Italy	3.9	1.3	2.6	5.0	4.8	5.7	10.8	19.1	17.0	16.7	19.3	12.3
United Kingdom	3.9	4.7	5.4	6.4	9.4	7.1	9.2	15.9	24.3	14.6	16.0	12.9
West Germany	3.0	2.6	1.9	3.4	5.3	5.5	6.9	7.0	6.0	4.5	3.9	5.3

Source: OECD-Main economic indicators (various issues)

Already in 1970, the rate of inflation has begun to increase with respect to previous years; it rises more dramatically later on—during the years of the commodity boom—and from there on hovers, at levels which are markedly higher than previous average figures.

Character-determining conflicts begin to play a decisive role in the evolution of the international situation: during the commodity boom, Third World countries realize that they could be capable of controlling prices and the consequent explosion of oil prices constitutes an example of their new aggressive role in international markets.

The argument here, therefore, is that the character of the present crisis in the world economic system is determined by the interaction of *crisis-provoking* and *character-determining* conflicts: an analysis of the five controversial areas in which they occur will result in a satisfactory profile of the current stagflation phenomenon. From this perspective the crisis can be seen as an historical process, rooted in the contradictory nature of capitalism itself, its principal characteristics—recession and inflation—are not a distortion of the system, but a consequence of its very structure.

(ii) THE UPSURGE IN WORKER MILITANCY

Full employment, high real wages, stability in prices—this appears an unlikely scenario for an upsurge in worker militancy. Nevertheless, in conditions such as these, Western Europe has experienced a proliferation of worker unrest, with the labour force pressing for wage increases, improved working conditions and a greater share in decision-making.

In fact, the behaviour of the labour force is understood as soon as it is placed in relation to its contradiction with capital, analysing the struggle centred on income distribution.

In the first place, in a full-employment situation, the spectre of unemployment cannot be effectively used by big business to moderate wage demands: this factor—normally crucial in labour/capital relations—loses all impact when demand for labour clearly absorbs the current supply.

Dobb (1963) summarizes the reasons for an aggressive behaviour on the part of the labour force; a full employment situation

"... means that the proletariat will be in a much stronger position than at any previous stage in its history to influence the terms upon which work shall be done. A sharp upward movement of wages and a growing share of the national income, will for the first time lie within the easy reach of organized labour to command. . . ."[28]

It is because of the strong position acquired by the labour movement that the struggle centred on income distribution reached a critical point towards the end of the sixties. The demands made by the labour force in Western Europe at this time led to a growing number of strikes and greater worker unrest; governments began to pay attention when they became aware of the possible consequences.

During these years leading businesses tended to accept unions' demands so as to ensure their share of a still expanding market; they adopt a similar behaviour to that described in the analysis of the conflict between large corporations and trade unions. On the other hand, governments—worried by the possible inflationary effects of wage agreements—began the implementation of short-term restrictive policies of a monetarist character.[29]

Braun (1977) underlines the fact that after this upsurge in worker militancy the character of government policies with respect to wages and employment began to be dominated by "the need for government (is) to bring some qualitative change in trade unions' demands—to somehow convince them of the 'need' to let real wages fall and to reduce the rate of growth of nominal wages".[30]

Short-term policy in almost every advanced country enters a restrictive stage which directly affected the possibility of output expansion in those years. The central problem is how to find an answer to the increasingly bitter conflict centred on income distribution.

(iii) THE MONETARY COLLAPSE

The official suspension of the convertability of the dollar into gold in August 1971 and the later adopting of floating exchange rates in March 1973, followed by a fundamental revision of the structure of the IMF concerning payments' regulations show just how critical the monetary situation had become in view of the lack of agreement among advanced countries.[31]

On the one hand, the United States' attempts to put measures into effect which would balance the increasing influence of other advanced countries—led by Federal Germany and Japan—try to further consolidate their position by demanding changes in the international payments' regulations.

The weakening position of the United States on the international markets precipitated the crisis of confidence over the dollar, opening up a period of intense speculation in which liquid capital tended to move rapidly, mirroring changes in the balance-of-payment situation in different advanced countries: this added factors of instability to the already deteriorating situation.

The fluctuations of exchange rates led to a further devaluation of the dollar *vis-à-vis* other strong currencies by the beginning of 1974. The question of the means of international payments—when the dollar is replaced in that function by a 'basket' of strong currencies—becomes a major source in the international transmission of inflation:[32] each individual advanced country begins to use floating rates as a medium of improving trade positions.

The new scheme which governs international monetary relations becomes more fluid than the previous one but, as a result, much less stable. Since unity among advanced countries is not fully restored by the alteration of the rules, their increasing internal instability—resulting from the growing conflict centred on income distribution—has the effect of aggravating competition for the dominion of world markets.

Even though the United States economy had enough power to reverse the unfavourable situation in which it found itself as a result of the new scheme, to destroy such a scheme and restructure it in such a way as to regain its dominating position would imply the creation of imbalances in other economies—mainly those of Federal Germany and Japan—which would constitute an even greater threat to the equilibrium of the world capitalist system as a whole.

At the point, the United States pressed for rather marginal changes in the international monetary system, accepting the modifications suggested by other advanced countries and preserving the overall structure of the organizations. Once again, fear of chaos *per se* acts as a stabilizing factor in the world economic situation.

Certainly, the scheme did not regain the stability of previous decades; later events—such as the oil crisis—add factors which make an uncertain and unstable structure the main feature of international monetary relations.

The confrontation between advanced countries in the monetary field shows how financial arrangements cannot become a central factor in restoring equilibrium in the world situation—a role they played in the 1940s with remarkable success.

The monetary collapse of the beginning of the 1970s is the most obvious sign of the disintegration of the international order which underpinned world economic expansion in the post-war period: it points to the fact that the resolution of the 1930s crisis has not succeeded, in the long run, in overcoming the main contradictions between advanced countries. Considered from the monetary point of view, the present crisis shows very similar characteristics to those of the great depression.[33]

The hazardous developments in the monetary sphere demonstrate that confrontation between the advanced countries had become critical: this allowed the expression of other conflicts which otherwise would have little impact on world economic affairs.

(iv) THE COMMODITY BOOM

The continuing conflict between advanced countries in the monetary sphere, the impossibility of overcoming this conflict through internal adjustment in each economy—given the degree of pressure focused on income distribution—and the urgent need to regain high levels of growth make the flood gates open for the transmission of imbalances to other branches of the world system.

In the early 1970s commodity markets are shaken by the increasing instability of the world situation. These markets had previously been dominated by tendencies which had led prices either to fall steadily or to remain relatively stable: the current supply of these goods seemed to exceed demand and the market, for long periods, operated without any fear of sharp rises in prices.[34] Nevertheless, from the beginning of the 1970s expectations began to change drastically.

The instability of monetary markets encouraged the movement of a large mass of liquid resources towards commodity markets, introducing an 'exogenous' inflationary factor with the development of speculative transactions in future markets.

The publication of the Meadows (1972) report—which warned of possible shortages in natural resources—created an atmosphere in which uncertainty becomes a major factor in the markets: the mere possibility of potential shortages changes the parameters of supply and demand due to the chaotic world economic situation.[35]

These changes in prospects which made price increases more likely must be viewed in the framework of the conflict between advanced countries. It must be stressed that the privileged position of the United States as a major producer of a wide range of basic commodities and a major operator in others enables this country to exercise a decisive influence on market transactions, contrasting with the relatively weak position of other advanced countries.

Thus the development of a "scarcity climate" in commodity markets—which encourages inflationary expectations—might help the United States in its struggle to regain world hegemony: it would allow this country to improve its own balance of payments position while damaging that of other advanced countries.

It is by no means coincidental that during these years the US Government initiated an attempt to redefine its policies concerning world economic affairs. The Commission on International Trade and Investment Policy (1971) produced a report to the President of the United States in which it recommended drastic changes in American foreign policy; it stated that:

"... our agricultural exports significantly affect our trade balance, and thus our balance of payments ... the economic health of US agriculture is likely to become increasingly dependent on world markets. ... We believe that our national interest demands agricultural trade policies that will permit and promote expansion of *both* US exports and imports of agricultural products while meeting income objectives for farmers".[36]

The message of this report is clear: the US must abandon the traditional agricultural policy which led it to stockpile surpluses of cereals—which had a downward effect on international prices—and allow stocks to run down in order to alter the operation of the market.

The US attempt to change its strategy is aided very considerably by the massive demand for cereals on the part of the Soviet Union. The controversial *Soviet deal*[37] is the very vehicle for implementing a policy of stock reduction by the United States. *The Economist* reported in April 1973:

". . . Canada announced the sale to Russia of $200m worth of wheat and barley. This was the latest instalment in the series of massive Soviet purchases of Western grain that has exceeded $2 billion in value over the past year. Half of this total has been sold by the United States; and last week controversy about the terms of the American sales was revived in Washington when a Democratic congressman, Mr. John Melcher, disclosed that the Administration had subsidised the wheat sales to Russia to the tune of $300m despite pleas from the Australian and Canadian wheat boards that Russia should be required to pay a proper market price. . . . Mr. Nixon is undoubtedly glad to get rid of the surplus grain attracted by the idea of improving the fuel outlook by arranging for supplies of Siberian gas, and eager to redress his country's balance of payments by developing new markets. . . ."[38]

The changing market situation opens up new perspectives for technological progress in agriculture, but also creates an atmosphere of uncertainty on the future stability of the market, because of the dramatic reduction in stocks.[39]

It is these changing circumstances that *all* basic commodities undergo a radical alteration in their price trends. Cooper and Lawrence (1976) in their thorough analysis of the new trends in commodity markets point out that, although one can detect specific changes in the conditions of supply and demand for each commodity, "they do not fill the need for some general explanation—a common cause, or strong linkages among commodities affected".[40]

The common cause must be found in the drastic change in expectations: the interaction of the appearance of speculative capital movements in commodity markets, the fear of scarcities and the drastic about-turn in US foreign policies led to the development of *structural* inflationary pressures. These pressures combined with increasing Soviet demand for grains and the sharp increase in aggregate demand in advanced countries[41] led to abrupt price rises.

The disruption of commodity markets during the first years of the 1970s can be summarized by performing a simple statistical exercise—see Table A.7. The series of basic commodities prices between 1960 and 1976 can be divided into three major periods: the first, between 1960 and 1971, characterized by relative stability; the second, between 1972 and 1974, showing abrupt upward movements, and the third between 1975 and 1976 presenting a succession of readjustments.

The development of prices during the 1960s shows that the movements which occurred during these years were governed by alterations within *each* specific market. Modifications of agreements between buyers and sellers and changes in the conditions of supply and demand give a good account of the reasons behind price movements: no major interaction between markets can be identified.

TABLE A.7
Commodity Prices
(index numbers Average 1960-71 = 100)

Specification	Commodity	Period 1960-71		Period 1972-4		Period 1975-6	
		Minimum	Maximum	Speculative step level	Maximum	Minimum	Maximum
East Afr cif Lon	Sisal	61	171 Apr. 63	82 Jan. 72	468	155	468
NY spot price	Sugar	38	325 Nov. 63	230 Jan. 72	1581	210	1070
Lon Met Exch	Lead	59	165 Mar. 65	123 Feb. 72	296	139	227
Mal cif Eur Port	Palm Oil	63	132 May 65	95 Mar. 72	369	153	262
All Coffee	Coffee	79	135 Sept. 70	140 Jul. 72	191	154	540
NY spot price	Rice	75	161 Sept. 67	110 Aug. 72	401	154	258
UK Dom c 64's	Wool	70	132 Feb. 64	120 Aug. 72	373	149	181
US No 2 HRW	Wheat	92	113 Mar. 67	123 Sept. 72	356	173	272
US No 3 Yellow	Maize	86	124 Sept. 70	111 Sept. 72	281	193	231
UK dom imp pr	Cattle hides	74	149 Apr. 66	274 Oct. 72	284	122	239
Sin No 1 fob	Rubber	64	187 May 60	73 Oct. 72	218	108	173
US No 2 yellow	Soya beans	78	129 Jul. 66	149 Dec. 72	302	165	239
Nig cif Eu port	Groundnuts	76	154 Feb. 71	158 Dec. 72	314	204	256
Lib BR con	Iron ore	91	129 May 70	128 Jan. 73	181	163	177
cif Lon any	Linseed oil	78	132 Jul. 61	117 Jan. 73	520	225	422
Nig cif Eu port	Palm kernels	81	140 May 68	94 Jan. 73	408	108	200
Phil cif Pot	Coconut oil	74	134 May 68	104 Feb. 73	379	102	173

TABLE A.7
Commodity Prices
(index numbers   Average 1960–71 = 100)

Specification	Commodity	Period 1960-71		Period 1972-4		Period 1975-6	
		Minimum	Maximum	Speculative step level	Maximum	Minimum	Maximum
Lon Met Exch	Copper	57	180 Apr. 66	117 Feb. 73	286	109	156
Dutch fob any	Soyabean oil	65	140 Aug. 71	122 Feb. 73	302	165	239
Phil cif Eu port	Copra	78	142 May 68	108 Feb. 73	429	908	195
NY/L ave price	Cocoa	45	178 Dec. 68	147 Mar. 73	317	172	517
WA cif EU port	Palm ker-oil	74	144 May 68	113 Mar. 73	497	222	203
Kho fas Casa	Phosphate R	96	108 Oct. 67	120 Mar. 73	535	412	577
Wol cif Eu port	Tungsten	25	250 Feb. 70	128 Mar. 73	323	236	413
Lon Met Exch	Zinc	66	144 Jul. 64	179 Mar. 73	668	226	301
Egy Menoufi FG	Cotton	78	123 Jan. 69	139 Apr. 73	306	205	298
cif UK Mn con	Mananese ore	75	115 Apr. 60	107 Jun. 73	190	185	211
Rott any origin	Sunflower oil	58	156 Jan. 71	173 Jun. 73	449	196	412
Nig/Gan cif Epo	Groundnut oil	72	158 Feb. 71	184 Jul. 73	314	204	256
BM spot NY	Pepper	6	159 Jan. 60	148 Jul. 73	203	185	228
Jk gra Eu port	Abaca	76	155 Feb. 60	172 Aug. 73	290	152	205
Lon Met Exch	Tin	69	140 Oct. 64	207 Dec. 73	297	198	268
Ecua cif Hamb	Bananas	61	139 May 63	107 Jan. 74	136	119	184
Can del UK	Aluminium	91	120 Dec. 71	126 Mar. 74	157	149	182
Lon auct price	Tea	68	149 Sept.60	125 Mar. 74	125	104	141
BWD fob Cbit	Jute	62	160 Dec. 71	153 Sept.74	172	107	174

Source: UNCTAD (1977).

The situation between 1972 and 1974 is radically different. One can define a "speculative step" as the *first* price increment during this period which is greater than 10% on a monthly basis, provided that the average in the following 6 months is greater or equal to the level reached by that increment. In symbols:

$$SS = \frac{p_t + 1}{p_t}$$

if and only if

$$p_t + 1 = 1.10\, p_t$$

and

$$p_t + 1 = \frac{\sum\limits_{k=t+2}^{t+7} p_k}{6}$$

where: p = nominal price (in dollars) for each basic commodity,
   t = time (month),
  SS = speculative step.

Changes of this kind *cannot* be found in the previous decade in any of the commodities covered by the exercise. Table A.7 shows that *all* the prices of basic commodities experienced a "speculative step" during the period 1972-4, followed by further sharp increases.

This behaviour points to a *general* tendency for prices to rise, showing similarities in the magnitude and direction of movements not exhibited by commodity markets since the Korean boom at the beginning of the 1950s.

The "speculative step" reveals the existence of a sort of rebound effect fuelled by the atmosphere of uncertainty in international economic relations. It was not clear at that time how the major economic problems were going to be solved; therefore, in the short term, price increases appeared as an adequate vehicle for secure profitability in a wide range of activities.

Even when none of the factors contributing to the upsurge of the commodity boom can by itself entirely account for its development it is possible to recognize an ultimate cause for *all* of them: that is, the need for the United States to reconsolidate its hegemony over world economic affairs. Certainly, accidental elements—like the drought of world proportions—have an effect on commodity markets, but, at that time, upward trends in prices were already driving them towards an uncontrollable situation.[42]

International monetary instability, fear of scarcities and changing US trade policies could be seen as manifestations of the rivalry between advanced countries for the dominion of world markets. Instead of using its superiority as a financial power, the United States exercises its strength as a producer of basic commodities to alter the balance of world power. As put by Rothschild (1976), the conditions of agricultural commerce "have changed from aid to trade" and "to some Americans, the possibility of agricultural power suggested extravagant opportunities".[43]

The strong reaction of the advanced countries towards the change in policy of the United States, the subsequent downfall trend in output throughout the advanced world and the threat posed by Third World countries in reaching agreements to unify their action in commodity markets, all call for a revision of the behaviour of the advanced countries on the international scene as well as in internal affairs.

The end of the commodity boom is the combined result of the advanced countries' awareness that inflation might become uncontrollable and the limits imposed by the market characteristics of each particular commodity.

Nevertheless, the commodity boom had two major lasting consequences. Firstly, which became rampant in the early 1970s, led to the imposition of more restrictive economic policies by governments in advanced countries.[44] They tend to use the argument of the international character of inflation in order to restrain wage demands, claiming that it is impossible to control price rises in any other way. The restrained tactics adopted by the unions show that this argument is having its desired ideological effect.

Rising unemployment and the internationalization of the inflationary process change the balance in the struggle for income distribution throughout the advanced world: unions find themselves in a much weaker negotiating position.

Secondly, Third World countries become aware that they can exercise some degree of control over the level of prices of basic commodities. Social forces in the Third World find themselves in a position to negotiate with transnational corporations and advanced countries on better terms. Thus they are encouraged by the situation to search for methods of improving their position on the commodity markets.

(v) THE EXPLOSION OF OIL PRICES

Further development in the commodity boom is limited by the characteristic of supply and demand of each particular product. Once the first stage in the structural "take-off" of general price rises is over, the markets resume the development imposed by the behaviour of exporters and importers. Nevertheless, one product—oil—is in an ideal market situation[45] and its price remains at a higher real level than that of the period prior to the commodity boom.[46]

The consolidation of a cartel among oil suppliers and the acute inelasticity of demand on the part of advanced countries allows the continuation of high prices.

The direct effect of the sharp rise in oil prices on the advanced economies are, firstly, a reinforcement of already existing inflationary pressures, and secondly, the exertion of a negative force upon the development and of effective demand—through the worsening of their balance-of-payments situation.[47] Nevertheless, these effects are not equally distributed among the advanced countries: it is the US economy which adapts most easily to the prevailing situation due to its position as a pre-eminent producer—even when it is still a large importer of oil—and its ability to attract liquid assets from Arab countries.

The OPEC countries suddenly find themselves with an enormous amount of liquid assets which obviously cannot be entirely and immediately channelled towards physical investment. Given the structure of international financial markets, the liquid assets in the hands of OPEC countries tend to flow to financial institutions in the advanced countries. Petras and Rhodes (1976) summarize the reasons why US financial institutions are the main recipients of those flows: the security offered by US institutions is superior to that which other countries can offer and the possibility of arms deals is greater if Arab countries place their assets in the United States.

In this way, the United States further improves its situation *vis-à-vis* other advanced countries. Thus, it is understandable that the United States should assume a pragmatic attitude towards the rise in oil prices, finally accepting the *de facto* situation and supporting the action of transnational corporations. Engler (1977) underlines the fact that US government policy, when faced with the dilemma of choosing an alliance with the other advanced countries or linking its interests further with those of the transnational corporations, prefers the second option.[48]

The explosion of oil prices leads to even greater changes in the balance of payments of advanced countries, reducing Western Europe and Japan's room for manoeuvre in their confrontation with the United States, while acting as a direct support for the dollar in view of the flow of capital from OPEC countries to American financial institutions.

Finally, as a consequence of the oil crisis, negotiations become even more frequent between organized groups of producers and importers: a widespread tendency to intervention characterizes the operation of markets in the second half of the 1970s.

(vi) THE GROWING IMPORTANCE OF NEGOTIATIONS ON THE NEW
      INTERNATIONAL ECONOMIC ORDER

The first half of the 1970s showed that it was extremely difficult to find a resolution to the major conflicts in world affairs without affecting output growth and price stability.

The failure to find a satisfactory solution through the use of market mechanisms gives rise to a growing reliance on direct negotiations. These negotiations differ from those which took place immediately after the war: they are not only restricted to the advanced countries. Bergsten (1975b), discussing the future of the international order, refers to the "new actors"—Third World countries, the socialist block and transnational corporations—who are going to play a decisive rôle in the process of negotiations.[49]

These "new actors"—whose behaviour exacerbates *character-determining* conflicts—break into the international scene because of the lack of resolution of *crisis-provoking* conflicts within the framework of market-oriented policies.[50]

The international division of labour cannot be reshaped without taking into consideration the problems emerging from the *five areas of controversy*. No successful alliance emerges from negotiations: all parties involved can exercise a *veto* power to obstruct alternatives put forward by others, but *none* of them is able to either impose its own strategy or find a way to implement an agreement that would result in increasing employment and reducing inflation.

In the advanced countries, macroeconomic policy increasingly relies on the application of incomes policies, using the implementation of restrictive policies as a threat to organized labour, forcing it to come to terms with governments' pay offers. A recent report prepared for the OECD (1977), even when defending the application of market-oriented policies to overcome the crisis, admits the need for pursuing incomes policies and recognizes that in the advanced economies:

"It (also) becomes possible for the government to try to influence the outcome (of pay policies) by threatening to raise taxes if wage settlements or price increases are excessive, or offering to lower them if they are moderate."[51]

Clearly, even the supporters of liberal ideas acknowledge that it is necessary to rely on government intervention rather than on market mechanisms in order to overcome inflationary pressures emerging from the dispute on income distribution.

The question of international payments is also increasingly in need of institutional interventing. The IMF in the late 1970s plays an even more regulatory role, in its attempts to moderate the effects of exchange rates fluctuations. Negotiations on the international monetary scheme demand an agreement among the parts that can only be achieved through consultations carried out in a framework of well-defined rules.[52]

The North-South dialogue attempts to find a compromise solution between advanced and Third World countries upon the price level and market operation of primary commodities. In this area—after the experience of the commodity boom—competition as such has been abandoned, suppliers and demanders are inclined to negotiate rather than let the market operate by itself.[53]

Transnational corporations are facing pressures by governments in advanced countries to pay more attention to expansion in their economies, while dealing with urgent demands from the Third World about the control of the supply of natural resources. As a result those corporations attempt to accommodate to the situation by reaching agreement with governments about their role in the accumulation process.[54]

Trade and investment involving the socialist block are considered by the advanced countries as a possible alternative in expanding their activities, in view of the current stagnation of capitalist markets. Once again, these developments involve negotiations where institutions play a significant part in determining their character.[55]

This process indicates that world accumulation is moving towards a *new* international economic order where disputes are settled by bureaucratic procedures. As indicated by Brzezinski (1974) "progress toward a freer and self-adjusting international economic system no longer seems very likely. Instead, we are likely to see increased governmental intervention, in part as a consequence of domestic pressures, resulting in the politization of international economics."[56]

After the turbulent first half of the 1970s, when the forces of the system in search of a solution led to acute recession and rampant inflation, a phase of *administered* accumulation restraining rather than resolving major conflicts is initiated: world capitalism enters a *sluggish* state without offering its components a clear alternative for progress.

No major advances can be seen in any of the forums of negotiations. The events of the early 1970s clearly marked what was *wrong* in the behaviour of the elements of the world economic system, but they did not offer any hint about what would be a *right* attitude to assume when faced with the task of restoring growth and stability.

Conclusions

Diagram C summarizes the arguments developed throughout this essay. It divides the past 30 years into two major periods: a *hegemonial* period where the United

YEAR	49 50 51	52 53 54 55 56 57 58 59 60 61 62 63 64 65 66 67	68 69	70 71	72 73	74 75	76 77 78 79
PERIOD	HEGEMONIAL PERIOD			NON-HIERARCHICAL PERIOD			
Output	Growth			Stagnation			
Prices	Stability			Inflation			
Main expression of the crisis			Upsurge in worker militancy	Monetary collapse	Commodity boom	Explosion of oil prices	New international economic order
CONFLICTS — Trade unions–corporations	Institutionalization of prices and wage structures		●				●
US–other advanced countries	Progressive weakening of US dominant position			●	●	●	●
Third World–advanced countries	Emergence of capitalist–type social forces in the Third World				●	●	●
Transnational corporations–advanced countries	Increasing control of transnational corporations on production					●	●
Socialist countries–advanced countries	Socialist block imposes constraints on capitalist expansion						●

● Means a direct incidence of the conflict in the appearance of the problem

Diagram C. The world economy in the post-war era.

States clearly dominated the world economic system in a framework of expanded accumulation and price stability and a *non-hierarchical* period where the exacerbation of *crisis-provoking* conflicts led to the disruption of the international economic order allowing the *character-determining* conflicts to emerge, the interaction of both sets of conflicts producing recession and inflation.

Notes

1. Throughout this study the term "advanced countries" refers to those which UNCTAD (1976) calls "developed market economy countries" and the term "Third World countries" to those UNCTAD calls "developing countries".

2. Lall (1975) describes the control achieved by the transnational corporations over the world economy in the 1970s emphasizing that more than one-fifth of the GNP in the non-socialist world is generated by transnational corporations and that almost 60% of trade in manufactured goods between developed countries is in the hands of these corporations.

3. Hussain (1977) makes the point that even the most trivial economic problem can be seen as a sign of the contradiction between productive forces and the relations of productions: this is why at each stage one must specify the way in which contradictions in the system are expressed, if one is to produce an effective analysis.

4. In order to make the argument more clear I have adopted a seemingly arbitrary approach concentrating on each separate conflict when, in fact, what really matters is the interaction of these conflicts. Nevertheless, the effort is made to integrate the analysis later on.

5. Page 708.

6. It has to be emphasized that the states as mediator does not imply the assumption that it plays a "neutral" role. A bias in the mediation is likely to emerge as long as the state policies express class interests, in the last analysis.

7. Williams (1952) presents an analysis of the international situation in the immediate post-war years, discussing the problems that emerged as a consequence of the implementation of the "Marshall Plan".

8. The interpretation of the payments deficit of the United States which is developed in the following paragraphs is based on the analysis proposed in the early sixties and developed later by Machlup (1968).

9. Drainages of reserves are necessary because, as Machlup (1968) states, "large financial transfers of the United States were not quite matched by its export surpluses" (page 197). Thus the position of the dollar as the means of international payments began to weaken as a consequence of gold losses.

10. It is difficult to establish to what extent military expenditure at the level of 3 billion dollars a year was *necessary* to secure the political situation in Europe; in the last analysis, it must be assumed as a political rather than an economic decision.

11. Page 186.

12. Page 154.

13. The question directly refers to liquidity in the world economy. On an international scale it reproduces the controversy that surrounds the determination of the money supply in a national economy, but since there is no such thing as a "world" currency the pressure is put on the monetary authorities of the United States since the dollar plays the role of international means of payments.

14. Einzig and Quinn (1977) emphasize the changed nature of the euro-dollar market, in that it creates a system of interest rates which do not come under the control of any national monetary authority, and which therefore gives rise to a monetary market which is organized "in parallel" with national markets. Thus the *dollar shortage* is more easily overcome, but at a risk of transforming it into a *dollar glut.*

15. Page 62.

16. Adam (1975) suggests that this behaviour is increasingly adopted by transnational corporations disregarding their country of origin.

17. For the motivations of business expansion of transnational capital see Aliber (1970).

18. Whether it is directed at supplying world markets—e.g. Hong-Kong, Singapore—or at developing internal markets—e.g. Brazil, India.

19. Barnet and Müller (1974) present an analysis of the American case, discussing the effect of the behaviour of private corporations on government policies—Chapter 10.

20. In her analysis of the possibility of price control on the part of the producers of basic commodities, Radetzki (1976) summarizes the conditions: control over the sources of supply and inelasticity of demand through a substantial range of prices. She concludes that only a limited number of commodities can be successfully handled by monopolistic practices: cocoa, coffee, tea, bauxite, petrol, manganese, phosphates, copper and tin. See also Gerling (1976).

21. In fact, exploitation through depression of prices paid to direct producers is *still* possible in many Third World countries as long as traditional forms of production and circulation continue to be prevalent.

22. This argument is developed in Braun (1976).

23. Sylos-Labini (1974) emphasizes the importance of armament production as an expansionary element in the US economic structure.

24. Page 108.

25. See Holzman (1976).

26. The struggle between labour and capital is an *essential* element of capitalism; the confrontation between advanced countries is an *historical* development.

27. Page 393.

28. Page 381.

29. See Maynard and Van Ryckeghem (1976), chapters 5 to 7.

30. Page 13.

31. For a detailed exposition of world monetary problems, see Bergsten (1975a).

32. See Triffin (1977).

33. For a presentation stressing the historical roots of the present crisis, see Hobsbawn (1976).

34. For a complete analysis of commodity markets, see Rangarajan (1978).

35. In fact the "scarcity climate" in commodity markets was developing since the end of the 1960s: the Meadows project started in 1968 and preliminary results were known by 1970.

36. Pages 153, 165 and 166.

37. For an account of the nature of these negotiations see Lutrell (1973), and for a study of their long-term effects on US food policy see Destler (1978).

38. Pages 27 and 28.

39. Grennes *et al.* (1978) stress the importance of the stock reduction as a key factor in the "transformation" of grain markets.

40. Page 672.

41. During these years—1972 and 1973—output expanded very rapidly in advanced countries—see Table A.4—as a result of governments' attempts to reactivate economic activity through monetary and fiscal measures.

42. All relevant analysis of the commodity boom—see, for example, The Brookings Institution (1974), that already mentioned by Cooper and Lawrence (1976), Harris and Josling (1974), Hone (1973)—underline the importance of the *interrelation* of factors in creating inflationary pressures. The drought appears *only* as an additional element in the explanation of price movements.

43. Pages 285 and 286. The author mainly refers to conclusions reached in a report of the Central Intelligence Agency's Office of Political Research.

44. Even at the cost of affecting output performance, governments choose the option of concentrating on inflation. The fear of social chaos dominates the management of the advanced economies. Even the monetarists recognize the social effect of inflation; for example, Friedman (1977) points out that in an inflationary situation: "Prudent behaviour becomes in fact 'reckless' and reckless behaviour in fact prudent. The society becomes polarized, one group is set against another. Political unrest increases. The capacity of any government to govern in reduced at the same time that the pressure for strong action grows." (Page 466).

45. Ideal in the sense that it has the advantages described in note 20.

46. Most other commodity prices, even greater in absolute terms, have lost ground in relation with manufactured goods prices. In average terms, the terms of trade of Third World countries did not improve very much after the commodity boom if one excludes oil from their calculation.

47. For a study of the impact of increasing oil prices on the advanced economies, see Fried and Schulze (1975).

48. "When the Secretary of State sought to develop an alliance of industrial nations to withstand a future embargo, there was no suggestion that the corporations would be removed from their pivotal position or might be a factor in the hostility of the producers." Engler (1977), page 131.

49. The complex problem of the new international economic order merits far more attention than the one devoted to it in the following paragraphs. My intention here is only to enunciate the major features of the problem.

50. It is the lack of unity among advanced countries and their disturbed internal situation which prepares the ground for the emergence of other conflicts.

51. Page 42.

52. Bergsten (1975a) points to the changing nature of these negotiations after the monetary collapse: he defines the new situation as a *non-hierarchical* one, contrasting with the *hegemonial* period when the United States imposed its own criteria on the arrangements—see especially pages 500 to 510.

53. Evans (1978) discusses the implication of these negotiations for the world capitalist system.

54. See Keohane and Ooms (1975).

55. On the nature of these agreements, see Holzman and Legvold (1975).

56. Page 64.

References

Adam, G. (1975) "Multinational corporations and worldwide sourcing". In H. Radice (ed.), *International Firms and Imperialism,* Harmondsworth: Penguin.

Aliber, R. Z. (1970) "A theory of direct foreign investment". In C.P. Kindleberger (ed.), *The International Corporation,* Cambridge, Mass: MIT Press.

Balogh, T. (1975) "The crisis of capitalism", *Mondes en Developpement,* 11.

Barnet, R. J. and R. E.. Müller (1974) *Global Reach: The Power of the Multinational Corporations,* New York: Simon & Schuster.

Bergsten, C. F. (1975a) *The Dilemmas of the Dollar,* New York: New York University Press.

Bergsten, C. F. (1975b) *Towards a New International Economic Order,* Lexington: Lexington Books.

Bienefeld, M. (1977), *Wages, Relative Prices and the Export of Capital,* IDS Communication 122. Brighton: IDS, University of Sussex (November).

Braun, O. (1976) "The new international economic order and the theory of dependency", *Africa Development,* 1.

Braun, O. (1977) *The Present Economic Crisis,* The Hague: Institute of Social Studies (August) (mimeo).

Brookings Institution, The (1974) *Trade in Primary Commodities: Conflict or Co-operation?,* Washington, DC.

Brzezinski, Z. (1974) "Recognizing the crisis", *Foreign Policy,* 17.

Commission on International Trade and Investment Policy (1971) *United States International economic policy in an inter dependent world,* Report to the President, Washington, DC (July).

Cooper, R. N. AND R. Z. Lawrence (1976) *The 1972-73 Commodity Boom,* Center Paper No. 235. Economic Growth Center. New Haven: Yale University.

Destler, I. M. (1978) "United States food policy 1972-1976: reconciling domestic and international objectives", *International Organization,* 32.

Dobb, M. (1963) *Studies in the Development of Capitalism,* London: Routledge & Regan Paul.

Einzig, P. and B. S. Quinn (1977) *The Euro-dollar System,* London: MacMillan.

Engler, R. (1977) *The Brotherhood of Oil,* Chicago: The University of Chicago Press.

Evans, D. (1973) *International Commodity Policy: UNCTAD and NIEC in Search of a Rationale.* IDS Discussion Paper No. 132. Brighton: IDS, University of Sussex (May).

Fried, E. R. and C. L. Schultze (1975) *Higher Oil Prices and the World Economy,* Washington, DC: The Brookings Institution.

Friedman, M. (1977) "Nobel Lecture: Inflation and unemployment", *Journal of Political Economy,* 85.

Gerling, M. (1976) *The Relevance of the OPEC Experience to Manipulation of Other Primary Commodity Prices.* Ithaca: Department of Agricultural Economics, Cornell University.

Grennes, T. *et al.* (1978) *The Economics of World Grain Trade,* New York, Praeger.

Hansen, A. (1945) *America's Role in the World Economy,* London: George Allen & Unwin.

Harris, S. and T. Josling (1974) "Can world commodity prices be explained?", *National Westminster Bank Quarterly Review,* August.

Hobsbawn, T. (1976) "The crisis of capitalism in historical perspective", *Socialist Revolution,* October-December.

Holzman, F. D. (1976) *International Trade Under Communism,* New York: Basic Books.

Holzman, F. D. and R. Legvold (1975) "The economics and politics of east-west relations". In C. F. Bergsten and L. B. Krause (eds.), *World politics and International Economics.* Washington, DC: The Brookings Institution.

Hone, A. (1973) "The commodities boom", *New Left Review,* 81.

Horsefield, T. (1969) *The International Monetary Fund 1945-65,* Washington, DC: IMF.

Hussain, A. (1977) "Crisis and tendencies of capitalism", *Economy and Society,* 6.

Hymer, S. and R. Rowthorn (1970) "Multinational corporations and international oligopoly: The non-American challenge". In C. P. Kindleberger (ed.), *op. cit.*

International Monetary Fund, *International Financial Statistics* (various issues).

Kaldor, N. (1976) "Inflation and recession in the world economy", *Economic Journal,* 86.

Keohane, R. O. and Van Doorn Ooms, "The multinational firm and international regulation". In C. F. Bergsten and L. B. Krause (eds.), *op. cit.*

Keynes, J. M. (1945) "The balance of payments of the United States", *Economic Journal,* 56.

Kuhn, T. (1963) *The Structure of Scientific Revolutions,* Chicago: The University of Chicago Press.

Lall, S. (1975) "Multinationals and development: A new look", National Westminster Bank Quarterly Review, February.

Lutrell, C. B. (1973) "The Russian wheat deal—hindsight vs. foresight", *Federal Reserve Bank of Saint Louis Review,* 55.

Machlup, F. (1968) "The transfer gap of the United States", *Reprints in International Finance No. 11,* Princeton University.

Maynard, G. and W. Van Ryckeghem (1976) *A World of Inflation,* London: Batsford.

Meadows, D. *et al.* (1972) *The Limits to Growth,* Boston: Universe Books.

Murray, R. (1975) "The internationalization of capital and the nation state". In H. Radice (ed.), *op. cit.*

Organization for Economic Co-operation and Development (OECD) *Main Economic Indicators* (various issues).

Organization for Economic Co-operation and Development (1977) *Towards Full Employment and Price Stability* (Summary of a report by a group of independent experts), Paris (June).

Petras, J. and R. Rhodes (1976) "The reconsolidation of US hegemony", *New Left Review,* 97.

Radetzki, M. (1976) "The potential for monopolistic commodity pricing by developing countries". In G. K. Helleiner (ed.), *A World Divided: The Less Developed Countries in the International Economy,* Cambridge: Cambridge University Press.

Rangarajan, L. N. (1978) *Commodity Conflict,* London: Croom Helm.

Robinson, J. (1977) "What are the questions?", *Journal of Economic Literature,* 14.

Rothschild, E. R. (1976) "Food politics", *Foreign Affairs,* 54.

Salant, W. *et al.* (1963) *The United States Balance of Payments in 1968,* Washington, DC: The Brookings Institution.

Salant, W. *et al.* (1977) "A supranational approach to the analysis of worldwide inflation". In L. B. Arause and W. Salant (eds.), *Worldwide Inflation. Theory and Recent Experience,* Washington, DC, The Brookings Institution.

Sylos-Labini, P. (1974) *Trade Unions, Inflation and Productivity,* Westmead: Saxon House.

The Economist (1973) "From the West's ability, to the East's needs?" April 14.

Triffin, R. (1960) *Gold and the Dollar Crisis,* New Haven: Yale University Press.

Triffin, R. (1977) *Le Nouveau système monetaire international,* Institut Universitaire de Hautes Etudes Internationales.

UNCTAD (1976) *Handbook of International Trade and Development Statistics,* Geneva.

UNCTAD (1977) *Monthly Commodity Price Bulletin,* Special supplement, Geneva (March).

US Department of Commerce, *Survey of Current Business* (various issues).

Wilczinski, J. (1978) *Comparative Monetary Economics,* London, Macmillan.

Williams, J. H. (1952) "End of the Marshall Plan", *Foreign Affairs,* 30.

CHAPTER 3

Malnutrition, Famines and the Drought

Any comprehensive study on the impact of climatic fluctuation on society or, rather, on the interactions between them, would cover a wide range of problems. The IFIAS project on "Drought and Man" selected only the most obvious link between climate and society, that is, the production of food and its availability for human consumption.

Within a given area, a decrease in food production, due to any "natural disaster" of climatic origin, may have a direct impact on the local population. The nature and the scope of the effects will depend on a number of factors, some of which are essentially local, while others are external and mainly conditioned by the insertion of the particular country into the world economy. If the "disaster" is widespread, affecting many areas in various continents, new factors will emerge and the combined effects may push the international system beyond some threshold of equilibrium. The regulation processes on the international markets, the world balance of power, world economic and political links of various types, international solidarity, and so on, will be called into play, to restore equilibrium or to aggravate the disequilibrium.

When "the 1972 Case History" was conceived as the focal problem for the "Drought and Man" project it seems that the year 1972 was chosen because it appeared to be a textbook example of the type of processes we have just mentioned. True enough, 1972 belongs to a rather complex period in the history of our contemporary world. The situation was described, in dramatic synthesis, in the statement by the US Academy of Sciences which had already been partially analysed: "In 1972, a year when the climate was particularly unfavourable for food production, millions of people starved to death."

And yet, in preceding chapters, we have provided conclusive evidence, in our view, to show that the statistics on the 1972 decrease in the production of food, the depletion of stocks and the sky-rocketing of prices of cereals on the international market cannot be taken as a basis to explain the drama of those countries where a proportion of the population was "starving to death".

In this chapter the problem has been considered from another angle: the people who suffered and died, or those who suffered and kept on living in sub-human conditions. We have considered this theme as being the focus of the Project. The welfare of man—of *each* man—and of the society—in so far as it is an organization of *people*—is the main concern of our study.

We must, however, make a few remarks in order to avoid some common misunderstandings. The analysis of what happens to an individual or a community when a particular phenomenon hits a given society depends on both the type of input of the individuals of the society and the structure of the society as such (see Chapter

5). From this point of view, in searching for those factors which are at the root of a specific situation, and which are to be taken as the cause of this situation, our frame of reference is the whole structure of the society at that place and during a certain period of time. This is why we have directed so much effort in analyzing the socio-economic structures and their historical evolution in our enquiries on the Sahelian disasters and on similar situations in Brazil or India due to, or attributed to, climatic events. However, our starting point is a concrete situation affecting *people,* not a low value of certain economic indexes.

When a statement such as the one quoted above is made, some questions spring naturally to mind. How many people actually died because of the drought? And how do we know this? The very serious difficulties we encountered in searching for acceptable answers to these questions led us to a type of study to which the Project directed a great deal of effort and which was not foreseen when the original plan was laid down. What were presented as clear, well-formulated, candid questions became the cross-roads of a number of very diverse subjects, placing formidable obstacles in our path.

The obvious answer to all the above questions appears to be: "Just go to the statistics for the countries and periods concerned and find out!" It seemed that, in the same way as we went to the FAO Year Books on production or to the UNCTAD Year Books on trade, it would suffice to ask for the relevant material from WHO in order to find out what happened in the field of nutrition. But this was just the beginning of our troubles: What material? Which statistics? The surprise of the non-specialist when he finds out that there are no world statistics of deaths produced by malnutrition changes into astonishment when he "discovers" that malnutrition, in actual medical practice is virtually ignored as a disease. In fact, malnutrition is not given its proper role in health statistics, that is, a cause of death or morbidity, despite the vast bulk of empirical studies linking it with bacterial and parasitic illnesses.

It was at this stage that the Project was fortunate enough to obtain the collaboration of Dr. José C. Escudero, who is a physician and a Public Health statistician as well as a sociologist, and who carried out or co-ordinated most of the case studies reported in Volume 2 of the present report. His analysis of the magnitude of malnutrition in the world and of the problems of measuring malnutrition, as well as an early draft of his paper on malnutrition in the Sahel, have strongly influenced the scope of the Project.

From there on, malnutrition became one of the focal problems of the Project, to the point that some collaborators from other fields became puzzled by the emphasis placed on this subject. Why is it that we made such an effort to carry out a sort of structural epidemiological analysis on a world-wide basis and, in particular, of some of the critical regions under study? In order to answer this question, we need to consider it from the overall perspective provided by the systemic approach developed in Chapter 5. Some preliminary comments may help, however, to clarify this point.

Our study is concerned with the impact of a natural phenomenon on society. With reference to the natural phenomenon itself, there is little doubt as to how it should be studied: we are in the natural sciences! Thus nobody is surprised—not even the layman—that an "explanation" of the drought in the Sahel, or of the failure of the Indian monsoon, would involve a detailed reference to the General Circulation of the Atmosphere, and an in-depth analysis of what are considered to be the "normal conditions" as well as a serious consideration as to whether there are signs of changing patterns in world climate. In the search for causal-chains, climatologists have introduced the expression "tele-connections" into their jargon, when trying to explain why serious anomalies take place in a region. This is clearly understood by everybody.

And yet, when a problem such as the famines in the early seventies is being studied, there is a tendency to consider that the reference to the "normal conditions" of malnutrition, its magnitude, its changing patterns and the causal relations with other social conditions, is not quite relevant. Tele-connections are readily accepted in natural phenomena, but very reluctantly in social phenomena.

Our view is that there exists a striking parallelism between the explanatory schemes for the drought as a meteorological event, and for the famine as a social event. To "explain" drought one needs a climatological analysis which automatically implies reference to large-scale space and time processes. It is only on this broad scale that the anomaly called "drought" can be given a meaning and a meaningful explanation provided. Likewise, famines occur as anomalies within large-scale processes in society which regulate the changing patterns at the level of nutrition. It is only with reference to this background that the famines have a clear meaning and a significant explanation of them given. The studies on malnutrition are, thus, the counterpart of the climatological studies.

The reluctance in accepting tele-connections when one is dealing with a *social* anomaly such as famine can be easily explained: one touches here a very sensitive set of issues. No one can blame the Soviets for having a longer than usual snow cover over Siberia, or the Arabs for a heating over the Persian Gulf, both of which may alter the Indian monsoon. Information about these natural phenomena is therefore not hidden. No country is, on the other hand, ready to expose its social diseases, and there are not very many people in the world who feel comfortable when one tries to find the "tele-connections" of social anomalies.

It is therefore not surprising to see the insistence with which Escudero endeavours to show that in the places where there are statistics there is no malnutrition and in the places where there is malnutrition there are no statistics. Hence the evaluation of the magnitude of malnutrition and, still worse, the assessment of the incidence of malnutrition on mortality is not an easy task. Notwithstanding this, it can be shown, beyond any reasonable doubt, that the magnitude of the problem is shocking.

As Escudero emphasizes, "malnutrition is perhaps the most widespread disease in the world". It has seldom been recognized as such, although there are periods when world malnutrition attracts public attention. The 1972 situation marks the beginning of a period of rather intensive studies on this subject, culminating in the 1974 United Nations World Food Conference. There was a similar world interest in malnutrition and famines in the early 1960s, as well as in earlier periods. This "periodic awareness" of the malnutrition problems in the world is one of the most depressing facts in the history of food supplies and "food aid" at the international level. For it is not so much associated with an effective periodic increase of malnutrition in the developing countries, as with changes in agriculture and in international trade policies in the developed countries. We have already referred to this problem in the preceding chapters. Here, we shall only quote without comment, a statement which presents the blunt facts:

> "Exaggeration of the extent of hunger in the developing world was clearly good politics for the USDA (US Department of Agriculture), faced as it was at that time with increasing and bothersome surpluses. Sales or gifts to the L.D.C.'s (Less Developed Countries) under Public Law 480 could postpone the day or more stringent controls or lower prices, or both, to American farmers."[1]

We do not entirely agree with Poleman's dictum because we do not believe in "exaggeration of the extent of hunger". The situation seems to be rather different. *There is* as much malnutrition and hunger as indicated in the USDA reports referred to by Poleman. The only thing is, the problem remains *hidden* until it is convenient to exhibit it for reasons such as those indicated by Poleman.

Ample evidence is provided in Volume 2 of this report to show that there is indeed no exaggeration in the figures provided by the USDA reports and elsewhere when they do care to exhibit the problem. Tables giving the estimated number of people in developing countries for whom food intake is below the minimum critical level show that, on average (for Africa, Latin America, Near East and Far East, excluding Asian centrally planned economies), 24% of the population, or over 400 million people, are below that level. The percentage does not change from the 1969-71 to the 1972-4 period (some increase in Africa is compensated by a decrease in Latin America and the Near East). When milder forms of malnutrition are included, the estimated population living below acceptable levels of food intake goes up to roughly 1000 million people. Some of them will die at a very early age, others will survive longer.

Drought or no drought, high prices of food or low prices of food, high levels of stocks of cereals in developed countries or low levels of stocks, the problems are always there, showing that they are not produced by contingent natural phenomena, nor by the elasticity properties of prices on the market.

From the point of view of our project, the fact we want to emphasize is that although we have rough figures on the magnitude of malnutrition in the world, as yet no reliable information is available on the number of people dying because of malnutrition. As Escudero points out, "the vital statistics systems of the world would record, in theory, all deaths which take place in certain defined geographical areas, as well as the causes of death. In practice, however, this does not happen." He indicates three main reasons (cf. Chapter 3 of Volume 2): (a) under-registration of deaths; (b) the unavailability of health services to much of the population (which prevents ascertaining the cause of death in many cases); (c) the existence of biases in the current system of determining the "basic cause of death" which significantly tends to underestimate the causal role of malnutrition. To these reasons, which alone would account for the fact that chronic malnutrition is permanently undermeasured, Escudero adds, in an illuminating analysis, the incidence of the epistemological framework of the medical profession and of their underlying

---

1 Thomas T. Poleman: "World food: a perspective", published by the AAAS in a special *Science* compendium on Food, 1975.

ideological biases. Here we shall only refer very briefly to the three factors mentioned above.

Concerning the under-registration of deaths we shall consider some figures for Africa and Latin America, referring to Volume 2 for further details. A survey undertaken in twenty Latin American countries in 1975 (which drew a non-response from ten of them) stated that "6 countries estimated their general mortality to be under-registered by at least 20% and 5 countries estimated a similar under-registration in their infant mortality". Other figures are even more serious. In 1955-60 the percentage of under-registration of deaths was 64% for Bolivia, 45% for Cuba, 40% for Honduras, 39% for Nicaragua.

The situation is much worse in Africa where in many countries statistics of causes of death are practically non-existent. In 1963 in the Arrondissement Nakmar (Sine Saloum, Senegal) only 12% of births and 1% of deaths had been registered, and in the Arrondissement Paos Moto only 4% of births and no deaths. In Upper Volta, the mortality rate as registered by vital statistics amounted to only one-seventh of the actual rate. In Ethiopia "precise figures indicating the mortality rates are not available. Registration of vital rates is virtually unknown in the rural areas of the country and even in the urban areas registration is carried out on a voluntary basis only."

The second contributory factor to the undermeasurement of chronic malnutrition and of death caused by malnutrition is the unavailability of health services. The physician to population ratios are generally very low in developing countries. In addition, of these countries, in those having market economies, physicians are very unevenly distributed "because, for lack of any other criteria, it is the 'market' that allocates them. They then drift towards those areas—mainly urban—and concentrate on those populations that can pay for their services" (Escudero, *ibid.*). We shall quote only a few references to some areas of Africa covered by our case studies. In Ethiopia, a country very hard hit by the 1972-3 famine, two-thirds of the hospitals, one-third of health centres and four-fifths of doctors and nurses are established in three provinces: Iboa, Eritrea and Haragué, it being estimated that no more than 5 million of an estimated 22 million Ethiopians were provided with ordinary health services. In Senegal, 75.2% of all physicians in the country are established in the Cape Verde region, with 18.55% of the country's population. A similar situation of uneveness of distribution of health resources occurs in the other Sahel countries. The implications are quite clear: "As a consequence of this maldistribution, there is a high percentage of recorded deaths whose causes cannot be ascertained as they are not certified by physicians, and most of these deaths from unknown causes occur in those geographical areas and social classes where malnutrition is the dominant pathology" (*ibid.*).

We now turn to the third reason for under-registration: biases in the current system of determining the "basic cause of death". The International Classification of Diseases (ICD) has adopted a world-wide uniform method for determination of causes of death by choosing *one* "basic cause of death" for every death. This decision undoubtedly facilitates the processing of information but "tends to underestimate malnutrition as a cause of death by allocating to another disease—usually an infectious one—the role of 'basic cause of death', even if both diseases are recorded in the death certificate". Escudero provides the following example: "Thus, an infant death 'caused' by a bronchopneumonia which is in turn caused by a measles infection in a child weakened by malnutrition will be assigned to 'measles', and malnutrition will not even be mentioned as a causal agent, even though it is well known that fatality from measles is a function of nutritional status, thus making malnutrition as much a cause of death as the measles virus."

The fact that malnutrition as a cause of death is seldom properly registered has a double consequence which cannot be overemphasized. Firstly, the magnitude of the problem remains hidden. Although we do not mean to say that this is the reason for a systematic under-registration, it is clear that many governments do not worry very much when these facts are ignored. As already stated, no country likes to expose the depth of its social problems. Nor does the world at large like it. People who are always avid for sensational news—natural catastrophe or otherwise—refuse to face a *permanent* situation of disaster affecting a large sector of mankind. Ignoring the problem is a well-known "defence" mechanism. Therefore one should not expect strong movements "in search of the truth".

Secondly, when there is a "natural disaster" such as the Sahelian drought, the deaths produced by malnutrition become too obvious. There is a tendency *to attribute all malnutrition-generated deaths,* and in fact malnutrition itself, *to the natural disaster.* The effects of natural disasters are thus greatly exaggerated. This goes well with the avidity for "sensationalism". Moreover, blaming the climate, or "nature" or some punishing God, leaves the conscience of the rest of the world with no other burden than piety and feelings of charity. These are not very heavy to carry and they might even help to reinforce the self-esteem of people.

We may now return to the questions asked at the beginning of this chapter. The difficulties in answering them are at this point quite apparent. We simply do not know how many people died in the Sahel in the early 1970s *because of the drought.* First, because we do not know how many people died in the Sahel in that period. Second, because even if we knew how many deaths were produced during the famine, it would be unfair to attribute all of them to the drought or to food scarcities, whatever the reason for the latter.

This leads us to our main reason for insisting on this background scenario in our studies on the impact of drought. Deaths "produced" by a drought have as a prerequisite, living conditions below a certain minimum level of nutrition. When a drought occurs it simply transforms a "normal" situation into a tragic one. But the relationship is by no means a direct one.

The most obvious effect of drought is found in the interference with food production. However, the impact is not proportional to the decrease in food production. It is, so to speak, *amplified* by the social structure. This is the reason for the occurrence, in well-documented cases, of vast famines which were started in connection with a climatic anomaly having only a moderate effect on food production. The natural phenomenon has, in these cases, the function of a "trigger", releasing a latent instability already present in the system. We shall deal with this problem more extensively in Chapter 5. From this perspective, the most important problem with which we should be concerned is therefore of pre-drought marginal conditions which render the society highly vulnerable when a drought situation arises. This problem involves, in fact, two different questions. First, what are the countries, regions, areas of the world where malnutrition prevails rendering their population highly fragile when drought strikes. Second, what are the characteristics of a given social structure which makes it either able to damp down or likely to amplify the effects of a perturbation such as a drought. This chapter is only concerned with the first question.

Where can one find victims of malnutrition. From what has been said so far, it is clear that we do not know for sure, since figures of nourished people are only estimates and at the level of national or regional aggregates. Little or no attempt has been made to relate its prevalence within demographic, social or economic variables or with a more comprehensive explanatory frame. In this connection, Escudero's remarks are worth quoting at length.

"This lack of solid data and studies leaves the field free for guesses which researchers can fill with deductive reasonings from their ideology and 'Weltanschauung'. If malnutrition is caused by low education it will be found among the poorly-educated; if it is caused by a death wish on the part of certain individuals it will be found among death wishers; if it is related to meteorological misfortune, to certain geographical areas of residence, or to certain occupations its prevalence will be correspondingly higher where these variables occur.

"If, as the conclusion of this Project strongly suggests, malnutrition can certainly be linked with many of the elements listed above, but there is also a higher explanatory level that encompasses them, then it will be found somewhere else. It will be found among those people who are surplus to a given form of social organization and a given productive process. Any increase in its prevalence will have to be searched for—lacking a reliable statistical monitoring system—in those countries whose capacity to make autonomous decisions is compromised, who are becoming increasingly poor, whose wealth is distributed in a less egalitarian fashion and whose social fabric becomes distorted by an encroaching profit-oriented international economy. But it will also have to be searched for *within countries* in those population groups who become irrelevant to the new organization of productive forces and therefore are remunerated at a level below subsistence by the societies in which they live. This is central because malnutrition studies are not only few, but those which exist have an overwhelming unilateral intellectual framework. Not only is malnutrition not recognized in its magnitude, but also very little empirical data has been gathered on the way in which malnutrition victims are linked to the productive process, the latter being either ignored entirely or treated in the most superficial way (as 'occupation', 'income' or 'economic level'."

The most accepted current explanation of the worldwide spread of malnutrition ignores the productive *process* and puts all the emphasis on food production: there are people who do not eat properly because their countries do not produce enough of the right food. And they do not produce enough, so it is held, for two main reasons: the lack of an adequate technology (backward, traditional agricultural practices) and a demographic expansion upsetting all achievements in increasing production.

The specific arguments on "backward" agriculture and demography are considered in other chapters. We shall refer now to the main argumental line contained in the assertion "people are under-nourished in some countries because they do not produce enough food'', taken literally, contains a gross over-simplification. We shall give an example. The amount of animal proteins contained in the average diet of a European is more than twice the average for Latin America. This does not mean, however, that Europe produces proportionally more meat than Latin America. In 1976 Western Europe *imported* (net!) 887,000 tons of meat, whereas Latin America *exported* 582,000 tons. This very simple arithmetic shows that the problem is certainly not *there*. In order to find out where the roots are, one must consider in some detail the production and trade structure of some representative countries. We shall take a few examples from Latin America.

The Central American countries are frequently mentioned as characteristic examples of a very high population growth and of deteriorating levels of nutrition. Let us consider the case of Honduras. The population growth is 3.6%, one of the highest in the world. Food production *per capita* decreased by 1.4% during the period 1970-76. The average intake of calories was 1987 in the period 1972-4 (to be compared with more than 3500 calories in countries like Belgium, Switzerland and the USA). About 38% of the population received an amount of calories lower than the critical limit of 1.2 M.B. Against this background, the structure of food production and trade is, to say the least, surprising, unless there is a high explanatory level which accounts for this surprise. The exports of meat, for instance, show considerable growth:

Exports of meat from Honduras
(millions of dollars)

1969	1970	1971	1972	1973	1974
8.9	8.7	12.5	15.9	21.7	16.7

This picture is by no means peculiar to Honduras. In 1973 the five Central American countries (Costa Rica, El Salvador, Guatemala, Honduras and Nicaragua) imported cereals from the US amounting to 59 million dollars, but they exported meat amounting to 139 million dollars and fruit and vegetables amounting to 146 million dollars, not to mention sugar and coffee amounting to 270 million dollars. A large amount of imported grain was used to feed livestock for export.

Can we go on pretending that the figures relating to trade in cereals explain the food situation in this region and to conclude that these people are undernourished because they do not produce enough food or that imports of cereals are forced by the demographic explosion? The total figures of the food trade of these countries with the US will dissipate all doubts regarding this.

Five Central American countries: Food trade with the US.
(millions of dollars)

	1960	1965	1968	1970	1971	1973	1974	1975
Exports to US	162	259	305	373	349	598	649	668
Imports from US	20	27	35	35	41	82	108	119

And yet, it would be unfair to put all the blame on exporting and on the forces acting on the international markets. True, when we divide the world in "developed" and "developing" countries, the two categories reflect a clear-cut difference in food-consumption patterns. However, to stop the analysis at this point would imply missing the core of the problem because countries cannot be considered as homogeneous units.

The *elite* of developing countries develop the same habits in their diets as those prevailing in developed countries. No wonder that countries like Mexico or Honduras use a large amount of grain to feed the livestock. Part of this livestock is for export, but another part is consumed by local sectors of the population.

Food production in these countries as well as in a large number of developing countries is sharply divided into two sectors: one, producing for export and for the local elite (only in a few cases for a more extended middle-class); the second, producing food for the large masses of population. The first uses advanced technology, receives strong support from the government (usually in the form of credits, public irrigation developments, etc.) and employs the labour force of salary earners; the second follows more traditional practices, does not have access to modern technology, nor to official support, and uses mainly family labour force. The first is oriented towards products having high market prices; the second is meant to produce cheap food for the country's labour forces.

The relevance of these considerations to the subject matter of the Project becomes evident when we analyse the vulnerability of these countries to the impact of an external factor such as drought. It seems clear from the above consideration that one sector of the population will be much more vulnerable than the other *to the same drought*. (On this important subject, see the paper by Portantiero in Volume 3.)

The above considerations show that in order to judge the nature and the scope of the "impact" of a drought one has to have a knowledge of the functioning of the society *prior* to the drought. Nutritional levels, their internal distribution within the country or region concerned, the characteristics of the productive system, and so on, are structural elements which carry considerable weight in defining its degree of vulnerability. They also determine the "normal" base line with reference to which the effects of anomaly have to be measured.

This leads us to a concluding remark to this chapter. The words "normal" and "normality" are generally used in a very ambiguous way. More often than not they only refer to long-term statistical averages. Nevertheless, when the expressions "back to normal" or "the conditions are now normal" are being used, people have a tendency to take them for synonyms of "the situation is now all right". The statistical meaning acquires, thus, a normative connotation. A proof of this could be provided by the fact that an expression such as "unfortunately, the situation returned to normal", somehow does not sound right.

And yet, the two meanings of "normal", the *statistical* and the *normative,* refer to quite a different realm of ideas. The former means "as it happened to be, on the average, in the past", whereas the latter has associated with it the notion of "acceptable standards". We can only talk in a purely statistical sense of the "normal conditions" in the life of a deprived child in Haiti, Mauritania or India, for whom every year is a bad year. They belong to segments of the human society living in a state of *constant catastrophe*. They may go through a period of greater "stress" when droughts, floods or earthquakes hit their territories. Some of them will die. Those who survive do not share the feeling of happy relief which the rest of the world experiences when the territory is officially declared "back to normal conditions".

CHAPTER 4

The Population-resources Balance

Statistics concerning population growth, food production, and consumption *per capita* are well known. When *projections* are made for the next decades, the situation looks dark enough to excite the malthusians: "While the gloomy predictions of the toll of wars, famines and pestilence associated with Malthus' principle have not come true under present conditions, in a sense we see even worse misery arising from his premise of population outrunning available food supplies, in the form of hunger and malnutrition on the increase."[1]

The alarm created by malthusian-type arguments has been widespread and has produced a growing conviction that increased malnutrition in developing countries is being caused by population growth:

"During the past 20 years or so, food production in the developing countries as a whole has, on the average, kept slightly ahead of the unprecedented growth in population. This is, of course, a tremendous achievement. But at the same time we must remember that in almost 40 percent of individual developing countries food production has failed to keep up with population growth and in almost two thirds of developing countries it has not kept up with the total increase in domestic demand. Again on the average, population growth accounts for about 70 percent of the increase in demand for food in the developing countries and 55 percent in the developed countries."[2]

The basic ideas expressed in the statements quoted above are widely accepted. Taken at their face value they lead, however, to misleading conclusions. Such is the case, for instance, with the authoritative analysis on "World Food Problems and Prospects", made by the well-known agricultural economist D. Gale Johnson. Under the sub-title "Reducing the birth rate" one finds the following statement:

"The government of the developing countries must be encouraged to realize that there can be no significant improvements in per capita food supply without declines in birth rates and reductions in population growth rates. Unless their birth rates are reduced, most of the efforts they are making to maintain a rate of growth in food production of 3 percent annually will simply provide approximately the current level of food consumption for a lot more people".[3]

Johnson's position has far-reaching consequences. For instance, he explicitly *regrets* the final clause of Resolution IX adopted by the World Food Conference (Rome, 1974) which "calls on governments and on people everywhere . . . to support, for a longer term solution, rational population policies ensuring to couples the

111

right to determine the number and spacing of births, freely and responsibly, in accordance within the context of an overall development strategy''.

Similar positions are even found at the highest levels of international organizations. Roy Jackson, in the address already quoted, concluded his remarks in the following way (it should not be forgotten that he spoke on behalf of the Director-General of FAO):

> "Let me re-state the two major points which I made. First, that action must be initiated now to reduce the rate of population growth if we are to have any chance at all of meeting the world's food needs 25 years from now. Second, while family planning and population policy are matters for individual governments, there is at the same time a clear need for international action."

It was already said that these conclusions are highly misleading and this requires some detailed explanation.

The above quotations, together with hundreds of other formulations of the population-resources problem in their multifarious presentations of neo-malthusian analysis, contain implicit assumptions which are never brought to the open. Malthus himself, a very conscious and clever thinker, regardless of the historical fate of his theory, did start his assertions with some "ifs" often forgotten by those who invoke him.

So far, reference has been made to those who look at the population-resources equation focusing the attention on the population side and preaching population control in order to keep the balance. Other authors, more realistically, take for granted that there is no hope of drastic changes in population growth in the near future and they focus their recommendations on the resources side of the equation: all efforts should be concentrated on increasing food production in developing countries. Perhaps one of the more explicit thinkers in this group is Roger Revelle who was Director of the Center for Population Studies at Harvard University. In his contribution to the Symposium on "The Food-People Balance" at the National Academy of Engineering,[4] he maintains that ". . . overall, the poor countries need somehow to find the means to produce food to meet the future demands of their people, one reason for this being that at least for the time being they have very little to export to pay for food from the rich countries".

His panacea, as we shall see, is the "Green Revolution". There is enough evidence today to prove that high technology agriculture was not *the* answer to the food production problems of developing countries. This is discussed below. Here we are concerned with bringing to the open the pre-suppositions we find in his quoted statement. They are shared by all those who believe that the food-population balance in developing countries can only be kept by decreasing the population growth or by increasing the capacity of these countries to produce more food. This seems to be very simple arithmetic. We question its logic. Scientists do not make mistakes in calculations, but they sometimes make mistakes in the logic leading to such calculations.

The current view, so forcefully represented by Revelle, and for which we have found no factual support, amounts to the following: Developing countries do not produce enough food to nourish their population. They cannot import from the rich countries either, because they are poor. They have therefore to resort to extraordinary ways to produce more. High agricultural technology is the answer. (This is paraphasing, not quoting.) These four basic postulates are unwarranted. To illustrate it we shall consider the case of two countries, India and Mexico, whose food problems are frequently presented by neo-malthusians[5] as confirming the validity of their arguments.

India is perhaps the example most often referred to as a case of a country with food problems attributed to population growth. The counterpoint between India and China, which is presented in Volume 2, seems to be clear enough to demonstrate that the Indian problems are by no means the unescapable result of a process originated in an excess of population and which becomes irreversible unless the population growth is drastically reduced. This historical proof would not suffice, however, for the purpose of this report, insofar as our aim is to show that the population/production balance has been wrongly formulated. We shall present, therefore, some simple facts concerning India's production and trade structure which show the myth of India's incapacity to produce enough food for her growing population.

Everybody knows that India is the first world exporter of tea and tobacco, not to speak of woven textiles. Much less known, and in fact rather shocking, is the fact that India's exports of animal feeding, fruits and vegetables, and fishery exceed the first two items. In 1967 India occupied the third place, after Peru and Argentina, in the list of developing countries exporting animal feeding (62,284 million dollars or the 4.27% of world exports). By 1973 the export of animal feeding stuff had more than tripled (210.9 million dollars) and was larger than tea exports (186.3 million dollars). The item of "Fruit and Vegetables" had gone up to 102.8 million dollars and the exports in the item of fishery reached the sum of 88.5 million dollars. Is this picture compatible with the idea of an India desperately in need of "food aid" because of her population growth?

Unquestionably India has a problem in her food trade. But the problem lies elsewhere. Her traditional hard-currency earning agricultural exporting product was tea. Her traditional imports were, in addition to manufactured goods, foodgrains. The progression of tea exports and cereal imports during the 1970s was as follows:

		1970	1971	1972	1973	1974	1975	1976
Tea	(1)	205	199	203	188	205	219	237
Exports	(2)	196	202	203	185	232	293	312
Cereal	(1)	4200	2500	660	3700	4458	7015	5832
Imports	(2)	350	242	82	501	711	1208	979

(1) Thousand tons.   (2) Million dollars.

A comparison of the years 1971 and 1974, just before and after the critical years 1972/3, is very revealing. In 1971 India's tea exports paid for 2.1 million tons of imported cereals. In 1974 her tea exports *increased* by 3%, but they could only pay for 1.5 million tons of the cereals she imported. This deterioration of the terms of trade of food products is a common feature of the trade structure of a large number of developing countries and appears to be the net result of the *new* food policy implemented by developed countries in the early 1970s (cf. Chapter 2).

The analysis of the "Indian case" would not be complete without an account of the historical reasons of why and how India devoted so much effort and valuable land to grow tea and tobacco instead of more staples. This would take us beyond the scope of this chapter. We shall only mention that such a study show that colonial and neo-colonial policies, not population growth, are at the starting-point of adverse agricultural production practices.

The Green Revolution was thought of as a panacea to cure Indian illness in agricultural production. In the paper already quoted, Revelle makes the following statement:

> "Just to give you some idea of the technical possibilities, at the present time in India, about 300 million acres are cultivated for a population of around 530 million people. The new varieties of wheat and rice, which have nothing miraculous about them, but which are simply highly responsive to fertilizers, are so productive, about four to five times as productive as the varieties used in the past, that in India, at least, the total amount of cultivated land could be reduced to about 100 million acres from the present 300 million acres, in other words, reduced by two-thirds. This would be sufficient to feed a population of 1.2 billion people, which is about the population expected in India by the turn of the century unless something drastic happens by way of fertility control. This would be sufficient to feed a population of 1.2 billion people at a level of diet twice as good as it is now, that is, with a diet of about 4,500 calories per day as opposed to the 2,200 that is now available per person in India."

History has shown, however, that this strong confidence in the new high-level agricultural technology was overoptimistic. The new varieties of rice, referred to in the quoted text, failed in India, like those of other crops except wheat, and yet the "Wheat Revolution" faced very serious limitations.

B. Dasgupta, in a detailed study of the Green Revolution in India between 1966 and 1976, considers three different phases during this period:

> "The first phase, from 1966 to 1971, was characterized by a rapid increase in the area under HYVs (high yields varieties), and in overall food production, and a decline in food imports. In 1971, the year the country's agriculture produced a record food production figure, production was large enough to accomodate the needs of the 10 million refugees who came from Bangladesh. Despite the impressive performance of the new varieties in some regions, there was no solid statistical foundation for the uncontrolled optimism of the government in the early seventies."[6]

Dasgupta finds here a misuse of the statistical information which, as we show repeatedly throughout the Project Report, distorts the facts and leads to attributing wrong causal relations among events. When the figures are more carefully looked at, the accepted explanations just dissolve. Dasgupta proceeds:

> "In fact, the figures suggested that most of the eight million ton increase of 1971 came from states which were poorly endowed with irrigation water and which had not been subjected to the influence of the new technology: Rajasthan (four million tons), Bihar, Madhya Pradesh and Gujarat (another three million

tons). In contrast, the production increase in Punjab, the heartland of the new technology, was no more than a hundred thousand tons in that year. The conclusion it drew from these figures was that the high figure of 1970/71 reflected the unusually favourable weather of that year, which showed the continued vulnerability of Indian agriculture to bad weather" (*op. cit.,* page 35).

What happened afterwards was a sad blow to overoptimistic views on the "Green Revolution":

"The second phase, from 1972 to 1975, was characterized by unfavourable weather, and vindicated the cautious stance of the Agricultural Prices Commission. While the overall acreage under HYVs increased substantially, yields declined. All the familiar problems of the pre-HYV era, dependence on food imports, harvest failure, and famine conditions in various parts of the country, were visible again."

To do justice to Revelle's position we should point out that he made it clear that technology alone cannot solve the problem. The sentence preceding the quotation we made above says just this: "The problem is not really a technical one, it is an economic and social and political one." We entirely agree with this statement, only when he clarifies what he means by it, we cannot go along with him. This point deserves some analysis as it goes to the heart of the controversy on the use of high technology to "save" the developing countries from starvation.

Let us see in detail what Revelle means when he talks about the economic and social and political problems involved:

"But if one looks into this a little more critically, one sees that what it really requires is a social revolution, because the new agriculture is primarily market agriculture and not subsistence agriculture. Farmers cannot grow large quantities of food unless they can purchase what the economists again call the factors of production, which are off-farm inputs such as fertilizer, irrigation water, the new seed varieties, pesticides, farm tools and farm machinery, and knowledge. In order to be able to purchase all these things, they have to be able to sell a considerable fraction of their crops, which means there must be customers available to buy these crops. The customers of course will be people who don't live on farms, but who live in cities or in towns and who do something besides farming."[7]

The reason why the Green Revolution has not succeeded in India, or elsewhere, was not because there were not enough "customers available to buy those crops".

Dasgupta points out that: "industrialists in India are deeply interested in a food policy which would provide their workers with a regular food supply at a cheap price, and would reduce the cost of food imports so that more of the precious foreign exchange could be made available to import materials for industrial development".

The introduction of high agricultural technology was therefore supported by industrialists, but with an important proviso: that it would not upset the existing balance of forces in the rural sector. In fact, the Green Revolution brought about a convergence of interests of the two powerful economic groups in the country: "the rural elite which is powerful at the local level, and the industrial elite which is powerful at the national level". In this sense, it reinforced the power of the rural elite:

"Whatever the influence of the industrial capital and the multi-national firms on the formulation of the new agricultural strategy, there is no doubt that its adoption has strengthened the position of the ruling elite in the countryside. Firstly, it has increased the profits and assets, and consequently the economic power of this group (see chapters III and IV). Secondly, through the new technology a new type of patron-client dependency relationship of the small farmers on the rich farmers has been created for the use of means of production which are owned by the latter, especially farm machinery. Thirdly, the rural elite has emerged as an intermediary through whose hands the inputs supplied by the government are delivered to the village. We have already noted the control of the rich farmers over co-operatives; in addition, in most villages retail shops for fertilizer, seed and other inputs are owned by the rich farmers."

It seems therefore that a "social revolution" is required, as Revelle indicates, but of a different nature, i.e. one which cannot be inspired by the past evolution of the countries which are *now* developed. The history of the relation between industrialization and rural development in developing countries does not follow such patterns.

A recipe which "worked" (regardless of social costs) in the period of industrialization of the leading industrial countries does not work in today's world conditions. This is the root of our dislike of terms like "developed", "underdeveloped" and "developing". C. Hewitt de Alcantara puts the problem in eloquent terms: "A type of rural change which was inhumane, but in the long run efficacious, in Britain or in the United States a hundred years ago, is proving inhumane and inefficacious in industrializing peasant societies of the twentieth century."[8]

The relations between agrarian and industrial sectors in developing countries that have started their industrialization process is neither simple nor susceptible of being reduced to general formulas valid for all such countries. We refer to the contribution by J. C. Portantiero included in Volume 3 (cf. also Chapter 6 below) for an illuminating analysis of this problem in Latin America.

Let us now turn to the second example. Mexico is often mentioned as a paradigmatic case of a country which has reached self-sufficiency in food production, but which later on was forced to become a food importer because of the demographic explosion. The key data generally quoted to "prove" the case is the figure of 2.6%, the rate of increase of cereals production in the period 1970-75, as against a population growth of 3.5%, one of the highest in the world. This shows, so it is argued, why Mexico started to import cereals during that period. This conclusion is, however, just wrong mathematics: it amounts to mistaking the value of the derivative of a curve at a certain point for the value of the function at that point. It is obviously true that if both curves continue with the same slope, in the long run the production will not be able to cope with the population growth. So far this has not happened. The figures are as follows: the production of cereals in 1975/6 was 119% higher than the production in 1960/61; the population in 1975 was only about 50% larger than in 1960; the production *per capita* in 1975 was therefore above the production *per capita* in 1960. These figures do not suffice though to provide the necessary insight to extricate what happened in Mexican agriculture.

By 1945 Mexico imported about 15 to 20% of the internal consumption of cereals (mainly corn and wheat). In the 1960s the situation had changed. From 1964 to 1969 Mexico exported 1.8 million tons of wheat and 5.6 million tons of corn. The wheat yields had increased from 75kg/ha in 1950 to 3200 kg/ha. The production of corn went up by 250%. The famous Green Revolution was in full force and the figures appeared to provide an irrefutable proof of its success. However, in the early 1970s Mexico went back to importing cereals. Why? "Population explosion" became a ready-made answer to explain this "catastrophe". The facts are, however, somewhat different.

What happened in the 1970s was in the first place an actual *decrease* of the absolute amount in the production of corn (in millions of tons):

1968	1969	1970	1971	1972	1973	1974	1975	1976
9.1	8.4	8.9	9.8	9.2	8.6	7.8	8.4	8.9

Source: FAO Production Yearbook, 1975 and *Monthly Bulletin,* February 1978.

Obviously, population growth has nothing to do with this decrease, since they are absolute figures. Nor is the climate responsible for the drop since 1971.

In the second place, the main argument used by the malthusians is the changes in the pattern of food trade due to massive imports of cereals starting around 1972. The figures are as follows:

Imports of coarse grains
(in millions of tons)

1971	1972	1973	1974	1975
0.173	0.140	1.513	1.571	3.065

Source: US Department of Agriculture.

Are the jumps from 1972 to 1973 and from 1974 to 1975 due to population problems? Not at all. The first difference is 1.373 million tons. But the production in 1973 was *lower* than the production in 1972 by precisely the same amount. The imports were just enough to compensate for the *decrease* in the absolute amount of production. What does the population growth have to do with it?

The second jump, from 1974 to 1975, was 1.550 million tons. But this difference corresponds exactly to the *increase* in the use of grains for animal feeding, the figures being as follows:

	Imports	*Animal feeding*
1974:	1.513	2.436
1975:	3.063	3.984
Difference	1.550	1.548

Source: US Department of Agriculture, *op. cit.*

Finally, in 1976, the *production* of grains (wheat plus coarse grains) *increased* to 15.4 million tons. The Mexicans had therefore 1 million tons more than in 1975. Did the population have more grain to eat? Hardly so. The stocks of coarse grain increased by 300,000 tons and animals ate 400,000 tons more.

The use of grains for animal feeding is indeed one of the keys to explain Mexican grain imports. These are the facts:

(a) From 1966 to 1976 the increase in domestic consumption of wheat and coarse grains was about 7 million tons, distributed as follows:

Animal feeding: 3.2 million tons
Human and industrial consumption: 3.8 million tons

(b) The imports of grain were *every year* inferior to the amount used for animal feeding.

The story does not end here. So far, we only talked about the production and trade of *cereals*. We have already considered at length (Chapter 1) the fallacy of taking what happens in the market of cereals as being representative of the food market.

The total figures for *food trade* shows that the picture of Mexico as a country which was forced to become a food importer (read: "cereal importer") due to the population explosion is totally wrong. The trade in the item "food and animals" (FAO's terminology) developed as follows:

Mexican trade in food and animals

	1969	1970	1971	1972	1973	1974	1975
Imports	52.6	123.5	100.5	182.8	357.8	737.5	815.3
Exports	525.7	521.2	527.2	642.1	712.9	795.3	738.9

Source: FAO.

In this table, FAO does not include the item of fishery. In 1973 Mexico *exported* 111.2 million dollars of this item (cf. *UNCTAD Handbook Supplement*, 1977, p. 147). This amount was equivalent to 12% of all fish exports of developing countries and 3.4% of the world.

It is too easy to jump to conclusions on the basis of the preceding table and play with the idea that food exports have already reached a ceiling whereas food imports must continuously increase. This would be again wrong logic. The figures in the table represent *values* in dollars. We already saw in the case of India that the picture is different when we look at the quantities which are imported or exported. The changing structure of Mexican food production, where tomatoes, strawberries and vegetables for export became privileged with reference to the traditional staples which were corn and beans, explains the difference. But this subject is treated in Chapter 12 and in more detail in Volume 4.

Once all this has been said, we are in a position to formulate the problem of the food-population race in more realistic terms. It would perhaps be wise to start by making clear what we *do not* mean to imply by our analysis. First, we do not deny that population growth is a problem which should be of serious concern for mankind as a whole and for some developing countries in particular. Second, we do accept the fact that population pressure is an important factor to be considered in the explanation of processes such as food scarcity, unemployment, desertification, insufficient educational coverage, and so on, in some places and some periods of time. Third, we do accept the fact that should the present conditions continue, the apocalyptic predictions of neo-malthusians may materialize in a not too distant future.

What we do specifically reject is the idea that population growth is the *cause,* or even *a* cause, of food scarcity for the developing countries, that malnutrition and famines are produced by it; that, in short, *any* of the social catastrophes originated by drought, floods, desertification or what not, could be explained in terms of the problems posed by the demographic explosion. Our position is that, in *all* cases, demographic pressure is no more than an *aggravating factor,* an additional burden, and sometimes a trigger of internal instabilities already present in a social system (cf. Chapter 5).

Putting together what we accept with what we reject concerning the "population problem", the obvious conclusion is that by proclaiming the control of population as the most important recommendation to be made to developing countries (cf. Johnson's statement quoted above) the whole problem is taken out of focus. One may or may not agree with the view that affluence brings automatic self-control of birth rates. If it is true, the problem will be solved once *the other* problems affecting the developing countries are solved. If it is not true, some specific action will be required by the governments concerned. But in any case, the so-called family planning could not be the starting-point of any serious attempt to solve the problems of the socially backward countries or regions of the world. They have to be considered *afterwards* or, hopefully, not at all.

Notes

1. P. V. Sukhatme, "The world's food supplies", Malthus Bicentenary Discussion on Fertility, Mortality and World Food Supply, held before the Royal Statistical Society, London, 16 February 1966. Mr. Sukhatme was Director of FAO Statistics Division (1951-71) and his paper published in *FAO Studies in food and population,* Rome, 1976.

2. Roy. I. Jackson, "Address to the World Population Conference", Bucharest, August 1974 (speaking on behalf of the Director-General of FAO).

3. D. Gale Johnson, "World food problems and prospects", in *Foreign Affairs Studies,* 20, American Enterprise Institute for Public Policy Research, Washington, DC, 1975 (second printing 1977).

4. Roger Revelle, "Aspects of the food-people balance", *Proceedings of the Symposium of Engineering at the Sixth Annual Meeting,* Washington, DC, 1970.

5. It should be pointed out that we do not consider Revelle as being a neo-malthusian, since his position appears to be much broader and open-minded. If we have taken his formulations to focus our criticism to a current view it is because he expresses it in a clear, synthetic and coherent way.

6. Biplab Dasgupta, *Agrarian change and the new technology in India,* United Nations Research Institute for Social Development, Geneva, 1977.

7. R. Revelle, *op. cit.,* p. 6.

8. Cynthia Hewitt de Alcantara, *Modernizing Mexican Agriculture: Socio-economic implications of technological change 1940-1970,* UNR/SD, Geneva, 1976.

CHAPTER 5

Responses to Drought-induced National Disasters

In the preceding chapter we put forward a theoretical frame as a proposal for a methodologically adequate diagnostic tool to be used in trying to find out "what really happened" in past examples of national disasters attributed to climatic factors. In Part Three of this Volume, attempts are made to use this tool in understanding the specific situations exhibited by the analysis of case-studies. It seems, however, that the proposed methodology may also be a very useful scheme to be applied in assessing characteristic responses, at both the international and the national level, to food shortages originated by drought.

Any attempt at classifying the countries or regions of the world according to their type of response to a drought situation ought to be started by drawing a line that separates societies of high vulnerability on one side, from societies of low vulnerability on the other side. The two examples given in Chapter 4 are, in broad terms, representative cases of each type.

In a society of high vulnerability, such as in Example 2, drought triggers off an instability which is latent in the system. The direct effects of the drought are amplified by the release of these instabilities. Once the system is taken away from its precarious "equilibrium" state, the pre-drought situation cannot be restored, even if enough food is brought to the place, unless the "natural" evolution is interfered with and structural changes are introduced in the proper places of the socio-ecosystem.

Example 1 describes, on the other hand, a case of *a stable system,* in which the social organization is such that it has ingrained response mechanisms to overcome the effects of either short or prolonged droughts.

The line between the two types of country is not always well defined as there are several kinds of intermediate stages. More important than that, the line itself, as well as the position of each country or region relative to it, are functions of time. The same country may be displaced in either direction at different periods in time. The Sahelian countries are typical examples of an evolution in recent decades towards more vulnerable conditions, as it is shown in Part Three and, in greater detail, in Volume 4. China provides an example of changes in the opposite direction and is, in fact, a remarkable case of a country crossing the line from high to low vulnerability within an impressively short period of time, as shown by Stavis in his paper included in Volume 2.

The present critical situation of a large number of developing countries, in particular those belonging to the M.S.A. (Most Seriously Affected) group, becomes clear when it is expressed in terms of *increasing fragility* due to the action of socio-economic factors which increase their *structural vulnerability*. International awareness of the semi-permanent crisis affecting these countries does not go beyond the recognition of certain symptoms, and very seldom is the real cause explored. The analysis remains, thus, at the level of "external" factors. When looking for the "culprit" among them, climate, population pressure and environmental problems come to the fore. The emphasis is placed on the production/population ratio or on the misuse of the soil, and the diagnosis misses the point, as the effects are taken for causes and vice versa. Even when, penetrating into deeper waters, the emphasis is shifted from production to *distribution* of food, the analysis remains superficial as long as the distribution problems are taken to be those associated with transport and storage, instead of those related to the *accessibility* of the food. The actual problem is the *distribution of means* which make the food accessible to people. This has much more to do with the structure of property, employment and incomes, than with transport.

No wonder that the measures usually proposed to cope with some critical conditions, when the situation deteriorates beyond the limits that the sense of decency accepted by international standards may allow, are no more than palliatives. We have coined the expression "Red Cross approach" (RCA, for short) to designate these types of measures. The expression is only descriptive and in no way derogatory. The RCA may provide a valuable set of instruments to help in getting out of serious emergencies, to aid people *in extremis*. Our criticism is twofold. In the first place, this approach only provides analgesics. Everyone suffering from toothache blesses the analgesics. But deep cavities in a tooth will get worse, not better, if only analgesics are applied. For instance, in Example 2, above, once the instability of the system is being released, the RCA *can* help *some individuals,* but will not stop, nor even slow down, the deterioration of the social sector concerned. This is a structural reason why RCA can be, at the best, of only limited value.

In the second place, the RCA, in so far as it is applied internationally, is merely an expression of aid-programmes which do not have the proper mechanisms to act promptly and efficiently. They are not specifically tailored to help countries, although they do accomplish this task on some occasions. As it is argued elsewhere (cf. Siotis' paper in Volume 3) they are an integral part of the foreign policy of each country. As such, they are directed by political and economic considerations, the humanistic motivations being subordinated to them. In this respect, past history of drought-induced famines is unmistakably clear in showing how the purely humanistically motivated help arrives too late, or never, or in time but hardly in the required amounts, or it is wasted because of mismanagement. Sahel 1973 is a pathetic example of this. The situation differs when there are political reasons pushing the donors to proceed quickly and efficiently.

During the Sahelian famine in the early 1970s, the roots of which are analysed in Part Three and in more detail in Volume 4, the insufficiency of the aid provided at the international level was justified either on the basis of "late information", which prevented the help from arriving in time, or of a world "food crisis", which prevented the help from being large enough. The first justification has been repeatedly denied by several authors and we only need to quote, without comment, an authoritative statement on this point:

"To the AID and FAO bureaucracies from 1968 onward came significant and ever-increasing intelligence on the catastrophe overtaking the Sahel. The scope, depth and momentum of the drought year by year were methodically recorded in the annual public reports by AID on disaster relief. The 1969 report spoke of the 'prolonged drought across West Africa', of 'drought conditions . . . general' throughout the region, 'complete crop failure' in Senegal. By 1970, there were more than three million people requiring emergency food. 'This was not a new disaster', the document that year explained for Mali, 'but a continuation of that which was reported' in the previous report. Famine in Upper Volta, continued the report, 'was brought on by the same drought problem which was plaguing other countries across West Africa'. 'Hunger, if not starvation, has become increasingly frequent (and) emergency imports have become the rule rather than the exception', concluded the 1970 report. A year later, the description had become almost perfunctory. 'Many African countries are plagued by droughts *year after year*' (emphasis added), observed AID's 1971 disaster relief report in describing emergency aid to over a half million victims in the Sahel."[1]

The second justification has also been disputed, but it deserves some further comments. It was eloquently expressed in the words of Lester Brown already commented on: ". . . now, during the seventies, the depletion of world food stocks has weakened both the capacity and the will of the international community to respond to food shortages" (Worldwatch Paper 8, page 7).

When we first read this remark we were sure that the depletion of abundance of stocks would make no difference to the Sahelian people. We wrote a note with this comment one year after the beginning of our Project (early 1977). Unfortunately, we now have "historical proof" that we were right: in 1977 droughts were again devastating the Sahel, and famines were present again. There was also a world "food crisis"; however, this time *it is not due to the depletion of stocks, but to excess surplus!* At the time we are writing these lines, the General Director of FAO has just called the attention of the world powers to the fact that the World Food Programme has not received the amount of grain which was promised at the 1974 World Food Conference. Once again, reports of famines in Sahel are an irrefutable proof that in the large series of euphemisms used in the international jargon, there is no one which is as misleading, and dramatically so, as the expression "international food aid". It should perhaps be recalled—for those who may consider our statement to be strong—that the amount of grain requested as relief aid for the Sahel, in 1977/8, as in 1972/3, was only 700,000 tons, i.e. little over one-tenth of 1% of the amount of grain used for animal feeding in developed countries; 2.7% of the grain bought by USSR in 1972/3; one-third of the "error" found in UNCTAD and FAO annual Statistics on grain trade.

This notwithstanding, the RCA may be applied with great success at the country level, where it may be locally organized and well planned. The Maharastra drought of 1970/73 in India provides a good example. The official response was quicker, more substantial and more opportune than in previous cases of Indian droughts (as compared, for instance, with the 1966-7 case). India did remarkably well in overcoming the drought effects of the 1972 period, which coincided with a year of minimum grain imports and no foreign help (except 1.8 million tons as a loan from the USSR). However, she used up most of her stocks of cereals. One cannot help thinking that a more prolonged drought would have created unsurmountable difficulties, of the Sahelian type. The low level of nutrition of large sectors of the population would not tolerate any reduction in the diet and, after the depletion of her stocks, the country would have been left at the mercy of international aid. . . . There is little doubt that this would have been the case. Why is this so? The various answers one finds everywhere are merely variations on the same theme: overpopulation. The country, so it is held, can barely produce enough to keep up with the population increase; any crop failure would quickly eat up the meagre stocks. And yet, as we have pointed out in Chapter 4, India is a *net exporter* of food! The appalling low level of nutrition in large sectors of her population is not reflecting a lack of capacity in her agricultural system to produce enough food to cover her needs. What is here at stake is rather the *structure* of production, distribution and trade. Once again the vulnerability to drought is a property of the whole system and cannot be explained away by referring to the *direct* "impact" of a drought on the crops.

It is clear that as the world's productive forces increase—as exemplified by an increased production of foodstuff, by an improvement in the communication network, and by quicker facilities for transporting such a bulky commodity as food over long distances—it can be expected that the RCA will be increasingly efficient, and that its defenders will point out this fact to justify its conceptual usefulness. But we need to go a little further.

It has been said that drought was the best possible thing that could have happened to a Maharastra peasant in 1970: he started participating in a work programme, his village probably had a water tank built, his cattle were provided with fodder, he was provided with cheap food. The same peasant, after the drought was over, saw himself go back to pre-drought conditions, which were bad and now probably worsening.

The RCA, even at its best, could not prevent the spectacle of a world in which drought victims are looked after, but their fate before and after the drought continues to deteriorate, and in which, for example, the world's *stable* death toll from malnutrition is probably higher, by a factor of 10 or 20, than that caused by the sum of all droughts. No one would expect the RCA to solve this problem.

One would expect, however, that malnutrition, being the background situation where severe droughts get most of their victims, would bring at least as much world attention as the drought victims themselves. This is certainly not the case—except in some periods and for other reasons already referred to (cf. Chapter 3 above)—and this is not a minor subject within the context of our analysis. Any attempt to clarify this issue should enter deeply into the roots of problems such as "development" and "underdevelopment", should take the pieces of the so-called "international economic order" apart, should exhibit the myth and the real meaning of "interdependency". All this goes beyond the scope of our study. But the problems lie there. Without this frame of reference we cannot hope to draw near to our goal, which is to disentangle the social, economic and political reasons for the catastrophic effects of climate anomalies (or, for that matter, any other "natural disaster") on certain countries or regions of the world. In this connection, the "case studies" presented in Volumes 2 and 4 undertake the task of determining diagnostically the long causal chains, the last link of which is a certain number of people, especially children dying of malnutrition.

The neglect of a permanent low level of nutrition as a precondition of the famines triggered by natural phenomena leads to typical distortions in the way any such a catastrophe is accounted for. In this respect, Dr. Banerji, in his contribution to Volume 2, presents a very disturbing picture. He suggests that a new pattern is emerging in the treatment of victims of drought *vis-a-vis* victims of malnutrition: while the former would be dealt with in an increasingly efficient way, through RCA measures, the latter would be kept, without help, at a level of bare physical survival, and they ultimately may die of malnutrition-related diseases. The defenders of the RCA will have reasons to be highly satisfied: they may be able to show that no lives are lost in droughts. Though this may happen, the history of drought-induced famines will not end in this simple manner. Unless structural measures are taken, the social conditions of the countries concerned will keep deteriorating. The structure of the social system will become more vulnerable, i.e. more unstable, and the instability triggered off by a drought will reach beyond the control of the RCA measures, which, at this point, will prove powerless. Evidence is supplied in Part Three to show that the Sahelian countries have reached this stage.

A typical malthusian-RCA attitude considers that unless there is a drastic way of controlling population, nothing can be done, except helping *some* people in emergency situations. The extreme form of this position goes as far as suggesting a "triage" method. This method was invented by military health services under war conditions and it has found widespread application each time the amount of wounded people exceeded the capacity of the available medical infrastructure. In such circumstances the wounded were to be divided into three categories:

(a) those who were to succumb regardless of any amount of care;
(b) those who were to survive only if adequate care was provided; and
(c) those who were to manage to survive anyhow.

The *help* only goes to those of the second category.

Countries, and societies within certain countries, should be divided, according to this view, into three corresponding categories. Only the second should receive any "aid".

There is, however, an antimalthusian RCA based on the growing conviction that human malnutrition and its aggravation under "climatic stress" are eminently preventable: that current agricultural resources available in the world could eradicate them if they were equitably distributed. Some of the figures, already given in previous chapters, provide strong support for this line of argument. We shall mention only a few:

1. The estimates made by FAO of the total annual "caloric deficit" in the developing countries is based on the difference between the country's supply and the needs per capita. For the 1972-74 period, the figures are as follows[2] (72 developing countries, excluding centrally planned economies in Asia):
   Deficit in calories (daily): 320,000 million
   Equivalent in wheat: 37 million tons
   (315 calories = 100 gr of wheat)

2. The figures given above represent about 3% of the total *grain* production in the world.

3. During the same period the amount of cereals used for animal feeding in the developed countries, per year, was 416 million tons (one-third of the total production). The developing countries themselves utilized 41 million tons of cereals for animal feeding.

4. On average, US citizens, whose diet contains a high percentage of animal food, utilize daily 11,886 calories, out of which a considerable proportion has gone through the animal cycle; while the citizens of India have, on average, a daily consumption of 2636 calories, almost exclusively in the form of vegetables.

It is tempting to jump from these figures to some "easy" conclusions: the amount of food needed to eradicate malnutrition in the world is ridiculously small as compared with the global production; some countries are overeating; it is enough to distribute what developed countries are eating in excess; animals could go back to pasture fields in many areas of the world, since they are now eating what should rather be used to feed people; and so on.

One finds the above position clearly expressed by Barbara Ward in her foreword to *Hunger, Politics and Markets*.[3] After a masterly presentation of some of the basic facts concerning food distribution in the world, she points specifically to the problems we mention above, in the following terms:

"It is also necessary to point out that they are overeating now. The increase in grain consumption in North America between 1945 and 1970 from about 1000 pounds of grain per capita to 1900 pounds of grain is due to a vast increase in meat and poultry consumption—in other words, grain eaten and digested by other animals to produce meat with something like a 70 per cent loss of food value along the way. The Indians' 400 pounds—which is grossly inadequate—is largely eaten directly as grain. It is this increased pressure of the affluent stuffing themselves with high protein that has helped to push grain prices up to three times their 1971 level.

So before we put all the blame for world inflation on OPEC's pricing of its major and often single resource, the peoples of North America, Europe and Russia could usefully ask whether the stomach, too, may not become an unconscious monopolist. The question is specially relevant when we recall that Norway has, for medical reasons, reduced high protein imports, based on feed-lot meat production and that a hardly radical organisation, the America Medical Association, has recommended a third less meat consumption for sedentary America. To have obesity a widespread disease in a starving world is itself a perversion of right order. 'Grain sheiks' we can all become, using our appetites to rig the market" *(op. cit., p. 14)*.

And she concludes:

"If the human race cannot agree on food, on what can they agree? If those self-proclaimed 'Christian' countries of the West who pray 'Give us this day our daily bread', are not prepared to give it to anyone else, they deserve the mockery and collapse that follow upon too wide a breach between principle and practice. If those who worship Allah, the all-Merciful, the all-Compassionate, do not spontaneously help those whom their new wealth most depresses, they, too, weaken the ultimate moral cement of their own societies. 'The peoples of the Book' who have monopoly control of what the world most needs—bread and energy—are directly challenged to go beyond 'the idols of the market' and to create instead a moral community for all mankind'' (*op. cit.,* p. 15).

No one can question the dramatic truthfulness of these statements. From the point of view of the analyses carried out in this Report, we agree, however, much more with Barbara Ward's diagnosis of the situation than with her eloquent appeal to the consciousness of the people. This does not mean to say that such an appeal should not be made, nor that we are not dealing here with a moral issue.

True, there is a profound immorality at the root of the problem we are considering in this volume. This immorality is not to be attributed to what powerless individuals do. The real immorality is to be found in the coercion, in the merciless exploitation, the sacking of certain countries by other countries, of certain sectors of the population by other sectors of the population gradually leading in the last centuries to the situation we have been describing. These methods, going hand in hand, in modern times, with much more subtle ways of taking advantage of initial differences in economic and political power, are the true immoral basis of the widespread malnutrition and famines in the era of scientific and technological wonders.

Nevertheless, the fact that the issue has indeed moral roots, does not imply that the solution has to rest on moral attitudes. "Immorality" may lead to sickness, but once the sickness is there, "morality" will not cure it.

This situation is now deeply rooted in a socio-economic system acting at the international level, among countries, and at the national level, within countries. The final expression of such a system is inequality of possibilities *to have access* to commodities, in particular to food. Large masses of people are deprived of such an access, or have it limited to below-minimum levels. Not because the goods are not "available", but because they are out of their reach.

Thus, the responsibility of the situation we are discussing does not rest on those who are overeating or wasting food in the affluent societies. *This is an effect, not a cause.* Once again, the causal order is inverted leading to wrong conclusions and unrealistic proposals. We cannot cast the blame on people who have acquired certain food habits, acting as normal citizens within an accepted type of society. Nor do we believe that these citizens have the solution in their hands.

The malnutrition in the world will not be solved by the peaceful meat-eaters of New York, London or Buenos Aires shifting to vegetables. This is, once more, a RCA taken up to the level of a world Crusade. This will not happen. If it happens, it will not do.

There is still another aspect of the problem which reveals both its complexity and the oversimplification involved in the purely "humanitarian" approaches discussed above. The point in question is that confining the analysis to differences among countries the formulation of the problem becomes very misleading. People still talk about rich and poor countries; countries with high and low income; countries with a high level of nutrition and with a high level of malnutrition. It is, however, a commonplace that "averages" have little meaning. Everybody knows how rich the oil countries are; but malnutrition has not disappeared, either from the Middle-East or from Venezuela. Gabon has an income close to the GNP of France, and yet it has one of the lowest life expectancies in the world (about 30 years). Argentina has always been a major exporter of wheat and meat and yet at least 20,000 children die annually of malnutrition or malnutrition-related diseases.

In fact, the differences found *between* countries are also differences existing within countries. This means, in the first place, that the actual situation is worse than is indicated in the tables of "daily per caput calorie supply in developing countries". The FAO study of malnutrition, already quoted, includes a table indicating the calorie deficits by regions. The note following the table provides a key element for an appraisal more realistic than the table itself:

> "It should be noted that this approach simply aims at a certain adequacy of total food supplies at the national level without confronting the problem of its unequal distribution within the country. Even if the average per caput availability were raised to the requirement level, there is no assurance that the problem of malnutrition would disappear. As a matter of fact, a number of developing countries (56) already has average supply levels equal to, or in excess of, their average requirement in 1972-74. Yet, many of them had a considerable proportion of their population with a calorie intake below 1.2 BMR, the critical limit adopted in the previous Section to estimate the number of the undernourished."

All this is well known and the case-studies included in this Report provide additional evidence that an adequate amount of food in the country will not guarantee an acceptable level of nutrition for the whole of the population. The food availability *per capita* in Brazil and Cuba is about the same, and yet the latter has eradicated malnutrition, whereas in the former the number of undernourished people is estimated to be 40 million.

The internal differences in developing countries add a new dimension—and a major one—to any rational approach to the ways of taking action which could be suggested as responses to drought effects. In order to focus the problem we shall consider the case of Latin American countries studied by J. C. Portantiero in his important contribution to the Project (cf. Volume 3). The central hypothesis in Portantiero's paper is that "Latin American agrarian problems are closely related to the problems of social costs determined by the path leading to industrialization (. . .) and the policies practiced by the State in order to follow this path. (. . .) This means that, in Latin America, land and the corresponding State policies must take charge of the costs of a dependent semi-industrialization process." Within this general frame, the agrarian sector participates in two quite different ways into the overall productive system of the country. On one hand, it is a source of high currency necessary to import raw materials, manufactured products and technology for the industrial sector. On the other hand, it must produce cheap food for the working class, inasmuch as high prices of food would have a direct and adverse effect on the minimum level of salaries and thereby on the cost of production. This double role of the agrarian sector implies that it must adapt itself to a double set of requirements corresponding respectively to the external and the internal markets. There is therefore a duality in the agrarian system which results in two quite different sub-sectors: the "modern", oriented to exports (and production of more sophisticated food for the urban elite), and the "traditional"—the "poor" one—which, as Portantiero points out, carries the burden of the industrialization process. More often than not, the support of the State, in the form of credits and investments, goes only to the former. Thus the coexistence of the two sub-sectors and, in particular, the permanence of the "traditional" one is not due to the "backwardness" of the population involved in it, but to the *effect* of State policies.

The relevance of this analysis for this Project becomes evident as soon as one realizes that the impact of a "natural disaster" on each sub-sector of the agrarian system produces entirely different effects. This poses a most serious problem for the Project, because any recommendation intended to reach the roots of catastrophic effects of droughts in the "backward" sub-sector of the agricultural system cannot help dealing with the profound *structural* problems of the society and, in particular, with the system of internal relations within the trinity of agriculture—industry—state. The whole problem of development is here at stake.

Notes

1. H. Sheets and R. Morris, *"Disaster in the Desert: Failures of International Relief in the West African Drought"*, Special Report, The Carnegie Endowment for International Peace.

2. FAO, *"The Fourth World Food Survey"*, 1977.

3. *Hunger, Politics and Markets: The Real Issues in the Food Crisis,* edited by Sartaj Aziz, NY: United Press, 1975.

ANNEX 3

International Multilateral Food Aid: A Critical Appraisal

by Jean Siotis

1. Introduction

A. Any attempt to discuss and evaluate the establishment, conduct and impact of international food aid programmes and, more particularly, those which are placed under the auspices of international organizations or consortia must begin by an examination of attitudes and policies of donor countries towards development assistance in general, as well as of the capacity of present international institutional structures to innovate and to embark on large-scale programmes likely to meet some of the dramatically growing needs of developing countries. At the same time, it is important to refer to the attitudes of recipient countries towards multilateral, in contradistinction to bilateral food aid. In this respect, it would also be extremely useful to attempt to answer a number of questions concerning the perceptions of various types of aid which we find in the Third World. In particular, we should try to answer the following question: Do developing countries' governments and informed elites make any value-oriented distinctions between bilateral and multilateral food-aid programmes?

In discussing development aid of any type we proceed from the assumption that it is part and parcel of the foreign policies of donor and recipient countries. We also consider that no matter how difficult it is to define the concept of "national interest", development aid programmes are launched and conducted in pursuit of national interests. Political, economic, strategic, ideological and other components of groups that make up the national interest of States must be taken into account when evaluating their performance in this, as in other fields of their foreign policies. No doubt individual policy-makers and opinion leaders, organized groups and even governments at times espouse attitudes and policies which place humanitarian considerations in the foreground. This does not affect, however, our basic proposition that foreign aid and, more particularly, international food aid policies reflect the overall political options of donors and recipients and that the national interests of States concerned represent the primary motivation for these policies. The fact that some donors give priority to humanitarian considerations simply indicates that *some* countries place their commitment to humanitarian ideologies ahead of strategic and economic interests. But, in all cases, development aid—and in this instance food aid—is a policy manifestation whose basic parameters do not differ from those determining the foreign policy of any given State.

This proposition is stated so emphatically because past and present discussions of food aid tend to be clouded by "moral considerations", whose proponents claim that they fall outside the field of foreign policy and are independent of the political, economic and strategic interests of donor countries. In our view, any attempt to analyse the behaviour of States which does not rest on a thorough grasp of their interests is bound to lead to distortions of reality. At the same time, we recognize that the various components of the national interest do not always point in the same policy direction. The wider the range of these components, the more likely it is that contradictions will arise when policy-makers try to formulate their options. In such circumstances, it happens that national decision-makers give priority to humanitarian considerations; either because of internal pressures or because of their ideological commitments but, in all cases, they first go through the process of evaluating any such programme in relation to other policy considerations. The humanitarian motivation is, in the best of cases, one of many in the range of factors that give rise to food aid programmes. However, it should not be taken in isolation from the other components of the national interest and, when it comes to bilateral or multilateral intergovernmental programmes, it should under no circumstances be considered as the only one which can lead to satisfactory policies. Good and generous intentions are not necessarily a guarantee for the success of international aid programmes; nor is it true, on the basis of the post-war history of such programmes, that if donors' motivations are political or economic they necessarily lead to results detrimental to the interests of recipient countries.

We thought it important to underline the basic assumptions on which we have undertaken this research, in order to avoid any confusion as to the place of multilateral food aid in the overall framework of international relations. Food-aid programmes are political and/or economic actions, undertaken by States, either on a bilateral basis or through international organizations. In both cases, however, they are part of the foreign policies of donor and of recipient countries. In regard to their motivations, food aid policies do not differ, whether they are conducted bilaterally or multilaterally. Their contents and impact may and very often do differ, but this is due to the very nature of multilateralism and *not* because of different motivations.

B. In any attempt to take stock of international and, more particularly, multilateral food-aid programmes, we should note that historically they were initiated when major producers of agricultural goods had accumulated such surpluses that ways and means had to be found to dispose of them, while at the same time maintaining the price levels of agricultural exports. Public Law 480 was adopted at a time when the US grain surpluses had attained a dangerously high level. And its authors clearly intended it to be of a temporary nature: as long as the surpluses lasted. Although this provision was dropped subsequently, the economic motivations of US food aid legislation have always dominated US policies. Programmes under PL 480 were the only large-scale actions in the field for nearly 15 years, until a second major agricultural producer, the EEC, was about to reach the stage of substantial surpluses, while Canada found itself in the same predicament as the United States towards the mid-sixties when it started accumulating large stocks of wheat. As for Japan, it faced a similar problem, at about the same time. Although it has been and continues to be a net importer of agricultural goods, it had accumulated by 1970 a large rice surplus (more than 7 million tons), largely as a result of changing food habits, which have tended to substitute wheat for rice. In this respect, we should also note that the decisive importance of producers' surpluses to the type and volume of food aid programmes is demonstrated dramatically by the sharp drop of commitments and deliveries as soon as the stocks are depleted, either as a result of major trade agreements (i.e. with the Soviet Union or with China) or because of unfavourable climatic conditions. By 1972, at the very time when the needs for food aid in drought-ridden areas of Africa became dramatic, world food production dropped, while the United States and Canada has undertaken to sell large quantities of wheat to the Soviet Union and to China. In addition, the effects of the sharp drop in cereal stocks were seriously aggravated after 1973, by international monetary instability and the devaluation of the dollar, which made sales by producers more and more lucrative while purchases of cereals by those who needed them most became more and more difficult. Between 1972 and 1974, the dollar value of cereals had increased by 200-400% and, although there was a drop in prices towards the end of 1974, they have remained at levels considerably higher than the rates of devaluation of the US dollar.

In addition to these factors affecting policies of donor States, the decolonization process having largely been completed by 1960, the new members of the United Nations started almost immediately exerting pressures for a substantial increase of aid and argued that it should be placed as far as possible under multilateral auspices. The World Food Programme was launched in 1961 and became operational in 1963. Following an initial period of 3 years, it was renewed in 1966 for an indefinite period. The WFP functions under the joint auspices of the United Nations and of the FAO. The next step towards partial multilateralization of food aid was the conclusion, in 1967, of the international food-aid convention, as part of the international cereals agreement negotiated in the framework of the GATT. This convention, renewed in 1971 and in 1974, aimed at assisting developing countries to overcome the difficulties raised by the price levels set for different categories of wheat in the convention regulating trade in wheat. Once again, however, it is interesting to note that international action in regard to food aid was closely linked to the over-all arrangements on trade agreed upon by producers and consumers. Moreover, the convention does not in fact impose any obligation favouring multilateralism vs. bilateralism in food aid, and with the notable exception of the launching of EEC's "bilateral" and multilateral programmes, the ratios between the two types of aid have remained unchanged, at least for the major donor countries.[1]

C. In the course of our discussion of multilateral food aid, we shall pay attention to the crucial issue of the relationship between aid and agricultural development programmes. In this respect, we shall examine the activities of the FAO, which is functionally committed to the assistance of developing countries in their efforts to increase agricultural production. At this point, we should simply mention that we are faced, in the case of food aid, with the more general question of the insertion of international assistance programmes into the framework of national development programmes of recipient countries. During the early periods of food-aid programmes and, to some extent, still today they have been and are linked to emergency humanitarian assistance to countries or regions suffering drought or some other calamity. While both in donor governments and in international organizations there are those who follow closely indigenous agricultural production, and research likely to improve its quality is supported by some of the donors, very often emergency actions and even "regular" programmes are undertaken which bear no relation either to the specific problems of the agricultural sector of these countries' socio-economic structures, or to the long- or medium-term development objectives set by national authorities. In some cases, laudable attempts have been made to overcome these shortcomings (for instance, "food for work" projects), but these have hardly been planned in close co-operation with the recipients. Finally, we shall raise some questions concerning the relationship between food aid and financial assistance. Considering the wide gap between nutritional habits and needs, on the one hand, and resources available for such aid, on the other, financial assistance enabling recipients to purchase food on the market has been considered by them as a necessary complement of direct supply programmes. Both bilateral and multilateral donors have been faced with such demands, but, for the time being, no truly satisfactory solution has been found. To the extent that direct supply of food has been almost always viewed by donors as part of the economics of surplus disposal, the role of financial assistance has been insufficiently linked to that of food-aid programmes.

D. Having discussed briefly the principal political and economic factors affecting multilateral food aid—and before presenting the existing programmes—it would be useful to mention an alternative approach to food aid: that whose starting-point is the concept of *basic needs*. This view was expressed most eloquently in the 1975 Dag Hammarskjöld Report, entitled *What Now.*[2] The authors of this Report, under the direction of the Swiss specialist Marc Nerfin, describe as follows the approach adopted to date in matters pertaining to international aid.

> "Since resources are limited, population increasing and it is impossible to feed everybody, they say, the poor must be divided into those who will die whatever is done, those who will survive whatever is done, and those for whom aid from the rich will make all the difference. Aid should be concentrated on the latter. . . . Such views are not only loaded with vested interests; they are politi-

cally impractical. They are in any case conceptually weak. They reflect a conservative view of reality; they consider only certain quantitative aspects of demographic and economic growth and fail to take into account its content."[3]

To the contrary, the authors of the Report believe that resources grow more rapidly than population and that *basic needs* can be satisfied without transgressing their outer limits. Over and beyond the optimism inherent in the thinking of those sharing this view, research carried out in various scientific settings[4] supports some of its premises; but multilateral decision-makers have not even begun to integrate its findings into their own policy-making frameworks. The Report states forcefully:

"In a world whose gross product trebled over the last twenty-five or thirty years, whereas population increased by barely two-thirds, resources are available to satisfy basic needs, without transgressing the 'outer limits'. The question is one of distributing them more equitably. However, over the next twenty-five years world population will probably increase from 4 to 6.4 billion inhabitants. It will be too late tomorrow to seek new solutions. The future depends on choices made today."[5]

Writing more specifically about food, the authors state:

"The 'food crisis' is not one of bad harvest years: it is a matter of permanent hunger and malnutrition. . . . Hunger and malnutrition are indeed due to the fact that the poor are deprived of the means either to produce or to purchase their food, the socio-economic mechanisms being so organized as to ensure that the lion's share goes to the rich and the powerful. The satisfaction of the need for food and its production cannot therefore be set apart from a transformation of political and socio-economic structures. . . ."[6]

E. In the preceding paragraphs we tried to present as clearly as possible the various motivations for and approaches to food aid which we find in examining past and present programmes, be they bilateral or multilateral. As for the differences between the two categories of programmes, although they should not be overestimated they do exist because of the very nature of international institutions. No matter how powerful the influence of donors within multilateral frameworks, there is always a gap that separates their motivations from the final outcome of institutional action, because of the way multilateralism affects the process and the complexity of decision-making in international organizations. Notwithstanding this caveat, however, we can say that international food aid can be approached from four different but not always mutually exclusive viewpoints: (1) the economics of "surplus disposal"; (2) the "charity" of "soup kitchen" viewpoint; (3) the developmental approach, inserting it in the larger framework of North-South relations; and (4) the "basic needs" approach, which considers the whole problem of nutrition supply as one of maldistribution to be remedied by radical transformations in political and socio-economic structures.

In the pages which follow, we shall discuss past and present multilateral programmes, before drawing some normative conclusions concerning their operations. In doing so, we shall naturally keep in mind our earlier statements concerning the relationship between food aid and foreign policy. However, when considering the parameters within which foreign policies are formulated and implemented, we should not ignore the fact that some policies are more effective than others. In the case of international organizations, we should also not lose sight of the fact that if at least *some* of those participating in the formulation and implementation of decisions share an approach which is not necessarily that of any individual donor, they may have an impact on the overall nature and contents of such programmes. This is why we believe that their critical examination is not a futile exercise, in spite of the formidable obstacles faced by those who consider that multilateral programmes must necessarily differ qualitatively from bilateral ones, both as to their motivations and as to their outcomes.

II. Multilateral Programmes in the United Nations Family

A. AN OVERVIEW

Historically, the foundation for international multilateral co-operation in the fields of nutrition and food production were laid at Hot Springs (Virginia) in 1943, when an international conference on food and agriculture was convened by the United States government. The FAO, established in 1945, is the direct outcome of the Hot Springs conference. Its present membership of almost 140 States does not include the Soviet Union and other Eastern European countries. FAO programmes cover a wide range of activities, including research and operations related to nutritional needs and food production. Its mandate covers agricultural resources on land as well as in the sea. At present, it is the largest specialized agency in the UN family.

The rapidly growing nutritional needs of developing countries and their massive entry into the UN and its specialized agencies after 1960 led, however, to the questioning of FAO's capacity to undertake a substantial expansion of its programmes and, even more so, to embark on qualitatively new activities, likely to meet the developing countries' dramatically growing nutritional needs. The establishment of the World Food Programme, jointly sponsored by the United Nations—acting through the General Assembly—and by the FAO was the response of the new majority in the United Nations to what was perceived to be the latter's inability to adapt its activities to the new circumstances.

More recently, the World Food Conference was held in November 1974, as a major renewed effort to draw attention of governments, international organizations and world public opinion to the plight of the hundreds of millions of people suffering from malnutrition and often facing starvation. The original formal proposal for holding such a Conference was made by Henry Kissinger, at his maiden speech before the General Assembly, in September 1973. We should note, however, that the Fourth Conference of the Heads of State or Government of non-aligned countries had called—earlier in September—for the holding of an emergency conference on the world food situation, to be sponsored jointly by the FAO and UNCTAD. The resolution convening the Conference was adopted by the General Assembly in December, following its endorsement by the FAO Conference and a recommendation by ECOSOC. Similar recommendations were made by the ILO Governing Body and by the Secretary-General of UNCTAD. The preparatory work leading to the Conference as well as the Conference itself should naturally be viewed against the background of the Sixth Special Session of the General Assembly, which led to the adoption of the Declaration of the New International Economic Order. The World

Food Conference was in fact one of the major events in the course of the multilateral examination of North-South relations to which we have been witness since 1973. At the same time, the Conference was held in the wake of the Sahelian drought which brought to the fore the serious failings of the system for international food aid which had been progressively established since the early 1960s.

Finally, before concluding this brief presentation of UN-related activities in this field, we should also note that several other institutions have been providing various forms of food aid. The UNDP has been steadily increasing its support for agricultural development and it has been involved in the financing of food-aid programmes; and the same can be said of the IBRD. The WHO has been working—often in co-operation with the FAO—in the field of nutritional standards and food safety. As for UNICEF, ever since its inception, it has been involved in food aid to children and to mothers. In this connection, and although they are not directly related to the United Nations family, we should also mention the activities of various regional Banks and other financial institutions which have been providing funds for food aid and agricultural development.

In the pages which follow, we shall present briefly the principal activities of some of these organizations; giving as often as possible specific data reflecting the evolution of their activities. We shall also be discussing the roles of some of the major actors in their decision-making processes, keeping in mind some of our earlier remarks concerning the nature of food aid policies which are part and parcel of national foreign policies.

B. THE FOOD AND AGRICULTURE ORGANIZATION

By the very nature of its constitution and functional orientation, the FAO has always been active in promoting policies in view of improving agricultural production the world over and of meeting the nutritional needs of those countries and regions facing serious imbalances in their food supplies. The ideological premises on which FAO's programmes were based ever since its establishment have been basically "Malthusian". Its first Director-General, Lord Boyd-Orr, was particularly outspoken in this respect and the tendency of its Secretariat has been to draw attention to the dangers of a rapidly growing world population in the face of limited food supplies. It is only recently that issues such as maldistribution of resources have become part of the FAO *problématique,* essentially because of the growing role of developing countries in its various bodies. Moreover, the FAO has had considerable difficulties to come to grips with the issues of appropriate technologies and patterns of production for at least some of the "most affected" regions of the world. During the first 30 years of its existence, the FAO activities reflected, to a very large extent, the views of those who sought the solution of the world's agricultural problems through an extension of technologies developed in the regions which prospered by using labour intensive production. This conceptual orientation of the FAO is of considerable importance for the understanding of the Organization's role in the overall framework of UN related activities in this field.

The formal structure of the Organization is similar to the ones we find in most UN agencies. The Conference meets every 2 years and it holds the responsibility for the approval of the budget and programme, as well as for determining its general policies. The Council, composed of forty-two member States, meets in its regular sessions once every year, and it may hold special sessions. It also meets before and after every conference. Naturally, most of the work is done in the various committees.[7] The Secretariat, headed by the Director-General, is composed of seven departments.[8] In addition to Headquarters staff, the Secretariat maintains an extensive network of regional and country liaison officers.

The FAO functional orientation could be summarized as follows: to elaborate proposals for and promote national, regional or international action in the areas of research, education, conservation, processing, marketing and distribution of food and agricultural products. Its specific tasks to meet these objectives include the collection, analysis and dissemination of data on agriculture, nutrition, forestry and fisheries. Moreover, the FAO has had a long-standing interest in the financial aspects of commodity trade.

The Organization's activities are financed by the regularly assessed budget, voluntary contributions which often take the form of trust funds and UNDP contributions. During the 1976-7 biennium, the regular budget reached $167,000,000, which represents an increase of 57% over the previous biennium level of $106,700,000.[9] It should also be noted that this amount represents approximately 20% of total FAO expenditures; nearly 80% are financed by the UNDP and various trust funds. In practice, this means that the intergovernmental organs of the FAO entrusted with the task of examining, approving and evaluating its programmes do not have a full view of the Organization's activities. We have, on the one side, the regular programme activities financed by the regular budget, which represents about one-fifth of total FAO disbursements and, on the other, a total amount of funds five times as large used to finance activities in the development field which very often are not related functionally with the rest of the Organization's programmes. Activities financed from sources outside the regular budget naturally entail administrative and other overhead expenses, for which the FAO is reimbursed in a less than satisfactory manner. Finally, to make the programme-budget situation even more complicated, we should mention that an amount of $18,500,000 was set aside in the regular budget for 1976-7 to establish a Technical Co-operation programme.

The result of this complex and cumbersome structure has been that the FAO has been unable to concentrate its efforts and carry out integrated programmes likely to have a decisive impact on any of the various "fronts" in the battle against hunger and malnutrition. The dispersion of the Organization's efforts has been a serious obstacle to the effectiveness of its development policies and has contributed to its inability to act rapidly when faced with requests for emergency action. This is certainly one of the principle reasons for the proliferation of parallel institutional structures which have been entrusted with tasks for which the FAO had both the necessary experience and the professional capacity.

In relation to the apparent reluctance of a majority of UN members to entrust the FAO with the tasks necessary to face the crisis in food supplies to developing countries, we should also mention the significant role played by agribusiness and other major industrial and trade groups in the Organization's informal power structure. The participation of organized business in FAO's informal processes has traditionally been recognized as being a necessary ingredient of intergovernmental cooperation. The absence of the USSR and other Eastern European countries certainly was one of the factors facilitating the "penetration" of FAO by agribusiness interests, but the Organization's "permeability" to the influence of private interests was essentially the consequence of the overall international pattern of food production and trade. The predominant role played by the United States and by several of its allies, both in production and in trade of foodstuffs, inevitably brought about a situation which could hardly be opposed by developing countries in dire need of international assistance. The presence of agribusiness interests in the FAO is formalized by the existence of the Industry Co-operative Programme, ever since it was established, in 1963, as an attempt to assure a continuous flow of information and exchange of views between the FAO bureaucracy and the multinationals involved in food production, processing and trade. At present, more than 100 private firms participate in the ICP and pay $5000 each, as an annual fee. In return, they obtain information on national and international projects in food production and distribution.

The very fact that the World Food Conference was called for outside the FAO structure and, even more so, that it was called for by the United States with the support of leading developing countries and of the Soviet Union, was perceived by the Secretariat's leadership and by the then Director-General, Dr. Boerma, as a disavowal of FAO's past performance and as a potential threat to its future activities. Although this perception of threat may have been exaggerated, it was largely founded. The sequence of events in the autumn of 1973—from Henry Kissinger's speech in the General Assembly in September, to the resumed fifty-fifth session of ECOSOC in mid-October, to the Seventeenth session of the FAO Conference in mid-November—clearly gave the impression that the powers that be were "forcing" FAO into the uncomfortable position of having to do the best of an embarrassing situation, resulting from what many considered as the Organization's poor performance in the recent past. This situation was particularly embarrassing for the Secretariat which tried and partly succeeded to attain two objectives: (a) to keep the preparation for the conference as much as possible under FAO's bureaucratic influence, if not under its control; and (b) to limit the Conference tasks to the assessment of the world food situation, based on research which had already been done, and to the examination of commitments by developed countries in the general field of food aid. The designation of Sayed Ahmed Marei as the Secretary-General of the Conference was considered initially as a success for the FAO, but the work of the Preparatory Committee and of the Conference Secretariat under Marei did not meet fully the expectations of the Rome-based bureaucracy. As for the Conference tasks, particularly in as far as the establishment of new institutional structures was concerned, events in November 1974 reflected the fact that the FAO Secretariat did not exert on delegations the necessary influence to avoid decisions which were perceived as a rejection of its proposals. During the preparatory period as well as during the Conference itself, the impact of expertise drawn from outside the FAO was often decisive and, knowing the importance of the "quasi-monopoly" of expertise claimed by international secretariats, this was a serious blow to the Organization.[10]

The election of Dr. Saumaa, in 1975, as Director-General of the FAO was, at least in part, the result of the conclusion reached by a majority of member governments that the Secretariat needed a *new* style of leadership as well as *new ideas.* Although it is generally more difficult to move international bureaucracies than to move mountains, the first years under the new Director-General have been characterized by a number of steps which are undoubtedly changing the image and the capacity of the

Organization to act effectively. The fact that the new Director-General had extensive "in-house" experience before being appointed at the head of the Secretariat has certainly been conducive to a smooth transition but, more significantly, Dr. Saumaa assumed his new functions under particularly favourable political auspices. The developing countries in majority, the United States and the European Community offered him the support which is indispensable for performing the formidable task of building on FAO's past achievements as well as of innovating in order to bring the Organization more in pace with the needs and expectations of the developing world. In relation to food production and distribution, there is no doubt that the capital of knowledge and unique experience accumulated over the years by the FAO can be invaluable, if properly channelled to provide the indispensble scientific, technical and administrative infrastructure for the implementation of multilateral programmes. Given this experience and the absence of any comparable expertise in the Secretariats of all other major multilateral and/or interagency bodies—World Food Council, International Fund for Agricultural Development, World Food Programme, United Nations Development Programme, etc.—the FAO could and probably should become the institutional focal point for all major international programmes in the area of food production and distribution. Moreover, it should be recognized that global conferences and other similar activities tending to mobilize governments and public opinion are necessary in order to overcome the obstacles to any significant developments in the various fields of international co-operation but, when the dust settles down, governments must be able to rely on institutions such as the FAO in order to move from the elaboration to the implementation of specific programmes. It would seem that this view is shared by most actors in the decision-making processes in this area as well as by the leadership of FAO. As soon as the present Director-General took office, he made it clear that he was determined to move in the direction of serious changes in FAO's style and content of activities. In 1976 he made this clear by refusing to be pressed into taking a stand on the programme and budget for 1978-9; and events since then indicate that this initial posture in his relations with major donors has had the positive effect of presenting a new image of the organization and of its potential for the future.

C. THE WORLD FOOD PROGRAMME

The WFP is a UN-FAO interagency programme whose goal is to help developing countries acquire the capacity to produce and/or to purchase adequate food supplies. Its assistance to and support for national activities in the field of food production and distribution are, theoretically at least, aimed at improving nutritional conditions by stimulating economic and social development. It is also authorized to provide food aid in emergency cases of drought and other forms of natural or man-made disasters.

Its governing body—formerly called Intergovernmental Committee of the WFP—is the Committee on Food Aid Policies and Programmes, consisting of thirty member governments, half of which are designated by the FAO Council and the other half by ECOSOC. The tasks of the Committee is to offer general guidance on policies and on operations, as well as to approve projects and the overall administrative budget. Moreover, following the World Food Conference, the WFP was entrusted with the co-ordination of food-aid policies. The Programme has its own staff, headed by the Executive Director who is appointed by the Secretary-

General of the United Nations and by the Director-General of the FAO acting jointly. The Secretariat comprises about 250 professional officers, 40% working in Rome and the remaining in the field. The WFP administrative budget for the 1976-7 biennium was close to $22 million but this did not include administrative expenditures directly related to field projects.

In the early 1960s more than 50% of contributions to the WFP in cash and food came from the United States, under Title II of Public Law 480. Progressively, this percentage dropped to less than 23% in 1976. However, the number of donors is still limited to a small number of States. In 1976, 84% of total contributions came from ten donors.[11] The total amount of aid channelled through the WFP since 1963 has been almost $2,000 million; beginning with $84,500,000 during the 1963-5 period and reaching $616 million for the 1975-6 biennium. In 1977 the value of foodstuffs shipped was $306 million. The proportion of cash payments and contribution in commodities has varied over the years; during the 1975-6 period, cash contributions were about $140 million. This represents a notable increase of donations in cash or services, as a result of the fact that some of the major oil -producing countries—particularly Saudi Arabia—have started making sizeable contributions to the WFP. None the less, in his report to the Sixth Session of the CFA, in October 1978, the Executive Director addressed a pressing appeal to donors to increase their contributions in cash.

In addition to direct contributions from individual donors, the WFP receives commodities and funds under the Food Aid Convention (FAC) and the International Emergency Food Reserve (IEFR). The Food Aid Convention was part of the International Wheat Agreement, concluded at the end of the Kennedy Round. It entered into force in 1968 for a 3-year period, and it has been renewed several times since 1971. The principal partners in agricultural trade—the United States and the EEC—as well as several other Western countries which had agreed on an increase of minimum prices for cereals, concluded the Convention, providing for total annual grants deliveries of 4.5 million tons, as a means to maintain price levels, without seriously affecting the nutritional situation in developing countries. At present, it is being renegotiated in the framework of the Tokyo Round. Since 1971 the WFP has received under the FAC contributions amounting to $136 million.

The IEFR was established following a Resolution by the Seventh Special Session of the General Assembly, in 1975. The target set by the Resolution was the establishment of a reserve of 500,000 tons and contributions, until October 1978, amounted to almost 560,000 tons. However, the replenishment of the Reserve is still under discussion. In as far as more than 400,000 tons have already been utilized, this is becoming an urgent matter for international food aid negotiations. During its October 1978 session, the CFA proposed specific measures for the replenishment of the Reserve and for the Management of its resources. The Federal Republic of Germany, Canada, Japan, the Netherlands, Norway, Sweden, the United Kingdom, the United States, Yugoslavia and the EEC are contributing to the IEFR.

The recipients of WFP aid since 1963 are to be found in Africa (north and south of the Sahara), Latin America, Asia and the Pacific and Southern Europe.[12] For the first 10 years of the Programme's operation, the aggregate percentages for the various regions were as follows: North Africa and the Near East 34%, Asia and the Pacific 28%, Africa (South of the Sahara) 17%, Latin America 13%, Europe 9%.

More recently, major donors as well as various UN bodies have been urging WFP decision-makers to concentrate their efforts on the category of "most seriously affected" countries and, since 1973, as a result of the Sahelian drought, a much higher proportion of aid has been directed to Africa. In 1975 the Committee on Food Aid and Policies stated the Programme's priorities as follows:

"First priority would continue to be given to LDC . . . and MSA . . . countries and to special hardship areas, to nutrition projects for pregnant women and nursing mothers, pre-school children and primary school children, as well as to projects which can effectively contribute through labour-intensive works and through training to increase agricultural and particularly food production."

Such a statement was clearly intended to demonstrate that the WFP was in line with the recommendations of the World Food Conference, as well as with the policies of some of the major donors. In practice, however, it has met considerable difficulties in trying to redirect its activities to the poorest recipients, basically because of two reasons: first, these countries often do not have the necessary infrastructure to absorb large amounts of food aid; and, second, the propensity of international organizations to favour the more advanced LDCs. As for the volume of food aid received by developing countries, its percentage in their total food imports dropped from 57% in 1961 to 21% in 1973, to 15% in 1975. This drop becomes particularly significant, if we take into account the fact that the annual average of cereal imports rose from 25 million tons, in 1961-3, to 50 million tons in 1973-5. At present, the total volume of food aid in cereals—bilateral and multilateral—is approximately 9 million tons annually, while the target set by the World Food Conference in 1974 was an annual minimum of 10 million tons. More recent WFP estimates, however, place the expected requirement for 1985 at 16-17 million tons. The growth in developing countries' food imports is estimated to be due, on the one hand, to growing nutritional needs related to their development—particularly of the oil-producing countries—and, on the other, to persistent and growing deficiencies in the distribution of indigenous food products.

In evaluating these figures, we should, however, keep in mind that recipient countries—taken as a whole—are net exporters of food stuffs; which simply means that food aid is used as a corrective for shortages caused by maldistribution and by economic distortions resulting from "savage" development policies followed in many countries of the Third World. We shall be discussing, at the end of this paper, the relevance of these trends to any evaluation of food-aid programmes. At this stage, we simply want to draw attention to some facts which are hardly mentioned in connection with the food situation of many developing countries.

WFP activities, can be classified under three principal categories: (a) "food for work" projects; (b) child and maternal feeding; (c) emergency actions. The balance among these three categories is very difficult to establish, essentially because of the wide discrepancy between declared priorities and actual practice. WFP rhetoric naturally suffers from the "ill" so widely spread among international organizations; that of declaratory "adaptions" to arising needs and bureaucratic and programme rigidity in practice.

The "food for work" projects were originally conceived in the framework of US bilateral aid, under Title II of PL 480, but they have also been an essential feature of

WFP activities ever since its inception. Commodities made available to the host country are used in lieu of cash payments for work done in certain rural development or other projects sponsored by local authorities. We should, however, note that according to a generally accepted rule such payments in kind cannot exceed a proportion of 50% of the total amount. The rationale underlying this type of activity has been that by introducing food commodities into the economic process, donors and the recipient government could maximize the value of donations by feeding the neediest groups, while at the same time contributing to the realization of certain projects, considered to be important for the country's development. Conceptually, such projects are undoubtedly attractive and, in many cases, the results obtained have met the host government's expectations. However, quite often the improvization forced upon the AFP teams by the absence of any real infrastructure capable of integrating "food for work" projects into a larger development perspective leads to waste and, in some cases, to the diversion of large quantities of commodities to the local "free market", which simply means to the black market. Such projects can produce the expected results to the extent that they are part of international as well as of national planning and that the interface between these two levels does not represent an insurmountable barrier.

The direct nutritional projects provide food for the neediest in particularly poor areas of some developing countries (the North-East in Brazil, urban areas in India, etc), or to "most seriously affected" countries taken as a whole. The recipients of such aid are usually children in school or of pre-school age and, very often, young mothers and pregnant women. The reasoning behind these projects is relatively simple (one may say even simplistic): it is not enough to identify countries or regions which have the greatest need for assistance, we must go a step further and identify categories of inhabitants who are the most vulnerable in the face of malnutrition. Some of the projects have been particularly successful, because they have combined food aid with alphabetization, scholarization or public health campaigns. In such instances, the distribution of food or the provision of free meals in school canteens has been a strong incentive for the participation of children and adults in the campaigns.

We should note, however, in relation to these two categories of programmes, that in spite of the relief and even the development effects of many of these projects, the WFP Executive Director has been realistic in evaluating their long-term impact.[13] A careful reading of a sample of evaluation reports for programmes in Africa and in Asia brings to our attention both their achievements and their shortcomings, particularly in terms of their development objectives. On the positive side of the balance sheet we find that such programmes have contributed to the improvement of the infrastructure necessary for the implementation of development schemes, to soil conservation, to the limitation of migration from agricultural areas, to the improvement of school attendance, etc. Notwithstanding these beneficial effects, however, the WFP reports also bring to our attention the fact that food aid often is a "disincentive to agricultural production". These disincentives can be summarized as follows:

(a) Inasmuch as free food is provided in schools, parents shift their responsibilities for feeding their children to school authorities; at the same time school gardens, which are common in many developing countries, tend to be abandoned when food aid is provided. These two consequences limit local food production and tend to act as disincentives for vocational training in the agricultural sector.

(b) The provision of temporary employment to marginal farmers leads them to neglect the exploitation of their own land. This has been particularly true when food
for work projects have extended over long periods, covering the critical periods
for farming.

(c) Food for work programmes have led to labour shortages in the agricultural sector

(d) Above all, however, such programmes have often led governments to postpone
essential decisions concerning the constraints on agricultural production.

The emergency assistance projects have received special publicity during the past
few years because of the apparent failure of international organizations and bilateral
donors to come to grips with the dramatic consequences of the recent droughts as
well as of other natural or man-made disasters. Considering the WFP structure, personnel and methods of work, it is not surprising that it has not always played an effective role in the face of such disasters. To the extent that its participation in
emergency actions fell short of being expected to mobilize resources on a world-wide
scale on extremely short notice, to co-ordinate the logistics of transportation, to
assure that the commodities provided by various donors reached their precise
destination—and not only a port in the stricken area—and to make sure that all this
be done while respecting the constraints that flow from co-operating with State
authorities jealous of their sovereign rights, to that extent one could say that the
WFP has performed in a satisfactory manner. In this respect, we should also note
that the WFP is but one of many channels through which emergency assistance is
sent to the stricken areas. Its allocation of funds for such actions, added to resources
provided by the International Emergency Food Reserve, amounted in 1977 to $85
million. This amount allowed the shipment of 323,400 metric tons of food to
disaster-stricken countries, which represents a little more than a third of total
emergency aid, bilateral and multilateral. In carrying out these tasks, WFP co-
operates with a large number of bilateral and multilateral public and private agencies, among which we should cite more particularly the FAO Office of Special Relief
Operations (OSRO), the United Nations Disasters Relief Office (UNDRO),
UNICEF, the UNHCR, the United States AID, etc. It would seem, however, that as
time goes by its role as the focal point for such operations is being increasingly
recognized and under its new Executive Director, the WFP may finally come to be
the agency most likely to succeed in co-ordinating the complex emergency operations which have to be carried out on an almost continuing basis.

This enumeration of positive and negative effects of food aid is only indicative.
On the one hand, it shows that those holding responsibility for their implementation
are not oblivious of their weaknesses and that they are prepared to bring them into
the open, drawing attention of both donor and recipient governments; while on the
other it underlines their mixed effects in relation to the need to increase and improve
agricultural production. In the medium and long run, food aid in itself cannot offer
solutions to the nutritional problems of so many developing countries. The WFP
seems to be perfectly conscious of this need and its recommendations for improving
the effectiveness of food aid always establishes a link between food aid and the patterns and level of local agricultural production.

At its session held in April 1978, the Committee on Food Aid Policies and Programmes proposed ten guidelines and criteria, both for bilateral and for multilateral
aid programmes. These are:

(a) "Food aid should be provided in forms consistent with the development objectives of recipient countries . . . and ensuring that it neither acts as a disincentive to local food production nor has adverse effects on the domestic market and international trade. . . ."

(b) In order to allow recipient countries to plan development and nutrition programmes, donors must be able to undertake long-term commitments.

(c) The need for forward planning is particularly great in relation to the use of food aid in support of socio-economic development projects.

(d) Priority should be given by donors to the MSA countries.

(e) Donors should undertake to help finance the infrastructure of the poorest recipients, to enable them to make the best use of food aid.

(f) In providing food aid to the MSAs, the proportion of grants should be considerably increased.

(g) Donors should channel their aid through the multilateral agencies and particularly through the WFP.

(h) Donors should also provide financial assistance earmarked for food, in order to facilitate the participation of developing countries' capable of exporting food in food trade processes.

(i) In the allocation and utilization of food aid, both donors and recipients should aim at meeting emergency needs, increasing agricultural production to meet basic needs and provide for special projects benefiting the most vulnerable groups in the recipient countries.

(j) Both donors and recipients should create and maintain food reserves, as well as storage and transport facilities, located in developing countries.

Before concluding this all too brief examination of WFP activities it should be stressed that aid channelled through the Programme has in fact increased over the past 5 years and, more particularly in 1977-8. During the 1973-4 period pledges by donors totalled $360.0 million, while the $750 million target for 1977-8 was almost met. However, if we consider the effects of inflation, in addition to the decrease of the dollar parity for purchases outside North America, these figures represent a very modest increase of food aid in the face of growing needs. In terms of shipments, the figure for 1973-4 was 1,121,400 metric tons; while in 1976-7 it rose to 1,731,200 metric tons. In this total, the shipments of cereals more than doubled between 1974 and 1977.

For the 1978-9 biennium, it was proposed to set the pledging target at $950 million, but at its May 1977 session, the Committee on Food Aid Policies and Programmes introduced a word of caution in its report:

"In this connection, they noted that the target of $750 million for the current biennium had yet to be reached, and therefore there was need for caution in fixing the quantum for the next biennium. Furthermore, they felt that the level of the pledging target needed very careful consideration, taking into account, *inter alia,* the absorptive capacity of recipient countries, effectiveness of resource management by WFP, relative emphasis on food aid within overall development assistance and the scope and limitations of co-ordination among the different sources of food aid."

The group of delegates expressing these views included the United States and other important donors who shared the opinion that the "target proposed by the Executive Director was not realistic". Delegations from most developing countries naturally did not follow the same reasoning and insisted on the adoption of the target proposed by the Executive Director, considering that an increase of 27% over the previous biennium would hardly meet the effects of inflation and the continuing decrease of value of the dollar. They also set aside any reservations concerning the WFP and recipient countries' capacity to absorb a larger amount of food aid.[14] No matter what the political motivations of the first group were, however, they certainly stressed the two essential shortcomings of WFP action: its own limitations in the area of resource management and the difficulties met by many recipient countries to absorb even the present level of food aid. Beyond these operational obstacles to the expansion of WFP activities, however, the major constraint on multilateral programmes is the absence of any meaningful advance planning, covering a period of more than 2 years. The World Food Conference of 1974 called for such planning and considered it to be one of the prerequisites for the expansion of food aid. Notwithstanding this pressing appeal to donors and recipients, with very rare exceptions both groups seem unwilling or incapable to come to grips with this issue. As a consequence, WFP actions remain punctual and its capacity to develop satisfactory resource management structures and methods is limited by the biennial cycle. Moreover, in as far as uncertainty concerning medium- or long-term expectations on the part of recipient countries is the rule, it is hardly possible to relate food aid to overall development assistance and to provide incentives for the improvement of the recipients' capacity to absorb such aid effectively.

Present efforts aimed at the restructuring of the UN development system may provide some solutions to the problems facing WFP, but we should have few illusions as to the effectiveness of blueprints for reform of bureaucratic establishments jealous of their autonomy and freedom of action. This has been particularly true of FAO, which has tended to be defensive in the face of attempts on the part of the central organs in the UN system to introduce greater institutional rationality and to increase the system's overall capacity to promote development assistance activities. As for the WFP, given its interagency nature and its considerable expertise in the field, it can only stand to gain from any action within the UN system likely to improve the coordination and planning machinery in the area of food aid.

D. THE WORLD HEALTH ORGANIZATION

We consider it appropriate to discuss briefly the World Health Organization's contribution to multilateral efforts to eliminate hunger and malnutrition both because of the relevance of its action in this field and because, by the very definition of its functions, it represents the qualitative element in the overall food-aid picture which bears the mark of quantitative demands and responses. The expansion and better distribution of food supplies are not enough to bring about a satisfactory solution to this global problem. The quality of food and its channelling to the neediest and most vulnerable groups are, in the medium and long run, equally important if we are to eliminate not only the causes of hunger and malnutrition but also their effects on the populations of developing countries.

Ever since 1948, WHO and FAO have been cooperating in various projects on nutritional requirements and WHO has carried out numerous studies on the effects on the health of undernourished groups and categories of people in developing areas. The thrust of its work in this field has been double: first, to study the energy/protein requirements and the effects of their insufficient intake on various age and occupational groups (particularly on children); and, second, the diseases provoked by malnutrition, such as xeropthalmia, endemic goiter, protein-calorie malnutrition and nutritional anaemia. In the context of these studies, joint WHO/FAO expert committees have made specific recommendations based on the relationship between energy metabolism and that of protein, which can serve as guidelines for the nutritional policies in developing areas. In addition to the availability of food in countries and regions, WHO has also tackled the problem of its distribution by social groups. Its conclusions clearly point to the fact that, in most cases, malnutrition and hunger are the consequence of maldistribution and not of over-all shortages of energy or protein supplies. More seriously, however, WHO studies have been pointing to the irremediable damage caused by maldistribution to the most vulnerable groups, such as children and pregnant women. In both cases, this damage often has important genetic consequences, particularly when the growth process is considerably slowed down in young children. According to its estimates, approximately 100 million children under 5 years are suffering from protein-calorie malnutrition, endangering their physical and mental future. Moreover, in Latin America, malnutrition accounts for over 50% of deaths of children belonging to this age group; and if similar studies were carried out in other developing areas, the conclusions would certainly be as dramatic.

In responding to the Plan of Action proposed to the World Food Conference, the WHO identified, in its own programme, five priority areas:

(a) The surveillance—at the local, national and international levels—of arising nutritional problems.
(b) The development of strong food supply and nutritional policies, in the context of over all planning.
(c) Emphasizing the nutritional component in the various sectors and at the very various levels of health services.
(d) Stepping up measures for the control and eradication of nutritional deficiency conditions, particularly through the control of vitamin A deficiency.
(e) Education and training of the personnel necessary for intensifying these programmes.

E. THE INTERNATIONAL BANK FOR RECONSTRUCTION AND DEVELOPMENT AND THE INTERNATIONAL DEVELOPMENT ASSOCIATION

The IBRD and its affiliate, the IDA, became involved in agricultural assistance programmes only recently, but they have jointly become the largest single source of international assistance in this field. Over the past 5 years they disbursed a little over $10 billion for agricultural and, more generally, rural development. In 1978 the figure was approximately $3.3 billion and, in a recent estimation, the Bank states that its 359 projects approved since 1974 will lead, by the late 1980s, to an increase of 13 million tons of cereals production. The Bank's activities in this area have been placing a heavy emphasis on rural development, which absorbs 55% of the total disbursements for 1978, as compared to 21% in 1974. The range of projects financed by IBRD or IDA lending covers irrigation, agricultural research, extension services, development of new crops, purchase of pesticides and fertilizers, agricultural credit institutions, etc.

Under the impetus given to the Bank group by Robert MacNamara, this is indeed a new departure. Compared to the earlier, almost exclusive attention paid to industrialization and infrastructure development, this reorientation of the Bank's policies is becoming, potentially at least, a major component in the overall picture of international assistance in the field of nutrition. The Bank does not, as a general rule, carry out food-aid programmes, but its financing of agricultural and rural development projects, if properly directed, may contribute both to an increase of indigenous production and to the creation of jobs in the rural areas of developing countries.

Notwithstanding the volume of lending by the Bank, its action has not yet produced the type of impact which recipient countries are expecting. There are numerous reasons for this failure to meet the Bank's declared objectives. First, the very fact that loans obtained from the Bank group are subject to conditions which are still difficult if not impossible to meet by most of the "most seriously affected" countries. Interest rates, repayment schedules and the recourse to commercial banks for channelling the loans presuppose not only a relatively healthy foreign exchange situation but also the existence of national banking institutions capable of handling effectively such loans. Second, experience shows, particularly in Latin America, that very often the beneficiaries of Bank loans are not the great majority of farmers and agricultural workers but a small number of land owners. In the case of live stock production, large-scale ranchers in Latin America benefited from such loans but the increased production did not benefit the countries' populations and simply led to a notable increase of exports. As for an increase of the number of jobs in rural areas and a wider distribution of income flowing directly from investments rendered possible as a result of Bank loans, it is generally recognized that these objectives have not been met because their beneficiaries have been exclusively export oriented.

Finally, criticisms of Bank policies has been focussed on the inappropriate production patterns and types of crops encouraged or induced by the Bank experts and decision-making bodies. Considering that the purpose of investments resulting from IBRD or IDA loans is the increase of indigenous agricultural production and, more generally, to promote rural development, the choice of technologies becomes a crucial variable. At the same time, these choices must take into account local physical conditions and traditional patterns of agricultural production, as well as the country's overall development objectives. Developing countries' agricultural policies generally aim at the progressive reduction of food imports and the attainment of a level of production covering minimum needs. In order to meet this objective, production patterns and techniques must therefore be such as to reduce as much as possible dependence, not only on imported food but also on imported technologies and their corollaries, chemical products. It is generally recognized that agricultural research specifically aimed to cover the needs of "most seriously affected" developing countries very often does not take into account their capacity to absorb its results. In many cases, had more attention been paid to the possibilities of developing and improving traditional crops, the results would have been much more encouraging. An example of misdirected agricultural development projects is to be found in Tanzania, where the Bank financed a programme under which a variety of maize was introduced, replacing more traditional crops. The production of maize, however, is dependent on imported seeds, imported fertilizers and pesticides, as well as on imported technological expertise. As a result, we have the substitution of food imports by a whole technological cycle which also has to be imported. The increase of production obtained through imported technologies which do not allow developing countries to put an end to their external dependence does not represent a satisfactory solution of the nutritional problems facing developing countries.

These and many other shortcomings in the Bank's programmes are increasingly recognized by experts and key decision-makers from within the Bank group. As a first step in the right direction, the IBRD's stated objective is to discontinue projects which have tended to benefit exclusively small groups of large landowners and to place a stronger emphasis on the need to distribute as widely as possible the increased income accruing from the Bank's lending policies. As for technological choices, there seems to be a growing realization among the Bank's decision-makers that the nutritional issues in the Third World cannot be tackled without taking into account the physical and socio-cultural conditions in the recipient countries. Moreover, several governments of MSA countries are scrutinizing much more carefully than in the past the projects elaborated by experts of international organizations, precisely in order to avoid the substitution of one form of dependence by another. To the extent that projects financed by the Bank take into account the particular characteristics of recipient countries—and this can only be done if the views of national experts are not only heard but are considered as a critical variable in the decision-making process—its role in contributing to the solution of developing countries' nutritional problems will certainly be enhanced. Over and beyond the minimum target of 10 million tons of food aid set by the World Food Conference of 1974, agricultural development in the Third World is also a matter of major transfers of financial resources. The estimate of minimum annual needs for the end of our decade made for the World Food Conference is $10 billion of international financial assistance, in addition to the mobilization of twice this amount of capital within the developing countries. If the Bank's lending expands at a pace comparable to that of the past 5 years, by 1980 it should reach a level of $5 billion. The destination and the overall direction of financial transfers under the Bank's auspices will thus represent a critical mass which will have a decisive impact on all multilateral and bilateral programmes.

F. THE WORLD FOOD CONFERENCE AND ITS AFTERMATH

We have already noted the conditions under which the Conference was convened, following the initiatives taken by Heads of State and government of the non-aligned, meeting in Algiers in September 1973, and, a few weeks later, by Secretary of State Kissinger speaking before the General Assembly of the United Nations. The decision to convene it was taken at a time of natural disasters and bad harvests which led to the dramatic shrinking of stocks, in the face of large-scale purchases on the developed food-importing countries such as the USSR, accompanied by spectacular increases in the prices of pesticides and fertilizers resulting from the jump in the cost of oil. To say the least, prospects were indeed gloomy in 1973-4 and many knowledgeable observers were predicting large-scale starvation in Africa and in Asia for the immediate future.[15] All these circumstances taken together gave rise to a sense of urgency for international action, shared even by the staunchest opponents of multilateralism. By the time the Conference met, at the end of 1974, this diffuse feeling of grave concern was still prevalent but in addition the preparatory work had generated some remarkable data and analyses, which were hardly questioned by any of the participants.

The World Food Conference deserves our attention for two reasons:

(a) it represented the first global effort—both in terms of participation and in terms of its agenda—to tackle the issues of food shortages and malnutrition affecting more than 500 million people, in Asia, Africa and Latin America; and

(b) it was one in the series of *ad hoc* international conferences convened by the United Nations in the 1960s and 1970s, in an attempt to draw attention to particularly acute global problems and to bring together decision-makers, plenipotentiaries and experts in order to initiate new courses of action capable of leading to their solution.[16]

In the context of this brief overview, it is impossible to treat exhaustively the multi-faceted aspects of the conference. We have therefore chosen to make some brief remarks about its conduct and refer to its institutional outcome, the establishment of the World Food Council and of the International Fund for Agricultural Development. We should also underline, however, that the Conference represented, in many respects, a milestone in the evolution of multilateralism. As compared with other global conferences, beginning in 1963 with the one devoted to the Application of Science and Technology for the Benefit of the Less Developed Nations to the recent conferences on Water Resources and on Desertification, it was probably the best prepared and its working documents truly served their purpose.[17] Little time was lost in the usual preliminary and often procedural debates and, from the outstart, delegates were in a position to discuss specific proposals for action, many of which were actually adopted and some of which entered the phase of implementation 1 to 4 years later. Moreover, in spite of serious differences of views on the precise measures to be recommended, there were few stifling ideological debates and, with rare exceptions, delegations agreed on its basic premises and on the urgent need for international action.

The composition of delegations to the Conference varied greatly but, on the whole, the principal donors and a great number of recipient countries sent cabinet-level officials as heads of delegations. In the case of the United States, the Secretary of Agriculture headed the delegation, but Henry Kissinger was also present and delivered the keynote address. The prestigious character of the US delegation was further enhanced by the inclusion of a number of prominent senators and members of the House of Representatives. Both Senators Humphrey and McGovern were members of the delegation but, in fact, the positions they took publicly were not always the same as those held by the delegation's leadership. On a number of key issues, particularly in respect to a larger US commitment of funds and of commodities, they and other members of the delegation publicly disagreed with the US administration's position and addressed public and private appeals to President Ford for a modification of his instructions. Such a diversity of views may be explained by the specific character of relations between the administration and Congress in the United States, but they are certainly not a common feature in the conduct of intergovernmental conferences. They were, none the less, an important component of the Rome proceedings because they contributed to the adoption by the US delegation of positions which would have been unthought of even during the preparatory period. They were also important because they reflected the deeply rooted concern over the issues of malnutrition and starvation to be found in important sectors of donor countries' public opinion and political forces.

Another element of critical diversity was the presence in Rome of representatives of a great number of non-governmental organizations. The presence of NGO's acting as pressure and lobbying groups was not a new phenomenon; in Stockholm, in 1972, in Bucharest, earlier in 1974, as well as in other global conferences in the past, NGO's were well represented. The novelty in Rome is to be found simply in the fact that rather than being isolated from the Conference itself and relegated to a different locus, carrying out polemical debates *among* themselves, in Rome the NGO activities were concentrated within the Conference, in permanent interaction with delegations and international bureaucracies. At long last, the leadership of NGOs seemed to have understood that the most effective way to have an impact on intergovernmental decision-making was to abandon their pious rhetoric and try to insert themselves into the processes, which are certainly not immune from non-governmental pressures. Western delegations were clearly influenced by such lobbying, as the final results of the Conference seem to indicate. An additional form of NGO action was the daily publication of a remarkably well-presented journal, *Pan*. Stockholm and Bucharest also had their "critical" newspapers but the journalistic quality, as well as the political maturity, of *Pan* remains unsurpassed. It is difficult to measure the precise impact of such a publication on the decision-making process, but the conclusion one draws from discussing its contents with delegates and international officials is that it certainly was not negligible.

We have already mentioned the high quality of the preparatory work, done under the direction of the Conference Secretary-General, Dr. Sayed Marei. During the Conference, as well, the role played by its Secretariat often had a decisive impact, particularly in the work of the committees. Moreover, the Secretariat behaved during the Conference in many ways which were quite uncommon for international bureaucracies.

According to Weiss and Jordan,[18] the flexibility shown by the Secretariat, when its own proposals for follow-up institutional action—essentially the "World Food Authority"—were almost unanimously rejected by delegations from developed and developing countries alike, was due essentially to two elements: first, Secretary-General Marei was not himself a bureaucrat, but a statesman of cabinet level and was immune from the all too common temptation of institutional "empire building" and, second, although he pursued with determination the substantive objectives of the Conference—and to a large extent succeeded in attaining them—he paid little attention to the form of the final outcome. The best demonstration of this success is to be found in the fact that although the World Food Authority never came into being, the wording of the resolutions and specially of those establishing the World Food Council and the International Fund for Agricultural Development replicated to a large extent the wording of Chapter 20 of the document submitted to the Conference. It is important to underline the course of action chosen by the Secretariat, because the relative success of the Conference can be largely attributed to the fact that it was not pursuing a policy of "empire building" and that this policy option was clearly perceived by the majority of delegations.

In the face of the small but determined and effective Secretariat, the FAO bureaucracy conducted a campaign against all proposals likely to lead to *any* new institutional structures. Not only did it oppose the establishment of a World Food Authority, even long after its fate had been sealed; its leadership worked hard to avoid any institutional follow-up outside the FAO organizational framework. Reliable observers of the Rome Conference were struck by the stubborn defence of institutionally vested interests which characterized the FAO Secretariat's action. At the same time, its experts provided the Conference with highly valuable inputs and, on the whole, delegates did not question the importance of their contribution. The problem lay elsewhere. The World Food Conference was a deliberate attempt to bring to the attention of decision-makers the urgency of the perceived crisis facing dozens of developing countries and hundreds of million people. Such a crisis could not be faced by recourse to institutional instruments dominated by the bureaucratic spirit which inevitably prevails in organizations which have not been confronted with any serious challenges to their structure, modes of operations and overall orientation of their activities. The very fact that limited though it was the institutional follow-up was not placed under FAO auspices had in itself a healthy impact on the Organization and on its Secretariat's approach and action in relation to the problems of hunger and malnutrition.

The Conference adopted twenty-two Resolutions, of varying relevance and practical value, in terms of their implementation 4 years later. Resolutions I and II set out the objectives, strategies and priorities for food production and agricultural development; while Resolution XVIII contained specific recommendations to governments and international organizations likely to improve the operation of food aid programmes. More particularly, we should mention that the target of 10 million tons of cereals set by Resolution XVIII has not yet been met.

Other Resolutions referred to the use of pesticides and fertilizers, food and agricultural research, nutrition, water and soil management, the relationship between population and food issues, international trade and food security, information and early warning systems, etc. Finally, Resolution XXII established the World Food Council and Resolution XIII contained the guidelines for the establishment of the International Fund for Agricultural Development (IFAD), as soon as the target of $1 billion of initial capital had been met.

The World Food Council, composed of thirty-six member States, met for the first time in June 1975 and it held its fourth meeting in June 1978. It is serviced by a small Secretariat, headed by the former Administrator of the US Agency for International Development and Deputy Secretary-General of the Rome Conference, John Hannah. Although its headquarters are in Rome, it operates independently of the FAO Secretariat. From the very beginning and even before it came into existence—during the debates in Rome—the WFC has been considered first by its sponsors and later by its members to be the "world's highest political body dealing exclusively with food"[19] and, in principle, it meets at ministerial level. Its functions were defined as follows, at its first session: "(a) To monitor the world food situation in all its aspects, including what international organizations and governments were doing to develop short-term and long-term solutions to food problems; (b) to look at the total food picture and determine in its co-ordinating role whether the world food strategy as a whole made sense; (c) to identify malfunctions, gaps and problem areas; and (d) to exert its influence, through moral persuasion, to get any necessary improvements made."[20] At the same time, the Council defined its Secretariat's tasks as follows: "Scrutinize, review and comment, frankly and impartially, on situations as it found them and should suggest improvements to the Council as and when necessary."[21] In accomplishing these tasks, however, the Secretariat should not carry out "major research" on its own and it should draw on outside expertise, particularly on FAO, "while exercising its own objectivity with respect to the conclusions it drew".[22] The increase of food production in developing countries was the first priority set at its first session; although the Council also referred to a number of other issues to be considered in the future. To a large extent, these issues reflected the recommendations of the World Food Conference.

At its second and third sessions, the WFC continued its efforts to identify the areas in which it was to become actively involved and it adopted its rules of procedure. It is fascinating to note, however, that, as the initial impetus created by the unanimous political support it had obtained at the Rome Conference withered away, its deliberations and reports started moving in the direction of bureaucratic routine. This is all the more interesting as the Council was established as "a high-level political body", precisely because of the need recognized in Rome to get away from bureaucratic patterns of behaviour, in order to obtain that decision-makers deliberate on the problems of hunger and malnutrition at a non-bureaucratic level. The principal items in the Council's programme of work, in 1976 and in 1977, were the following: (a) production, distribution and consumption of food; (b) the assessment of the world food situation, based on existing research resources; (c) the "weaving together" of international agencies' actions aimed at raising nutritional levels, in view of establishing an overall plan of action; and (d) international trade in food and international food security. At its fourth session, held in Mexico in June 1978, the WFC also considered progress made towards the constitution of a 500,000 tons of cereals reserve stock, to be used in cases of emergencies and particularly acute shortages. As time went by, the Council's sessions became more "businesslike", but the principal conclusion to be drawn, after 4 years of existence, is that its establishment has not led to a breakthrough in international food-aid policies, likely to bring them closer to the needs recognized by all participants in the Rome Conference.

As for the IFAD, it finally came into existence in 1978, once the $1000 million target had been met. When its establishment was first proposed in Rome, by the OPEC countries and a few Western donors of food aid, it certainly did not draw support from the United States and most Western delegations. Today, however, it is recognized, even by the US administration, that it is a potentially important step forward, to the extent that it is contributing to mobilize resources from the oil-producing countries. Countries like Iran and Saudi Arabia are, in this respect, particularly important contributors to the Fund. The principle on which the Fund is based in that of an approximate parity of contributions from OPEC and from OECD countries. In 1975-7 the plenipotentiary and other preparatory meetings were characterized by a rather depressing series of tough bargaining sessions, in order to determine which one of the two groups was going to provide the $30-50 million to meet the $1 billion target. At the end, both sides made additional pledges and the Fund has now become operational. One last point to be made about IFAD is that it is held in particular favour by the US Congress. Its objective of increasing the productive capacity of Third World countries is one considered to be of particular importance, both among donors and among recipients, who often view direct transfers of commodities on a concessionary or grants basis as attempts to fill a bottomless pit. The Fund has its headquarters in Rome but it is very jealous of its independence *vis-à-vis* the FAO organizational framework.

III.   Donors' Policies and Multilateral Programmes

Having reviewed the principal multilateral programmes aimed at the improvement of the developing countries' nutritional conditions, we should now ask ourselves how these programmes are viewed by the donors. Given the intergovernmental nature of their decision-making bodies, it would be impossible to draw any conclusions as to their significance and future development, without discussing the policy objectives and motivations of those who "hold the purse strings". We shall therefore first attempt to present and analyse some global data concerning the principal donors, before examining more closely the cases of the EEC and of the United States.

A. AN OVERVIEW

Although food aid is also channelled through other intergovernmental and nongovernmental organizations as well, we shall refer basically to donors' policies in the WFP and, among the donors, we shall discuss the policies of OECD member countries and, more particularly, the United States and the EEC, whose contributions for the 1977-8 biennium represented approximately $660 million out of total pledges to the WFP of $716 million, made by eighty-five countries. The only other major contributor was Saudi Arabia, which pledged $50 million. Among the OECD members, France and Italy were proportionally far behind the others in contributing to multilateral programmes outside the EEC framework.[23]

The eighteen donors about which we have data (for 1975-6) used multilateral channels for their food aid to a varying degree. Two of these countries—Austria and Norway—channelled 100% of their aid through the WFP; the Netherlands (85%) and Denmark (67%) channelled a great proportion of their aid through the WFP; five more use UN channels for 25% or more of their aid (EEC: 25%, Sweden: 26.4%, Finland: 37.8%, Canada: 44.8% and Switzerland: 49.5%); while the proportion for the remaining ranged between 18.3% (New Zealand) and 0.38% (France). The United States contribution to WFP represented 4% of total aid. These figures, though incomplete, nonetheless reflect the extreme diversity of donors' policies towards multilateral programmes under UN auspices.

In regard to forward planning, whose need has so often been stressed by multilateral bodies, it still remains largely a matter of wishful thinking. Beyond the biennium pledges to the WFP—often made several months after the beginning of the biennium—it would seem that such planning for 3-4 years in advance is to be found in only three countries: Canada, the Netherlands and Sweden. As for the EEC, the Commission, the European Parliament and some member governments would like to see more forward planning. The whole range of subjects related to this question are presently being discussed in Brussels, but the constraints of the budget cycle render extremely difficult if not impossible such planning in the European Community. The inability—but sometimes also the unwillingness—of most governments to make financial commitments beyond the following fiscal year represents a major obstacle to the satisfactory operation of the IEFR. To the extent that such a reserve must be replenished on a regular basis, while governments state that they are unable to make commitments going beyond one or, at the most, 2 years, its value as an instrument of emergency action is greatly diminished.

A last point of interest is to examine briefly the priority objectives of donors, in the context of their policies within multi-lateral organizations. Twelve out of eighteen donors give priority to emergency aid and three simply accept WFP priorities. Japan does not seem to have any clear priorities, while the United States gives precedence to the expansion of international trade and export markets for US agricultural commodities. Practically all donors also recognize the need to use food aid as an instrument for economic and social development, but only a few of them place emphasis on the use of such aid to develop indigenous agricultural production. As for the geographic distribution of aid, most donors give high priority to the most seriously affected countries, while members of the European Community tend to take seriously into account the balance of payments situation of potential recipients.

This all too brief overview of donors' attitudes and policies in regard to food aid does not allow us to generalize and to draw meaningful conclusions concerning their political and/or economic motivations to do this, we would have to go beyond the limited scope of this study and introduce analyses of donors' decision-making in the field of development assistance policies. At the same time, even a study with limited objectives would be incomplete if we did not refer to the policies of the two major donors, the United States and the European Community, as they have evolved over the years.

B. THE UNITED STATES AND MULTILATERAL PROGRAMMES

Historically, the United States was the first country to embark on massive food-aid programmes and, ever since its establishment, it has been a major donor to WFP. United States participation in the WFP is based on the provisions of Title II, of Public Law 480, adopted in 1954 and amended on several occasions. Title I of PL 480 regulates trade in agricultural commodities, while Title II authorizes the President of the United States to purchase American farm products and donate them to foreign governments, American voluntary agencies and the World Food Programme. Actions under Title II have come to be known as "Food for Peace" programmes. In this connection, it is interesting to note the objectives of United States policy, as set out in section 2 of PL 480. In a Report for the Committee on Agriculture and Forestry of the United States Senate, published in 1976, these objectives are presented as follows:

—expanding international trade;

—developing and expanding overseas markets for American farm products;

—preventing and ameliorating malnutrition and surges throughout the world;

—encouraging economic development and improving food production in less developed countries;

—providing an additional outlet for the products of American farms and ranches;

—advancing the objectives of US foreign policy.[24]

The same Report also states that "P.L. 480 traditionally has been used to increase the export of US agricultural commodities and support farm income by providing concessional terms for countries unable to buy on commercial terms". Although a distinction is made between Title I (sales) and Title II (donations), the Report adds that programmes under Title II also "have market development implications".

In examining the objectives of P.L. 480, we should note that the prevention of malnutrition and hunger occupies the third position, after the commercial objectives of US policy. At the same time, this list refers to the "objectives of US foreign policy". This is a realistic and straightforward presentation of motivations underlying the United States participation in multilateral food-aid programmes, which is supported by the practice of US authorities every time the country's political or commercial interests are at stake. During the Nixon administration, in particular, Secretary of State Kissinger was perfectly explicit in setting the guidelines for US international food-aid programmes: their "humanitarian" objectives were always subordinated to the overall objectives of US foreign policy. Such a posture is not unique to the United States; the difference lies simply in the fact that US authorities, as a rule, spell out the objectives about which most other donors prefer to remain discreet.

More specifically, in respect to multilateral food-aid programmes and the WFP, the United States has always succeeded to maintain its rights to determine the recipients of its contributions. At the same time, it has been the policy of US agencies "to keep a very close eye" on all WFP operations. Though such a policy is not surprising—given the importance of US contributions—the tendency for US policy-makers and administrators has been to seek institutional recognition of the right of US authorities to intervene actively at all stages of WFP decision-making and operation procedures and to place on WFP's relations with recipient countries constraints likely to ensure that US interests are taken in account at all stages of programme formulation and implementation.

Responsibility for US participation in WFP is shared by three executive agencies: the Departments of Agriculture and State and the Agency for International Development. At the same time, both the Senate and the House of Representatives have consistently paid particular attention to US participation in multilateral programmes. In addition, on several occasions, special task forces or advisors have been instructed to scrutinize US policies in this field. More than any other donor, the United States has been explicit both in spelling out its objectives and in undertaking policy initiatives likely to promote them. The explicit nature of policy debates over food aid is certainly part of a wider pattern of public policy discussion in the United States; but it is also strengthened by the interest shown in these debates both by powerful economic groups and by those who share a strong humanitarian concern over the plight of regions and countries affected by natural disasters and/or permanent malnutrition. Groups and organizations belonging to both categories are well represented in Congress, the media and the Administration. The scope of this paper does not allow us to discuss in detail the various facets of US policy. We shall therefore concentrate our remarks on the declared objectives of US participation in the WFP and on some aspects of their implementation.

The examination of numerous Reports, studies and unpublished papers—originating in Congress, the administration and non-governmental groups—leads us to the following conclusions:[25]

(a) The United States should pursue a policy aimed at introducing "a clear set of programme priorities and a long-range programming system".
(b) No WFP project should be approved if it conflicts with US objectives.
(c) In considering projects, their effects on "current and developing markets, particularly on US exports" should be given high priority.
(d) The approval of a project should be subordinated to the existence of an appropriate structure for its management in the recipient country, as well as to the assurance that the WFP field staff is in a position to monitor the project.
(e) The auditing and evaluation procedures should conform with, or at least should not contradict similar US procedures.
(f) The most directly concerned US agency, the AID, should play an active role at all stages of WFP activities. Its field staff and its Mission in Rome, as well as headquarters in Washington, should exert their influence on WFP, in order to assure the conformity of its decisions and of their implementation with US policy objectives.

During the last year, a reappraisal of US policies in relation to food aid has led to the amendment of P.L. 480, in order to place greater emphasis on the need to improve—through donations—the nutritional conditions in developing countries. The amendments, both to P.L. 480 and to the Foreign Assistance Act of 1961, adopted in September 1978 include provisions authorizing the President to undertake actions in the fields of agriculture, rural development and nutrition which go beyond the terms of previous legislation. Concerning more particularly P.L. 480, these amendments are motivated by the lack of success "in meeting the food needs of those suffering from hunger and malnutrition" and are aimed at an increase of food aid under Title II of the Law. It would, however, be too early to speak of a change in US policy, which would imply a more "humanitarian" posture towards food aid. Foreign policy and trade considerations still represent the yardsticks by which international food-aid programmes are appraised. It remains to be seen whether the reexamination of the basic assumptions on which US policy has been developed over the past quarter of a century will be modified, as a result of a more general reexamination of US international development policies.

C. THE EUROPEAN COMMUNITY

The second largest donor of food-aid programmes is the European Community. As the same time, these include its own "bilateral" programme and those of its member countries. The Community and member states are involved in three different types of food-aid programmes: (a) Bilateral-member state to recipient state; (b) "Bilateral"—Community to recipient state; (c) Multilateral-Community to WFP and other agencies. However, when we refer to EEC food aid, we have in mind all three types of programmes. To the extent that member states' national actions are co-ordinated within the Community Council and that international commitments undertaken by the EEC are carried out both through direct Community programmes and through those of member states, to that extent it is appropriate to consider that they are part of a comprehensive Community food-aid policy.

The starting-point for EEC action in this field was the signature of the Food Aid Convention in 1968. At that time, the Community undertook the obligation to provide 1,287,000 tons of cereals, but this target was not reached until 1973. Ever since, this level has been maintained, but the Commission has been pressing the Council for an increase in the face of growing demands from recipient countries and from multilateral agencies. The proportion of national and strictly Community contributions has varied, but the latter has increased over the years. In 1969 approximately 30% of the total was covered by the Community, while in 1977 it had reached 60% and in 1978 it was slightly below that level. In this respect, we should also note that during the first years following the conclusion of the first FAC, funds necessary for the "Community" component of EEC's programmes were made available by member states; while at present they are provided under the Community budget.

Beginning in 1970, the EEC increased and diversified its activities in this field by providing massive quantities of food products other than cereals. These included essentially milk products—skimmed milk powder and butteroil—as well as sugar. The ratio between cereals and other products has varied greatly over the years, largely as a result of market conditions within the EEC. In 1970 non-cereals accounted for almost 85% of total EEC aid, the following year the Community provided only cereals and in 1972 their proportion grew to almost 60%, to drop again in 1973 to approximately 20%. In 1977 the ratio stood at approximately 1/3 for products other than cereals. We should also note, however, that milk and other non-cereal products are drawn from the EEC's surplus stocks and are part of the "Community" component of its food-aid programmes.

As for Community contributions to multilateral programmes—including national actions—they have grown steadily over the years. Since 1970 the principal beneficiaries have been WFP, UNRWA and the League of Red Cross Societies. In 1976 the Community contributed 105,000 tons of cereals and 85,000 of milk products while the total cash value of these deliveries was approximately 331 million units of account. In 1978 its contribution to multilateral programmes in cereals alone was 141,000 tons. This represents slightly less than 11% of total Community food aid, while in 1970 it represented less than 2%. In addition to pressing for an overall increase of food aid, the Commission has also been insisting on the need to increase the Community's contributions to multilateral programmes. However, in this field, as in so many others, the Community is faced with a very real dilemma: on the one hand, food aid given bilaterally is one of the means through which it can affirm its position and its image *vis-à-vis* developing countries; on the other, the Community is desirous to appear "disinterested" in its relations with recipient countries, which should normally lead to greater participation in multilateral programmes. This dilemma is discussed in various Commission documents and the conclusion one draws is that the Community will have to live with it for some time to come.

It is none the less important to note that in spite of the level of the Community's participation in multilateral programmes—which is considered unsatisfactory by the

Commission and by some member states—the fact that a large proportion is constituted by milk products represents a qualitatively very important contribution to WFP and other multilateral programmes. The diversification of food-aid components is generally recognized to be a high priority objective and Community action is particularly important in this respect. Its value would, however, be enhanced if it was not largely subordinated to market conditions within the Community. Forward planning is absolutely necessary, if food aid is to play fully its role in the efforts to remedy the present situation; but the value of Community action is diminished because of the uncertainty which presides over its internal market conditions.

Decisions concerning food aid are taken by the Council, on the basis of proposals submitted by the Commission. As a rule, the Council reduces considerably the amounts included in the Commission's proposals, but it does not modify the proposals qualitatively. This means that, on the whole the recipients of the Community's actions and the components of specific programmes are largely determined by the Commission. The criteria on which such decisions are taken can be summarized as follows:

(a) A chronic nutritional shortage, either at the national level or within a given region in the country.

(b) A GNP *per capita* below a certain level. This level has varied and it is now set at $450.

(c) An important balance of payments deficit.

Finally, we should note that while during the first 5 years the trend was towards an increase of the number of recipients of EEC aid, since 1974-5 its programmes have been concentrated on the most seriously affected countries. This means that, as a result of the Council's refusal to increase the overall quantity which has remained at the same level since 1973, several countries originally benefiting from such aid no longer do so. On the whole, EEC food aid has not fluctuated as much as US or Canadian programmes, but its cereals component has not increased in response to growing needs in any way comparable to the increase of US aid during the past 3 years. Quantitatively, the EEC programmes are lagging behind, but qualitatively their importance has been growing, both because of the diversity of products they include and because they are perceived to be unrelated to the pursuit of political objectives. We shall discuss this aspect in greater detail in our conclusions; at this point, we simply want to mention this qualitative characteristic of EEC food-aid actions.

IV. Multilateral Programmes and Recipient Countries

A. FOOD AID AND DEVELOPMENT

Chronic food shortages in most developing countries can be attributed to one of or a variable combination of four causes. First, the rapid and unplanned development of the industrial and service sectors of their economies; accompanied by an unprecedented rate of urbanization and massive shifts of population from the countryside to the cities, or rather to their peripheries. Second, a grave imbalance between investments in these two sectors and those in agriculture. Third, a distortion of agricultural trade circuits and an ever-growing concentration both of production and consumption of agricultural products in certain highly industrialized regions of the "North". Fourth, climatic events, which have tended to compound the effects of the Third World's "mal-development".

Although no serious observer of the world nutritional situation would disagree with this enumeration—and the texts adopted at the World Food Conference as well as on many other occasions clearly recognize the linkage between "mal-development" and food shortages—donors' and recipients' policies have been remarkably unsuccessful in implementing programmes likely to contribute to the structural causes of malnutrition. Lip service is certainly paid to the need to relate food aid to economic and social development; but such statements are, as a rule, kept at such a level of generalization that they are hardly ever translated into specific actions. We shall be discussing this question at greater length in our conclusions; at this point we simply want to note the fact that food-aid programmes have not, on the whole, contributed significantly to the elimination of the most important causes of malnutrition.

If the donors—multilateral and bilateral—gave a high enough priority to the need to insert food-aid programmes in a planning process aimed at the necessary transformation of the patterns of food production and trade, authorities in the recipient countries would have had an incentive for the implementation of measures likely to redress a constantly deteriorating situation. This not being the case, however, food shortages tend to increase and food aid is becoming a lasting and self-perpetuating feature in North-South relations. Moreover, governments of most recipient countries act—more often than not—in the face of urgent needs, as they arise and in the absence of any forward planning. The absence of such planning on the part of donors and international organizations both explains in part but it also is an easy excuse for authorities in developing countries.

Such a statement on our part does not represent an attempt to "strike a balance" between donors and recipients, for their failure to draw the optimum benefit from food-aid programmes. It simply reflects the situation most recipient countries are in; which represents an important constraint on the quantitative and qualitative development of such programmes. Observers have often noted that local authorities are not in a position to assume the responsibilities for their logistics and administration. The breakdown of transportation when emergency situations arise, corruption and the tragic imbalance between the urban centres and rural areas in terms of food supply are all phenomena which have drawn attention of well-intentioned observers. However, not enough attention has been paid to the roots of these problems, to be found in the very link between the socio-economic, political and administrative structures of these countries to the post-colonial system of dependence.

Major donors occasionally call for better planning, but the term is used to designate better "technical" arrangements, in view of maximizing the benefits of food aid. This is not surprising, to the extent that the very same actors who make decisions in relation to such programmes are, at the same time, entrusted by their constituencies with the task of pursuing objectives which generally place in the foreground the long-term interests of donors and the short-term interests of recipients. As they are presently conceived and implemented, food-aid programmes cannot make a significant contribution to the achievement of goals likely to transform the structures which are at the root of growing food shortages, which tend to become chronic.

Given these constraints on donors and recipients, we consider that those responsible for multilateral programmes—both at the decision-making and at the implementation levels—must undertake the task of introducing into the food-aid debates the types of pertinent questions in relation to such programmes' functions, in the context of an overall development strategy aimed at the elimination of the structural causes which perpetuate the present vicious circle. In our view, beyond the research and operational activities presently carried out by multilateral agencies, no matter how valuable they are, it is their responsibility to go several steps further and identify the complex mechanisms of the food production—trade—consumption cycle. As Gunnar Myrdal put it more than two decades ago, "truth is wholesome" in itself, no matter what the immediate practical effects of publicizing it are. Before and during the World Food Conference, there were serious reasons to hope that some "elementary truths" concerning the world nutritional situation were at long last going to find their way into donors' decision-making procedures and into recipients' planning for a more effective use of food aid. These hopes were certainly misplaced, essentially because major donors refused to implement the Conference recommendations concerning the qualitative aspects of food aid programmes. In the presence of "qualitative stagnation" in the multilateral policy bodies—which was well illustrated by the performance of the World Food Council at its fourth session, in Mexico, in June 1978—it would seem appropriate for the Secretariats of multilateral agencies to work closely with some forward-looking donors and the authorities of recipient countries, in order to develop strategies for future action. The willingness to do so seems to be present, both in the Rome-based organizations and in the European Commission. It remains, however, to be seen whether the governments of recipient countries will accept to set aside some of the inhibitions stemming from their insistence that nothing should be said or done which could affect their sovereignty. The multinational corporations which carry such weight in the donors' camp pay little attention to such "outdated" concepts and the persistence of views to the contrary in so many developing countries simply weakens their bargaining positions.

In our view, the present deadlocks can only be broken through the establishment of effective coalitions between recipients, some donors and international Secretariats. To that extent, the dilemmas facing decision-makers in this field are the same as those facing them in the wider policy areas of restructuring the international order. This is not surprising, if we recognize that food-aid programmes should become part and parcel of the more comprehensive efforts towards the establishment of a new international order.

B. RECIPIENT COUNTRIES AND THE POLITICS OF MULTILATERALISM

We have already seen that food aid programmes were originally launched as one of the means used by the government of the United States to solve the problems it was facing as a result of the accumulation of massive cereals surpluses. The WFP was established in the early 1960s and, since 1968, the EEC has been an important donor. The initiative taken by the United Nations and the FAO to establish the WFP represented an attempt to place such programmes under multilateral auspices.

Moreover, the important role played by the EEC, particularly after its enlargement to include two long-standing donors (Denmark and the United Kingdom), introduced an additional multilateral dimension to the overall food-aid situation. The volume of aid channelled through multilateral agencies has been growing steadily, but the question which deserves our attention is whether or not this particular type of aid is "different" from traditional bilateral aid, at least as it is perceived by recipient countries.

No doubt, developing countries—whether or not they receive such aid—as well as some of the "rich" members of the United Nations have been pressing for more multilateralism in foreign assistance, precisely because it does introduce a "different" dimension in the donor-recipient relationship. The fact that a third party—the Secretariat—intercedes between the donor and the recipient and that decisions concerning individual country projects become part of an overall approach to the issues and are not, formally at least, considered in the sole framework of dependence relations does make a "difference" in the eyes of recipients. This is not the occasion to discuss the perceptions of and expectations raised by the development of multilateralism; we should note, none the less, that in this very sensitive field of food-aid governments and elites in recipient countries have always shown a clear preference for multilateral programmes. Whether or not this perceived "difference" corresponds to the reality of donor-recipient relations in the framework of multilateral programmes is important, but to the extent that perceptions are an essential part of power relations—that is of politics—they cannot be divorced from reality.

When examining the way decisions are made in multilateral bodies in the UN family, it becomes clear that, in the last resort, no food aid is channelled to recipients which are not approved by the authorities of the country where the aid originates. The very nature of this type of assistance, which is largely composed of goods and services whose origins are identifiable, gives the major donors a leverage which is much greater than in other UN-sponsored activities. The WFP and other agencies do dispose of limited funds made up of cash contributions from some Western countries, but they represent a very small percentage of the total value of food aid. In spite of repeated calls for an increase of financial contributions to WFP, donors have been, on the whole, reluctant to diversify their participation by placing at its disposal funds which would make possible "untied" purchases of agricultural products, more adapted to the needs of recipients. The result has been that, on the one hand, deliveries continue to be "tied" politically and, on the other, the range of food products placed at the disposal of recipients continues to be limited to the surpluses held by donors.

In this connection, however, it is worth mentioning that the nature of the European Community's surpluses, added to its institutional structure which places the Commission in a central position in its decision-making process, brings the EEC food-aid activities closer to the needs and to the expectations of recipient countries than other multilateral programmes. First, the fact that the EEC is the only major donor which supplies the WFP and other multilateral agencies—as well as the recipients of its "bilateral" programmes—with large quantities of non-cereal products introduces into its food-aid activities the diversity which is almost totally absent from other programmes. This qualitative aspect, due essentially to the nature of

EEC's surpluses, represents a great asset in the eyes of recipients. Second, the role played by the Commission in the establishment and in the implementation of EEC's programmes introduces an element of "objectivity" which is also appreciated by recipient countries. No doubt the Commission takes into account the views of member governments when it puts forth its proposals, but the very nature of Community decision-making tends to "dilute" the political or trade interests of any single member state. This last characteristic in itself, which is also reflected in the Community's development assistance programmes, distinguishes its food activities from those—bilateral or multilateral—which are "tied" as to their contents and as to their destination.

Seen from the viewpoint of recipient countries, multilateral food aid possesses certain qualities which make it more "attractive" than bilateral aid. With few exceptions, however, the differences between the two types of programmes, in terms of their political "acceptability", are limited. Recent developments, which have brought into the donors' group some oil-producing developing countries, and the insistence on the part of some of the traditional donors—Scandinavian countries, the Netherlands, etc.—to diversify and to "untie" multilateral programmes may eventually have an impact. But, for the time being, their domination by the United States is still a fact with which recipient countries are faced, in the day-to-day operations of the programmes.

V. Conclusion

The very fact that we have considered this paper as a "critical appraisal" led us to draw all along partial conclusions. Little can be added at this stage, but we should underline some points which may otherwise escape the reader's attention.

First, international food-aid programmes—no matter what their origins and nature—cannot possibly have a decisive impact on the nutritional situation of developing countries. This is true independently of their volume, of their functional effectiveness or of their organizational efficiency. Although this has not been the principal form of our paper, we have repeatedly referred to the inadequacy of all such programmes, when faced with the structural causes of malnutrition. The problem of hunger is but one facet of the overall structure of maldistribution of resources which characterizes the present international order. Other papers written for this Project offer convincing evidence that, in the last analysis, there is no real shortage of food supplies in those parts of the world which receive food aid. Maldistribution of international, regional and national resources is part of the same structure, which finds its expression in the patterns of international foodstuffs trade, as well as in the "savage" development of many Third World countries. Moreover, the persistence, at the national level, of social structures which tend to perpetuate and which draw their strength from maldistribution of wealth is also characteristic of the present international order. In this context, food-aid programmes are not only quantitatively inadequate; they serve the purpose of "filling the gaps" in the nutritional supplies to developing countries, whenever the shortages reach certain thresholds. Emergency programmes are usually launched when the perception of human suffering reaches a threshold which is considered unacceptable by public opinion and decision-makers in donor countries. As for "regular" programmes, they are generally related to the thresholds leading to national or international unrest and/or violence. When food exporting countries like Brazil or India receive food aid, these are typically actions aimed at "filling the gaps" created by the structural deficiencies we mentioned above.

Having made such a categorical statement, however, it is not our intention to suggest that these programmes are unnecessary. Quite to the contrary, in the face of large-scale human suffering in so many developing countries—no matter what its origins are—those who control food surpluses or are able to acquire them should be induced to increase the volume of aid and to improve its quality. At the same time, we consider it important, from a policy viewpoint, to stress the fact that such programmes can only bring about temporary relief; because the roots of chronic food shortages are to be found in the structure of the international order, which in turn is the mainstay of national socio-economic structures perpetuating the maldistribution of resources.

This leads us to our second conclusion that any significant improvements in multilateral action in this field can only come about if food aid is integrated into larger international development strategies and programmes. This particular point does receive extensive lip service, but little has been done up to now to make it part of specific policies and actions. We should note, in this respect, that the structural obstacles to the solution of developing countries' nutritional problems are compounded by the organizational and bureaucratic structures in donor countries' and international administrations. The fragmentation of international development activities is essentially due to the inability or to the refusal of policy-makers to adopt a comprehensive approach to international development co-operation. However, the vested interests of national and international bureaucracies in keeping control of "their" programmes is a factor which must also be taken into account. To that extent institutional reform in the United Nations system can have a beneficial impact on the formulation and conduct of international food-aid policies. A closer integration of food-aid actions into larger agricultural and rural development programmes should become a policy objective of bilateral and multilateral donors. The non-separability of international activities aimed at the solution of developing countries' nutritional problems should be recognized as a guiding principle by donors and recipients alike; but we should not lose sight of the socio-political implications of policies whose success would be dependent on the transformation of the international and national food-production and food-trade structures.

Notwithstanding the constraints which prevent international organizations from engaging in activities which endanger the interests of key decision-makers, our examination of multilateral food-aid programmes leads us to the conclusion that their persistent failure to bring about any lasting solution to the developing countries' nutritional problem is already having an impact on multilateral decision-making. The evolution of the IBRD's policies over the past 5 years and its apparent willingness to modify them in the light of its experience is but one indication which confirms this point. Naturally, much more can and should be done in this direction. In our view, the next steps should be to obtain a higher degree of programme integration involving the Bank, the WFP and FAO. These institutions perform different but complementary tasks and the emerging United Nations development structure should become the focal point for the formulation of long-term comprehensive policies in the field of nutrition. In stating this objective, we are perfectly aware of the difficulty to bring into the new structure institutions jealous of their "independence'', such as the IBRD and the FAO. We do believe, however, that the coalitions of secretariats, some donors and some recipients may, if properly motivated, move the United Nations system in the direction of greater policy integration.

Our third and last conclusion is that in the face of the formidable obstacles lying in the way of any meaningful long-term actions in this field, scholars and other observers of multilateral organizations have the responsibility not only to analyse, but also to evaluate and formulate normative conclusions. No matter how ''unrealistic'' some of our recommendations may appear, we are firmly convinced that they ultimately do have an effect on decision-makers. This is particularly true when certain myths are destroyed, as is the case in the studies conducted by Rolando Garcia and his colleagues. Policy-makers may refuse to draw the appropriate conclusions when presented with analyses and evaluations which tend to ''demystify'' reality, as it has been perceived over the years. We should, however, pursue our efforts in this direction; because in the last resort, ''truth is wholesome'' in itself.

Bibliography

I. SOURCES

A. *Governmental documents*

1. Executive

United States International Economic Policy in an Interdependent World—Report to the President submitted by the Commission on International Trade and Investment Policy, Washington, 1971, 307 pp.

The Overseas Food Donation Program—Its constraints and problems—Report to the Congress by the Comptroller General of the United States, Washington, General Accounting Office, 1975, 57 pp.

The World Food Program—How the U.S. can help improve it—Report to the Senate Committee on Governmental Affairs by the Comptroller General of the United States, Washington, General Accounting Office, 1977, 40 pp.

2. Congress

(a) US Congress Hearings

US Foreign Agricultural Trade Policy—Hearing before the Subcommittee on Foreign Agricultural Policy of the Committee on Foreign Agricultural Policy of the Committee on Agriculture and Forestry United States Senate, Washington, US Government Printing Office, March 1973, iv-650 pp.

Export Control Policy—Hearing before the Subcommittee on Foreign Agricultural Policy of the Committee on Agriculture and Forestry United States Senate, Washington, US Government Printing Office, July 1973, 363 pp.

World Hunger, Health, and Refugee Problems, Part 1: Crisis in West Africa—Hearing before the Subcommittee to Investigate Problems Connected with Refugees and Escapees of the Committee on the Judiciary United States Senate, Washington, US Government Printing Office, July 1973, 140 pp.

World Hunger, Health, and Refugee Problems, Part II: Food Scarcity, Nutrition, and Health—Hearing before the Subcommittee to Investigate Problems Connected with Refugees and Escapees of the Committee on the Judiciary and the Subcommittee on Health of the Committee on Labor and Public Welfare United States Senate, Washington, US Government Printing Office, October 1973, 370 pp.

World Hunger, Health, and Refugee Problems, Part III: Development and Food Needs—Hearing before the Subcommittee to Investigate Problems Connected with Refugees and Escapees of the Committee on the Judiciary and the Subcommittee on Health of the Committee on Labor and Public Welfare United States Senate, Washington, US Government Printing Office, October 1973, 152 pp.

World Hunger, Health, and Refugee Problems, Part IV: Famine in Africa—Hearing before the Subcommittee to Investigate Problems Connected with Refugees and Escapees of the Committee on the Judiciary and the Subcommittee on Health of the Committee on Labor and Public Welfare United States Senate, Washington, US Government Printing Office, March 1974, 218 pp.

Disaster Relief—Hearing before the Committee on Foreign Relations United States Senate, Washington, US Government Printing Office, March 1974, 87 pp.

Foreign Food Assistance—Hearing before the Subcommittee on Foreign Agricultural Policy of the Committee on Agriculture and Forestry United States Senate, Washington, US Government Printing Office, April 1974, 111 pp.

National Nutrition Policy Study—Hearings before the Select Committee on Nutrition and Human Needs of the United States Senate, Part 1 - Famine and the World Situation, Washington, US Government Printing Office, June 1974, 269 pp.

National Nutrition Policy Study—Hearings before the Select Committee on Nutrition and Human Needs of the United States Senate, Part 2 - Nutrition and the International Situation, Washington, US Government Printing Office, June 1974, 424 pp.

World Population and Food Supply and Demand Situation Hearings before the Subcommittee on Department Operations of the Committee on Agricultural House of Representatives, Washington, US Government Printing Office, July 1974, 188 pp.

World Hunger, Health, and Refugee Problems, Part V: Human Disasters in Cyprus, Bangladesh, Africa— Hearing before the Subcommittee to Investigate Problems Connected with Refugees and Escapees of the Committee on the Judiciary and the Subcommittee on Health of the Committee on Labor and Public Welfare United States Senate, Washington, US Government Printing Office, August 1974, 208 pp.

Food Relief Programs—Hearing before the Subcommittee on Department Operations of the Committee on Agriculture House of Representatives, Washington, US Government Printing Office, November 1974, 67 pp.

Implementation of World Food Conference Recommendations—Hearing before the Subcommittee on Foreign Agricultural Policy of the Committee on Agriculture and Forestry United States Senate, Washington, US Government Printing Office, May 1975, 95 pp.

Exemption of Foreign-owned Reserves from Export Controls—Hearing before the Subcommittee on Foreign Agricultural Policy of the Committee on Agriculture and Forestry United States Senate, Washington, US Government Printing Office, May 1975, 34 pp.

Food Problems of Developing Countries: Implications for US Policy—Hearings before the Subcommittee on International Resources, Food, and Energy of the Committee on International Relations House of Representatives, Washington, US Government Printing Office, May 1975, 355 pp.

World Hunger, Health, and Refugee Problems, Part VI: Special Study Mission to Africa, Asia and Middle East—Hearings before the Subcommittee on Refugees Connected with Refugees and Escapees of the Committee on Health of the Committee on Labor and Public Welfare United States Senate, Washington, US Government Printing Office, June 1975, vi-617 pp.

Implementation of World Food Conference Recommendations—Hearing before the Subcommittee on Foreign Agricultural Policy of the Committee on Agriculture and Forestry United States Senate, Washington, US Government Printing Office, November 1975, 128 pp.

US International Grain Policy: Sales and Management—Hearing before the Subcommittee on International Resources, Food, and Energy of the Committee on International Relations House of Representatives, Washington, US Government Printing Office, December 1975, 34 pp.

Future of Food Aid—Hearings before the Subcommittee on Foreign Agricultural Policy of the Committee on Agriculture, Nutrition, and Forestry United States Senate, Washington, US Government Printing Office, April 1977, 137 pp.

(b) US Congress: Reports

1. 93rd Congress - 1st Session

Agricultural Trade and the Proposed Round of Multilateral Negotiations, Washington, US Government Printing Office, 1973.

2. 93rd Congress - 2nd Session

Report on Nutrition and the International Situation, Washington, US Government Printing Office, 1974.
Malthus and America, Washington, US Government Printing Office, 1974.
National Nutrition Policy: Nutrition and the International Situation-III, Washington, US Government Printing Office, 1974.

3. 94th Congress - 1st Session

Hunger and Diplomacy: A Perspective on the US Role at the World Food Conference, Washington, US Government Printing Office, 1975.

4. 94th Congress - 2nd Session

Implementation of Recommendations of the World Food Conference, Washington, US Government Printing Office, 1976.

Use of US Food Resources for Diplomatic Purposes - An Examination of the Issues, Washington, US Government Printing Office, 1977.

5. 95th Congress - 1st Session

The US Proposal for an International Grain Reserves System - II, Washington, US Government Printing Office, 1977.

B. Intergovernmental International Organizations documents

1. United Nations

(a) General Assembly

Report of The World Food Council, 1975, General Assembly, Official Records: Thirtieth Session, Supplement No. 19 (A/10019), 23 pp.
Report of The World Food Council on the work of its second session, 14-17 June 1976, General Assembly, Official Records: Thirty-first Session, Supplement No. 19 (A/31/19), 79 pp.
Report of the World Food Council on the work of its third session, 20-24 June 1977, General Assembly, Official Records: Thirty-second Session, Supplement No. 19 (A/32/19), 40 pp.
Rapport du Conseil Mondial de L'Alimentation sur les travaux de sa quatrième session, 12-15 juin 1978, Assemblée Générale, Documents Officiels: Trente-troisième Session, Supplément No. 19 (A/33/19), 53 pp.

(b) United Nations World Food Conference

Assessment of the World Food Situation present and future, E/CONF. 65/3, 1974.

(c) United Nations World Food Council

Review of the World Food Situation and the Critical Issues with which the Council Should Be Concerned, doc. WFC/6, 2 May 1975, 5 pp.
Review of the World Food Situation and the Critical Issues with which the Council Should Be Concerned, doc. WFC/5, 5 May 1975, 3 pp.
Progress Report on the Implementation of Resolutions Adopted by the General Assembly and the World Food Conference, doc. WFC/3, 15 May 1975, 4 pp.
Review of the World Food Situation and the Critical Issues with which the Council Should Be Concerned, doc. WFC/12, 20 May 1975, 9 pp.

2. Food and Agriculture Organization (FAO)

Ten Years of World Food Programme Development Aid, Rome, 1973, 72 pp.
Council—Food and Agriculture Organization of the United Nations—Rome, CL 65/6, March 1975, 8 pp.
Food Aid Bulletin, No. 2, April 78, 70 pp.

3. World Food Programme

(a) Intergovernmental Committee

Thirteenth Annual Report of the United Nations/FAO Intergovernmental Committee of the World Food Programme to the Economic and Social Council of the United Nations and to the Council of FAO, doc. WFP/IGC: 27/18, April 1975, 21 pp.
Interim Evaluation Report, doc. WFP/CFA: 1/10 Add. C2, January 1976, 31 pp.
Interim Evaluation Report, doc. WFP/CFA: 1/10 Add. B4, February 1976, 18 pp.

(b) Committee on Food Aid Policies and Programmes

Interim Evaluation and Terminal Reports—Studies of the Role of Food Aid in relation to Trade and Agricultural Development in Botswana, Lesotho and the Arab Republic of Egypt, doc. WFP/CFA: 1/10 Add. 1, April 1976, 30 pp.
Interim Evaluation Report, doc. WFP/CFA: 1/10 Add. C7, April 1976, 66 pp.
Food Aid and Habitat—World Food Programme Assistance for Human Settlements, doc. A/CONF. 70/B/9, May 1976, 32 pp.
Fourteenth Annual Report of the IGC/CFA to ECOSOC and the FAO Council and First Report of the CFA to the World Food Council, doc. WFP/CFA: 1/21, June 1976, 7 pp.
Coordination of Bilateral and Multilateral Food Aid, doc. WFP/CFA: 2/7-B, November 1976, 10 pp.
Annual Statement of the Executive Director on the Development of the Programme, doc. WFP/CFA: 3/4, March 1977, 26 pp.
Food Aid Policies, Including in Particular a Review of the Implementation of Recommendations Adopted, doc. WFP/CFA: 3/7-A, March 1977, 14 pp.

Assessment of Food Aid Requirements and of Food Aid Targets for Cereals—Possible Approaches, doc. WFP/CFA: 3/7-B, March 1977, 10 pp.

Establishment of Minimum Food Aid Targets for Dairy and Fish Products, Oils and Fats—Further Consideration, doc. WFP/CFA: 3/7-C, April 1977, 21 pp.

Annual Statement of the Executive Director on the Development of the Programme—Information on resources updated to 31 March 1977, doc. WFP/CFA: 3/4 Add. 1, May 1977, 19 pp.

Second Annual Report of the CFA to ECOSOC, the FAO Council and the World Food Council, doc. WFP/CFA: 3/16, May 1977, 7 pp.

Interim Evaluation Summary Report, doc. WFP/CFA: 3/14 Add. All, Revision 1, November 1977, 18 pp.

Annual Report of the Executive Director on the Development of the Programme, doc. WFP/CFA: 5/4, February 1978, 23 pp.

Annual Report of the Executive Director on the Development of the Programme—Information updated to 28 February 1978—Contents, doc. WFP/CFA: 5/4 Add. 2, March 1978, 5 pp.

Review of Progress towards the Implementation of an Improved Food Aid Policy in Accordance with the Recommendations of the World Food Conference and the World Food Council, doc. WFP/CFA: 5/5-A, March 1978, 18 pp.

Interim Report on the Assessment of Food Aid Requirements, Including the Question of Food Aid Targets, doc. WFP/CFA: 5/5-B, March 1978, 26 pp.

A Survey of Studies of Food Aid, doc. WFP/CFA: 5/5-C, March 1978, 69 pp.

Third Annual Report of the CFA to ECOSOC, the FAO Council and the World Food Council, doc. WFP/CFA: 5/17, April 1978, 6 pp.

Report of the Executive Director—Outline, doc. WFP/CFA: 6/4, July 1978, 29 pp.

Annual Report of the Executive Director on Transportation, Progress Report on Partial Self-insurance, doc. WFP/CFA: 6/12 Add. 1, July 1978, 5 pp.

Annual Report of the Executive Director on Transportation, doc. WFP/CFA: 6/12, August 1978, 10 pp.

Report on Budgetary Performance—1977—Submission by the Executive Director, doc. WFP/CFA: 6/13, August 1978, 11 pp.

Report on Budgetary Performance (1977)—Comments on the FAO Finance Committee (May 1978). doc. WFP/CFA: 6/13 Add. 1, August 1978, 2 pp.

Report by the Executive Director, Contents, doc. WFP/CFA: 6/6, September 1978, 26 pp.

4. Organization for Economic Co-operation and Development

Food Aid, Paris, OECD, 1974, 134 pp.

II. WORKS

Huguel, Catherine, *L'Aide alimentaire—Analyse comparative,* Paris, Presses Universitaires de France, 1977, 103 pp.

Weiss, Thomas, G. and Jordan, Robert, S., *The World Food Conference and Global Problem Salving,* New York, Praeger Publishers Inc., 1976, xii-170 pp.

World Hunger—Causes and Remedies, Amsterdam, Transnational Institute, 1974, 64-xix pp.

Notes

1. We use the term "notable exception" because, in fact, EEC's programmes are multilateral in their very structure, whether the aid is channelled through other international agencies or directly. We shall devote a special section of this paper to the EEC programmes.

2. *What Now?* Report prepared on the occasion of the Seventh Special Session of the General Assembly under the auspices of the Dag Hammarskjöld Foundation, published in *Development Dialogue,* 1975, Nos. 1-2.

3. *What Now? op. cit.,* p. 25.

4. The recently established International Foundation for Development alternatives, with headquarters in Nyon, Switzerland, aims precisely in carrying out such research, in co-operation with a wide network of research centres the world over.

5. *Ibid.,* p. 26.

6. *Ibid.,* p. 30.

7. These are: the Programme Committee, the Finance Committee, the Committee of Agriculture, the Committee on Commodity Problems, the Committee on Fisheries, the Committee on Forestry, the Committee on World Food Security and the Committee on Constitutional and Legal Matters.

8. Department of Economic and Social Policy, Agriculture, Forestry, Fisheries, Development, General Affairs and Information, Administration and Finance.

9. It should be noted, however, that approximately half of this increase was due to the devaluation of the US dollar, and the remaining additional amount became necessary in order to enable the Organization to meet its obligations following the World Food Conference.

10. See Thomas G. Weiss and Robert S. Jordan, *The World Food Conference and Global Problems Solving,* published in co-operation with the United Nations Institute for Training and Research, Praeger Publishers, New York, Washington, London, 1976, 170 pp., for useful information on these issues.

11. These were: Canada, Denmark, EEC, the FRG, the Netherlands, Norway, Saudi Arabia, Sweden, the United Kingdom and the United States.

12. In Europe, aid has been given to Turkey and Cyprus.

13. The WFP evaluation activities are, in many respects, unique in the UN family. Not only are evaluation reports published, but the informed reader draws the impression that they contain the "unembellished" conclusions of the evaluation teams. To that extent, they are valuable sources of information and analysis of the impact of food-aid programmes.

14. As of 31 March 1978, $626.9 million had been pledged for 1978-9 and $689 million for 1979-80.

15. Whether or not these predictions were entirely founded is another matter; the important fact was the perception of imminent catastrophes on the part influential sectors of western public opinion, as well as of many decision-makers.

16. More detailed information on the Conference is to be found in: Thomas G. Weiss and Robert S. Jordan, *The World Food Conference and Global Problem Solving,* published in co-operation with UNITAR, New York, Praeger, 1976, 170 pp; and Committee on International Relations, US House of Representatives, Report submitted by the Agency for International Development, "Implementation of Recommendations of the World Food Conference", Washington, Government Printing Office, 1976, 76 pp.

17. This is true, in spite of their authors' inhibitions when they were faced with the need to discuss critically the prevailing food trade structures.

18. *Op. cit.,* p. 99.

19. Report to the General Assembly, United Nations, *Official Records,* Thirtieth Session, Supplement No, 19 (A/10019), New York, 1975, par. 62.

20. *Op. cit.*

21. *Op. cit.,* par. 64.

22. *Op. cit.,* par. 65.

23. The data in this sub-section are drawn essentially from various documents of the WFP and, more particularly, from documents WFP/CFA: 3/7-A, March 1977 and WFP/CFA: 6/4, July 1978.

24. See: *American Foreign Food Assistance, Public Law 480 and Related Materials, Report to the Committee on Agriculture and Forestry,* US Senate, US Government Printing Office, Washington, DC, 1976, pp. v-vi.

25. One of the most comprehensive reports on this subject is the one presented by the Controller General to the Senate Committee on Governmental Affairs on 16 May, 1977, entitled *The World Food Programme—how the US can help improve it.* ID-77-16.

CHAPTER 6

A Structural Approach for Diagnosing the Impact of Climatic Anomalies

"Drought and Man" was intended as a study focused on the social, economic and political impact of a specific type of climatic fluctuation known as drought. This formulation, simple, direct and innocent in appearance, may, however, lead to misunderstandings. One obvious interpretation is that drought is a purely natural phenomenon, independent of society, which is in turn the victim of its occurrence. Were this the case, we should have, on the one hand, a physical agent operating on a certain territory and, on the other hand, a society receiving its impact. This scheme has been questioned by many authors. We believe, however, that the criticism has very seldom been pushed sufficiently far to identify clearly the weakness in the argument, and to point the way to a more adequate methodology.

An increasing number of ecologists and economists are becoming aware of the role of socio-economic factors in some processes leading to a deterioration of the environment as, for instance, in the case of desertifiction. However, conflicts between man and nature, presented as an ecological problem on the one hand, and as a socio-economic problem on the other, have more often than not been approached as if both components were autonomous. Ecologists — even those using the most sophisticated models — as well as sociologists and economists, deal with the symmetrical problem (i.e. the socio-economic problem for the ecologists and the ecological problem for the sociologists and the economists) as something injected from outside into their models. But the two problems are only two aspects of a complex situation which may be better described with reference to the internal interactions within an all-embracing *system*. For here, we are evidently faced with a type of phenomenon where causes and effects, interactions and inversions, linear chains and feed-backs are mixed in an integrated, complex whole. The soil of a certain territory, the atmosphere above it, and the human settlements located and working on it, are not entities to be considered in isolation. They cannot be studied independently of each other, nor can the results be assembled in a unidirectional explicative scheme. They constitute a totality, a single system; they are only "parts" or "elements" or "components" interacting all the time within the system.

We may analyse the components of the system in quite different ways, each component being itself a subsystem which has, at a certain moment, a given structure and varying number of constituent parts.

In a first approximation, we may consider the whole system as constituted by four components or subsystems which for the purposes of this discussion we call:

(a) A *physical component,* which we shall refer to here as the "atmosphere".[1]

  (b) A *physico-biological component,* briefly called the "soil" (including the basic physico-chemical structure and the recycling of nutrients by the natural fauna and flora).
  (c) A *man-generated biological component.*
  (d) A *socio-economic component,* which we shall designate as "human activities".

The four components are interrelated in the way shown in Fig. 6.1. The diagram represents the set of interactions which determine the state of the system at a given moment. Some of the interactions, represented by double arrows in the diagram, such as those between human activities and the biological subsystem, are rather obvious. The cycles (a) and (b) are perhaps less obvious.

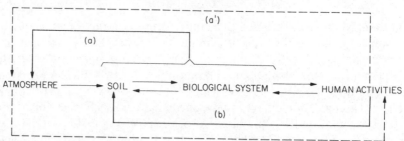

Fig.6.1 Interrelations and cycles among the components of an integrated ecological system.

Cycle (a) represents the interdependence between the soil and its vegetation cover, considered to be a unit, and the atmosphere. The upper branch refers to feedback processes such as those originating in modifications of the albedo (Charney's theory, see discussion in Chapter 9 of Volume 1).

Cycle (b) takes into account the modification of the soil resulting from human activity. A typical example may be certain cases of salinization processes produced by irrigation.

As a result of this double cycle, the soil receives water from the atmosphere, but its accumulation and distribution capability is conditioned by the biological system as well as by the way humans use the soil. In turn, the soil surface may induce changes in the field of motion of the atmosphere above it which may either favour or oppose cloud formation and precipitation. The biological system, which emerges in equilibrium with certain conditions of water accumulation and distribution and certain soil properties, constitutes, together with the soil, a single entity interacting with the atmosphere, on the one hand, and establishing the production options open to human activities, on the other.

Cycle (a') represents the direct action of man on the atmosphere leading to changes in the composition (e.g. increase in CO_2), which modify the radiation balance and may lead to significant changes in the atmospheric circulation and thus alter climatic conditions.

A change in the system may therefore be generated in any subsystem, and lead to modifications in all the other components through the chain of interactions and positive or negative feedbacks.

Our specific problem can therefore be formulated as an analysis of the conditions under which a system of interactions and cycles remains unchanged or undergoes significant changes. But an adequate integration of physico-biological and socio-economic factors in a coherent system, with an internal dynamics determined by the actual interactions among its components, has proved to be a difficult task.

Current methods of system analysis do not carry us far enough. It also should be kept in mind that numerical models are not explanatory models. They are only research tools to investigate possible explanatory mechanisms of a given process, to make long and interrelated calculations too tedious to do by hand.

There is, however, another way of looking at the problem and we shall deal with it below.

A second approximation to a model of interactions in a complex system formed by a natural and social environment requires a higher degree of desegregation of the component units. The definition of the system itself also requires more detailed consideration. The following explanations refer to Fig. 6.2.

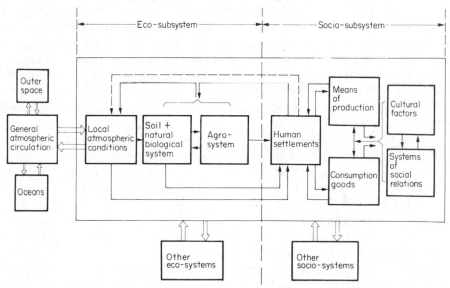

Fig.6.2. A socio-ecosystem as an open system with in- and outflows.

It should first be emphasized that the definition of a system is somewhat arbitrary. It may refer to a country, or to a region within a country, or to a continental region including more than one country. Sometimes it is useful to consider a system which coincides with a geographical area, having an identifiable ecological, economic or political unity. A more structural characterization of a system is, however, preferable, and will be given below.

The large rectangle in Fig. 6.2 represents the boundaries of a given system, however it may be defined. We shall call this system a *socio-ecosystem*. In an earlier version, we used the expression ecosystem, in an extended sense, to refer to the whole system. Although we would prefer to keep this terminology, we found it liable to lead to misunderstandings. Ecosystems are therefore considered, in this report, in the narrower sense, as subsystems of the whole system.

The human activities of Fig. 6.1 have been spelled out in their various components, going down to the system[2] of social relations and to the cultural factors, which determine production relations, utilization of certain means of production, consumption habits, and so on, and, in turn, are modified by them.

At the other end of the diagram, it is shown how the local atmospheric conditions (local climate) are the result of a quite complex set of interrelations.

The double arrows indicate the interactions of the given system with other systems. The latter will be called, briefly, "the external world". These interactions are fluxes entering the system or coming out of it. It may be fluxes of matter such as air masses, running water, products, migrations of animals or people, etc. Or fluxes of energy in any of its forms. Variations of these fluxes will be called external fluctuations or external perturbations.

There are also sources and sinks inside the system: population changes (people die, children are born); political and economic power may be displaced, changing production patterns for instance; and so on. Variations of all these factors will be called internal fluctuations or internal perturbations.

The complexity of a given system depends quite obviously on the kind of its components. For instance, the ecological subsystem may be richer or poorer, in any sense of these words. But it also depends on the kind of interrelations among the components. In fact, it is through the set of all interrelations among the components that a system is defined as such. They determine the structure of the system. They provide the criterion to consider a set of elements as components of one entity having the "unity" referred to above which is necessary for identifying it as a single system.

A socio-ecosystem is therefore a single entity which is characterized by a number of components having among them a definite set of internal relations that define its structure, and which is in relation with other systems through exchanges (fluxes) of matter, energy, etc. The emphasis here is on the structure, rather than on the components themselves. As a structured entity, the system has properties which do not result from a simple addition of all component properties. In fact, the most significant aspects of the evolution of a system are the changes in its structural properties. This is an essential point to which we shall return.

In order to clarify the assertions made above, we now need to make a brief incursion into a theoretical approach to the dynamics of systems which, as indicated below in a footnote, departs from the current methods of system analysis.[3] Recent advances in several fields dealing with the evolution of natural systems - covering a wide range of disciplines including Biology, Physico-Chemistry, Fluid Dyamics, Populations Dynamics - have led us to a much deeper understanding of their dynamic properties. The theories which have been developed in this connection now offer a new conceptual framework to approach the analysis of highly complex systems such as those we are dealing with.

We shall introduce a certain basic terminology, borrowed from Thermodynamics, which will help to fix ideas. From a thermodynamic point of view, systems are classified in three broad categories: *isolated* systems, confined within boundaries that do not allow exchanges of either matter or energy with their environment; *closed* systems, exchanging only energy with their environment; and *open* systems, exchanging both matter and energy. Classical thermodynamic theory deals only with isolated or closed physical or physiochemical systems. The theory is mainly concerned with systems that, starting from a given initial state (defined by the values of the state variables), evolve towards steady-state conditions, i.e. they go asymptotically towards a certain state, the properties of which do not change with time (equilibrium conditions). Perturbations introduced into the system, i.e. departures from equilibrium conditions, may be such that the system returns to equilibrium by a succession of states which repeat in reverse order the changes produced by the perturbations. The system is said to have undergone a reversible process. Classical thermodynamics is by and large a thermodynamics of reversible processes. Strictly speaking this applies, conceptually, only to laboratory-controlled experiments. However, it is a remarkable fact that some natural systems, under carefully specified conditions, behave as closed sytems. Even the atmosphere may be treated as such for short periods of time.

When a system is open, i.e. exchanges matter and energy with its environment, the situation becomes much more complex. It is only in the last 20 years or so that important progress has been made in the study of such systems. Open systems may undergo processes which may be classified into two very characteristic types. One class of phenomena obtains when the variables defining the state of the system fluctuate in such a way that their values do not depart very much from the values they have under equilibrium conditions. The system under these conditions has a characteristic configuration, i.e. a distribution of its macroscopic properties, which is called an equilibrium structure.

A system in equilibrium has mechanisms of response to peturbations. The changes introduced by a perturbation generate forces opposing the changes. A well-known example is provided by the principle of Le Châtelier-Braun: "Any system in chemical equilibrium undergoes, as a result of a variation in one of the factors governing the equilibrium, a compensating change in a direction such that, had this change occurred alone, it would have produced a variation of the factor considered in the opposite direction." Internal responses of this type are usually called negative feed-backs. In biology they are called homeostatic mechanisms, a term which is now being used by ecologists. These mechanisms are responsible for the stability of the system, i.e. for its capacity to return to equilibrium after departing from it.

The second type of process obtains when an external perturbation or internal fluctuations of the state variables occur beyond a certain threshold, and take the system away from equilibrium. In such a case the internal responses arise which amplify the perturbation. The structure is no longer stable. The released instabilities lead the system to a new state of self-organization. The system may thus acquire a new structure which is then kept stable if the fluxes of matter and energy (i.e. the exchanges with the environment) are kept constant. The new structure of the system, which, we repeat, is kept stable by the flows of matter and energy into the system or out of the system, is called dissipative structure.[4]

The self-organization of matter in open systems which are far from an equilibrium state is a subject which has led in recent years to very striking results. It has served to clarify the internal mechanisms of natural systems jumping from one state, with a characteristic structure, to another state, with a different structure, in a typical time sequence. The theory of dissipative structures has also provided an explanation for the spontaneous emergence of order in a previously structureless system. It has been shown, for instance, that a non-linear chemical system not in thermodynamic equilibrium, can assume a very variegated spatial organization and pattern formation and that the introduction of diffusion leads to a spontaneous self-organization process in a previously homogenous medium.

The analysis of the stability concepts we have just summarized when applied to the system described above (Fig. 6.2), conceived as an open system, lead to several relation notions. We identify three elemental characteristics of a system:

(i) *Endurance*: the power or capacity which a given system has of undergoing a perturbation without departing from near-equilibrium conditions.

(ii) *Resilience*: the capacity of resuming the original equilibrium conditions after a departure produced by a perturbation.

(iii) *Fragility*: the property of a system that makes it liable to structural changes under the action of low endurance and low resilience.

The fragility of a system is the manifestation of a property of its structure which we shall call *vulnerability*. In this precise sense, vulnerability is the property of a structure that makes it unstable under the action of perturbations.

A few comments may serve to clarify the above definitions:

—Systems of high resilience and high endurance are only altered under very strong perturbations, but they recover the initial state.

—Systems of high resilience and low endurance are easily altered, but they recover the initial state.

—Systems of low resilience and high endurance are resistant to perturbations, but once they are altered they may not return to the initial state when let alone after a perturbation. They have a vulnerable structure.

—Systems of low resilience and low endurance are fragile, hence they are easily altered, have a low capacity of recovery, and may not return to their initial state when they are let alone after a perturbation. These are systems with a highly vulnerable structure.

To sum up: a system may be more or less *fragile*; a *structure* is more or less *vulnerable*; a process may be reversible or irreversible; for a given *perturbation*, a system may be *stable* or *unstable*.

Let us apply these concepts to the analysis of some concrete situations. We shall first consider examples of processes which start as "natural phenomena".

Natural ecosystems are pre-adapted to climatic fluctuations. There are a number of well-known adaptation strategies which allow living organisms to survive, for instance, through drought pulses: deciduousness, hibernation mechanisms, high seed production in dry periods, etc. Agrosystems, i.e. systems of primary and secondard production created or managed by man, may have only very weak adaptation strategies for surviving drought. However, when an ecosystem is taken to a state of far-from-equilibrium conditions (for instance in the case of a prolonged drought) it may become unstable, i.e. there is no recovery to the original equilibrium conditions. The system may then undergo a complete change leading to the onset of new structures, i.e. new forms of organizations, under new equilibrium conditions. In the case of prolonged droughts, such an irreversible process may lead to desertification. In such cases, however, drought is one of the factors entering into the process, but not the only one.

Processes leading from drought to desertification can be seen in operation generally in territories with limited water resources and large seasonal variability, i.e. in semi-arid zones. Droughts operate in this case on natural ecosystems which are of low endurance and low resilience, i.e. highly fragile. But the vulnerability increases in *agro-systems* when the exploitation of ecological resources is extended beyond certain limits of risk which would thereby lead to disastrous conditions under a climatic stress. Since the agro-systems do not have in general homeostatic mechanisms to neutralize the drought pulse, they are the first to collapse. Natural ecosystems, even though they possess adaptation strategies to live with drought, may, however, retrograde when the drought brings an increase in the grazing pressure (either wild animals or domestic livestock) on a system which has naturally reduced its plant cover as a temporary adaptation mechanism to the drought.

Let us consider now an example where the "action" starts from the socio-subsystem.

A typical case is when foreign markets and capital investment set in motion certain processes which have a profound influence on the productive structure and "the way of life" in a given region. The starting-point may be the introduction of highly technological agricultural activities, oriented to the export market, which take the place of native subsistence economies. The space available for the pastoral systems and subsistence agriculture is reduced. These native systems are pushed to areas of very high fragility where they play a destructive role in the natural environment and generate a desertification process. A dramatic example of this type of situation leading to drastic socio-economic changes in the local population (regression in the income distribution and the social stratification, in the levels of living, in health and nutrition) can be found in the studies made by G. Martins Dias and also by D. Gross on north-eastern Brazil (cf. the Report on "Drought and Man", Volume 3). The advancement of agriculture using high-level technology—both dry farming and irrigation agriculture—has been the origin, directly or indirectly, of desertification processes which have been well documented in the Caatinga of Brazil, in the Columbian Goajira, in the Argentinian Chaco (Formosa), in the Paraguayan Chaco, and in many areas of Africa (cf. J. Morello, "Enfoque Integrado y Niveles de Analisis en la Zona Semiarida de America Latina").

The examples given above are intended to illustrate in what way we refer to the structural properties of the system as a whole to explain the effect of a given perturbation acting on the system. In both examples the "action" starts in one of the sub-systems (the ecosystem in the first case, and the socio-system in the second example), but the whole process can only be explained in terms of interactions between the sub-systems. In diagnosing a given situation with reference to a particular system, we have to make a careful distinction between:

(a) the factors that make the structure of a given system as it is;
(b) the properties that make the structure of a given system more vulnerable to certain perturbations.

With reference to (a), we should like to refer again to the theory of dissipative systems. Their essential characteristic is that they are open systems which adopt specific patterns of self-organization structure, as a response to the fluxes of matter, energy, etc., into and out of the system. At a given moment the structure is maintained by the fluxes. If the fluxes are cut off, the system becomes isolated and evolves towards a certain equilibrium structure. If the fluxes do not change beyond a certain threshold, some homeostatic mechanisms may provoke rearrangements in the internal components of the system, keeping the structure essentially constant. If the changes in the flux are large enough, the system will suffer more profound rearrangements leading to new patterns of self-organization, i.e. to new structures. The greater the stability of the system, the larger the perturbation needed to modify the structure of that system. An unstable system is therefore a fragile system which changes its structure under the action of small perturbations. Stable and unstable conditions correspond therefore to what we called above, low and high vulnerability respectively, of a given structure.

For a given perturbation, the stability properties of the system will determine whether or not the homeostatic mechanisms will function, keeping the structure constant. Moreover, once a perturbation is large enough to destabilize the system, the evolution of the process is no longer determined by the perturbation itself but by the nature of the system and the properties of the structure. This is the reason why relatively small perturbations may produce very large departures of a system from its initial conditions.

This is also the reason why the methodology of impact studies should be the analysis of processes and not the description of states, and these studies must go far beyond examination of the initial perturbation.

We may now go a little further in applying the notions referred to above to complex socio-ecosystems schematically represented in Fig. 6.2. We shall consider two typical examples of systems having quite different structures and undergoing similar "perturbations" which for obvious reasons we take to be some serious climatic anomalies.

Example 1 is a country with an agro-system which makes it self-sufficient for food. It has, in addition, an advanced social organization and a high economic level. A drought produces a failure of the crops. But the country either has enough stocks or is in a good position to import all the food needed. Moreover, there are social mechanisms to prevent side effects such as unemployment or underemployment, to provide credits for farmers and social assistance to rural workers. The country as a whole will feel some effects of the drought on the overall economy, but no direct effects such as shortage of food will be felt in any sector of the community. The social security schemes, on the one hand, and appropriate technologies, on the other, will act as homeostatic mechanisms to reverse the changes produced by the drought and restore equilibrium when the "perturbation" ceases. The system is *stable*. A good example was England in the 1976 drought.

Example 2 is a country with a food-producing system composed of large farms where most of the labour is undertaken by rural workers on a wage basis and with no social security schemes. The country has food stocks available on a commercial basis. A drought or a flood partially ruins the crops. The price of food goes up and speculation begins. Inflation sets in and salaries remain far behind price increases. The rural agricultural workers become unemployed. The food, although available, passes out of the reach of large sectors of the community. There are migrations of rural workers, to towns or to industrial centres, searching for jobs and food. The distribution of both the urban and rural population may undergo profound changes. After the "perturbation" is over the system is not restored to the previous equilibrium conditions: once the system passed beyond the point of instability, it evolved to a new form of self-organization, i.e. a new structure.

It is clear that in this example the society did not have homeostatic mechanisms. The perturbation did not need to go too far from the (precarious) equilibrium conditions to become amplified by the internal response mechanisms. The society had a *structural vulnerability,* which has nothing to do with the vulnerability of its crops to droughts or floods. In a situation like this, if the nutritional level of the population concerned was already low before the perturbation, the situation may end up with starvation even though there is no actual scarcity of food.

Notes

1. A more complete discussion of the climate system, of which the atmosphere is just one part, is found in Chapter 9 of Volume 1.

2. The use of the word "system" to refer to this subsubsystem does not present any ambiguity. We follow here the common practice in set theory where a subset is also called a set, so that one may talk without ambiguity about "the set of sets such that . . ." or "a set of subsets such that . . .".

3. The fact that natural systems can have several levels of self-organization is not depicted by current theories of "systems analysis". In fact, classical thermodynamics also fails to provide understanding for this feature of complex, highly-interactive systems. Classical thermodynamics, for example, through the famous second law, leads to the prediction that, given enough time, systems degenerate into homogeneity. Energy is equally distributed throughout the system. Thus we would always expect evolution towards the lowest degree of organization of the system. The tendency of biological systems to evolve such as to continually increase the level of organization had been a paradox. In attempts to reconcile biology with basic physics, Prigogine was led to new insights and new concepts in thermodynamics, for which he was awarded the Nobel Prize in Chemistry in 1977. We may compare this extension of classical thermodynamics as analogous to the work of Einstein in extending the concepts of Newton. The Climate system, as discussed in Chapter 9 (Volume 1 shows similarities to the new thermodynamic structures discussed by Prigogine.

Newton's explanation failed to be applicable to known astronomical problems as well as to later discoveries: atomic forces and the behaviour of particles at speeds approaching the speed of light. Einstein introduced new ideas which, for the case of large masses at moderate speeds, reduced Newtonian mechanics, and also explained the newly discovered phenomena.

CHAPTER 7

The Roots of Catastrophe
(Regional and National Case Studies)

A. Introduction

The aim of IFIAS studies, like the present Project, is to reach a deep understanding of the problems of the contemporary world and of the possible solutions for them. The ultimate motivation can only be expressed in terms of the well-being of mankind. Not of mankind as an abstract entity, a product of intellectual speculation. Not as a set of fictitious statistical parameters, but mankind as an ensemble of concrete individuals with their needs and their desires, their hopes, their satisfactions and their frustrations.

In this regard, the basis of our analysis is in direct opposition to a number of current analyses mainly made by "developmental" economists. We do not accept, for instance, that the increase of the GNP of a country should always be considered as an accomplishment (although economists often do so even when this increase meant that large sectors of the population had decreased their real salary below the limit required to have a decent life by any acceptable standards). When we look into food, we often find analyses along these lines. They would look into the demands on the markets, would consider the level of stocks and the current production of certain privileged foods, and on these bases will decide whether or not the situation is "normal", will predict variations and will make forecasts of "good years ahead" or "bad years ahead". The child of Mauritania or Haiti for whom every year is a bad year does not enter into these "estimated values". That child, as we have repeatedly emphasized, is an implicit integral part of the definition of what is considered to be a "normal situation".

However, when a "disaster" comes, it is that very child, whose parents will be blamed for bringing him into the world, who will be held responsible for his own suffering and the suffering of other hungry children. "If there were not so many children, there would be enough food for everybody." A very simple arithmetic presides this thought, simple-minded, more than simple, profoundly misleading and, more often than not, demonstrably false. Less simplistic explanations would include of course "external" factors: any combination of the apocalyptic horsemen referred to in the Introduction.

The position we have just outlined goes hand in hand with a certain brand of individualism according to which the solution of the social problems rest on the individuals as such. Education is usually called upon: each individual has to learn how to "adjust" himself to society, to work more, to produce more, to reproduce himself less, and to look after his environment. This fallacious position mixes up causes and effects. It can never provide the appropriate remedies, as it starts with the wrong diagnosis.

In the preceding chapter we have attempted a reformulation of the problems from a quite different approach. Neither a statistical average, nor a singular autonomous case, each individual is an element of a certain structure, of a totality, the properties of which are not the simple addition of the properties of the elements, and are such that they become "averaged-*out*" by the current statistical analysis. In the present chapter we intend to apply these ideas to the specific study of concrete cases. We shall endeavour to find out what type of structures are characteristic of some given countries or regions, what their laws are, how they operate. This can only be studied with reference to each particular society, having specific features, at a certain historical moment, but being also the result of an evolution which differs from the evolution of other societies appearing to be "similar". We do not claim that our study has succeeded in reaching the depths of all problems involved in each case study. This would require a time-scale and resources far beyond the strict limitations of this Project. Notwithstanding, we believe that we have assembled some examples which are sufficiently clear to provide a solid background to the working hypothesis which led most of the research carried out in this Project.

In selecting the cases to be studied, we had to make a difficult choice. As it is well known, to select means to exclude. The selection of the cases which will be analysed below was made on a combination of several criteria: the intrinsic importance of the case, its representativeness, the availability of information, the availability of research teams or individuals willing to undertake the study and having similar motivations. Some case studies were carried out because they were a good example of how strongly a drought may disrupt the life of a society. Other case studies were undertaken to show how similar disruptions have occurred in the absence of drought or any other *natural* disaster. We wanted to show how easy it is to blame the climate for events which would occur without the presence of climatic anomalies, and to illustrate how the response of different societies actually differ from each other under the impact of similar climatic disturbances. It should be kept in mind that the aim of each analysis is to provide an illustration of the main ideas put forward in the preceding chapters of this Report and to provide solid grounds for our conclusions and recommendations. There is no claim of having made exhaustive analyses.

The material included in this chapter is by and large the product of the work of a large number of researchers and research groups throughout the world. The organization and co-ordination of this work has been one of the focal points of the Project and, undoubtedly, that to which the largest amount of efforts and resources were devoted. The special contributions from the regional study groups and individual researchers have been incorporated in Volume 3 of the Report of the Project, under the same title as this chapter. In addition to this written material, the discussions with the authors at some of the Project workshops as well as in personal meetings were a source of precious information. These discussions also provided enough interactions to result in a relatively large number of contributions that present convergent views and a common denominator allowing for fairly safe generalizations.

We have given high priority to the studies on the Sahel as the current views on the drama of the countries in this region, during the period covered by our Project, epitomize the "fallacies on natural disasters" brilliantly exposed in another IFIAS study by Michael Glantz.[1] We believe that this case study illustrates, perhaps more clearly than any other case, the basic hypotheses put forward in the foregoing chapters and according to which drought is not simply a climatic anomaly, but *the social perception of a natural phenomenon*.

B. The Sahelian Drama: Breakdown of a Socio-ecosystem

The Sahelian countries have had the unwanted honour of becoming the most typical example of what is believed to be the devastating effect on a territory of a combination of climatic stresses, population pressure and human negligence. Elsewhere in this Report we have called this the "official version".

The Sahelian drama starting in the early 1970s also marks the beginning of a serious consideration of environmental problems by international institutions. In a way, it was also a major factor influencing IFIAS' decision to embark on a climate programme, as indicated in the Preface to this Report.

When we started our studies for the "Drought and Man" Project, we thought not only that the Sahelian case was a textbook example to be taken as a reference point, but also that the textbook had in fact already been written; that this case had already been exhaustively analysed; that it was only a matter of learning what had been done in order to see whether or not "the same things" happened in other countries or regions.

We therefore began to read the literature on this subject, just for information. Our assumption proved to be wrong. From the enormous mass of literature referring to the Sahelian drought we drew some rather embarrassing conclusions. First, it became more and more evident that the official version was untenable. Second, there were alternative positions but mostly in the sense of penetrating criticisms or piecemeal studies of small areas, rather than of a comprehensive alternative interpretation. Third, there was an attempt at a comprehensive alternative explanation for the Sahelian drama (produced in France by the "Comité Information Sahel", mainly based on the analysis of cash-crops as the most important single cause); this analysis was clearly insufficient to account fully for the actual facts.

This was why it was necessary for the Project to make a considerable effort, not contemplated in the original plans in connection with the Sahelian case, and to commission some special studies. These studies were undertaken bearing in mind some basic ideas which began to take shape from other sectors of the Project and with a view to finding either confirmation or information of the underlying hypothesis.

Three papers emerged from these studies by P. Bonte[2], H. Gambarotta[3], and F. Sabelli[4]. They are included in Volume 3. A fourth paper by R. Green was unfortunately not in final form for publication at the time Mr. Green left the Project, but we have drawn valuable information from his draft and from personal discussions with him.

In this chapter we present an overview of the main ideas contained in the aforementioned contributions. A good deal of the material is taken from the detailed paper by Bonte, a French anthropologist who spent a considerable time in the Sahel and who is considered one of the foremost experts on nomadic societies. Several of the following sections are merely abbreviated versions of selected parts of the paper prepared by him and his group for the IFIAS project.

1. PRE-COLONIAL TIMES

Food production in Africa, South of Sahara, has been based traditionally on two different production systems: livestock rearing and agriculture. The two systems are generally found in association with different ecological environments somehow related to an aridity gradient. Their distribution is not however determined only by climatic and soil conditions. It is also the result of a specific historical evolution. We shall only mention two clear examples of historical events having a decisive influence on ecological changes.

The first example refers to the region of Zichitt in Mauritania. In this region there is evidence of agricultural settlements in neolithic villages during the first millenium B.C. Within a few centuries, agricultural areas were transformed into pastureland occupied by cameleer nomads. The domestication of the dromedary and its spread in the Saharan and sub-Saharan regions is an important historical event to which we shall refer later. Here we only want to take it as an example of an ecological change induced by the development of a pastoral society.

> "The social and political dynamism of this nomadic population carried along a progressive extension of the grazing ecosystem. This evolution may only partially reflect some climatic trends. This is confirmed by the fact that cultivated land was again extending northwards after the beginning of the twentieth century, i.e. after colonization which broke down, the political capacity of expansion of nomadic populations, who were often a major obstacle to colonial conquest" (Bonte, *op.cit.*).

A second example is found in the Ayr region (Niger) where there is evidence of cereal production during the nineteenth century in areas having an annual rainfall of little more than 250 mm. The yields were poor, but the productivity was high as only a little work was needed to grow the crops. These cultivated lands were transformed into pasturelands when the caravan routes between the nomadic regions and the *Hausa* country were developed, between the end of the nineteenth century and the beginning of the twentieth. There were two reasons for this transformation: on the one hand, herdsmen needed the land for grazing while, on the other hand, they could easily obtain the cereals from the *Hausas*.

The distribution of the land between herdsmen and cultivators was not therefore entirely determined by the climate and the soil, and the characteristic of the ecosystem became the resultant of various factors involved in the production system. This is an important element to be considered later on in connection with the analysis of the vulnerability of the Sahelian socio-ecosystem and its evolution in time.

This eco-transformation had, however, well-established boundaries: climatic conditions impose restrictions upon the productive system by establishing thresholds beyond which agricultural production becomes impossible or extremely fragile. These thresholds may change from time to time. The ruins of villages in territory which today is completely arid (as in the examples of Kumbi-Saleh and Audaghast in Mauritania, mentioned by Bonte) are witnesses to such shifts. As far as the outer limits are concerned, the pastoral systems penetrate well into the Sahara, whereas the agro-pastoral systems extend far south into the Sudanese Savannah.

Rainfall variability and drought were so engraved in Sahelian societies that they were essential elements already incorporated in the organization of their production and in their social structures. The effect of droughts with similar *natural* characteristics may therefore be shown to vary historically as a function of the dynamics of the production systems and the corresponding frame of social relations. It is therefore clear that purely climatological parameters do not suffice to characterize a drought situation. Climatic conditions, which were perceived as a drought in the neolithic agro-pastoral economics of Zichitt referred to above, were not taken as such by the cameleer nomads in the same territory a few centuries later. The latter pastoral societies offered a typical example of how the effects of climatic fluctuations are determined by the receptive social structure and, in particular, by the organization of the production system. In spite of the differences among the various kinds of pastoral societies, there are important features common to all nomadic populations in the region.

Of these features, that most often referred to is transhumance which allowed for an optimum utilization of dispersed natural resources. Sub-Saharan pastures rich in salt, very much needed by the herds, were only accessible during the rainy season, whereas dry spells required searching for permanent water sources and southerly grazing land. Displacements, which were on average about 200 km per year, might go up to 700 or even 1000 km in unfavourable years. The capacity to displace themselves was the best immediate answer to droughts which only seldom had the extent and the duration of those in the 1914/16 period or in the early 1970s. Livestock could be taken to graze in better environments, escaping from drought. In addition, the animals provided the best way to store food and to transport it.

This mobility of the pastoral population, although providing it with clear advantages over the more sedentary agricultural groups, would not, by itself, explain the effectiveness of the response to climatic constraints. At least equally important was the fact that the work of these pastoral societies was always organized within the frame of complex and rather compulsive social relations. The system would not work without agreements among groups to use each other's territories as needed. The organization of *pastoral communities* and the agreements among communities was the way of assuring all productive units (domestic groups) of equal access to all natural resources.

The system of social relations at the community level performs yet another important function. A stockbreeder very seldom keeps his herd concentrated in a single place. A system of loans (animals may be lent for milk, or given on a reciprocal basis, or taken to another herd as part of established family relations, etc.) resulted in a dispersion of the herds and played a double role: strengthening social relations -particularly important in periods of climatic stress - and decreasing the vulnerability in periods of natural catastrophes.

It was therefore the whole of the social structure which provided an insurance against drought. And it was precisely this organized social system of responses to climatic variations which suffered most during colonization and after independence, leading to a catastrophic increase in the vulnerability of the whole society.

As already mentioned, livestock provided the best way to store food in this environment. The size of the herds was therefore larger than the actual needs, as a safeguard against bad periods. The problem of herd sizes has, however, much more complex connotations.

Current conceptions relating to the dynamics of nomadic societies are based on the idea of a necessery equilibrium between human and animal populations on the one hand and natural resources on the other. The assumption, sometimes made explicit, is that the stockbreeder would always use the so-called "carrying capacity" of the land to the maximum. One can see clearly how this conception results from an illegitimate transposition to a nomadic society of the capitalistic principle of maximizing profits. As Bonte shows, this ideologically oriented interpretation blocks the way to an understanding of the functioning of the nomadic system of social relations and production.

The comprehension of nomadic behaviour requires proper consideration of both the domestic groups, which are the production and consumption units, and the community groups to which they belong. Production patterns and levels were not determined by domestic requirements alone. Quite the contrary! It is the community which establishes what will be considered as the needs of the group. In so far as belonging to a community represents a collective utilization of the means of production, the community should be understood as a production community. The *reproduction* of the community has therefore a higher priority than the reproduction of the domestic groups. Livestock has certainly a value for food consumption, for exchange, and as a means of production. However, its *social value* is placed at the same level or even higher, since it is related to the system of social relations within the community. This includes the need for sacrifices and ritual ceremonies, marriages, tributes, the "loans" already mentioned, and so on.

The social needs predominated when stockbreeders decided to increase their pastoral production. In addition to the needs of the domestic groups, necessary for their subsistence and reproduction, a surplus was required for social uses and for the reproduction of the community as a whole. Each productive unit will use its own surplus to reinforce and to enlarge its system of social relations. The level of the production is thus socially dependent.

The above does not prevent, but rather stimulates, social competition and unequal accumulation. This, together with a rather weak development of the level of the productive forces, puts some severe limitations on the adaptability of a nomadic society to its environment (sometimes exaggerated by dogmatic "ecologist" views), having some extremely peculiar characteristics which acquire their full significance when one compares the historical effects of drought with the 1972 case.

Bonte explains how the accumulation takes place in both classless pastoral societies (such as the Peuls communities) and those with social stratification (Maures and Tuaregs). In both cases socially oriented surplus requirements and strong social competition among groups very often result in overproduction. This, in turn, produces a situation of disequilibrium with the ecological environment, the nature of which illustrates and confirms some of the basic hypotheses put forward in this report.

First and foremost, one cannot overemphasize the fact that increase of livestock production carries with it a demographic growth. What has been called a demographic pressure is therefore an *effect,* not a cause. The economic expansion can only be carried out by an increase in the labour force, i.e. either by enlarging the size of the family (new wives, more children), or by acquiring more slaves. The socially determined production system is therefore the cause of the demographic changes, not vice versa. This does not ignore the interactions with each other, and the fact that at a certain moment the causal chain may be reversed.

In any case, overproduction introduces a disequilibrium with the environment which may not be noticed until a drought strikes. Droughts *do not* generate the disequilibrium, they merely *reveal* a pre-existing one.

Secondly, as Bonte has shown, droughts perform an extremely important regulating function in nomadic societies. In fact, every time they attempted to expand their production system too much, they paid a very high price for it. Serious droughts which are recurrent in such an adverse environment caused heavy losses of human lives and drastic reductions in livestock. However, contrary to what happened in the 1972/3 case, no past drought, however serious, disrupted the system, jeopardizing its capacity to reproduce the structure of the pastoral society itself.

Nomadic societies appear, then, as being subject to recurrent periods of expansion and contraction, the former being caused by social pressure (not primarily by demographic pressures), the latter by climatic stresses. Bonte points out that every time that a nomadic population was "contracted" by a drought, it emerged from this situation with a greater impetus and a renewed capacity to reproduce its internal social relations and productive organization. An historical overview may consider the periods of maximum expansion as a "decadence" of the society. Droughts may not be taken, from this perspective, as a catastrophic, unforeseeable phenomenon, but rather as an integrated factor of the pastoral productive system and one which is perhaps decisive in preventing its complete decadence and dissolution.

Let us now turn to the Sahelian populations using an agricultural production system. They were, in general, agro-pastoral societies to which can be applied, *mutatis-mutandis,* a large number of the above remarks concerning social relations and social structures. We shall only emphasize the differences.

The agro-pastoral Sahelian societies settled, in general, on a more favourable territory, characterized by longer rainy spells and larger amounts of rainfall. In return, they were more vulnerable to climatic fluctuations on account of their relatively sedentary character.

The most important problem facing the agro-pastoral systems was how to secure availability of food between two crops. They had to bridge a gap the duration of which was a function of the climatic conditions both before the harvest and after it. The former determined the amount of grain which was harvested; the latter the period of time until the next adequate crop. Sufficient reserves and adequate storage were needed to keep food for periods sometimes as long as 3 years and for seeding. Bonte points out several ways of dealing with this problem. In some cases collective land was cultivated by the villagers under the authority of the chief. The crops were kept in stock and redistributed. The storing places were considered to be under the control of gods and could only be opened after rites and sacrifices.

Storing grain was not, however, the only defence against drought. Here, as was the case with the nomadic societies, one finds that the whole agrarian system was organized as a structural response to climatic stresses. The magnitude and nature of the effects of drought were, once more, determined by the receptive social structure: keeping land fallow for long periods, as well as soil which could be reclaimed when needed; preservation of large zones with trees and bushes between the various political agro-regions; association with herdsmen who could use their land and would provide, in turn, the manure to enrich the soil; a mixed agrarian and pastoral system, conceived as a form of association already described but also in order to have "stored food" in the form of livestock. All of these mechanisms are key elements of the adaptability of the agrarian organization to the climatic constraints.

In periods of scarcity, the redistribution of herds took place under a series of norms which were implemented under strong social pressures.

An interesting and important feature of the agrarian organization was that, although here the production unit is also the domestic group (extended family), the land appropriation takes place at the community level. There was no "private property". It was only through the community that the producer had access to the land. A distinction should therefore be made between "real appropriation" which takes place during the agricultural production process at the level of the one who produces (i.e. the "extended family") and the "formal appropriation" at the community level.

For most agro-pastoral societies, the term "masters of the land" as an institution is very often mistakenly regarded as being linked to actual rights on the land. In fact, the institution symbolizes, through ritual practices, the rights of the community to the land and the pre-eminence over individuals or domestic groups which utilize it. This pre-eminence is materialized by the ritual practices in the sense that "real appropriation" requires a series of rites which will guarantee the success of the production. This community structure may also give rise to social stratification when an organized social group, whether or not established as a state, is able to determine conditions for the formal appropriation of land and obtains part of the surplus, without intervening in the production process itself.

The differences between Sahelian pastoral and agro-pastoral systems, important as they are, did not imply the existence of isolated, mutually exclusive systems of food production. They were in fact highly complementary in two quite distinctive aspects. In the first place, at the level of exchanges, herdsmen got from the agricultural areas not only cereals but also cotton goods, henna, tobacco, etc.; in turn, nomads provided livestock, cheese, leather and handicraft goods (mainly derived from cattle, but from wood and metals as well). In the second place, there was a more intimate mixing of both types of societies: in former times, the agricultural societies provided slaves to reinforce the productive capacity of the pastoral groups; in turn, herdsmen took care of the herds of the farmers and also served as caravaneers for them.

In this way, differentiation and complementing between both socio-ecosystems formed the basis of complex social formations within which there were important inter-regional and inter-ethnic exchanges. In some cases, strong ethnic, economic and political differences led to the establishment of states and empires which marked the domination of pastoral groups over the more sedentary agricultural society (e.g. the Peuls established in the eighteenth and nineteenth centuries a series of states between what is today Senegal and Cameroun). The social formations under the control of a State developed two types of characteristic relations: internal relations, both inter-ethnic and inter-regional, based on specialization of work and a well-established network for the circulation of products; and international relations directed towards the north (trans-Saharan), bringing to the Mediterranean their own products as well as products from further south (meridional regions of West Africa where they could get gold and slaves). These trade routes and the commercial relations with countries outside the region also played an important role as a safeguard for periods of local scarcities.

2. STRUCTURAL CHANGES INTRODUCED BY COLONIALISM— THE EXAMPLE OF ADRAR IN MAURITANIA

Problems started before colonization of the region, as a result of the French domination in the south. When the French arrived in Adrar they found a territory disturbed by political and military troubles and by the interruption of some of the exchange routes. There already began to be a scarcity of food in 1904 (500 deaths out of a population of 20,000). The drop in food production became a major problem. Malnutrition was chronic between 1904 and 1932, with superimposed famines (1914/17), "caused" by droughts, and in 1927/31, "caused" by the international economic crisis.

The French administration introduced, under glamorous names, two key elements which will gradually destroy the social and economic structures of the traditional society: administrative *autonomy* and *free* utilization of pasture lands.

"Autonomy" was indeed "autonomy of the budget" (i.e. "self-supporting" budget); it meant taxes to support the administrative personnel and occupation forces and requisitions for the transport of military equipment and men.

"Freedom" to use the pasture lands meant the abolition of the land control of traditional hierarchies and the beginning of an abusive utilization of the best grazing land which was often used to "tame" rebel nomads in the arid "Far North". The establishment of a spoliatory administration and the destruction of the traditional political framework was accomplished, in part, by setting up an intermediate layer of chiefs who acted as "relays" between the administration and the people. But the real mechanisms which disrupted the economic pre-colonial structure was the cutting off of the ancient trade routes and the monetization of markets. In the first place, Senegal and the Ivory Coast became the main administrative and commercial centres, and the Atlantic Ocean the route to the Mediterranean. Newly manufactured products would come massively from the Metropolis to ruin the local crafts condemned thereafter to remain as suppliers for the tourist market.

The international economic crisis of the thirties found the colonies with the old structures dissolved and the new ones paralysed. Prices slumped, livestock prices dropped to one-fourth or one-fifth of previous levels. Money obtained in the market was barely enough to pay taxes. There was a final rebellion of the old indigenous aristocracy, definitely subdued when they refused to be "bought". When the international situation became normal, prices of imported products went up to former levels whereas the prices of exported products never recovered.

A similar picture was repeated in the 1942-6 crisis. This time the direct cause was the war and the defeat of France, with one aggravating factor: drought. Famine became a permanent companion until 1950.

The most important alteration in the economic life of Sahelian territories under colonial power was undoubtedly the rise in agricultural and pastoral markets and the monetization of the trade. The markets, as such, prolonged traditional exchange practices established in very early times. In addition to the introduction of money, colonization incorporated some new features with far-reaching consequences.

Professional and ethnic specializations, particularly in metallurgy and textiles, were destroyed or reduced to a subsidiary role oriented to the tourist market. Some Hausa tanneries disappeared, others were kept to produce tanned leather for European firms. Moreover, old exchange networks were destroyed and replaced by new networks which were geared to the supply routes from Metropolitan France. Thus a coherent regional and inter-regional network for the circulation of goods simply disappeared. Cutting the territory by imposing arbitrary frontiers and orienting the trade towards administrative centres finished the job. The establishment of customs at the frontiers was, of course, an additional measure.

As a result, certain regions remained isolated and therefore extremely vulnerable. The frontier between Niger and Nigeria, for instance, cut off a part of the Hausa territory (then in Niger) from the Hansa villages in the south (then in Nigeria). This was considered to be the main cause of the famine in the Hausa region of Niger during the 1914/17 drought. On the other hand, as already mentioned, the suppression of the trans-Saharan trade was the basic cause of the Mauritanian famines of 1942/8.

This rearrangement of traffic created a double dependency for the Sahelian population. On the one hand, there was a dependency with reference to the world capitalistic system. On the other, a dependency with reference to new social groups (or ancient groups with new roles) to which we refer below. Moreover, the emergence of urban centres on the coast (Senegal, Ghana, Ivory Coast) created a new demand for food which was particularly reflected in the increase of the livestock trade.

As already stated, this fundamental alteration of trade networks took place together with the implementation of a policy of extortion and constraints which gave rise to the following practices:

—Requisition of products. The prices paid were as low as one-third or one-fourth of the current prices. The amount was fixed before harvesting, on the basis of the area sown with crops. This lead to a simple type of speculation: farmers had to buy, sometimes the same cereal, at much higher prices.

—Requisition of people, allowing the French administration to use any labour force deemed to be necessary - refusal lead to prison. The more serious cases were the forced migrations of workers to the plantations in coastal territories.

—Requisition of money. Sahelian populations were obliged to contribute to the reconstruction of France after the 1914-18 war and to the victims of disasters in Southern France in 1930, just during the serious famine in Niger.

—Taxes. Neither droughts nor famines spared the payment of taxes. A report by Harranger, Inspector of Colonies (cited by Bonte), indicates a fourfold increase of taxes between 1924 and 1928. In the last year of this period, taxation amounted to 40 to 50 kg of millet *per capita* (compared to an annual consumption per capital of 150 to 200 kg).

The most important effect of colonialism was the transformation of food into merchandise. The circulation of food entered the monetary circulation system, subjected to capitalist rules. This is described by Claude Raynaut as "the change from a 'substantive' to a market economy"[5] and explained as follows: "The 'substantive' economy is closely tied to the functioning of society, manipulating, producing and exchanging goods to meet material and social demands; the market economy is centered on the creation and circulation of currency (expressed in a monetary form) which eclipses the significance of the particular goods concerned."

This transformtion has pronounced social effects at two different levels, as described by Raynaut:

—"At the inter-personal level, this new situation means an increasing emphasis on notions such as competition and personal fortune, which have taken the place of a sense of belonging to a community, of reciprocal responsibilities, and of family alliances with the spirits, which became difficult to reconcile with the spread of commerce and trade."

—"On the collective level there is a breakdown of the old social structures, that is, of the dominant institutional frameworks within which social relations flourished in particular, kinship ties, village organization and ethnopolitical grouping."

The final result of this trend is twofold. On the one hand, "through the breakdown of the fabric of society, collective control over material conditions of life has been taken away". On the other hand, "the aim of the production and circulation of goods is less the satisfaction of needs linked to subsistence and the functioning of social groups, but more and more the acquisition by individuals of badly needed money". The relevance of this analysis to an understanding of the catastrophic effects of droughts thereafter is quite apparent. As Bonte emphasizes famines were less due to scarcity of food than to the lack of money to buy it.

The breaking down of social relations at both the domestic and the community levels, including the traditional practices of land appropriation and land use, hinged on some fundamental changes:

—The emergence of private ownership of the land, particularly by individual appropriation of formerly collective soil.

—The confiscation of stocks and storage places of collective land and their appropriation by administrative officers, sometimes for their own benefit.

—The decrease in the size of the domestic production unit.

—The "liberation" of a considerable migratory working force, feeding the increasing demand for a labour force from the coast and from the Metropolis.

Curiously enough, as Bonte clearly explains, the profound disruption of the community structure by the monetization of the market did not imply a change of the productive system into a capitalistic mode of production. Bonte suggests that the underlying reason is the devaluation of agricultural labour. Food was sold, for the market, at prices below production costs. Labour productivity became extremely low and the productive forces were blocked. Those earning salaries, who form the core of the capitalistic mode of production, could not compete with the domestic production units.

3. THE PERIOD OF INDEPENDENCE

After independence, most colonial interests at stake remained unchanged. In most cases neo-colonialist methods used local administrations simply as relays between the metropolis and the population. A Carnegie report synthetizes the situation as follows:

"The primary French influence in the Sahel was the pervasive cultural and administrative presence that has been the special legacy of French colonialism in Africa. In the years following independence, there remained in the area substantial numbers of French governmental advisors, teachers, merchants, and military instructors. The régimes of the Sahel were made up of French-speaking African politicians and civil servants closely tied to France both culturally and politically. In Chad, French military aid was crucial in containing an obscure but bloody insurgency in the late sixties.''

There were, however, new conditions which introduced some departures from colonial times. At the political level, the most important change was the development of social groups which were blocked by colonialism.

Both colonial and neo-colonial domination was characterized by the fact that it was exerted through particular social groups started by the colonial administration by making use, whenever possible, of traditional "chiefs" already tamed and bribed. These groups were as much agents of foreign capitalism as genuine representatives of an incipient national bourgeoisie.

The transformation of the powers and functions of the ancient hierarchies during colonization was just one aspect of the changing structures of social relations. Their role in the management of collective land, for instance, disappeared as a result of the introduction of individual rights on the land. The main function of the old chiefs under the new rules - or of those replacing the chiefs who remained loyal to their communities and rebelled - was tax collection, an activity that was a source of income proportional to their capacity of exaction under the protection of bodyguards. Such a group was thus favourable to the colonial ruling at the moment of independence, as they were afraid of losing their priveleged position and feared the revenge of the population.

Merchants and traders were a second group for whom the monetization of the markets, brought about by colonialism, provided the means for accumulation, but found their further expansion limited by the colonialists themselves. Political independence, strongly supported by this group, offered them the possibility of becoming real capitalists and entrepreneurs.

The new social groups emerging after independence took control of the State administration. A heavy bureaucracy was established. It had to be supported by the peasants. Not only did taxes increase, but a better control allowed for a still larger increment in the number of people and goods under taxation. The following figures are taken from Green's paper. Between 1964 and 1965, in Chad, the number of people paying taxes increased from 629,000 to one million; the number of cattle under taxation increased from 2,432,170 to 3,482,034; and the number of sheep from 1,996,950 to 3,003,698. In the same country, the number of administrative employees doubled between 1962 and 1965.

Taxes weighed heavily on the peasant farmers. At the time of the drought crisis they became unbearable: "At the village level the effects of reduced rainfall thus included crop failures and exhaustation of water supplies, loss of livestock, and a drying up of cash income. At the same time demands for cash spending were unabated, including the collection of personal tax, continuation of which during the drought years was one of the greatest scandals of the crisis."[6]

4. THE 1973 FAMINE

There is a large number of well-known descriptions of the famines and social disruptions in the Sahel during the early seventies. We shall not repeat them here. The drought situation which culminated in 1972/3 was in fact a "detector" of the contradictions which developed within the Sahelian production systems during and after colonization. The disequilibrium pre-existed in the socio-ecosystem, which had already reached a very unstable state when the drought arrived. The system blew up under the impact of the drought. The drought did not generate the instability—the drought triggered it off. But the drought lasted a long time and acted upon the evolution of the system, after the instability was released, aggravating the effects of the process that followed.

The internal contradictions which pre-existed within the whole socio-ecosystem had developed at two different levels:

(a) The contradiction between the productive system and the natural environment which developed in a irreversible way once the old response mechanisms were broken. The dissolution of traditional social structures made it impossible to reproduce the former association between the ecosystem and society. The degradation of the ecosystem was mainly due to:

—abandonment of the practice of fallow land and reclamation of marginal land;

—extension of cash-crops with gradual impoverishment of soils (Senegal and Chat);

—increasing deforestation as a result of land reclamation and urbanization (utilization of wood for energy);

—overutilization of pasture land, particularly in connection with wrong hydraulic policies and the abandonment of traditional rules of pasture land utilization;

—disruption of the close association between pastoral and agricultural communities with the reciprocal reinforcement influence already described.

(b) The contradiction between the development of productive forces and the organization of production relations, with the result that production remained pre-capitalist, whereas the capitalistic development of the market implied the circulation of food transformed into merchandise. Production became stagnant mainly as a result of the devaluation of agricultural labour which, as already pointed out, appears to be the key element in the interpretation of the process leading to the degradation of the whole socio-ecosystem.

As a result of these trends, a fundamental opposition arose between a blocking action on the productive forces leading to a decreasing labour productivity, on the one hand, and "a rapid and continuous increase in the demand for agricultural produce", on the other. The latter was "not only due to population growth, as has been stressed so often, but also a consequence of the spread of so-called 'cash-cropping' and increased marketing of traditional food crops, as the constantly increasing need of the rural population for money could only be satisfied by a simultaneous increase in the level of agricultural production" (C. Raynaut, *op.cit.,* p.19).

The explanation of the 1973 famine is therefore to be found not in a detailed analysis of the climatic conditions and of their effects on the quantitative output of the agricultural sector, but in the economic and social situation prevailing in the 1960s, before the drought. Gambarotta's paper offers a clear-cut description of this situation and shows how it is dominated by the "double-squeezing" dynamics of the economic process: growing dependence on the outside world and widening disparities in income distribution inside the countries. The result was a clear pattern of exploitation of the lower strata of the population, i.e. of those who then will be the victims of the famine. The economic policies tended towards the extraction of the surplus generated by agricultural productions and its transfer to the urban occupational groups. From this perspective we reject the kind of analysis made by the supporters of the "official view" that accounts for the catastrophic effects of the drought as being primarily due to the constraints of the natural milieu, aggravated by the disproportionate population growth and the irrational behaviour of the peasants who are responsible for the deterioration of the environment. As Gambarotta rightly points out: "This behaviour of the peasantry is by no means 'irrational', but results from the fact that, confined to a marginal role in society, the conservation of the environment does not enter into its economic calculation, which is centred on the dilemma of *survival*. It is the marginalization of the peasantry by the social system, and not the behaviour of the peasantry itself, which appears as the ultimate cause of the destruction of the environment."

During the mid-term workshop held in Geneva by the present project, a group of specialists made the following striking remark:

> "Traditional societies seem to be less affected by droughts, as was the case of northern Sahel bordering on the Sahara, where suffering was relatively low during the 1972 drought. The critical area was that where rainfall is between 500-1200 mm/year and where cash cropping in cotton and ground nuts has greatly increased."

The critical area also coincides, and this is the essential fact, with that where the disruption of the traditional societies and the reinforcement of the "laws of the market" were more profound. It is the area where the farmer had lost the control of his own production, i.e. of the basis of his survival in the old times.

5. PROSPECTS

The analysis of the Sahelian drama could not stop at the level of the diagnosis only. This Report has already questioned the meaning of international aid in emergency situations. Here again the Sahel case study offers a textbook example of what has been maintained in Chapter 5, as well as in Chapter 1 (the latter, in connection with the so-called "world food security"). The first question we asked ourselves when we became acquainted with the descriptions of the Sahelian famines was why the international response arrived so late and was so little. The supporters of what we called (in Chapter 1) the "official view" about the 1972 food crisis provide only indirect answers: "depletion of stocks", "sky-rocketing prices". But this is just not true. The emergency situation started at a moment when there was an *excess* of stocks and the prices were quite steady.

Both the US Government and FAO knew about the situation from the very beginning, i.e. already in 1968. There were between thirty-five and seventy-five US AID officers since 1967 and over 100 medical doctors and other experts related to a US Public Health Service Programme since 1966. How could they ignore the problem? In fact they did not. The Report by Sheets and Morris provides a clear account of information received by the US Government and by FAO about the Sahelian situation. In particular, on pges 15 and 16 the authors say:

"to the AID and FAO bureaucracies from 1968 onward came significant and ever-increasing intelligence on the catastrophe overtaking the Sahel. The scope, depth and momentum of the drought year by year were methodically recorded in the annual public reports by AID on disaster relief. The 1969 report spoke of the 'prolonged drought across West Africa,' of 'drought conditions . . . general' throughout the region, 'complete crop failure' in Senegal. by 1970, there were more than three million people requiring emergency food. 'This was not a new disaster', the document that year explained for Mali, 'but a continuation of that which was reported' in the previous report. Famine in Upper Volta, continued the report, 'was brought on by the same drought problem which was plaguing other countries across West Africa.' 'Hunger, if not starvation, has become increasingly frequent (and) emergency imports have become the rule rather than the exception,' concluded the 1970 report. A Year later, the description had become almost perfunctory, 'Many African countries are plagued by droughts *year after year*' (emphasis added), observed AID's 1971 disaster relief report in describing emergency aid to over a half million victims in the Sahel.

On the basis of numerous field reports, the Director-General of the FAO told an intergovernmental committee of the U.N.'s World Food Program later that spring of 1972 that drought in the Sahel had become 'endemic,' making it necessary to give the area 'special treatment' in providing emergency food aid."[8]

Strangely enough, the Director-General of FAO, Addeke H. Boerma, in his press conference at FAO Headquarters, on 1 February 1973, told the correspondents: "Recently there have been articles in the press mentioning the threat of famines in some parts of the world (. . .). In my view, based on a number of careful assessments by our experts over recent months, there is not—I repeat, *not*—a likelihood of immediate widespread famine at this time - that is to say, not for the next few months."[9] Not a single reference to the Sahelian situation. However, in March, the six countries in the region set up a Permanent Inter-State Committee to meet the crisis. Governments and non-governmental groups had already started providing aid. Following a meeting in Rome on 20 May between A. Boerma and Secretary-General Waldheim, FAO was designated as the focal point for all action by the UN system in the emergency phase of assistance.[10]

As far as the US is concerned, it is only towards the end of 1972 that the aid to the region started. This tremendous delay is hard to explain. Raul Green has carefully studied this problem during the period of his association with the Project. He conjectures that the interaction of the US takes place only after the inability of France, the dominant power in the region, to meet the crisis, became manifest. The US steps in, followed by other European countries and Japan. A new era starts in Sahel: the period called by Green "the internationalization of domination".

Green analysed the known information about foreign investments in the exploration of natural (non-renewable) resources in the region since the early 1960s, and even before. He also made a comparison of the development programmes proposed for the region since 1973 by a number of international and national organizations (FAO, Club des Amis du Sahel, US AID, MIT). What we may infer from these analyses—coincidence with the appraisal made by Gambarotta in his paper—is not very promising for the Sahelian countries.

We shall only mention a few points.

—Perhaps the first remark to be made is clearly expressed by Giri[11]:

"It is surprising to note the multiplicity of measures of all kinds which are proposed in the various studies considered, and also the lack of any order of hierarchy for these measures. Sometimes the expert's conclusions give the impression that all things need to be done, and straight away. The orders of priority do not always clearly emerge. . . ."

—The kind of approach to the problems of the region tend to offer solutions that cannot be implemented without heavily depending on the magnanimity of advanced countries. According to the US AID proposal about 17,000 million dollars will be needed until the end of the century for its implementation.

—The goals of the projects appear to be linked with the "modernization of agriculture". This means the acceptance of a well-defined model of rural development based on an intense use of technologies brought in by the donors. This "modernized" agricultural sector is expected to insert itself in the framework of the international division of labour envisaged by the advanced countries.

—In this connection the following two quotations from the MIT paper are very revealing:

"Since it is inevitable that economic development will give rise to a rapid growth of import demand this underlines the need for export development. In turn export growth will require an agricultural development of livestock for the world market."[12]

". . . the number of people (and families) who can be directly employed in agriculture and have a reasonable income in this example of an agricultural strategy is less than half of the total at present and will decrease as higher activity levels are introduced into the agricultural production system. Labor intensive production systems may absorb some of the imbalance. Welfare camps can be established but ultimately some meaningful employment will be required for millions of people."[13]

—Paradoxically enough for the supporters of the thesis of "natural disaster" as the main cause of famine and poverty in the Sahel, the proposals show that the region has the real alternative of being converted into a centre of large-scale meat production.

—But the proposals have little concern for the fate of large sectors of the population. The remark of the MIT report quoted above summarized a common feature. For instance, the FAO proposal which is excellent at the "technical" level, implies about 48% of unemployment for the rural population in Upper Volta, and 32% for Mali.

With these remarks in mind, and within the context provided by the analyses made by Bonte, Sabelli, Gambarotta and Green, it is hard to avoid a conjecture that, if it is true, will mean a very dark future for large sectors of the Sahelian population the very existence of which is here at stake. Meat production will be taken over by international corporations. Their aim - as everywhere else in the world - will be the reduction of costs by taking advantage of the possibility of exploiting cheap labour and idle natural resources. The modernization of a sector of the agricultural production will leave large masses of the rural population unemployed or out of the "modernized" sector, i.e. reduced to a precarious agricultural production for self-consumption, without change of the present conditions. If this is linked with the exploitation of mineral resources in the region now under way (Niger is already the fifth producer of uranium in the world), the obvious conclusion is that at least part of the unemployed rural masses will provide cheap labour for the mines. The rest may die after successive crises. This may turn out to be the end result of the Sahelian droughts.

Once again climate will be blamed for it. And the very people who died will be held responsible for contributing to their own fate because they "refuse to modernize." But the region may become at that time a great exporter of natural resources, including food. The GNP of the countries will undoubtedly increase, to the joy of "developmental" economists. And the international organizations as well as the "donor" countries will place on record their satisfaction for the great achievements.

We know that quite a few readers may react to the above comments in the usual way: "Oh! Yes. Once again the 'conspiracy' theory!" We strongly reject this idea. No actual complot of a certain number of individuals or institutions is needed to materialize those sad auguries. We, in turn, call "naïve" those who believe that an actual conspiracy is required. This belongs to what we have called "second-level" explanations in the Introduction. The explanation we suggest belongs to the "third level": it is a structural problem, the unavoidable consequence of a *system* that operates that way. When you put together the prevailing "international economic order". plus the "international division of labour", the application of the "comparative advantages" plus the prevailing ideas on international aid, you do get such a result.

C. Drought in Eastern Africa[14]

The three East African countries, Ethiopia, Kenya and Tanzania, which are presented as case studies in Volume 3 of this Report,[15]not only offer a regional contrast with the Sahelian arca but also extreme national divergences of the impact of drought on society. The contrast between the impact of drought in the three countries helps us to illustrate the pseudo-relationship between drought and famines. The extent of the drought, and the preparedness of the countries to satisfy the food and nutritional requirements of the people, provide a logical framework for a discussion of drought and society. To understand this relationship requires knowledge of the physical features of the countries and above all an appreciation of their socioeconomic structures.

THE EXTENT OF DROUGHT

There is an implicit assumption, not supported by meteorological information, that the drought of the 1970s prevailed over the *whole* of East Africa and in particular over the *entirety* of Eithiopia. The evidence available shows that even in Ethiopia, which was the most seriously affected of the three, only *parts* of the country were affected by drought. Both Ayalew and Mascarenhas emphasize this fact and depart from the misleading but popular notion of their countries suddenly seared by drought and consequently afflicted by famines. Odingo illustrates that in Kenya, despite drought, there was no officially reported famine.

The physical geography of Ethiopia does not dictate a nation-wide drought. The splintered highland massif is surrounded by lowland areas which not only have very low precipitation (0-600 mm) but where the variation is also great. An area of moderate rainfall surrounds and juts between the highlands. The juxtaposition of mountains and plains causes a variation in rainfall due to the local rainshadow effect. Another aspect for consideration is that there are two rainy seasons. In the north and west the rains come from June to September and March to April; in the south the rains are from March to May and October to November. But even here one must be cautious. In Tigre the rain patterns permit only one planting season, May to August. In contrast, the most parts of Wollo there are two agricultural seasons—the harvests coming around July and December.

Briefly, one can summarize by stating that aridity and semi-aridity are not uncommon features in parts of Ethiopia. Similarly, variation and fluctuation of rainfall are not unusual. Between the extremes of those areas which receive adequate rainfall and those under the stress of aridity are the marginal areas of growing population and where the people are even more susceptible to risk from crop failure.

The full extent of the variation of rainfall and the impact it has on the people is complex. In the 1972/3 season, at a provincial level, both Wollo and Tigre were badly affected. Even in normal years they receive less rainfall than the highlands because they lie in the rainshadow of the vast highland massif. Elsewhere, the severity of the drought was not exceptional. Thus during the rainy season (*belg*) of 1972, 62% of the *awrajas* (subdivisions of provinces) received below normal rainfall. In the second rain season (*keremt*) of the agricultural year, nearly 75% of the *awrajas* received *normal* rains.

In some aspects the rainfall pattern in Kenya is not too different from that of Ethiopia. There is a central core of highland (also splintered by the rift valley), which receives adequate rainfall. The arid and semi-arid areas almost surround the highlands. Proportionally, they cover a much larger area of Kenya than in Ethiopia. However, on the eastern and western extremities the presence of the Indian Ocean and Lake Victoria break the monotony of low-rainfall areas. Based on the mean annual rainfall, nearly half of Kenya, mainly in the north and south, is arid to semi-arid. In this area drought is not abnormal. Another third of the country is agriculturally an area of medium potential. Rainfall varies from 500 mm to 900 mm per annum and the risk of drought is high. The northern part of Kenya is arid, the Rift Valley (mainly Turkana) and Kajiado, Narok, Machakos and Kitui districts all fall into this category. In the 1970s the arid and semi-arid areas experienced an even greater decline of rainfall.

In Tanzania, the climate pattern is different. To begin with, extreme aridity is confined to a small area in the north which borders Kenya but there is a tongue of semi-arid area which extends from the north into the centre of the country. Areas of reliable to marginally reliable rainfall are found in the periphery of the country. These include Mounts Kilimanjaro and Meru, and the Pare and Usambara mountains in the north and the Uluguru mountains continue the system southwards into the vast Southern Highlands. On the western side, most of Rukwa Region, especially the Ufipa plateau, is an area of net precipitation surplus. Parts of West Lake region receive over 80 inches of rain per year. The distribution of rainfall has a complex pattern. In 1972 many of the arid and semi-arid areas received less rains than normal but areas of reliable precipitation such as the Ufipa plateau and southern highlands received adequate rainfall. Others, such as the western slopes of the Usambara and Pare mountains and the plains areas of the Kilimanjaro and Meru, experienced greatly reduced rainfall. In good years, such as in the mid and late sixties, most of the semi-arid and marginal areas received adequate rains for the purpose for which the lands were being used.

In all three countries there has been a long history of meteorological droughts over many parts of the countries. The occurrence of drought often coincides in each of the three countries. Thus, periods of low rainfall in Lake Stephanie (Ethiopia) corresponded with low rains in Lake Rudolf (Kenya) and Lake Victoria (Tanzania). However, none of the countries has embarked on any systematic study of drought and the meteorological information is patchy. In the few studies that are available, there is a tendency to focus on periods of abnormally low rainfall. However, even assuming that there was more meteorological information available it is unlikely that the impact of the drought would have been found to be too different from what actually transpires in the existing literature simply because the other more important variables which link drought to famines were ignored.

THE IMPACT OF DROUGHT

The impact of the drought in the three countries in Eastern Africa are in complete contrast of each other. The drought which prevailed in parts of Kenya, Ethiopia and Tanzania had an impact on the agricultural production of all three countries. However, drought offers only one explanation for decline in agricultural production and in some crops there may be no explanation. Ethiopia experienced catastrophic food shortages and between 100,000 and 250,000 persons perished. Tanzania also experienced a food deficit of major proportion in 1974 and the importation of food affected the economy negatively. Kenya could contain the food shortages experienced in some parts of the country but there was decline in the production of some agricultural crops. Such contrasting patterns of famines of food availability, despite the fact they they all experienced drought, only helps to confirm that between drought and food shortages there are many interventions. These interventions offer the explanation for the adequacy of food or the lack of it. Since the background factors are different in each country it is best to seek explanations at a national level from the case-studies presented in this work and from other sources.

THE ETHIOPIAN TRAGEDY

There are two contributions to the "Drought and Man" Project concerning the situation in Ethiopia during the drought in the early 1970s. One of them comes from S. Ayalew, an Ethiopian medical doctor deeply involved in the public health problems of his country; the other one, from R. Odingo, a Kenyan geographer with vast experience in Eastern Africa. These contributions are complementary to each other, but they are widely different, as they consider the Ethiopian drought from two quite diverging perspectives.

Ayalew's concern is more about the causes and consequences of famines. He emphasizes that famines and food shortages are socio-economic phenomena and can be explained largely by socio-economic variables. This is a consistent theme throughout his presentation. It seems that perhaps it was not necessary for him to use global political principles and generalizations in order to explain the unequal exchange and distribution of wealth which prevailed in feudlistic Ethiopia, since there is enough evidence in his country about these facts. Nevertheless, his conclusions are worthy of serious considerations because his explanations sustain the fact that the root cause of famines is not nature but man's socio-economic systems.

Richard Odingo's account focuses on the physical aspects of drought. While Ayalew makes no attempt to explain it, Odingo gives three observed causes of drought. These are: the expansion of population in previously marginal lands, the significant growth of urbanization which has created a fuel crisis and the exponential increase in stock number. This may give the impression that he supports a neo-Malthusian cause. The postscript added to his paper clarifies the issue, as he states: "It is therefore important to admit that in examining drought I was only looking at one of the consequences of a much more complex ecological, social and even political situation. Any impression given of cause-effect relationship between human and livestock increase, ecological destruction and the inevitability of drought effects was therefore unbalanced." There is, therefore, complete agreement on this basic issue between both contributors to the Project.

It seems also necessary to mention two significant accounts of the Ethiopia famine: Abdul Hussein's *Drought and Famines in Ethiopia* and Jack Shepherd's *The Politics of Starvation*. Since the accounts by Hussein and Shepherd were written for a different purpose and contain dimensions not contained in those of Odingo and Ayalew, it is worth elaborating on them because they provide additional evidence supporting the main thesis of this work.

Shepherd's account of the famines in Ethiopia explores the conspiracy of silence. The first cover-up was by the Imperial Ethiopian Government (IEG) of Haile Selassie. The IEG acted slowly even after knowing the truth because it believed that drought and famine were *normal* for Ethiopia. A charitable view is that some ministers and even the Emperor himself did not wish to be embarrassed by another "Sahel" and hoped to be saved by a good harvest. The other cover-up was by the national and international relief agencies. They had the facts, the means, and the expertise to take action, but they remained silent. According to Shepherd, the only reason for their silence was diplomatic tradition and practice. Two questions are raised by Shepherd—Would queries by the international communities be regarded as unwarranted interference in the internal affairs of a State? Were Ethiopian lives expendable to maintain the traditional diplomatic practice of non-interference? The fact remains that "one authoritative voice might have saved thousands; their silence condemned tens of thousands". There were many ways to have made the world aware of the tragic events. The Ethiopian famine was not a local affair, for starving peasants had moved out to Sudan, Somalia, and into Kenya. Therefore, the famine had become an international affair. Secondly, the international agencies could have conveniently "leaked" the information as they have sometimes done. While the world was being told about the modernization of Ethiopia and millions of dollar poured in as aid or out as purchases for armaments the people of Ethiopia starved. It seems interesting and important to compare this situation with what was done in Tanzania at about the same time, as indicated below.

A dimension also not covered by the two case-studies on Ethiopia but discussed by

Shepherd are the after-effects of Ethiopia's drought and famines. The whole question of Ethiopia's ability to sustain itself becomes a crucial issue. Given the fact that the UN civil service bureaucracy is so slow and cumbersome and in any case the demands being made on them make it unlikely that they will have the capacity or the means to provide immediate solutions. Meanwhile, as a result of the centuries of neglect and the physical damage to the ecology of the country as well as to the health of the people and the problems of resettlements, one must not expect immediate results from recent reforms by the new government of Ethiopia, even under the assumption that they are sound.

Apart from reforms there are other areas requiring attention. Since most of the food crops were destroyed in the traditional food-supply areas in Tigre and Wollo there is need for massive assistance for seed. The problem with livestock (needed for transportation, ploughing and as food) is even more serious because as the Ethiopian livestock and Meat Board stated, the effect of the drought on the people would be "long range since sufficient recovery of livestock numbers cannot be expected for 3-5 years". To remedy the damage from denudation of the country and deforestation requires colossal inputs. Similarly, the Ethiopian peasant-farmers who constitute the majority of the people of Ethiopia need to recover from past famines. This means special attention to the young and the very old, improved water facilities and great increase in the availability of nutritious foods. Finally there is the problem of land reform. One of the first major decisions of the new military rulers of Ethiopia was to promulgate a law in land reform and this opened the door for far-reaching structural changes in the countryside. But as has been pointed out by a writer, land reform has proceeded unevenly and it continues to be the most important issue in Ethiopian domestic politics.

The work edited by Hussein, and which came one year after Shepherd's is a collection of articles ranging from technical, such as basic zonal rainfall patterns in Ethiopia, to socio-economic studies, such as health problems resulting from famines in Ethiopia. In the preface he points out that thousands of peasants died in Ethiopia but many more were saved. He reiterates the view found in most of the contributions to the IFIAS study that: "the prolonged drought was only part of the reason for the catastrophe whose major causes are to be sought in the economic, political and social structures of the society and in the responses of the imperial government in power at that time". He also underscores that Ethiopia is still affected by famine conditions in many parts of the country. The other main value of Hussein's work is the documentation and citation of works originating from within Ethiopia itself including works by the UN agencies. Therefore, the tragedy of Ethiopia is not one based on ignorance but the fact that the poor and the oppressed were not even an item on the agenda in the priorities of the Ethiopia Government during the régime of the Emperor.

The value of Hussein's work is that, although he too is a geographer, he is not intimidated by drought. By separating aims from consequences of decisions, he does not get misled. Nowhere is this more apparent than in the two accounts of the Awash Valley project. Odingo's account begins by describing it as one of the "most successful commercial agricultural projects" but there were problems in implementing the "lofty aims" of the Awash Valley Authority. He acknowledges that the efforts of resettling the Afar people were half-hearted. One is also struck by the admission that "the great mistake was to offer land in the project to the concessionaires". Yet commercialization of agriculture in Kenya was given as its main strength. Odingo is concerned with aims not so much with consequences and this is perhaps the reason why he readily accepts the official view. Thus he states:

"The original aims that the Awash Valley Project were concerned with were laudable. It was hoped that as the production of grain in the valley rose, storage facilities would be built to deal with carrying over stocks from season to season. Secondly, it was hoped that the valley should provide the government with one of the areas in which strategic famine relief reserves would be built to serve the drought prone districts of Wollo and Shoa."

Odingo's source of information is the Awash Valley Authority, UNDP/FAO, A. Shaw and others.

Hussein, writing about the same valley, is concerned about the consequences. He documents the adverse effects of commercialization of the subsistence economy. Writing about the valley he notes:

"Out of an estimated total of some 200,000 ha of irrigable land, 25% was developed in 1970/71, mainly for the production of cotton and sugar. It was precisely those areas most frequented by the 'Afar - traditionally their grazing - which were converted into the profitable cashcrop production enterprises. However, this also proved to be *excellent land for irrigation!* Hence, concessions were given to various private individuals as well as big companies, the latter mostly Dutch, Italian, Israeli, or British. A lion's share also went to the feudal autocrat of the 'Afar, Sultan Ali Mirah, who cultivated over 14,200 ha. The eviction of the 'Afar from their well watered grazing pastures led to a relative over-population of the less fertile parts of the valley to which they had been forced to move. This is how the over-grazing, diminishing herds, malnutrition and starvation much talked of by the 'experts' came about". (Hussein, p. 19).

But the most severe indictment about the famines of the Ethiopian drought was that there was grain in the world and there was grain even in Ethiopia. Shepherd writes:

"For one thing, the State Department kept shifting the arrival dates for grain shipments to Ethiopia. Ironically, most ships hauling grain from the United States in 1973-74 were heading for the Soviet Union and not the hungry nations of Africa. But the more serious charges were that "while peasants died, some Ethiopians thrived. . . . This was the ultimate, bitter irony about the famine, unlike the Sahel, or any other starving nation in the world, Ethiopia always has available within its borders, the resources for halting famine. Throughout 1973 and during the first half of 1974, while tens of thousands starved, other Ethiopians hoarded and exported grains . . . there were between 20,000-30,000 tons of grain in commercial warehouses. . . . Those 20,000 or more tons were at least half the amount needed to keep all the starving peasants of Wollo and Tigre alive throughout 1973 . . . classic market fluctuations were played careful. . . . Sorghum prices in places . . . jumped from $5 per quintal to $20 per quintal during 1973. . . . There was little concern for the impact of this on the starving . . . long after careful documentation of the extent of the food crisis—Ethiopian merchants exported hundreds of tons of grains, beans and even milk to Western

Europe and the Saudi Arabian peninsula. In 1973, while 100,000 of its people starved to death, Ethiopia exported 9,000 metric tons of grain (food for 100,000 people for 3 months)—almost double its 1972 exports . . . the country was additionally exporting 177,000 tons of pulses—a staggering amount of exports for a country whose people were begging for food and dying from starvation.''

Shepherd quotes his figures from the National Bank of Ethiopia, the *Ethiopia Herald* and various relief organizations. What were the priorities of the IEG and the world press? Once again Shepherd points out the irony:

"The high-politics of this hot corner obscured the fact that Ethiopia wanted guns and needed grain, but was only willing to pay for guns. While high-level policy planners in Washington and other world capitals weighed and the world press focussed on the major issues: the arms build up in Ethiopia; the Russian presence in Somalia, the strategic significance of the Babel Mandeb straits; Red Sea, Persian Gulf, Indian Ocean - scenarios involving the Soviet Union, the United States and Arab States, and Israel - Ethiopians starved.''

The priorities of deployment of resources is a much more crucial factor in the consideration of famines than drought. If the priorities are not food and self-reliance then drought serves as an excellent excuse for the deaths of thousands and the malnourishment of millions.

THE SITUATION IN KENYA AND THE STRENGTH OF ITS AGRICULTURE

Richard Odingo is the author of the paper on the Kenya case-study. Odingo puts more emphasis on the 1961/2 famines than on those of the 1970s. Perhaps this could be justified on the grounds that the famines of 1961/2 were more severe than those of 1975/6. In 1961/2 Kenya spent over £10 million in importing famine-relief food apart from the free famine-relief supplies from the United States. In the 1970s, Kenya was much more prepared to deal with the situation and only £1 million was spent on famine relief. Once again Kajiado District and especially Masailand were hit. Similarly, the people of the north-east part of Kenya also experienced food shortages. Altogether some 2.4 million people live in areas considered to be of medium potential. Covering a far larger area but with about only a fifth of the population is the area defined as arid and with a low potential for agriculture. An important difference between Kenya an Ethiopia is that the number of people in semi-arid areas is small in Kenya. Secondly, Kenya, as Odingo points out, "has a strong agricultural base in at least one-third of the total land area and where a policy of self-sufficiency in food has been pursued and achieved for some years''. But the strength of Kenya's agriculture is not merely one of land suitable for agriculture; rather it is a story of massive investment of resources into agriculture. The origins of this success story are not too different from those which initiated "successes'' in the agriculture of Europeans in South Africa, Rhodesia, Mozambique, Angola or pre-independence Tanzania. What distinguished Kenya is that the heroic fight for land led to independence but a privileged "white'' farmer class gave way to a Kenyan privileged class. Consequently the old system was preserved. Commercialization of agriculture has intensified to a degree which makes Kenya an important centre for multinational activities. This is a pattern also found in Mexico, Colombia, Philippines and other countries.

Odingo stresses several times in his paper that the Kenya Government was much more prepared to deal with the situation in the 1970s. Thus while there was an overall reduction in some agricultural crops in some years due to drought, there has been a steady to dramatic increase in maize production from 240,000 tons in 1967 to 373,000 tons, 440,000 tons, 365,000 tons, 487,000 tons in 1972, 1973, 1974 and 1975, respectively.

Kenya seems to have embarked on the commercial cultivation of maize and maize has become big business. As a result the surpluses of maize are so ensured that Kenya uses maize for secondary and tertiary purposes rather than for human consumption alone.

In the context of preparedness, the Kenyan case-study also shows how the infrastructure in the arid and semi-arid areas has improved. The government has constructed appropriate storage facilities close to the drought-prone areas of Machakos, Kitue, etc., and where famine-relief distribution has to take place there is close liaison between the Maize Marketing Board and the Provincial Administration. Since the semi-arid north-eastern part of Kenya is also politically vulnerable, and indeed Somalia has on several occasions made territorial claims to these parts, it has also become important for political and strategic reasons to pay attention to an area formerly neglected. Therefore, communications and infrastructure have had to be improved.

Notwithstanding the above facts, the pastoral people of Kenya continue to be afflicted by famines. The explanation in the case-study is that these famines are a result of "previous government efforts to sedentarise the population and to introduce agriculture in the district, in addition to the very marked reduction in the livestock mortality through diseases like rinderpest and East Coast Fever". Small irrigation projects and formal grazing schemes were started in Turkana, Masailand and Samburu. Obviously, such measures are not intended to halt drought! Therefore, one is surprised by the first half of the statement that "the meteoric rise in cattle populations which must partly be blamed for the drought and the high stock mortality during the drought". Both in "the colonial period and even today the main blame on pastoralists like the Masai is their extreme conservatism". However, this impact of drought on livestock is not specific to Kenya. The total livestock mortality figures in Australia, for instance, during periods of drought are many times higher than in Kenya. The explanation for pastoral activities in semi-arid areas in Kenya or Australia or Tanzania is that it is a convenient form of land use. To blame the Masai for loss of cattle on conservatism and to spare his colleagues in the developed world is in fact applying double standards. The negative attitude to pastoralists is not uniquely Kenyan. For instance, an Ethiopian notes that:

"The pastoralists, in Ethiopia and elsewhere (Oxby) are usually blamed by armchair 'experts' for keeping too many herds as this causes over-grazing degradation of the soil leading to erosion and the now popular terms—desertification and the 'encroaching desert'. However, it is not that simple. Pastoralists everywhere have found through centuries of accumulated experience that a large number of animals is an insurance against a severe drought. What is more, livestock are their major form of property with all the political and social significance attendant on this" (Hussein, p. 19).

Kenya has managed to achieve "national self-sufficiency in grain ostensibly even during periods of drought. Such 'national' self-sufficiency can only be short term. The long-term improvements can only come about if groups which are marginalized are identified and the root causes of poverty are attacked."

TANZANIAN FOOD SHORTAGES AND ATTEMPTS FOR SOLUTION

There were two contributions to the Project about drought in Tanzania, by R. Odingo and by A. Mascarenhas. We have included only the latter in Volume 3, as it is more comprehensive and provides some relevant examples supporting the main theme of this Report.

The common features about the studies on Kenya, Ethiopia and Tanzania is that they experienced a drought and a decline in agricultural production around the mid-1970s. However, in Tanzania there were no deaths attributed to drought. As has already been stated, Kenya managed to ride through the drought because of a strong agricultural base. Tanzania did not have the technically sound agricultural foundation which had been created in Kenya. The emphasis on "cash" or export crops during the colonial period undermined whatever food security which might have existed in Tanzania. It is not surprising that some contradictions in this respect still exist in independent Tanzania as the extent to which this country can achieve self-sufficiency depends much on the international situation. The fact remains that there was no human calamity despite the drought in the 1970s and therefore it becomes important to know how this was achieved.

In Tanzania attempts to improve the quality of life in the rural areas had begun in 1967. One aspect of improvement is related to settlements. The period of drought threatened to disrupt a massive political programme, which had started some years ago to resettle people. For centuries most of the people lived in scattered homestead and while this ensured a certain degree of minimization of environmental risks, including drought, there was little room for any significant improvement to the quality of life. The first villagization programmes took place in regions prone to environmental hazards. The majority of people in Tanzania now live in nucleated villages and the essential social and economic services are increasingly becoming a reality. The resettlement programme is just one aspect of a process in which the central theme is the development of people. Capitalistic trends such as land speculation and exploitation of labour have been curbed. The essential services have all been taken in the hands of the state. Mascarenhas recognizes, however, that the major beneficial impact on all people will take decades to materialize.

There was no loss of life from food shortages in Tanzania because the problem of food shortages was openly discussed by the government. Several months before the food crisis loomed there were reports in the local papers about crop failures, food shortages and even food relief in some districts.

This is in clear contrast with the attitude of the Ethiopian government in 1973, as indicated above. In September 1974 the President made an appeal to the nation and launched the *Kilimo cha Kufa na Kupona* (Agriculture for Survival) programme. Most of the food required was *purchased* but a considerable amount also came in as famine relief.

The response made to the food shortages in the 1970s is clearly not a long-range guarantee against famines. Neither is it enough to have institutional reforms without developing a technical competence and adequate infrastructure.

The constraints to Tanzania's food security are numerous. They range from social factors such as lack of recognition of the significance of the role of women in food production both at domestic and farm level to the appropriateness of technology; from economic factors such as unstable prices and unequal exchange to purely technical questions such as the correct use of fertilizers or seeds.

Notwithstanding the above facts Tanzania still has options. These include, that a higher priority be given to the investments made to production of food crops, encouragement of simple technologies as well as the more sophisticated ones, greater efforts to encourage settlements into high potential areas. Food security is a long-term goal because it is a multi-sectoral problem of which drought is but only one dimension. The food security of Tanzania will be assured if there is development, but in order to develop it cannot afford to ignore issues connected with both food and export crops. This duality has created problems and the question that Tanzania will have to repeatedly ask itself is whose interests are being served in the long run and change directions when the balance is not in favour of Tanzania. For example, research in food crops might well be expensive but getting loans for tobacco expansion is relatively easy. Should it risk expansion on tobacco in order to earn foreign exchange? Clearly, there is more room for studies which explore options and policies for long-term food security. Similarly more efforts should be made to look into the realities of solving nutrition and food problems rather than stagnate in the various permutations of past exploitation. In this respct the policy of having strategic grain reserves is excellent but what are the emerging logistic and administrative problems?

Kenya seems to have made impressive gains on the side of sheer production especially of cereals. Given the right policies there should be no famines or malnutrition. Tanzania falls at the other end of the spectrum in which past neglect of food crops and its weak production infrastructure has demanded a reorientation. Being an underdeveloped country this reorientation has been painful in the short term. The Ethiopia tragedy highlights the price which had to be paid for not regarding famines as a socio-economic problem. Finally, with so much hindsight shown in the case studies is there any way to ensure that in the future the rational choice is made? This is more a political question than an environmental issue.

D. Drought in America

Part Five of Volume 3 contains six papers dealing with the impacts of droughts on some Latin American countries:

1. J.C. Portantiero: "Land, state and industry in Latin America: some hypotheses" (Chapter 11).
2. G. Martins Dias: "Drought as a social phenomenon in Northeastern Brazil" (Chapter 12).
3. D. Gross and N. M. Flowers: "The political economy of drought in Northeastern Brazil" (Chapter 13).
4. E. Nunes: "Social and political aspects of the drought in Northeast Brazil" (Chapter 14)
5. A. O. Villarreal and M. A. E. Ortiz Cruz: "Drought and man in Mexico: the historical case of 1972" (Chapter 15).

6. O. Maggiolo: "Venezuelan atmospheric anomalies and its food supply in 1970-1975" (Chapter 16).

Portantiero's paper includes two case-studies, on Argentina and Mexico, written in collaboration with Carlos Abalo and Santiago Funes, respectively.

1. LAND, STATE, INDUSTRY AND THE STRUCTURE OF AGRICULTURAL PRODUCTION IN LATIN AMERICA

We consider Portantiero's paper as one of the most important conceptual contributions to the Project. His central hypothesis is that "Latin American agrarian problems are closely related to the problems of social costs determined by the path leading to industrialization (. . .) and the policies practised by the State in order to follow this path. (. . .) This means that, in Latin America, land and the corresponding State policies must take charge of the costs of a dependent semi-industrialization process." Within this general frame, the agrarian sector participates in two quite different ways in the overall productive system of the country. On the one hand, it is a source of high currency necessary to import raw materials, manufactured products and technology for the industrial sector. On the other hand, it must produce cheap food for the working class, inasmuch as high prices in food would have a direct adverse effect on the minimum level of salaries and thereby on the cost of production. This double role of the agrarian sector implies that it must adapt itself to a double set of requirements corresponding respectively to the external and the internal markets. There is therefore a duality in the agrarian system which results in two quite different subsectors: the "modern", oriented towards exports (and production of more sophisticated food for the urban élite), and the "traditional" - the "poor" one - which, as Portantiero points out, carries the weight of the industrialization process. The support of the State, in the form of credits and investments, goes mainly to the former. Thus, the coexistence of the two subsectors and, in particular, the permanence of the "traditional" one is not *caused* by the "backwardness" of the population involved in it, but the *effect* of State policies.

The relevance of this analysis for the Project becomes evident as soon as one realizes that the impact of a "natural disaster" on each subsector of the agrarian system produces entirely different affects. This poses a most serious problem to the Project because any recommendation intended to reach the roots of catastrophic effects of droughts in the "backward" subsector of the agricultural system cannot help dealing with the profound *structural* problems of the society and, in particular, with the system of internal relations within the trinity agriculture-industry-state. We find therefore that the analysis of the differential effect of drought or any other "natural disaster" coincides with the analysis of the roots of underdevelopment.

The study would thus be led to enter another field: the evolution of agriculture in developing countries in relation to the successive phases of the international division of labour. We shall only make a few remarks. The present situation is outlined by Portantiero in section 4 of his paper ("Agriculture and the New Accumulation Pattern"). He refers to the new trend in agriculture and livestock activity that transforms it in just one of the links in a complex chain of activities within agro-industry. The chain as a whole is controlled by transnational companies or their local affiliates. This irreversible trend springs from a deeply rooted orientation in the "central" countries as regards the establishment of a new international economic order. In those countries where it is in operation the initial effects of the new model have already aggravated the food situation for the low income of urban and rural masses. We share in this regard Portantiero's position whose final remarks put the problem within a proper frame:

"While production increases for export and for local high-income consumers, furnished with food from large, modern agricultural companies—supported by the State with loans and investment for infrastructure - the traditional *campesino* economy languishes, the sector faces increased problems of proverty and poor diet until it gets to the point where basic foods must be imported in order to prevent famine, while at the same time sophisticated products and cereals for animal fodder are exported to the central countries. It seems that it is impossible to curb the path of agroindustry in its current role for developing countries. It is obviously not the aspect of modernization that could become detrimental to the countries, but the orientation given to this aspect. It is not a question of crying over the disappearance of a *campesino* economy with a low productivity rate, but of seeking to render the inevitable role played by the industrialization of agriculture into more rational use in terms of the food requirements of the majority of the population."

2. DROUGHT IN MEXICO

The Mexican case-study has been approached by the Project in two different ways. A global approach is found in Portantiero's paper referred to above. The section entitled "The case of Mexico", written in collaboration with Santiago Funes, presents a condensed and clear-cut overview of Mexican agricultural problems, their historical roots, and their relations to natural disasters.

The authors consider that Mexico is the richest laboratory in the continent for the study of agrarian problems. "Extremely vulnerable against any 'natural catastrophe', Mexico is an excellent example of the significant influence of such 'human' factors as the selection of state policies, the distribution of income and, in short, each and every item that may be included under the concept of 'development pattern' for the analysis of the reception and processing of natural disasters."

We refer the reader to the original paper for an account of the historical evolution leading to the present crisis of the Mexican agriculture. Here it suffices to quote some revealing figures showing that the roots of the crisis of this sector of Mexican economy are not found in natural catastrophes, nor in the population explosion, but elsewhere.

—At present, the animal fodder absorbs more agricultural products than 20 million *campesinos*: in 1976 more soybeans were used in cattle feed than the total amount of beans and legumes consumed by the population.
—Between 1939 and 1965 agricultural production had risen to an average annual growth of 5% (higher than the population growth rate).

—Between 1964 and 1970 the growth rate dropped to 2%, but the animal growth rate for livestock reached 5.4%.

—Between 1970 and 1976 there was a drop of -0.9% in the annual growth rate of agricultural and livestock products as a whole, although livestock production rose by 3%.

—In the food industry the situation is similar: during the period between 1970 and 1976, manufacture of cereal products registered an annual growth of 1.6%, whereas the manufacture of protein and canned products showed a growth rate of 4.5%.

The explanation provided by the authors for this panorama is quite simple. While commercial agriculture flourished under the protection of availability of credit, capital, irrigation and infrastructure, the *campesino* economy underwent an increase in decapitalization and a drop in productivity. Meat, eggs and milk are not important parts of the diet of the majority of the population, but beans and corn are. "Thus, the role of the agrarian sector seems increasingly clear: to produce for export, to feed cattle well and to feed the medium and high income urban population."

When this pattern is applied to the analysis of the drought effects the conclusions we may arrive at appear as a rather obvious consequence of the following remark. Thus two totally different areas must be outlined to be used as the basis for a study of official activities and concrete government policies regarding drought. The evidence shows that most past experience involves reducing the coefficient risk for commercial agriculture; in other words, increasing the accumulation rate in the agrarian capitalistic zones. The rainfall-dependent zones with predominantly "simple-merchant" forms of production have not received official assistance in regard to weather risks.

With this background the contribution made by E. Ortiz and A. Oñate becomes very illuminating. They carried out a second approach to the Mexican case-study envisaged by the Project, the materialization of which involved a long process. First, an agreement was reached with the "Centro de Ciencias de la Atmosfera" of the National Autonomous University of Mexico (UNAM). A group under the direction of Eng. Pedro Mosiño collected the best available rainfall data set for Mexico and Central America, and carried out an analysis of the 1972 rainfall anomalies in the whole area. They applied a powerful statistical method developed by Mosiño and Garcia based on computation of the gamma function.[16] On the basis of this climatological information three regions were selected in Mexico that presented at the same time a serious rainfall deficiency in the period under study and distinctive characteristics of the agricultural production system. These regions were located in the States of Guanajuato, Baja California and Oaxaca.

At a second stage, another agreement was reached with the Metropolitan Autonomous University of Mexico (UAM) in order to undertake the study of the three regions. A multidisciplinary team of ecologists, sociologists and economists was set up by the University to that effect. They visited the three states to make some field research on each of the fields of study. Their results, presented in the extended paper by Oñate and Ortiz, provide a striking illustration of the general picture described in the preceding section and in several other sections of this chapter concerning the "differential" effects of drought on different sections of the population.

In two zones, Baja California (Norte) and Guanajuato (Bajio), the population does not seem to have registered the 1972 drought as a specially significant catastrophe. In the Bajio, 1972 was not considered an abnormal year as far as rainfall was concerned. It seems that there is an adaptation to periodic reductions of rainfall. There is a fairly solid economic integration in the region and a rather stable infrastructure that has been developed after many years.

In the case of Baja California, 1972 was in fact considered an anomalous year. Unirrigated cropping was reduced to practically zero. This had, however, no serious effect as the economy of the region as a whole is based on high technology agriculture, under irrigation and highly capitalized. It was, therefore, not disrupted. The environment itself did not suffer any damage either.

The region of Oaxaca is in sharp contrast with the preceding two. The 1972 drought was really perceived as a disaster. The authors characterize this region as having a socio-ecosystem with very marginal stability conditions. The drought destabilized the system and started a process with serious consequences for the population, out of proportion with the actual marginalization of the physical phenomenon itself. We find here a clear illustration in a concrete actual example, of the theoretical interpretation put forward in Chapter 6.

What followed after the instability of the system was released is the common well-know pattern:

—migration of part of the rural population to urban centres;
—governmental aid to the region, creating jobs for the unemployed (construction of roads, dams, channels, etc.), and providing cheap (subsidized) food for the victims.

The authors analyse the consequences of these two effects. They both act in the same direction. Migrations to the urban centres generates a cheap labour force available to the local industries and service enterprises. It helps keeping salaries down. On the other hand, the benefit of the governmental "aid" does not really go to the peasants. Here again, cheap food and subsidized labour keep costs down for those who control the power structure in the region. The net result is an increase of capital accumulation.

The striking similarity of the process described by Oñate and Ortiz with the picture that emerges from the case studies on north-east Brazil (cf. next section) makes it unnecessary to go into further details. We shall only add an important remark made by the authors about the preservation of the environment. In a fully capitalistic society the elements of the ecosystem are considered as a merchandise. This is because the process of capital accumulation is linked to the reproduction of the whole socio-ecosystem. Preservation of the environment is thus a way of accumulating capital. In a society which is in a transitory stage, as far as the capitalistic system is concerned, capital accumulation requires only the reproduction of the social relations, not of the ecosystem. The elements of the ecosystem do not reach the level of merchandise. There is therefore no interest in reproducing the ecosystem which is thus subjected to a destructive use.

This is very far indeed from the naive perspective of those who believe that "education" alone is the answer to the destruction of the environment that is characteristic of marginal societies.

3. DROUGHT IN THE BRAZILIAN NORTH-EAST[17]

Few regions in the Americas have been the object of greater public attention and studies than the North-east of Brazil since the early fifties. The reason for such great interest lies in the fact that this area has always been one of the poorest and most backward in the Continent. This is an extraordinary fact when we consider that Brazil itself has reached one of the highest levels of economic growth in the West in the last 20 years.

In contemporary Brazilian history the North-castern region has remained as a huge pocket of underdevelopment, underemployment, poverty and ignorance. Indeed, the word *Nordestino* (North-easterner) has therefore become synonymous with "inferior and undersirable qualities" throughout the rest of the country. The scientific literature concerning the region, resulting from its unique suffering, has grown and is part responsible for the increase in the number of scholars, politicians and government officials, both inside and outside the region, searching for and suggesting solutions for this drama of the Brazilian North-east.

The drama can partially be understood through the physical and economic characteristics which divide North-east society into three subregions. The area next to the Atlantic is humid and is called *a zona da mata*, or forest zone. There is a long intermediary subregions between the humid coastal belt and the semi-desert inland region, it is called the area of rough countryside or *o agreste*. The semi-arid interior is called *o sertao* which can be translated as the hinterland. The occupation and utilization of these subregions at the end of the sixteenth century by the Portuguese gave rise to widely differing economic, social and political forms. Notwithstanding being part of one colonial system only, the ecological differences which characterized them were seen to subject them to completely different forms of both land and political domination; while the large estate owners controlled the economic, social and political life of the forest region, turning it into one of the world's greatest sugar-cane-producing areas; the other two subregions were subordinate and soon became a mere appendage to the "zona da mata's" economy and political power, especially the "Agreste", which concentrated in food production for internal consumption, mainly cassava and cattle ranching. This livestock farming, augmented by the pastures of the sertao, has since widened both the agricultural as well as the political frontiers of the region as a whole.

However, not only do the soil's characteristics distinguish the coastal zone from the inland area of the North-east, for, even by the end of the sixteenth century, Portuguese colonizers had already reported terrible droughts occurring in the "hinterland". These droughts resulted in that part of the colony receiving little or no attention. This neglect was to remain for the next two centuries until cattle ranching and cotton became profitable because of the American civil war. Certainly, only from the end of this epoch can we see a rise in the demographic growth of the *sertao* and above all only after this period that the droughts in fact had large-scale and catastrophic effects.

Economic development in the last three decades has resulted in important changes in the physical environment and in the social structure of the region. There has been:

1. a process of rapid and widely spread urbanization;
2. the beginning of industrialization in the big coastal cities;
3. a substantial decline in the numbers and the area of very large rural establishments;
4. a considerable expansion in the number of the medium-sized and the small rural establishments;
5. a very substantial expansion of the impoverished subsistence agriculture which represents the major source of North-easterner livelihood;
6. a considerable expansion in the network of roads and water reservoirs, making possible the expansion of rural frontiers;
7. more recently, the development of large-scale cattle farms which tend to occupy the best agricultural lands in the dry *sertao*.

These changes altogether have contributed to transform the region in a very noticeable way. Although we can notice a correlation between social and physical changes (in spite of the fact that these changes may have helped to strengthen old privileges and make life still poorer to the peasant and to the urban poor in the North-east region) we could not state with any degree of scientific precision that there is a correlation between these transformations and the contributing physical and biological causes.

The papers on North-eastern Brazil included in Volume 3 are intended to bring the reader a combination of information and perspectives providing a retrospective and analytical picture of the phenomenon of droughts of the Brazilian North-east.

Through the three contributions we are introduced to some of the very central questions of the drought challenge in spite of the different emphases and distinct perceptions of the phenomenon by the authors. Indeed, we are dealing here with the relationships that men are forced into with the environment and consequently we are looking into the patterns of relationships which society establish with the ecosystem.

Even so, we still have to insist on the fact that all three essays are attempts which seek to establish the social, economic and political dimensions of a natural disaster, and in doing so they try to qualify the vulgar understanding that such phenomenon can be dealt with exclusively with physical solutions. Indeed, the most essential argument used in the three essays is that phenomena such as drought can be, and frequently are, manipulated by social, political and economic interests. Therefore, the drought excuse is used in such a way as to perpetuate socio-economic structures and existing privileges, or even to create new ones. Many instances of similar natural disasters in different societies have resulted in very distinct social, economic and political consequences. Thus earthquakes, floods, epidemics or droughts produce effects which are distinct not only by the physical characteristics of their agents but over all by the recipient or affected social group characteristics and/or by the way the social structure of the community is organized.

The first paper, by G. Martins Dias, covers the social, political, economic interactions and the changes in economic and political structures in the region during the last 50 years. It concentrates on the examination of the functioning of the droughts *secas* in the present socio-economic context of the country and the roles being fulfill-

ed by the North-east region in the actual process of development of Brazilian society. Accordingly the drought is seen here as a phenomenon which by its systematic
manipulation by the regional oligarchy results in the maintenance of the social,
economic and polictical structures of the region. Therefore the survival of the
regional and conservative élites results to a large extent from the existence of complex mechanisms of interaction between them and the central government. Through
the transfer of financial resources and political power decisions which can be
justified through the overdramatized plight of the *secas* and the existing power structures are reinforced through the selective use of public funds in such a way as to ensure ever-increasing privileges to region "chieftans". That is why it is argued that
the sad, social, economic and political consequences of North-eastern droughts have
as their causes as much as the lack of rains, the very social structures which it creates
and helps to maintain.

The second paper is both an ingenious and original piece of research and is by the
eminent Brazilian scholar Edison Nunes. The picture of the droughts provided by
his research enable us to envisage the phenomenon in its social, economic and
political aspects, portrayed above all through the testimonies of those who witness-
ed, at first hand, these dry periods. It is above all through the careful analysis of
reports of journalists who actually experienced "the heat of the moment" that this
work is illuminating in so many respects. Edison Nunes through his original approach presents this repeating drama, its eternal players, the exploiters, its
mediators and the State. It is a testimony above all that is not limited by the simple
areas of drought but extends far beyond. Indeed, the author through a clear analysis
provides us with a schematic approach of the relationships which are created and
strengthened between the different social groups during such traumatic times. Also
he gives an insight on the inter-regional consequences, especially on the growing
dependence of the North-east in relation to the centre/south region of Brazil.

In the case of Edison Nunes' contribution, we can perceive the sorrow and the suffering of the population although through the eyes of journalists, whose urban bias
became transparently clear when they wrote about topics they have selected and
those contents concern basically also urban interests and fears. Indeed, what is more
dramatized by journalists' reports, analysed in the paper, tend to be those aspects of
the drought whose consequences can threaten or disrupt life in town. Pillage,
violence, assaults and epidemics became the object of more attention although they
would represent very little in relation to the deep suffering represented by unemployment, loss of status, personal and social impotence and dependence, not to speak of
the almost perennial insufficiency in food, land and water. We find in this contribution a very good complement to the paper by Martins Dias who, in a different
fashion, tends to concentrate on the political and economic effects of drought leaving aside the very way the phenomena is perceived by its victims.

The study by Daniel Gross and Nancy Flowers is very illuminating not only for the
indisputable anthropological competence shown by the authors but also because of
the differences with the former papers, particularly with reference to the proposals
made.

Gross and Flowers have been working for many years in the Brazilian North-east,
and the standard of their research and methodology can only compare with the very
best ever done on the region. We only need to mention in this connection the

pioneering studies made by Gross on the ecological, anthropologica, social and economic aspects of sisal cultivation. In their paper, the authors, beyond supplying a comprehensive perspective about the North-east region and its recent development, permit us to see the amount of work done by a large number of scholars, mainly foreigners who have advanced considerably the research into the causes and the effects of drought in the region. By comparing the views, arguments and proposals made by these scholars with those of Martins Dias and Nunes, we can detect a clear distinction between those who are very much part of the local *milieu* and look at the problems from inside the country and within the context of the internal national inter-relations among regions, on the one hand, and those who have a more detached perspective, on the other. Each group may detect in the other an element of ethnocentrism.

4. DROUGHT IN VENEZUELA

Maggiolo's contribution is twofold. In the first place, he accepted the responsibility for undertaking the calculation of the severity of droughts in the areas of the world studied by the Project. He developed his own method of assessing the "return time" of a drought or flood in order to make the comparison possible. This part of his work is reported in Part Two of the present volume. Here we shall only mention his findings about the climatic anomalies in Venezuela during the period we are considering, reported by him as follows:

> "1. Between the years 1967 and 1974, atmospheric anomalies have occurred in Venezuela. These consisted of seven consecutive years of great precipitations or severe droughts, with a return time greater than 4 years. This fact has not been observed in the last 50 years, for which hydrometeorologic records are available.
> 2. In 1972, very intense atmospheric anomalies occurred in important regions for Venezuelan agriculture, as in the Unare low plain, in the high central plains, the low plains, the high western plains, and the Orinoco river basin. These anomalies were characterized by low precipitations in the Unare low plains, and in the high central plains, while in the western plains and in the Orinoco river basin there were very heavy rains.
> 3. The return time of both these anomalies were very high: twenty or more years.
> 4. In 1973, the droughts covered all the regions previously mentioned, and in some of them, which during 1972 were rainy areas, the effect was lessened as a consequence of the stored water in the underground (High West Plains).
> 5. The return times of the observed droughts are of the same order as those which were calculated for the African Sahel region during 1972 and 1973."

After these findings, Maggiolo turns to an analysis of the Venezuelan agriculture. The period between 1971 and 1973 were considered as years of an "agricultural crisis" in Venezuela. He comments as follows:

> "The coincidence that exists between these three years, and the strong atmospheric anomalies, analysed in the previous chapters, which affected the

whole national territory, led us to establish a close relationship between the agricultural crisis of 1971-73, and the water excess or scarcity for crops. However, it is amazing to see that the majority of the analyses related to the theme give little importance to the climatic factor. The fundamental responsibility of the agricultural crisis is attributed to the lack of a national political stimulus for agriculture and cattle activities.''

He concludes that it is necessary to distinguish between two kinds of factors that explain the Venezuelan agricultural crisis of the years following 1971, namely the structural ones, which are of a political and economic nature, and those related to special climatic anomalies. he rightly points out that ''if unfavourable climatic factors are prolonged more than usual, as has been the case of Venezuela after 1967, a structurally weak system could collapse if rapid adequate political and economic measures are not taken''. This is quite in line with the analysis made in other case-studies.

Maggiolo adds, moreover, a very important point deserving, we believe, further analysis. This would take us, however, beyond the scope of our study. He considers that ''the structural crisis of the Venezuelan agricultural production is related to the decrease of the invested capital on this activity, with respect to the investments in manufacturing industrial activities of the same country, or in the great multinational industrial enterprises, through the international banking system''.

We may agree with this, but we should take exception to his following statement:

''This situation is also very similar to the one observed in some food producing countries of South America like Uruguay and Argentina, where the stagnation of meat production is responsible for the troubles observed in the political and economic life of these countries.''

We believe that the assertion is far too strong, that agricultural production and meat production cannot be put in the same basket, and that the problem has to be reformulated in a larger context such as, for instance, the framework provided by Portantiero's contribution. With some minor modifications we would agree, however, with Maggiolo's final conclusions:

''Only great agro-industrial and commercial complexes which include everything from production to sales through industrialization, packing and transportation to highly remunerative markets, are able to overcome this permanent crisis which affects agriculture. In the case where populations of low income levels must be fed, private enterprises do not seem to provide economic means for food production, except by transgressing the basic principles of free enterprise, through a compulsory intervention of the state via subsidies and price and wage control. In summary, if the conclusions of the Venezuelan and the South American case could be generalized to the Third World situation where hunger is permanent, a hypothesis could be established: the food crisis as well as the danger of a world famine which has been so much discussed in recent years, is mainly the crisis of the private agro-production system, since it is not able to create the adequate stimuli to increase the activity in the agricultural sector, and, at the same time, to produce food at prices that can be reached by most of the world population.''

D. Drought in Asia

1. Part Four of Volume 3 includes the following special contributions on Asia:

   1. P. Spitz: "Drought and social classes in Asia" (Chapter 8).
   2. P. R. Pisharoty and P. Sharma: "Drought and man in India" (Chapter 1)
   3. G. Etienne: "Possibilities and prosects of reducing drought effects in India and China" (Chapter 19).

These papers are preceded by an introduction, written by Pierre Spitz, on "Drought, aridity and society", having a very wide scope and being therefore applicable to all case studies.

There is no paper concerning the problems of the rice-producing countries in South East Asia and the Far East. A special project on "The impact of climate change on agricultural production and socio-economic conditions of rice-growing countries in Asia" is underway under the leadership of Dr. Shinichi Ichimura, Director of the Center for Southeast Asian Studies of Kyoto University, the results of which will be made available to IFIAS.

2. In the paper by Pierre Spitz, an assessment is made of the impact of drought on the production and the consumption patterns of various groups of agricultural producers in India. His approach is original and highly illuminating. By making very simple and realistic hypotheses about actual situations, he is able to show - through direct calculations - the magnitude of some important differential effects which are sometimes known in purely qualitative terms but seldom appreciated in their real dimensions.

It is well known, for instance, that the effect of good and bad years are not felt with the same intensity by all producers. One is shocked, however, when numbers are put into this assertion.

Spitz considers the case of families who own lands of different degrees of fertility. He assumes three families having areas of land in three different kinds of rice-fields, the size being inversely proportional to the yields in a good year. The actual calculations show the following situation.

—In a good year, the three families produce the same annual crop (this is obvious, since the figures have been chosen that way). There are, however, important differences. "Family Z has to work twice as hard as family X. If this double work is done entirely by the family labour force, it is not paid for it. However, it involves increased consumption, since consumption on workings days is higher than on non-working days. The differences between the two families X and Z may be due to climatic constraints which require the work to be done within a specific period of time. If, for example, the work force of family X (the most privileged family) is such that full employment is possible during a working period whose duration is fixed (by the arrival of the monsoon, combined with a bioclimatological constraint), family Z will have to procure additional manpower (and animal traction) and pay for them. The same problem may arise in an even more acute form at the planting stage, since planting has to be done quickly and requires many hands. Thus, a real cost item emerges."

—In a year of drought the differences between the three kinds of rice fields is strongly accentuated. Under the assumptions made (e.g. the three families have the same level of self-provisioning) the surplus of X is reduced to only one half, but that of Z is almost entirely eliminated.

Theoretically, if there is an alternance of good and bad years, family Z could ensure a level of self-supply provided that stocks are laid in during a good year. However, in the case of a failure in this alternance (two successive bad years, not enough carry-over from the good year) the only way to make the necessary adjustment in the provision of food is by way of an interest-bearing loan, which reduces for the next year the share available for consumption or stock. The gap between family Z and family X is thereby widened. The widening of the gap is further increased if - as it is often the case - family X acts as a lender.

> 'Thus—concludes Spitz - between these two families which have the same gross income in a normal year, we find a lopsidedness due to the effect of yearly variations between yields in lands of unequal fertility. This lopsidedness was inherent in the fact that the lands were of different value, but it was concealed in a good year by the equality of the harvests, and it is accentuated by a cummulative process.''

The consumption patterns are analysed in a system of agriculture directed towards self-provisioning, i.e. direct consumption by-passing the market. The production is not measured in terms of total production, but in terms of the number of months of self-provisioning. Spitz shows the strong effects of the seasonal cycles in agricultural work. It is reflected in the need for building up intra-annual reserves (as distinct from inter-annual security stocks):

> "In the Chota Nagpur region, the varieties of rice used in 1962-1963 had a vegetative cycle of about five months (more recent varieties have a shorter cycle). If the months following the harvest are numbered from 1 to 12, the first soil preparation work begins with the monsoon in month 7 (May-June). The peak period for agricultural work is in month 8. During this period, the unit of production has its full complement of labour. The members of the family who are working away from the village return, and those who are engaged in a craft interrupt that activity. Month 8 is therefore a month in which monetary income is at its lowest. It is also the month in which food consumption is at its highest both because of the number of workers and because of their increased consumption level resulting from the hard physical labour required of them. Observation has shown that, in order to cope with this situation, families of types E and F tend to build up food reserves for this period, voluntarily breaking off self-provisioning whenever monetary resources can be found. These resources are then used to buy basic foodstuffs, particularly cereals, at a lower price than they would cost later, since prices rise steadily up to harvest time."

Thus each family is at the same time part of an agricultural system directed towards self-provisioning, and of a monetary economy. The insufficiency of any analysis that does not take this fact into account is quite apparent:

> "The point of departure for a correct analysis consists, on the one hand, of the establishment of a budget in physical terms and a budget in monetary terms and, on the other, of the establishment of a multiple calendar which makes it possible to register changes in stocks and flows, discrepancies between

resources and employment, variations in nutrition levels, the connexion of these nutritional variations with work distribution (festivals, ceremonies, pregnancies), migrations, indebtedness phenomena, discrepancies between the working periods of draught animals and availability of fodder resources etc.''

Spitz works out an example, by assuming various families whose production is expressed in different numbers of months of self-sufficiency. In order to assess their economic behaviour, he takes into account the average production characteristics (in relation to family characteristics, consumption levels and work opportunities outside), the variability of such characteristics in different years (i.e. basically according to climatic variations), price variations, distribution and size of deficits and surpluses, and the probabilities associated with them. He is then able to show how certain farmers may maintain or improve their incomes in a drought situation, whereas others suffer even before the effects of a drought are felt in their stocks. In this connection he quotes the following remark made by N. V. Kameswara Rao in respect of the Andhra Pradesh drought (1971-3):

"While the drought situation was disadvantageous to the lower sections of the society who mainly depend on manual labour, the well-to-do sections . . . found it advantageous to them. As they were getting labour at a cheaper rate, they took the opportunity to get their irrigation wells repaired and new ones dug at a much lower cost.''

The striking similarity of this situation with the descriptions of the drought situations in North-east Brazil described above shows that the effects of the socio-economic structures prevail over the wide differences of geographic, demograhic or cultural nature.

3. The paper by Pisharoty and Sharma, as well as Etienne's contribution to the Project may acquire a new dimension when they are looked at from the perspective offered by Spitz. They provide a straightforward analysis of factual material concerning the drought problems in India and China, and the remarks they make are indeed very sound from a technical point of view.

Their case-studies remain, however, incomplete inasmuch as the socio-economic analysis is not pushed, in our opinion, far enough. One exception is found in the section on the Green Revolution, by Pisharoty and Sharma, where they show how a social reality changes entirely the theoretical prospects of a purely technological approach:

"Most of the new varieties have to be raised on irrigated areas. With the availability of short-ripening varieties, multiple cropping has become much more extensive than it was before. Earlier results showed that by using multiple cropping employing the new varieties, yield of land was almost doubled. It was postulated that small farms were likely to be cultivated more intensively and hence the new technology would benefit small land holders more as compared to large land holders.

"It was thus thought that the "green revolution" would reduce the relative disparities between large and small land holders in irrigated areas. However, subsequent findings showed that it did not yield the anticipated results in this respect, although it saved India from large food imports. The success of green revolution did develop the rural parts although the wealth of the poor did not increase. In an "experimental" farm the tests conducted by scientists may indeed conclusively establish that small farms are as capable of benefitting from the new technology as big ones, but in the existing socio-political conditions in rural India the necessary inputs could be provided only to the relatively rich farmers with large holdings. The small farmers could not find the necessary inputs, partly due to lack of funds and partly due to official hurdles, which became unsurmountable for the poor.

"In adopting the new technology, a small farmer is not on par with a big farmer due to stringent requirements of irrigation, use of improved varieties of seeds, fertilizers, pesticides etc. which need capital investment. A number of Co-operative Agencies are in the field to advance credit to the farmers. However, it has been a common experience that large land holders manage to corner lion's share of the money. The small land holders are left with no alternative except to resort to borrowing from private money lenders and either pay back along with exorbitant interest on the loan or else part with a substantial part of the produce to the money lender in lieu: in either case it is the money lender who is benefitted financially more than the farmer. Similarly, big farmers manage to get priority in acquiring irrigation facilities whether it is by canals or tubewells. These circumstances have even provided a tendency to increase the financial disparity between the small and large land holders."

These are precisely the type of problems that require special attention in assessing the impact of droughts on a certain society. For as it is repeatedly shown in all case-studies which have been approached from a socio-economic viewpoint, it is the differential effect of droughts on certain segments of the population and not only the nature of the physical phenomenon that determines the conditions for what is called "a climatic disaster".

Notes

1. "Nine fallacies of natural disaster: the case of the Sahel", in *The Politics of Natural Disaster,* edited by Michael H. Glantz, New York, 1976.

2. *"Drought in the Sahel: transformation of the Sahelian pastoral and agricultural systems"* (Chapter 2 of Volume 3).

3. *"The Sahelian region: splendor yesterday, famine today. What will happen tomorrow?"* (Chapter 3 of Volume 3)

4. *"A few proposals for research-action concerning West African societies which have been the victims of drought"* (Chapter 4 of Volume 3).

5. Claude Raynaut, "Lessons of a Crisis", in *Drought in Africa,* edited by D. Dalby, R. J. Harrison Church and F. Bezzaz (International African Institute).

6. Jonathan Derrick, "The great West African drought 1972-1974", *African Affairs,* No. 305, October 1977.

7. IFIAS International Workshop on "The Drought and Man Project", Geneva, 19-22 September 1977, Report of Working Group B.

8. H. Sheets and R. Morris, *Disaster in the Desert: Failures of International Relief in the West African Drought.* Special Report. The Carnegie Endowment for International Peace.

9. *A Right to Food,* a selection from speeches by Addeke H. Boerma, FAO, Rome 1976, p. 132.

10. Comment by Colin Mackensie, editor of Boerma's speeches, *op.cit.,* p. 141.

11. J. Giri, "An analysis and synthesis of long-term development strategies for the Sahel", OECD, 1976.

12. W. Seifert and M. Kamrany, "A framework for evaluating long-term strategies for the development of the Sahel-Sudan region", MIT, 1974, Annex I, p. 52.

13. *Ibid.,* Volume II, p. 237.

14. We are greatful to Dr. A. Mascarenhas for his collaboration in the writing of this section.

15. We refer to the following papers:
    "The Ethiopian famines of the 1970s. Causes and consequences" by S. Ayalew. In Chapter 7 of Volume 3.
    "A background and a postscript to the food shortages in Tanzania in the 1970s" by A. Mascarenhas. In Chapter 6 of Volume 3.
    "A study of the causes, consequences and policy recommendations on drought in Ethiopia and Kenya" by R. Odingo. In Chapter 5 of Volume 3.

16. A paper describing the method was presented by the authors to the IFIAS Workshop on "Drought and Man", Geneva, September 1977.

17. This section was written in collaboration with G. Martins Dias.

CHAPTER 8

Conclusions and Recommendations

A. Conclusions

1. CLIMATIC FLUCTUATIONS AND THE 1972 BASE-HISTORY

1.1 It is normally assumed that during the year 1972 widespead food shortages and famines as well as serious disruptions in the international food market were the direct effects of extended and simultaneous droughts affecting various continents. Some speculations went even further and one finds quite definite statements, from authoritative sources, warning about the "growing evidence that the world is entering a new climatic régime". The prolonged Sahelian drought was considered by some climatologists as indicative of such changes.

The Project considered and discarded the assertion that we are witnessing a period of profound climatic changes. Such a contention is based on statistical analyses of mean atmospheric temperature changes. Quite apart from the difficulties which are inherent to the problem of climatic prediction, there are serious difficulties in reaching an agreement on the changes that *already occurred* in the atmosphere in the last 30 years. A survey of the results, published by several authors, show large disparities in defining the large-scale variations of atmospheric temperature (cf. Smagorinsky's paper in Chapter 10 of present volume). On this subject the Project supports the conclusion that there seems to be no clear evidence that the amplitude of climatic variability during the recent decades is significantly different from the natural variability of the past century.

Once the idea of dramatic climate changes is discarded there remains the need to explain the whole set of events assumed to be associated with the 1972 droughts. The Report makes a distinction between two categories of problems which are put together in current explanations of the 1972 crisis, but which belong to two entirely different realms: the events related to the profound changes which took place on the international food market in the early 1970s, and the events associated with the droughts affecting several regions of the world at about the same period. Both sets of events, the Report maintains, are originally independent of each other. They interacted at a later stage, although the latter played only a minor role in the evolution of the former.

1.2 Climatic events *per se* are not the root cause, in our times, of great disasters, famines, increased misery.

All our case-studies provide confirmatory evidences that droughts, long and severe as they may be, are not the sole or even the primary cause of internal disequilibrium in the society. They merely reveal a pre-existing disequilibrium. The

219

evolution after the drought has "stricken" is much more determined by the structure of the *whole* socio-ecosystem than by the drought itself. The Report devotes a whole chapter to propound a theoretical frame for a structural analysis of these problems (cf. Chapter 6).

In accordance with this approach, a classification of countries or regions of the world which takes into account their types of response to a drought situation ought to begin by drawing a line that separates fragile societies (high structural vulnerability) on one side, from societies of low structural vulnerability on the other. In a society of high vulnerability, drought triggers off an instability which is latent in the system. The direct effects of the drought are amplified by the release of these instabilities. In the extreme cases it may not be possible to restore the pre-drought situation, even if enough food or other emergency aid is brought to the place, once the system is taken away from its precarious "equilibrium" conditions, unless some structural changes are introduced in the society itself. A society having a socio-economic structure of low vulnerability is a stable system in which the social organization is such that it has ingrained response mechanisms to overcome the effects of either short or prolonged droughts.

The line of separation between both kinds of countries as well as the relative position of each country or region with reference to this line are functions of time. The Sahelian countries are typical examples of an evolution in recent decades towards more vulnerable conditions. China provides an example of changes in the opposite direction.

1.3 The foregoing analysis does not intend to minimize the importance of droughts for some countries. Quite to the contrary, the Project emphasizes the decisive influence of a drought on the whole life of a fragile society. The release of internal structural instabilities does in fact *amplify* the effects of even a mild natural perturbation starting in the ecosystem. Under certain conditions, a not very severe drought or flood may thus have catastrophic consequences, out of proportion with the intensity of the anomaly. This means that climate and its variations should play an important role in a rational planning of a society striving for a preservation of adequate minimum standards of living for all of its population.

On the basis of what is known today about climatic variability, it appears that a rational use of climatic information should have to take into account three different kinds of phenomena.

(a) First, there is a normal, expected fluctuation around some mean value referred to a long period of at least many decades. These first kind of variations have generally a range which we can determine for long-term records. They have some oscillatory character (not cycles), more pronounced in some regions than others. Relationship to other geographical phenomena (influence of solar activity, wobble of the earth's axis, etc.) is still very much an open question. But we do know enough about them to use information on their range of variation so as to design the food-production systems, for example, to operate in such a way as to allow for margins of safety for down turns, droughts in particular. Some technical developments will help, in some places, such as dams, wells, control and re-use of water supplies. They should be designed also with the normal climatic fluctuations in mind. The measures to be taken are not, however, restricted to the physical aspects that determine the output of the production, but they should include the whole problem of accessibility to food by all sectors of the population during the periods of low production (marketing, stocks, distribution, employment of rural population, are here some of the main problems). Although it is not known when exactly these periods will occur, it is known that they will occur. The society should be prepared to absorb the climatic anomaly when it comes, with some hardship, to be sure, but not catastrophe.

(b) A second class of climatic variations are the rare and large events - great floods, very prolonged droughts, etc. We can examine historical evidence to obtain some idea of their frequency of occurrence. Needless to say the boundary between the first and second kind of climatic variability is arbitrary, and it is a matter of judicious judgement, for each socio-ecosystem, to decide whether or not a certain range of variability is explicitly planned for. The "rare" events that are left out of the plans do call, when they arrive, for emergency measures which may include international solidarity, aid programmes and regional co-operation agreements.

(c) A third class of variation is of a long trend, a cooling or warming, over a century or longer. In the past, these occurred and had strong social effects, such as migrations or even wars to enable populations to migrate. We are studying today mechanisms that might induce trends—use of fossil fuels, deforestation, urbanization, concentration of energy generating plants, etc. Our knowledge of climate forcing mechanisms is too incomplete to give any reliable prediction at this time. If fossil fuels continue to be burnt, we will continue to increase carbon-dioxide (CO_2) in the atmosphere, which in turn is likely to lead to warming (increase of the mean value of the temperature of the earth atmosphere). How much this will be, what will be resulting changes in the general circulation of the atmosphere, how the large-scale and regional-scale patterns of temperature, cloudiness and precipitation will change, are matters that we cannot answer now. We do not share the view of those who predict catastrophic effects for mankind as a whole of the type of changes that may occur. If a general warming takes place, some regions, undoubtedly, will get better climate and others will become worse. We could imagine possible scenarios, with some assumed changes, and try to figure out the implications for some countries and some regions, as well as for the interrelations among them. No matter how rational and judicious these assessments may be, we should not fool ourselves into believing that we are really assessing the possible effects of an increase in CO_2. As far as the developing countries are concerned, the events in Africa, Asia and Latin America on the socio-economic and political side are, and will continue being, of such a magnitude that they are going to shape the future of many of those countries far more and more abruptly than any change in climatic conditions during the coming decades. We have provided evidences, in this Report, of the difficulties in assessing the actual climate impact of a known nature under known social conditions. We have also shown that the actual impact depends, in developing countries, at least as much, and in many cases much more, on the conditions of the recipient society than on the actual magnitude or nature of the climatic perturbation. It would be childish, therefore, to analyse possible future scenarios taking the climate as the only variable and believe that we are predicting anything likely to occur. The actual possible scenarios would rather be the cartesian product of two sets of possible events, one set being climatic variations, the other referring to the relevant feature of the social structures. The former are little known, the latter still less.

2. THE FOOD CRISIS

2.1 A climate particularly unfavourable for food production (droughts hitting several continents), a soaring demand for food, spurred by continuous population growth and rising affluence, have been the reasons normally adduced to explain the food crisis that began in 1972 and which resulted in declining food reserves and sky-rocketing food prices. This was the basic assumption accepted in the UN World Food Conference (1974) and in a large number of well-known reports from official institutions at national and international levels, as well as in influential articles and books. On this basis we have called it "the official view".

We did not find that the figures themselves on world food production and trade supported the "official view". World food production had been generally rising sharply, much faster than population growth, with two pronounced peaks, one in 1971 and another in 1973. In this long-term context, we cannot accept the relatively small drop in 1972 as a "crisis", especially on a global scale. This realization led us to examine a broader body of information.

2.2 On the basis of the FAO and other official figures, we conclude that there is adequate global food production to rise nutritional standards everywhere to acceptable medical levels, and that the food-production potential is in advance of population tendencies, at least for this period.

Food trade figures show another important factor. Many of the countries that were hard stricken by the climatic events in the 1970s, and asked for food aid, were net exporters of food. There is no other conclusion except that unavailability of food to some segments of the population was a consequence of national policies. The changing of eating habits of Europeans, Soviets and North Americans, or the placing of fallowed land in the USA back into production, will not solve the problem of those segments of national populations which are the victims of policies, advertant or not, of their own governments and of those who control the agricultural productive system. The droughts only exacerbated their situation; the press exposed their plight to the rest of the world; food aid shipped in from other countries (much of which did not get to the famished anyway) only helped for a short time. When the rain returned, some pastures and marginal lands could again be placed into production of food for the local population, who then could recuperate from starvation to be faced merely with severe malnourishment. The "productive" sectors of the national economies continued to develop and further isolate the poor sectors from participation in the various profit-making productive processes: either the raising of "commercial" food or the opportunity to be employed in activities that supplied enough purchasing power to feed their families and adequate diet.

2.3 Further investigation and, in particular, discussions with researchers familiar with a large variety of social and political structures in Africa, Asia and Latin America, convinced us that availability of food in these areas to a significant segment of the population was only marginally related to world production amounts and grain trade. Indeed, for a large segment of society there is in effect no or insignificantly little purchasing power at the local level.

We conclude that structures - i.e. social organization; political systems; control of credit and capital; large-scale production arrangements, such as the multinational agro-business; international inter-governmental organizations and their bureaucracies, and the "needs" of these bureaucracies; national power sectors, their bureaucracies and their needs; cultural patterns and forces; etc.—developed by humans into social, political and economic ways of life, have a fundamental role to play in "how things work": who has access to food and other essential elements for a minimum decent life, and who does not.

Evidences have been given in several of the case-studies to show that, at least in some instances, these structures only survive by paying an irreducible price: some part of society, some population segment must remain outside the cycles of work, money flow, productivity that characterize the structure to which they belong.

The production of these people play no role in the overall figures of world food production. The role in the local economies is, however, quite significant and it is erroneous to think of these sectors as being out of the productive system as such. They are marginal in the sharing of benefits within the society, but well integrated into the system as far as their contributions to the development of other sectors are concerned.

2.4 The whole conception of development has to be drastically revised. International programmes aiming at increasing the participation of developing countries in world trade and finance, as well as national plans setting national priorities for development, are no more than screens to protect or to increase profit-making activities of powerful economic and political forces, unless they can include in their plans the marginalized population segment referred to above. The price to be paid for it may have to be a slower development (in the conventional sense) and a lower GNP.

Governments and all types of organizations that have the power to decide how these matters are directed, as well as economists advising them or publishing their own studies on development, may have to realize that the commonly used economic parameters are meaningless when applied to the marginalized population of the Third World. They may be forced sooner or later to introduce non-monetary values into their expectations and plans.

3. DIAGNOSIS OF THE CRISIS

The "official version" offers the following sequence of events to explain the 1972 food crisis: as a result of the fall in world food production, the Soviet Union and the developing countries purchased large quantities of grain, which led to a depletion of stocks and the exceptional price increase of grain and other foodstuffs. This version is questioned by the Report.

The fluctuations in the international grain trade and, in particular, the price variations, during the period 1972-5 do not reflect a deficit in food production nor changes in the food requirements of the developing countries. They are the result of a changing policy concerning the structure of world food production and trade, and not the accidental effect of climatic phenomena or the inevitable consequence of a gradual increase in demand due to demographic pressure.

The key element in the alternative explanation offered by this study is the set of measures adopted in the US by the Nixon Administration, which introduced fundamental changes in international economic policy and particularly in international trade. The history of this process is briefly reviewed on the basis of two official US documents: the Williams Report (July 1971) and the International Economic Report of the President to the Congress in March 1973.

The changes in the trade policies were clearly reflected in the total amount of the agricultural exports of the US. Moreover, the product composition of the US food trade underwent structural changes which were quite in line with the analyses and recommendations of the Williams Report concerning the comparative advantages of the US productive system.

One could still think that the 1972 drought played a major role in the sharp increase in the value of US food exports between 1972 and 1975. The Report maintains that it did play a role, but the drought was neither the starting-point of the process nor the dominant factor in the subsequent developments. In light of the analysis of this Report the sharp price rise would have occurred even in the absence of the climate anomalies of 1972.

4. FAMINES, MALNUTRITION AND THE DROUGHT

4.1 Malnutrition has been one of the focal problems of the Project. It became a central subject after it was found that there was no reliable answer to questions such as "How many people died in Sahel during the drought?" There exists a striking parallelism between the explanatory schemes for the drought as a meteorological event, and for the famine as a social event. To "explain" drought one needs a climatological analysis which automatically implies reference to large-scale space and time processes. It is only within this long scale that the anomaly called "drought" can be given a meaning and can be provided with a meaningful explanation. Likewise, famines occur as anomalies within large-scale processes in society which regulate the changing patterns at the level of nutrition. It is only with reference to this background that the famines have a clear meaning and that they can be given a significant explanation. The studies on malnutrition are, thus, the counterpart of the climatological studies.

4.2 The evaluation of the magnitude of malnutrition and the assessment of the incidence of malnutrition on mortality is an extremely difficult task. As a general rule, in the places where there are statistics—there is no malnutrition and in the places where there is malnutrition—there are no statistics. This notwithstanding, it can be shown, beyond any reasonable doubt, that the magnitude of the problem is shocking. Malnutrition is the most widespead disease in the world. The estimated population living below acceptable levels of food intake goes up to roughly 1000 million people.

4.3 Although there are rough figures on the magnitude of malnutrition in the world, no reliable information is available on the number of people dying because of malnutrition. The vital statistics systems of the world would record, in theory, all deaths which take place in certain defined geographical areas, as well as the causes of death. In practice, however, this does not happen. There are three main reasons for this:

(a) Under-registration of deaths

Examples provided in the case-studies (cf. Volume 2 of this Report) show that the percentage of under-registration of deaths in some Latin American countries has been as high as 40% and even 60%. The situation is much worse in Africa. In Upper Volta, the mortality rate as registered by vital statistics amounted only to one-seventh of the actual rate. In Ethiopia figures indicating the mortality rates are not available; registration of vital rates is virtually unknown in the rural areas of the country and even in the urban areas registration is done only on a voluntary basis.

(b) The unavailability of health services to much of the population

As a consequence of the maldistribution of health services, there is a high percentage of recorded deaths whose causes cannot be ascertained as they are not certified by physicians, and most of these deaths from unknown causes occur in those geographical areas and social classes where malnutrition is the dominant pathology.

(c) The existence of biases in the current system of determining the "basic cause of death"

The International Classification of Diseases by WHO has adopted a world-wide uniform method for determination of causes of death by choosing *one* "basic cause of death" for every death. This decision tends to underestimate malnutrition as a cause of death by allocating to another disease—usually an infectious one—the role of "basic cause of death", even if both diseases are recorded in the death certificate. Thus, an infant death "caused" by a bronchopneumonia which is in turn caused by a measles infection in a child weakened by malnutrition will be assigned to "measles", and malnutrition will not even be mentioned as a causal agent, even though it is well known that fatality from measles is a function of nutritional status, thus making malnutrition as much a cause of death as the measles virus.

To these reasons, which alone would account for the fact that chronic malnutrition is permanently undermeasured, one should add the incidence of the epistemological framework of the medical profession and of their underlying ideological biases.

4.4 The fact that malnutrition as a cause of death is seldom properly registered has a double consequence which cannot be overemphasized. Firstly, the magnitude of the problem remains hidden. Secondly, when there is a "natural disaster" such as the Sahelian drought, the deaths produced by malnutrition become too obvious. There is a tendency *to attribute all malnutrition-generated deaths,* and in fact malnutrition itself, *to the natural disaster.* The effects of natural disasters are thus greatly exaggerated.

5. THE POPULATION-RESOURCES BALANCE

There is a growing conviction that increased malnutrition in developing countries is being caused by population growth which is therefore responsible for the catastrophic effects of droughts or other natural phenomena on some societies. Neo-Malthusian arguments have created great alarm and led to the conclusion that there can be no significant improvements in *per capita* food supply in developing countries without declines in birth rates. This Report maintains that although demographic pressure will be in the long run a serious problem for mankind, it cannot be held responsible for any of the national or regional catastrophes of recent times, including those of 1972. Examples are provided of countries which are often mentioned as suffering from food shortages due to excess of population, and yet are net exporters of food even in periods of famines. Underpopulation has also been the cause of serious disruptions in food production, leading even to ecological degradation and desertification. The detailed analysis of the Sahelian case provides a striking example of pre-colonial societies where the expansion of the productive system, which is determined by social requirements other than demographic pressures, generates a population growth. The diagnosis that emerges from this case-study rules out demographic pressure as the actual cause of overgrazing and misuse of agricultural land, often referred to as an explanation for the magnitude of the damage produced by the drought in the early 1970s.

6. THE CASE-STUDIES

The selection of the regional case-studies carried out by the Project was made by combining several criteria: the intrinsic importance of the case, its representativeness, the availability of information, the availability of research teams or individual researchers willing to undertake the study, etc. The case-studies which were actually carried out correspond to countries or regions (either regions within a country, such as North-east Brazil, or regions covering several countries like the Sahel), which differ in their historical and geographical context as well as in their socio-economic conditions.

In spite of the differences, the conclusions of the case studies always point to the same direction, showing the pre-eminence of the receptive social "structures" over the purely physical and biological factors in determining the nature and the scope of the effects of the drought.

Sahel offers a textbook example of what is called "the social dimensions of drought". The pre-colonial pastoral and agro-pastoral ethnics has response mechanisms ingrained in the structure of social relations which were at the basis of the production systems. An analysis of the historical evolution of the system of social relations and the disruption of the response mechanisms provides a solid foundation for the diagnosis of the Sahelian catastrophe in the early 1970s.

Latin America presents clear examples of how two different agricultural sectors of the same country under similar conditions of climatic stress over their respective territories are affected in entirely different ways. Interpretations of the food production problems in these countries usually present an opposition between both sectors: one being "modern", "progressive", "technologically advanced", whereas the other is "traditional", "backwards". The Project analysis leads, however, to the conclusion that both play an essential role in the process of industrialization. Their coexistence is thus the *effect* of state policies.

This poses a most serious problem for a Project like the present one because any recommendation intended to reach the roots of catastrophic effects of droughts in the "backward" sector of agriculture cannot help dealing with the profound *structural* problems of the society and in particular with the system of relations within the trinity agriculture-industry-state. This means nothing less than an analysis in depth of the roots of underdevelopment.

B. Recommendations

1. FURTHER STUDIES ON CLIMATE AND SOCIETY[1]

1.1 In our foregoing conclusions we emphasized the fact that enough is known about climate and its variability to give some useful basis for planning further development and evolution of production systems, especially food and also to aid in other questions of energy use, water resources, human habitation, etc. We stressed that more use can be made of information now available, and more information can be obtained at reasonable effort. How this should be done is, however, far from obvious. It requires nothing less than an adequate diagnosis of the actual direct and indirect effects of climate variability on a given society and this, as some of our case studies have so clearly revealed, is a function of socio-economic factors as much as a function of climate itself. We claim that there is not enough knowledge available concerning the nature of these effects and that much research is needed in this direction. We therefore recommend that further studies should be carried out on the interrelations between climate and society and that they should be directed to answer the following kinds of questions in properly selected areas of the world:

(a) What is the *direct* effect of climatic fluctuations or climatic anomalies on the output of a *given productive agro-system under specified socio-economic conditions?*

(b) What is the *direct* effect of a *given climatic phenomenon* (e.g. a drought of certain characteristics) on the output of various types of productive systems and socio-economic structures?

(c) What is the *indirect effect* (e.g. effects on labour markets, prices, food accessibility, migrations, etc.) of certain climatic features on various types of societies?

(d) How different the various segments of the agricultural system of a given country or region react to the impact of the same climatic phenomenon. What are the structural reasons for these differences?

(e) What are the characteristics of the structure of a given socio-ecosystem (cf. Chapter 6) that makes it more vulnerable or more resilient to climate variability?

(f) How effectively the traditional agricultural and pastoral societies have incorporated the climatic and ecological features of their territories into their agricultural practices and socio-economic structures. What has been the effect of the application of modern technology in the agriculture of those countries. How a synthesis could be achieved that would allow a full application of scientific knowledge and technological innovations together with a wise utilization of the natural environment.

1.2 Any study of the nature we have referred to above presents serious difficulties. We shall enumerate them, and shall add some brief comments that condense our experience.

(a) First and foremost, these type of studies are by essence of an interdisciplinary nature. The high degree of specialization prevailing in the scientific community makes it difficult to find researchers for this kind of work. It is commonly believed that interdisciplinary studies need only a team of specialists in the related fields. But this is hardly sufficient. The real problems are found, in these studies, not so much within each one of the specialized field, but at the *interphases* between them. And there is only one way of working at the interphases: each "specialist" or, at least, the coordinator of such a team should know enough about the other fields to be able to ask meaningful questions that cut across the borders, to be able to pose the problems on one field as seen from the perspective of the others and requiring specialized knowledge from each one of them.

(b) Second comes the search for data. There are here two important questions. The first question to be asked is what kind of data are needed. In some cases the answer is obvious. For example, in order to find out rainfall anomalies in a certain area, one must look into the records of rainfall stations as well as in records of variations in levels of rivers and lakes. In this respect we know what data to look for and the only problem is to find them.

In other cases, however, the answer is not at all obvious. The relevance of some basic information to the explanation of certain problems may by itself be an important part of the problems. To put it bluntly, in these cases we do not know what data to look for until we have found them. Then we look for more—or more reliable—data of same kind.

It is clear that between the two extreme cases we have mentioned, there are intermediate cases in which we have hints, we guess, we may infer the data that are needed. Here the important warning is not to fall into the trap so clearly described by Dr. Escudero with reference to malnutrition problems (cf. Chapter 3, Volume 2 of this Report).

The second question to be asked about the data is how to get them. In the case of climatological data there are internationally agreed rules to register the information, to concentrate it in national, regional and international centres, to publish it in conventional form. We have described, however, in our Report the serious difficulties we encountered in finding rainfall information in some critical regions, and the appalling insufficiencies of internationally kept records. The actual gathering of known data has been one of the most painful and costly efforts the Project was forced to make (cf. Chapter 9).

In other fields, where there are no agreed rules on what to observe, how to observe and how to keep and exchange the observations, one finds various degrees of difficulties. There is, however, an immense reservoir of information, sometimes published, other times existing only in the form of accumulated experience of field research workers. We have found this to be particularly the case, as far as our study was concerned, with reference to anthropologists who have been working for many years in regions such as the Sahel. In these cases, the task of a researcher conducting impact studies, may very often be, not only to find adequate information to answer his questions, but to find the proper questions that could be answered by the existing information.

(c) Studies on the interrelations between climate and society cannot be confined, in general, to predetermined boundaries. We refer to Chapter 6 for a description of the complex set of interrelations of a given socio-ecosystem to be taken into consideration. There are undoubtedly examples of impact studies that could be limited in a very precise manner. The impact of a drought on the food system of a highly industrialized country, with a diversified productive system and a stable economy is an obvious example. This is not the case, however, in a large number of developing countries heavily dependent on agricultural production and having a highly vulnerable socio-economic structure. Here one should be expected to take into account aspects of such structures that may appear to be rather distant of the specific relation drought/agricultural output. The kind of studies proposed in recommendation[2] below may provide an idea of the very wide scope such impact projects may have.

(d) The political dimensions of the problems involved. Within the wide range of problems that an impact study might need to deal with, there are some having quite obvious political dimensions. In fact, as it has been repeatedly asserted in this Report, the real difficulties in decreasing the catastrophic consequences of climatic anomalies in some areas of the world are not technical, but political. This imposes clear limitations to the feasibility of certain studies, particularly when they are conducted by international governmental institutions. Independent scholars may have more freedom to perform such studies but may also find difficulties in the access to relevant data. The scientific community acting through such non-governmental institutions as ICSU or IFIAS may find appropriate channels of actions.

(e) The insufficiencies of theoretical frameworks for the case-studies is at present one of the serious obstacles to the design and implementation of impact studies. A special recommendation is made below, (5), to foster research in such a direction.

2. THE SAHELIAN CASE[2]

2.1 The Sahelian case-study reported in Chapter 7, has provided a large number of important lessons from the past. Moreover, the diagnosis of the present situation and the prospects for its evolution in the foreseeable future are such that it justifies a maximum effort in the search for an adequate solution to the problems of the region. We have strongly criticized the plans for development that have been proposed by various international institutions or research groups based on conventional economic ideas about "development". We believe that an entirely different approach is needed.

The Sahelian social organization and dynamics were better adapted, in the historic past, to the climatic variability and the ecological conditions of their territory. We consider that an alternative to the conventional approach should begin by inquiring what aspects of such structural adaptations could be valid today, given that some conditions have changed dramatically. We urge, therefore, that a study be made of the past and present of Sahel, as a conceptual case-study, to try to look into historical methods as they, *mutatis mutandis,* might be applied today.

2.2 In more specific terms, we recommend a project having the following characteristics:

2.2.1 The project should comprise, initially, a few small-scale research studies to verify empirically, by taking suitable examples, some of the hypotheses and theoretical presuppositions which have been put forward by researchers in the region, such as those reported in Chapter 7, it should then be possible to study the different kinds of actions to be taken, according to the specific regional characteristics and the political constraints.

2.2.2 The main objective of the research would be to assess the feasibility of regional plans based on measures such as:

(a) Restructuration of the regional economies by a progressive reduction of their dependencies on a market economy.
(b) Revalorization of agricultural and pastoral work by a reappropriation of the material conditions of production and by redefining the agricultural system now mainly directed to create an exchange value. This revalorization of agricultural and pastoral work should be designed on the basis of a fundamental change in the concept of productivity of the agricultural system. The productivity in this sector should not be measured merely in terms of quantities of output (relative productivity), but it should be expressed in terms of its contribution to the stability of the system (vulnerability or resilience of its structures). The term "structural productivity" has been suggested for this concept (cf. F. Sabelli's paper in Volume 3 of this Report).
(c) Reintroduction and enhancement of various modes of productive organization by co-operation and mutual aid in agricultural work. They have always played an important role, being perhaps the main factor in the process of social and economic reproduction in the region. They emerged, historically, as means to overcome the constraints imposed by the natural environment.

2.2.3 The final goal of the project should be a set of recommended policies to restructure the local agricultural productive system in such a way that they would be capable of again making the people masters of their environment.

2.3 The policies with regard to the action to be taken should be conducive to the main goal of regaining the material conditions for the reproduction of the social systems of the Sahelian agricultural and pastoral productive sectors so seriously affected by the crisis in the early 1970s. The readaptation of the productive structures to the climatic hazards is subordinated to this goal being achieved.

2.4 We are quite aware that the type of research we are proposing goes against the fashionable strategies for development prevailing in this region. The development programmes criticized in Chapter 7 are conceived, as we have tried to show, with complete disregard for the need to restructure the local economies in such a way that it would be capable of again making the people masters of their environment. We recommend a judicious choice of the researchers selected to conduct the work. They should be quite aware of the pitfalls of conventional development programmes, but should not fall either in the utopian attitude of naïve "ecologism" or in the traps of dogmatic preconceived patterns.

3 MALNUTRITION AND HEALTH[3]

3.1 National and international groups involved in health programmes must be made to revise their thinking about malnutrition. It is a disease, not an infectious one, to be sure. The cause is insufficient food. It does not need highly trained medical specialists or expensive equipment to diagnose it. The therapy is simple: more quantity of appropriate food. The therapy does not have to be administered by licensed or even trained personnel.

Without recognition of malnutrition, as the widest spread human disease all over the globe, and without systematic treatment and permanent measures to eradicate it, the far more costly medical treatments, by professionals, using expensive supplies and technology, of the large-scale infectious diseases, is not justified in large areas of the world. A child can be vaccinated against measles, but if the child is malnourished below a critical threshold, death will merely be transferred from measles to another infection. Measles will be eradicated, but death rates will remain equally high.

Along with recognition of malnutrition as a disease, and as a major common agent in death, there must be a revision of reporting procedures of cause of death. The internationally recommended forms must be revised to allow the designation of malnutrition as the significant contributing factor. It may seem ironic, and antithetical to conventional medical wisdom, but it appears that *malnutrition* should be designated as the *primary* cause of death when accompanied by an otherwise non-fatal infection (measles, disentery, etc.). In this connection, the International Classification of Diseases (ICD) should have its rules for selecting "basic cause of death" modified, in order to be able to reflect the real weight of malnutrition in causing a death. The ninth revision of the ICD has just come into operation virtually unchanged from the eighth revision, the shortcomings of which have been analysed in Chapter 4 of Volume 2. It will be the task of WHO to undertake the next revision of the ICD, and an IFIAS/ICSU proposal for modification to be effected along the lines explained by this Project could be very useful.

As a complementary measure, medical schools should be urged to stress the importance of courses on nutrition and its relation to infectious diseases in their curriculum. The teaching of medicine to professionals who are to practice in developing countries particularly must emphasize adequate nutrition as a primary requirement for the treatment of other diseases.

3.2 Governmental efforts in public health in developing countries (as well as in "marginal" society sectors of industrialized countries) should include improvements of nutritional levels as a major early goal. It may be found, if nutritional levels can be adequately established, that the costs and manpower needed for combating other diseases may be appreciably reduced. Studies should, therefore, be encouraged on the various medical and practical aspects of nutrition, with a goal of setting basic standards for nutrition, including gross caloric content, provision of adequate amino-acids, mineral and vitamins, and bulk characteristics (e.g. fibre content) of foods. The cultural aspects and potentials and limitations of local food-production systems must be included so that authoritative recommendations can be made to governments, appropriate to specific regions, as targets for their national health programmes. The tendency should be reversed to regard the European and North American diet as the desired goal. Animal proteins should not be labelled "quality" proteins, with the obvious implication that vegetable proteins are necessarily inferior. A better set of dietary recommendations should be developed as guidelines for minimum healthy, as well as practicable, diets for various regions. This would require a permanent updating, in the light of the most recently gathered evidence, of the nutritional needs of humans. This is a task for joint WHO/FAO Committees, which periodically produce reports on the subject. It is likely that we already know everything that is to be known on the subject, but recent developments (i.e. the 1973 Committee Report) seem, for example, to have produced guidelines on protein needs which were less demanding than previous ones, a decision of great technical significance due to the high amount of energy and resources needed everywhere to produce animal proteins.

In a rational world this recommendation would precede all others, and would in turn dictate the magnitude and structure of the food that is to be grown and the mechanisms for its distribution. It is perhaps too much to ask for this type of rationality, but IFIAS can insist of having updates of those estimates of needed nutrients for humans, and then can proceed to do a thing that the WHO/FAO Committees do not do—translate this biological need at planetary level into a worldwide agricultural policy to satisfy it.

In this connection, the ultimate recommendation—as utopian as it may appear in most free market economies, although quite natural, *in principle,* in centrally planned economies—would be the interdiction of utilizing some basic food production as a commodity subjected to the "market forces". The so-called market laws are not natural laws as the law of gravitation or of the increasing entropy in closed systems, but rather the result of human manipulations of socio-economic structures where *then* they appear as "laws".

It is hard to think that the solution of malnutrition problems in much of the Third World could be achieved without some drastic measures that will put the food necessary to keep minimum acceptable standards of nutrition, out of the action of those who speculate with human hunger.

3.3 Other recommendations are related to the failure of the conventional health statistics to monitor the extent of malnutrition and of other diseases in the population, to ascertain their chronic level or the increase in them as the drought takes hold. The tremendous under-registration of vital events—births, deaths and their causes—make vital statistics very bad indicators of the health of the population, and the fact that the system as it exists is heavily biased towards recording events which occur in urban areas—which in turn are not only unrepresentative of countries that are mostly rural, but are also biased against malnutrition - make any extrapolation on their findings seem even harmful if the objective is to arrive at a nationwide determination of health problems. The statistical data that derives from Health Services activities suffers from the same biases, which can be compounded by the fact that, in many cases, what is offered to people through the Services - and which is later recorded as data which presumably measures health levels - can have little bearing on what people *need* in terms of health: due to the scarcity of health resources everywhere in the developing countries, any kind of medical speciality is going to be crowded by patients seeking care, and to immediately produce statistics showing the magnitude among the population of the problem which it is treating. This is a case in which supply would generate its own demand, both conceivably being unrelated to health needs as measured by any objective criterion.

It would be utopian here to advocate improvements of an incremental kind for the Vital and Health Statistics systems of most of the countries reviewed in Volume 2 of the Project. Even in the very unlikely case that they could be implemented, an 80% target for registration of births and deaths in, for instance, the Sahel countries,

Ethiopia, Sudan, Brazil and India, would be a misapplication of priorities. The resources that would be needed for this extensive effort would be channelled away from more pressing national needs. The limitations on coverage by statistics of Health Services are a function of the incomplete coverage of the Services themselves: if coverage of population by the Services were nearly complete it would be paradoxical but true to state that the health statistics of that coverage would be less needed, as the total Health needs of the population would more or less be looked after. In any case, the incomplete coverage of Health Services is part of the fabric of lack of resources which envelops these nations and one that is very difficult to change.

What would be imperative for these countries would be the setting of an alternative statistical system for health to the one evolved over the centuries by the affluent Western countries. What should be proposed would be the establishing for the countries of a basic survey frame on a sampling basis whose findings would be as representative as possible of national situations and which would become a basic statistical infrastructure for the whole Public Administration, one that should be made as inexpensive as is compatible with the deducing of correct decisions for the administration of the countries, and which could be utilized in turn by different users—sectors like education, health (by investigating such topics as causes of death, professional attendance at births, somatic and psychic growth rates in children, immunization coverage, prevalent morbidity, etc.), communication, agricultural development, etc.; to draw statistical inferences of nationwide coverage and of a reasonably probablistic nature. In the case of nutritional problems, for example, a periodic nationwide sample survey of the nutritional status of the population, using simple procedures like somatic growth measures, weight/height ratios, etc., could be undertaken, and frequency of recording could be increased in the face of a natural catastrophe like the 1972 drought.

What IFIAS should propose then is a monitoring system of nutrition and health status to centralize all of the information pertaining to the nutrition of the population and to complement the Vital and Health statistics systems currently in operation.

The monitoring system should be comprehensive in scope, covering all aspects of the society relating to nutrition and health problems, such as food production, reserves and distribution; employment, salaries and food prices, nutritional status of the population, especially children, and incidence and prevalence of nutrition-related diseases. Much of this information can be gathered from the government agencies responsible, and the task of the monitoring system—one that can be done very cheaply—would be the collating and interpreting of the data and the putting forth of technical recommendations for their improvement; that information to be gathered directly would be collected through the survey infrastructures mentioned above, through the use of time- and resource-saving techniques: different types of sampling procedures and simplified instruments of demographic analysis (such as the Brass methods).

The monitoring system should be designed in a co-ordinated effort between IFIAS and ICSU, who may then elaborate a complete proposal for submission to the UN. From then onwards, the steps to be taken can only be hazarded, but a possible UN co-ordinating group for this effort could be the Statistical Office of the United Nations, which could direct the establishing of an *ad hoc* Working Group set up from members of the statistical sections of the different international agencies: WHO and UNICEF (those most directly concerned with health and nutrition) UNESCO, ILO, etc.

4. INTERNATIONAL AID FOR FOOD PRODUCTION SYSTEMS

4.1 Recent projects supported by such national organizations as USAID, and international ones such as the World Bank, should be studied and documented, with a view to understanding the criteria for establishing the project, the goal of the project, and the sectors of the local economy that were expected to benefit from it. The objective of such studies should be to develop a constructive critique of the projects, their benefits and possible disbenefits. For example, were the projects designed by taking into account the known local climatic variability of the region so that the productive sector concerned would be resilient to expected fluctuations?

At least one case was mentioned in this Report of an aid project for which substantial credits were given, that does not seem on the surface to have been directed at the most practical way of solving nutritional problems in the country. We refer to the World Bank credits for maize production in Tanzania. Considerable credits had to be included for technological aspects (fertilizers and machinery, water systems, etc.). It is known that by using high-yield hybrids of maize with adequate fertilizers, pesticides and water supply, the peak yields are impressively high. However, this maize is not drought resistant, i.e. is less productive than millet and sorghum, the traditional indigenous grains, under drought conditions (normal semi-arid or subnormal conditions). What is the best long-term strategy for such regions? Emphasis on higher yields in good years, high yield per agricultural worker, but also high energy requirements and fragility of the system in some years, versus lower peak yields but satisfactory average production and less vulnerability in bad years. Moreover, who is in a position to obtain the credits? What sectors of the country actually got them? Who finally benefits most from high technology aid: companies and governments through taxes? How could alternative approaches through less glamorous and lower technology projects spread benefits to wider segments of the population? We know enough today about the "green revolution", its limitations, drawbacks, as well as the benefits, when properly applied in the restricted conditions where it really works, to be able to conduct these assessments on solid grounds.

4.2 The Sahelian countries present also here a clear-cut case-study on the way the international institutions conceive their aid to the least-developed nations. We have given arguments, in Chapter 7, to cast serious doubts on the soundness of the development plans of the agricultural sector in the Sahel elaborated after the crisis in the early 1970s. The plans which are known to us focus the attention on the increase of the agricultural output: "modernization" of the production system, investments through foreign aid, production targets to ensure, statistically, enough food for the population. Some of them - like FAO's plan - stress the need for complementary social changes (e.g. the need to open up new opportunities and new ways of life for the local population) but this appears, to us, contradictory with the likely effects of the implementation of the plan.

We therefore recommend that a study should be made of the social consequences of implementing plans of the type mentioned above (we suggest that FAO's plan be taken as a reference). The study should analyse whether there are ways of implementing such plans that would not imply, for instance, marginalization of segments of the rural population. It would also explore the soundness of the technology to be imported, with reference to the local environment and the local wisdom in adaptation to the characteristics of such an environment. Finally, the study should explore the feasibility of integrated development plans for the region, where the exploitation of natural resources may minimize the need for foreign dependency in the implementation of agricultural plans leading to food self-sufficiency.

5. THEORETICAL STUDIES[4]

The contributions to the Project discussing specific case-studies are only partial answers to one of the major issues of the drought phenomenon, namely the relations between society and its environment. To answer this question one must go further in terms of the existing methodology and social sciences theories. The link between society and its physical environment and the patterns of relationships and transformations which result from those exchanges between man and nature cannot be fully examined within the limits of our present knowledge of social science. Therefore new ways of analysing the question are required for, as technological advancement takes place, the possibilities of human intervention in the environment increases with no, or little, possibility of assessing its consequences. Certainly, the first step in that direction would be to discover and study the patterns of exchange between society and the environment within a dynamic framework; and the model for society and environment are permanently changing. Such a model, however, cannot afford to take advantage of the existing stock of knowledge on social structure and its functioning.

What we propose in Chapter 6 is basically a structural model, including society and its ecosystem, through which the study of phenomena like natural disasters can better and more accurately be understood. To do so, we have to look into what is then called the socio-ecosystem, or the complexities resulting from the interaction of man and his changing environment. It would be impractical to try to detect all its possible components and the exact weight and influence of each element which constitutes the socio-ecosystem. In different stages of interaction those elements play roles of distinct importance and functions. In answering this challenge we have approached this fundamental question by classifying the component elements of the socio-ecosystem into some major categories. The next problem was to identify the most relevant constituent part of those components and the external elements with which they are interacting. In doing so we soon realize that there is not a single socio-ecosystem but a multiplicity of subsystems. These correspond to the particular ways in which the socio-ecosystem manifests itself, resulting in specific formations, which derive from given stages of historical, technological development and the peculiar geographical characteristics. The specificity of the way the socio-ecosystem thus manifests itself results in the establishment of frontiers to other subsystems in which the interaction of the major component categories do not occur in the same way. However, in no circumstances does the socio-ecosystem develop any autonomous behaviour, since it is an indivisible part of a much larger system to which it is constantly interacting.

From this point the next step would be to detect and to study both the regularity and the way by which the component parts of the system interact. If it is done successfully it would become much easier to evaluate the likely role of each component on the phenomenon under investigation. In the case of the Brazilian North-eastern droughts, the possibilities for a full understanding and evaluation would be considerably increased, if the social, economic and political aspects of the phenomenon were considered systematically and scientifically in relation to its physical, biophysical and biological traits. Certainly the acknowledgement of the existence of interactions and links between them is not enough. We must also evaluate the ways in which physical and culturally determined components are interacting.

The approach suggested in Chapter 6 needs much further elaboration. It has some fundamental differences with current models of "System Analysis". A structural analysis is formulated in terms of patterns, taken as totalities, the laws of which are not directly implied by the laws of the component elements. For a structure is a system of relations among elements, and a property of the structure is a property of the relations, not of the elements.

There is an urgent need for research on the theoretical aspects of these problems that may lead to an adequate modelling of the behaviour of socio-ecosystems, taking into account the complex sets of internal and external interactions. The report (cf. Chapter 6) suggests that there is here a field for the application of ideas and techniques which have been developed in recent years in the theory of dissipative systems. IFIAS may contribute to this kind of study by sponsoring a theoretical project linked with empirical studies carried by other institutions. We recommend, for instance, an association with the UNRISD programme on "Food System and Society", the basic views of which are clearly convergent with the lines of thought emerging from the present Report.

Notes

1. The ideas put forward in this section have been presented by the author in discussions held in some international meetings preparatory of the World Climate Conference held in Geneva, February 1979. In particular they have been represented in the Report of the International Workshop on Climate Issues published by the US National Research Council under the title "International Perspectives on the Study of Climate and Society", Washington, 1978 (cf. specially Chapter 6).

2. We are grateful to Mr. F. Sabelli for his contribution to this section.

3. We are grateful to Dr. J. C. Escudero for his contribution to this section. We refer to Chapter 12 of Volume 2 for further elaboration of these ideas.

4. We are grateful to Professor G. Martins Dias for his collaboration in the writing of this section.

Part Two

The Climatic Dimension of Drought

Introductory Remarks

The originators and designers of the Project were mainly physical scientists, deeply interested in the physical aspects of natural phenomena affecting human life, such as drought. It was natural, therefore, that a physical emphasis was given to the Project.

As the work progressed, some features investigated on the societies impacted by the drought made it clear that the physical events were strongly inter-related to societal ones, the physical and human elements forming a complex interactive system. The physical aspects of the drought period took on new dimensions as triggering forces set loose far-reaching human reactions and changes. As discussed in the preceding chapter, these triggers may have increased the instabilities in precarious economic and political structures that were close to disruption anyway, and thus forced peoples living in human conditions that were already marginal and inadequate to conditions that became totally miserable and that led to fast death. As it is shown at length in this Project Report, these deaths linked with the droughts should not be directly and solely attributed to the droughts. They stem from the entire social-physical structure.

As the project developed it also became clear that, as far as the available resources allowed it, the study of the physical elements was to be mainly designed to provide a physical context for a wider investigation of the human elements. To this purpose a number of special meteorological projects were undertaken to identify, acquire and analyse relevant physical information, especially new information. These projects are briefly reviewed in Chapter 9. This type of work was deemed to provide sufficient factual information for the specific case-studies undertaken by the Project. However, they do not answer some of the important questions posed by the originators of this study. Food scarcity and famines as well as sky-rocketing food prices on the international market in the early 1970s were attributed to climate, as we have already seen in some detail. At that time, there was great concern about the possibility of a repetition of the 1972 events. Some leading climatologists went as far as diagnosing an actual change in the climatic conditions over the world. The Proceedings of the Toronto Conference Workshop (17-22 November 1975), one of the most important international meetings held on this subject, was published under the title "Living with climatic change". The foreword to the text starts with the following words: "There is growing evidence that the world is entering a new climate régime. Both the rate of change of the climate and the amplitude of short period climatic variations will be much more pronounced."

The idea that climate is changing is widespread and has already reached deep into public opinion. It seems that it has also influenced the thinking of high-ranking decision-makers in international institutions. We thought therefore that the present Report should contain an appraisal of these climatic forecasts as well as an authoritative presentation of what can be said today, on solid scientific grounds, about climatic variability and climatic changes. We must express our great indebtedness to Professor Joseph Smagorinsky, Director of the Geophysical Fluid

Dynamics Laboratory of Princeton University, for his contribution included in this Volume as Chapter 10. On the basis of an unpublished presentation made to the Swedish Academy of Sciences, Professor Smagorinsky, one of the world leading authorities in atmospheric dynamics, elaborated the subject in order to adapt it to the characteristics and the needs of our Project.

An introductory chapter to Smagorinsky's monography was considered necessary to summarize current knowledge on the climate system and to link it with the specific findings of the Project on the 1972 droughts. Stanley Ruttenberg, of the National Center for Atmospheric Research (Boulder, Colorado, US), an unfailing collaboratory of the Project from its very inception, undertook the main responsibility of writing this chapter (Chapter 9). The level and scope of the contents were discussed time and time again, and the text itself was revised several times. We hope it will be a useful synthesis for the learned non-specialist reader.

Climate, Climatic Variability and 1972

1. The Climate System

Climate itself is generally understood to be the average "weather", that is, how warm, cool, wet, dry, windy or calm we may expect it to be for any given region for a specified season or month of the year. It is often said that climate is the statistics of weather. We may also turn around this definition and say that weather is the statistics of climate, that is, for a given climatic régime, what kind of storms will occur, what will be their average frequency of occurrence, their average duration, magnitude, their maximum amplitude; we also need to know what will be the periods of non-stormy weather, their duration, their temperature and cloudiness characteristics.

Weather and climate are actually our perceptions of those aspects of the motions and workings of the atmosphere that affect us: temperature, moisture, wind. In actuality, the atmosphere itself cannot be isolated and understood all by itself. The oceans, land surface characteristics and geological features, the snow- and ice-covered regions, and the vegetation of the earth (the biosphere), all are affected by and in turn affect the state of the atmosphere, in various degrees and with various delays in time. We call the complicated interaction of these various elements the climate system, and shall in later sections describe some of the physical relationships important to describing how it works. By that we mean what energy source is responsible for the motions and changes that we observe, what are the transformations from one kind of energy to another, how is energy transported or distributed within the system?

2. Time Response of the Climate System to Changes

Different parts of the climate system have quite different time scales of response to external changes. During an eclipse, when the solar energy is shut off in the path of the total eclipse for several minutes, very sudden changes take place in the very thin upper atmosphere, where the state of the atmosphere (thermal and electrical) is very sensitive to the kind and amount of immediate energy input. The lower atmosphere, which is more dense and contains much water vapour (which has a high heat capacity compared with dry air), responds more slowly, since a given energy change causes a smaller change in temperature. Nevertheless, at the ground in clear weather, one can feel a cooling in an eclipse, even over a few minutes - the ground cools a little and so does the air, not much, but a little. The change from day to night is more pronounced, but at night the atmosphere does not cool to absolute zero, it cannot radiate energy that fast. The cooling and warming rates are a few degrees per day.[1] These rates depend very much on the state of the atmosphere. At winter locations, with cold surfaces, snow or ice, the air will cool very quickly if there are no clouds overhead and the relative humidity is low. In desert climates, which are very hot in the daytime, night-time is often very cool because the ground cools quickly through the clear, dry air. These effects illustrate that if one is to calculate heating and cooling rates, one has to know a great deal about the water content of the atmosphere, and about the cloud cover—its type, amount of the sky covered, height of the bottom and upper layers, and even the amount of dust contained in the cloud.

Ocean heating and cooling rates are far slower than in the atmosphere, since water has a very high heat capacity and is much denser than air. The surface temperature of the sea can change by a degree or so under a large cloud, or in a heavy rainfall. This temperature change, however, is generally confined to a very thin layer of the ocean surface. Strong winds can stir up the ocean surface and mix temperature changes downward, but this is confined to about the upper 100 metres of the water. In lower layers, the water temperature changes very slowly, as slowly as geological time scales for the very deepest layers.

The major large-scale ocean currents are driven by the great atmospheric wind systems. As an example, the Gulf Stream, driven by the Atlantic Ocean Trade Winds, transports warm tropical water to the far north and east, being responsible for the fact that the climate of the British Isles, Ireland and North-west Europe is far milder than that of the corresponding latitudes of North-east North America. Any pronounced change in the trade winds over the Atlantic would have pronounced effects on the climate of these regions. The oceanic and atmospheric circulations interact strongly. Any successful model for long-range weather prediction and for climate studies must include both the atmosphere and the oceans and their interaction.

There are smaller-scale features of the Gulf Stream that illustrate how the oceans may interact with the atmosphere. The Gulf Stream is not a completely uniform flow. It interacts with the weather systems of the Caribbean and Atlantic areas and with the coastline of North America. The flow is in large part laminer, but more like a series of ribbons or fibres in a band, the whole of which undergoes sinuous wave-like motions. There are temperature gradients between individual ribbon elements and a large gradient between the Stream and the surrounding cooler and more static boundary regions.

Interaction between the stream and the boundaries, or other kinds of interactions, produce small-scale rotating irregularities, such as whorls or eddies. These eddies are observed from satellites, and their development and movement is thereby tracked easily. Their rotational motions may extend to depths of a hundred or so metres; they may have diameters of up to several hundred kilometres; they maintain their rotational motion and temperature structures while they move away from the main stream, over considerable distances. Their temperatures thus may be several degrees higher than the colder waters of the North Atlantic. If they move into more tropical waters, they may be cooler than the surrounding waters. Such eddies, generated by several processes, are found in almost all areas of the oceans. It is thought that they are responsible for a considerable part of the oceanic transport of heat, especially from the warmer tropics to the cooler polar regions.

There are even larger and more persistent eddies in some parts of the ocean, especially in the Pacific. These may be 1000 or 2000 kilometres in diameter and persist for several years. Many studies are underway to try to understand how these larger eddies are related to atmospheric behaviour. What has been learned this far is that the relationship is not simple. It seems that the ocean eddies are generated by some anomalies in the motion of the atmosphere. Once the eddies appear, since they clearly are a large-scale anomaly in temperature and affect the exchange of energy between the ocean and atmosphere, they have a strong feedback upon the atmosphere, the changes in which, in turn, influence the eddies. However, the relationship between such eddies and average atmospheric behaviour is complex. It is not a straightforward matter, at least yet, to forecast longer-time atmospheric changes, such as seasonal anomalies, on the basis of ocean eddies.

Turning to land surfaces, there clearly are many feedbacks between atmospheric changes and changes in land surface conditions that relate to perceived climatic anomalies. The time scale of such changes may cover a large range.

Snow cover over land, for example, can be established in a short time (a day to several days) over large areas. Depending on meteorological conditions, the cover may persist for a long time, such as an entire winter. It is also quite different year to year. It may well be that an intensive and persistent snow cover over a large continental area may influence weather patterns for the season or even the year ahead. A climatic anomaly that produces an anomously larger or smaller winter snow cover probably thereby induces further anomalous climatic behaviour, and so on. We can only suspect that these inter-relations occur; we have as yet no good theory relating seasonal anomalies from one year to another.

Natural or man-induced changes in land characteristics may also propagate in time to influence further changes. If a large region that has been vegetated becomes denuded of cover, either from a prolonged drought or from man's use of the land, then it is postulated that the change in the land surface relative to surrounding areas will serve to amplify the drying effects.

It is known that land which is vegetated absorbs more incoming solar energy than land which is bare, especially when the land is dry and somewhat sandy anyway, as in semi-arid regions. Thus, if a vegetated region is denuded, there will be established a heat balance between the denuded area and the overlying atmosphere that will be different from surrounding regions. A detailed model analysis has been made[2] on the large-scale dynamic processes (air motions) to study the possible effects of such relative changes in a regional heat balance. The studies show that the resulting changes in air motion over the region tend to suppress the formation of clouds and hence reduce precipitation. Thus it is postulated that removal of vegetation can influence atmospheric motions to an extent that could initiate a drying of the region. Moreover, once a drying were to commence, the soil surface would become more dusty. Under the influence of any surface winds, dust would enter the atmosphere. Other studies have indicated that increase in dust content of the lower atmosphere also acts to suppress precipitation and thus the drying-out process is given further impetus.

Thus, a seasonal climatic anomaly, acting over a large region, and changing the land surface significantly, could be amplified through this mechanism to cause a long-term effect. Man's agricultural and pastoral activities in regions where rainfall is marginally sufficient anyway may decrease the rainfall further in such regions by these mechanisms.

Studies have shown that the decrease in vegetation could very well have been amplified in the Sahelian situation, for example, and be a major contributing factor in desertification processes in general. Studies in India in the Rajastran Desert region indicate that the dustiness of that region, attributable to the intense dry agricultural practices there, could have been an amplifying factor in the gradual deterioration of local agricultural possibilities.[3]

Desertification is of considerable concern in many parts of the world today. It is not a simple process. It is not merely a climatic result, at least in the short-time scales we are considering. It is a process that seems to be a result of complex interactions starting with incipient marginal conditions, to which are added triggering events such as a prolonged drought, and man's activities. These activities may be long-term ones arising from changes in cultural patterns induced by demographic changes or from development pressures. They can also be results of nearly uncontrollable human action undertaken in desperate attempts to survive under harsh temporary climatic variations if other avenues of remedy are non-existent.

For example, in Roman times much grain was supplied from North African regions bordering the Mediterranean Sea, large cities flourished, and the region was also a favourite place for vacations for the élite - pleasure palaces flourished. Now it is essentially barren. The pleasure palaces are covered by drifting sand, and the large agricultural lands of Carthage do not lend themselves any longer to production. Other examples could be cited. The biblical land of "milk and honey" has for centuries lain in sandy, agricultural non-production. Modern understanding and improved land-use practices are now bringing it back to life. The Mesopotamian region once fed a large population; now the region provides only subsistence land use. How many of these changes can be attributed to climate variability, how many to man's agency? We do not see concrete evidence that climate changes alone, as between those earlier times and today, account for such changes in agricultural possibilities.

3. Some Factors Influencing Change

Modern investigations of tree rings, pollen analysis in bogs, lake and sea levels, cores of deep ice in Greenland and Antarctica, deep ocean sediments, and other geological and palaeobotanical evidence, as well as human historical records of the past several thousands of years, allows us to reconstruct past climates. Considerable detail can be extracted for the past several thousands of years, in which seasonal changes can be identified and correlated over large regions. As we go further back in the record, the time resolution degenerates quickly, but even so we can identify in the various climatic régimes of past geological epochs short and severe climatic perturbations of a few hundred years, with the average climate returning to normal after these sharp excursions. Can we discern some of the factors involved in changes of régime?, in the shorter perturbations within a regime?

We know that in its history the earth has undergone great geological evolution, with associated climatic periods. There was, for example, a long period of many tens or hundreds of millions of years of relatively uniform and mild climate, very conducive to plant growth, with great and warm shallow seas and evidently little if any mountain building. The fossil fuel we burn today comes from that time. The distribution of land masses in those times was far different from the contemporary geography; perhaps there was essentially one major continent. Then, at some time, perhaps about 200 million years ago, the earth became geologically active, the protocontinent began to break up, large parts drifted apart to form the Atlantic and Pacific Ocean basins. Crustal blocks of continental material moved differentially. In some places mountain chains were formed where these blocks encountered each other. Mountain building is still in progress, partially balanced by erosion, and it is believed that continents are still on the move. New techniques make it possible to detect the very small annual or decadal motions. But the movements are very small indeed, and we may safely assume that the continental distribution over the past several hundred thousand years has not changed appreciably enough to trigger significant climatic shifts, at least on a global basis.

However, there have been several rather regular glacial and interglacial periods in the past several hundred millenia. We cannot invoke vast geological activity to explain them. We could invoke changes in the sun, extensive volcanic activity, and the ever-present slow and predictable changes in the geometry of the sun-earth movements with cycles of 19,000-23,000, about 40,000 and about 100,000 years, as described below in section . But we have not always had, as read in the climate record, regular climatic variations of these periods. Perhaps the orbital changes were just not quite enough in themselves to force climatic shifts, but served to bring the climate system close to the point of instability. At those times, other factors that had the appropriate magnitude and effects might then have been the triggering mechanism to induce a climatic change.

In this regard, allowance should be made for the possible small change in solar radiation, the occurrences of which is still an open scientific question. There is some good evidence that the sun has a cycle of dynamic activity, manifested, for example, by the appearance and disappearance of sun spots on a cycle that averages about 10-11 years; some cycles are much more intense than others. This cycle of sunspots has been observed regularly since the time of Galileo, *circa* 1600. It is also known that sunspots and solar activity are related to cycles of the aurora borealis and australis, the former of which has been well observed and recorded for the past 2000 years or so. There is good evidence for a marked reduction in solar-cycle activity for an extensive period spanning 1650 to 1715, and there is enough written evidence on auroral activity to suggest an even longer period of solar quiescence around 1100. Thus, we may not rule out changes in our sole energy source, the sun.

Volcanoes are very unpredictable geological phenomena. A violent volcanic eruption, such as that in the Yellowstone region of North America, ejected hundreds of cubic kilometres of material into the atmosphere, some 350,000 years ago. An eruption that violent must have sent material upwards well into the stratosphere, where it would have had a lifetime of many years before it slowly fell back to earth.

Early in the nineteenth century the famous European "year without a summer" followed shortly after a volcanic eruption in the East Indies had ejected something like 20 km^3 of material into the atmosphere. Was there a connection?

A dust layer in the stratosphere, it is generally believed, would result in a cooling of the earth, by serving as a partial reflector for incoming solar visible light radiation, while not inhibiting very much the outward loss of heat from the earth by infrared radiation. An extensive period of strong vulcanism would surely produce a climatic effect, especially if the entire climatic system were in a condition of near instability caused by an independent process such as the change in the earth's orbit around the sun.

Periods of extensive volcanic activity have occurred in the past that most likely induced some climatic effects. There are many active and quasi-active volcanic regions around the earth in this contemporary period, and we cannot rule out the possible resumption of extensive volcanism at any time. We have no way of anticipating such possibilities, however.

Human activities in the aggregate may also influence climate especially if the climate system is near instability anyway. Possible human roles in desertification processes are mentioned earlier. Human drives to cultivate land has led to deforestation of Europe and eastern North America, to the ploughing under of vast grasslands in central North America and Asia, and to diversion of many river systems for irrigation of large regions. Our current understanding of the workings of the climate system do not permit reliable prediction of climate changes caused by such human activity. It is sure, however, that society will continue to press more land into production and use increasing amounts of energy as we attempt to raise the nutritional and well-being standards of the world population and as population itself grows.

Could the emergence and spectacular growth of human civilization following the last retreat of ice cover in the temperate regions have been a factor that will influence the timing or magnitude of the next glaciation, if there is to be one? Unfortunately, we will not be able to tell, for even though we have detailed evidence of several relatively uniform glaciations in the recent past, that in itself does not allow a linear extrapolation to the next in the series. The Pleistocene series of glaciations began, it seems, with little evidence of any remarkable change in external conditions.[4] It could end just as mysteriously in our times. If the next ice advance does not come on time, we probably shall not know explicitly what, if anything palpable, prevented it.

There is also much speculation today about products of man's rapid industrial development, particularly the introduction into the atmosphere of gases that absorb infrared radiation and thus would increase the temperature of the lower atmosphere. Carbon dioxide from the burning of oil and coal is the dominant gas of this kind, but there are others that in the aggregate are nearly as important, such as nitrogen oxides produced in the soil from agricultural fertilizers, organic chemicals used as solvents, refrigerants and propellants, etc. It is not a simple matter to predict what the effect will be of continued introduction of these gases. A doubling, which might occur in the next century, will probably induce some warming trends on a global average, but regional cooling and warmings might be considerable, and many of them beneficial rather than harmful. This one matter is now receiving considerable attention, but the scientific problem is complex and we cannot look forward in the near future to a reliable estimate of climatic perturbations or actual changes, especially with regard to such essential details as how much and where.

4. Some Stability Considerations of the Climate System

In some respects, the earth's climate system is remarkably stable. Extreme events occur that do not seem to affect subsequent periods. Europe had its famous year without a summer in the 1800s. The Rocky Mountain region of the United States had its year without a winter in 1976/7. The summer of 1976 was the warmest and driest recorded in England in some 200 years, followed by the wettest and coldest winter in that time span. Yet these extreme years will probably not affect noticeably the 30- or 100- year statistics.

We are in a period called an inter-glacial, with reference to the record of the past several hundred millenia. Yet within this short period, since the northern-hemisphere continental ice sheet began its retreat some 22,000 years ago, there have been many incidents of quite cold weather, cold enough to presage another ice age. Several very cold winters occurred in North America around the turn of this century; there was a longer period culminating in the middle of the last century, when Alpine glaciers were very well developed and extended. This was the so-called "little Ice Age" in the period around 1550-1850.

Besides excursions to the colder side, the climate system also seems to permit extended spells of warmer weather, such as the very long altithermal period centred at about 6000 years ago. Norse seafarers were able to colonize parts of Greenland in the medieval warm phase of about 800-1200. Many runs of favourable weather have also been noted in the recent past, the most recent being those in the 1950s and also in the late 1960s.

Thus, the climate system can permit rather abrupt and severe excursions from long-term averages as well as rather long-term shifts from these averages, and return to the average condition of the climate régime.

It is also important to note that the atmosphere is a global entity. There is a global continuity that must prevail in such aspects as air motions. Change of motion anywhere must be compensated by reverse changes somewhere else. Such circulation adjustments will produce changes in temperature and rainfall régimes. Global averages may not portray the complete picture of climatic events. Regional changes can be larger in magnitude, and of diverse nature. Not all of our record of the past climatic fluctuations can be analysed on a regional basis, but we do know from contemporary instrumental records that even one hemisphere can show a general warming while in the other a general cooling can prevail. Moreover, even though the global atmospheric content of carbon dioxide is increasing, there seems to be a general cooling right now, but whether this is really a trend or a short-term fluctuation cannot be distinguished.

There seems to be evidence that the climatic system tends to be stable, with regard to changing from one régime to another. We have no evidence that the next ice period is imminent. Based on the climatic record, however, we can expect short-term departures, changes, or fluctuations, whatever we wish to name them. We may also not preclude the possibility of the onset of a trend, regional warmings, coolings, or even a global warming or cooling. Such trends happened in the Medieval Warm Phase, in the Little Ice Age, and earlier, within our current climatic inter-glacial régime. Even if we disregard possibilities of changes in the sun, volcanism, or other natural factors that influence the equilibrium state within a given régime, we cannot rule out the possibility of human influences, as described above. There is little evidence, however, that such influence would have sudden effects, as we are changing the physical factors very slowly. We have to assess their possibility of occurrence and learn how to monitor their evolution. Human institutions, in the time scales of half a century or so, may be able to evolve to keep up with perceived trends, in such way to minimize harmful or optimize beneficial effects of any perceived slow trend in climatic equilibrium conditions.

5. The Physical Elements of the Earth's Climate System

In the previous sections we have given some examples of the ways in which the climatic system may change its equilibrium conditions, and have mentioned some of the factors involved, without going into a more physical discussion of how these elements actually enter in. In this section, we will discuss in very general terms some of the physical principles involved to give the interested reader some further insight into the challenging complexities of the physical part of the system that we are trying to understand.

We first start from a basic assertion, first recognized by Galileo, and formulated in mathematical terms by Newton: any change in motion of a physical system must have a direct physical cause, namely a force. Later work revealed a corollary basic principle: any time a force acts to produce a change, energy must be supplied from somewhere. The supply of energy to the climate system, and its flow through the system is one of the basic principles first to clarify, so that we can appreciate how and why some parts of the system work the way they do.

5.1. SOURCE OF ENERGY

To a very good approximation, the radiant energy from the sun is the only source of the energy that heats the earth's surface and evaporates water from the oceans, lakes and rivers. These processes drive the motions of the atmosphere and oceans. To give a context for the importance of solar energy, moonlight is less intense than sunlight by a factor of one million; starlight is less important still by another factor of one million. The interior of the earth is very hot, but the average over the globe of heat loss from the interior to the surface is very low. The earth's internal heat energy is conducted outward through thick rock and sediment layers very slowly and the amount of energy reaching the oceans and atmosphere from below can be ignored completely.

The sun radiates energy over a very wide range of frequencies, from the very low frequencies of radio waves (the lowest frequencies we detect regularly are some hundreds of millions of cycles per second) to high-energy X-rays (some million million million cycles per second). That part of the frequency range (spectrum) to which human eyes are sensitive lies in the frequency range of 1000 million million to about 3000 million million cycles per second. These large numbers are hard to grasp. For comparison, television programmes are transmitted at frequencies of about 100 million cycles per second. It will not help either to give these figures in terms of the wavelengths of the waves, for then they become nearly incomprehensibly small, in terms of human experience. For comparison, television frequency wavelengths are about 3 metres. The wavelengths we are talking about here, for visible light, are 10 million times shorter.

The atmosphere itself absorbs directly very little of the incoming solar energy, since air is very transparent to visible light. Clouds and dust, of course, reflect some part of the incoming visible solar radiation, on the average about 30% over the earth as a whole. The solar radiation not thus reflected back to space thus impinges on the earth's surface (see Fig.9.1). There, the major mechanisms of transfer and transformation of solar heating are:

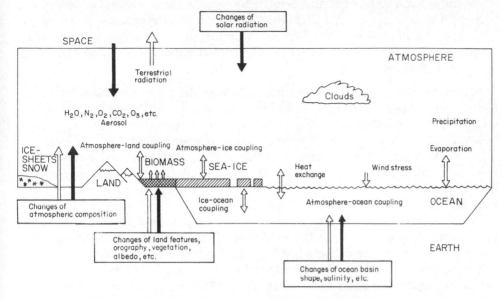

Fig.9.1. The physical basis of climate and climate modelling.

(a) Direct absorption, which heats the surface. Air in contact with the surface is then heated directly by conduction. Heat transferred directly in this way to the atmosphere is called sensible heat, which accounts for the smallest portion of atmospheric heating.

(b) The land and ocean surfaces, heated by incoming solar radiation, emit radiation, as explained in the next section. At the normal surface temperatures of the earth, this radiation is in the infrared wavelengths for which many atmospheric gases absorb strongly; they thus become heated themselves. Carbon dioxide and water vapour are the two most important gases in this respect; there are some other natural gases, such as methane and nitrogen oxides, as well as gases produced by man, such as the chlorofluoromethanes, and nitrogen oxides arising from the bacterial decomposition of nitrogenous fertilizers. Even though these gases are present in small quantities, they absorb infrared energy to cause significant atmospheric heating in the lower atmosphere. Since the infrared radiation is also emitted outwards to space, being absorbed and re-emitted by successive atmospheric layers on its way, there is also a cooling in the upper layers. The total amount of energy received from the sun is ultimately radiated back to space, but an equilibrium is reached in which the lower atmosphere is warmed.

(c) Evaporation from water surfaces always takes place. Regions strongly heated by incoming solar radiation, in particular the tropical oceans, account for most of the water vapour released into the atmosphere. Since water molecules attract each other strongly, each evaporating molecule must have acquired additional energy to escape from its liquid state. This escape energy is called the latent heat of evaporation which, for water, is one of the largest for any known substances. It is estimated that about half of the energy that reaches the earth's surface is transformed into latent heat of evaporation and thereby introduced into the atmosphere. Wherever the water vapour condenses and forms clouds, then that latent heat is released. Since the atmosphere has large horizontal motions, the release of the heat is often far distant from the place of evaporation. Thus the transport of water vapour is a critical part of atmospheric motions.

In this discussion we are concerned mainly with the portion of the solar energy centred on that part of the solar radiation range that we call the visible part, extending from the near ultraviolet to the near infrared. This portion of the solar radiation spectrum contains about 99% of the total solar energy reaching the earth.

We do know that there are large variations of the radiation outside this part of this range of solar energy, in the far ultraviolet and in the radio-wave portions. These variations may be large, but the total energy is small compared with the portion centred on the visible portion. We also know that these radiations, especially those in the ultraviolet and even shorter wavelength portions, do affect the earth's outer atmosphere considerably, but we do not know if or how such variations affect the inner part of the atmosphere in which weather and climate occur.

To the best of our current knowledge, the solar output of energy is constant in magnitude or at most has a variation of about 1%, which has been the limit of accuracy of measurement. Radiation instruments on satellites will be used in the coming decades to measure the solar energy and its variations with an improvement in accuracy of at least a factor of 2 and possibly a factor of 10.

5.2. LOSS OF ENERGY BY THE EARTH TO SPACE

The sun, as the sole energy source, is far enough away so that it is nearly a point source. The rest of space surrounding the earth is very cold, at a temperature of only a few degrees above absolute zero. Thus, we may consider here that space is an infinite sink of energy.

We know from the laws of physics and radiation that any body at a temperature above absolute zero radiates energy, the magnitude and central wavelength of which is determined by the body's temperature. The average temperature of the earth, as seen from space, is just over 300° absolute. At this temperature, the radiation from the earth to space is centred in the infrared portion of the spectrum.

5.3. ESTABLISHMENT OF TEMPERATURE EQUILIBRIUM

If the earth were a simple homogenous body, with constant and known radiation properties, it would be easy to calculate its annual average equilibrium temperature. With a knowledge of the thermal properties of the surface, we could also predict regional temperature variations arising from the earth's rotation, as well as those arising from the annual cycle of revolution around the sun in an orbit with well-known ellipticity and well-known geometrical relationships between the plane of the earth's own rotation and the plane of the earth's revolution about the sun. These orbital parameters, however, do not stay strictly constant over long periods. The plane of rotation, the direction of the earth's rotational axis, and the direction of the major axis of the earth's orbit around the sun slowly precess in space, with cycles of about 100,000, 40,000 and 14,000-23,000 years, respectively.

However, the earth is far from a simple homogenous body, as we shall discuss below, and its orbital characteristics, with respect to the sun, do change with time as mentioned above. These changes, in effect, cause a change in the magnitude of the energy arriving at earth and its time distribution through the day and through the seasons. Let us discuss this latter matter first so as to dispose of it within the context of short-term changes in climate.

The orbital changes of the earth's motion about the sun are understood from astronomical considerations. The various orbital changes mentioned above can be calculated to a good approximation. We cannot make exact calculations because it is not possible to obtain a completely exact mathematical solution to the motion of a body under the gravitation influence of several bodies. That is, the complete Newtonian description of the motions of the sun, moon, earth and near planets can only be approximated. However, we can say with some assurance what the general character of the motions are. We know that they do not vary in abrupt ways. Many scientists believe that the slow change of the earth's orbital motions account for some of the climatic changes we can reconstruct from geological and palaeobotanical evidence. The recent cycle of glaciations, with periods of about 100,000 or so years, for example, may well have arisen from such orbital changes, for evidence shows that other geophysical processes, such as mountain building or continental drift, did not change much in that time span. Such orbital changes may well have caused changes in input energy and its distribution throughout the year sufficient or nearly so to change the average annual temperatures enough to induce advances or retreats of polar ice sheets. But such changes are not what we are concerned with in this study, although knowledge of details of the climate changes or variations in the past climatic régime of withdrawal from the last ice age are very helpful in understanding some aspects of climatic variations, as discussed below.

Turning back to the earth, it is in reality a very complex body, the radiation properties of which are quite variable in time and space. The presence of a surrounding atmosphere, for example, is the first complication. The atmosphere contains some gases that absorb and emit infrared radiation, and the atmosphere contains a highly variable component, water, that exists in three forms—vapour, liquid and solid. Water has a very high capacity for absorbing heat energy (that is, it takes a great deal of heat gain or loss to raise or lower the water temperature) and it also absorbs or releases a large amount of heat when it changes from one form to another, as when it evaporates to form vapour, condenses to form clouds, freezes into snow or ice, or melts. Water as cloud droplets is a very good reflector of visible light, and water vapour as well as droplets are very good absorbers and emitters of infrared radiation. Water as a solid (snow, ice) has a very high reflectivity for visible light. Thus it is easy to understand how complicated it is to calculate, predict, or even to measure how much of the incoming radiation from the sun actually reaches the entire surface of the earth to be absorbed and changed into direct or infrared heating, or be absorbed by water and then transported to other regions by motions of the atmosphere in the form of latent heat of vaporization.

5.4. RELATIONSHIP BETWEEN ELEMENTS OF THE EARTH'S CLIMATE SYSTEM

The sections above touched on a few of the ways in which energy is modified, transformed and transported in the earth-ocean atmosphere climate system, that is, how the climate system works to remain in approximate equilibrium with the sun and space. It is beyond the scope of this report to present a scholarly review of the various processes involved; in addition, such a review would overemphasize our understanding of the complexities of the entire climate system. Moreover, an excellent review already exists of the state of knowledge of the many physical factors involved and their many positive and negative interactions.[5]

Figure 9.1 is taken from this publication and illustrates schematically the various physical factors and the flow of energy. Rather than describe this figure and elaborate on it, we wish here to make a few points to set a context for the discussion that follows on variations of climate. The "external" forces (sea, mountains) shown are those factors or processes that can be assumed to remain constant for the short time scale of climate variations treated in this report, namely inter-annual, inter-seasonal variabilities, short trends of a few years, within the context of a century or so. We assume that the solar output is not changing enough year to year to influence climate, but as mentioned earlier, this question is under study, for solar changes would indeed force climate changes. We assume that mountain building and movements of continents are negligible within the time frame that we have set. Of course, over millions of years these have been very important geophysical factors indeed.

The other elements (such as clouds, water vapour, snow, ice) are called internal to the system—their most important attribute, from the viewpoint of this discussion is that they may change from causes that are solely internal in the system. For the most part, they are also highly inter-related. Sometimes we can understand chains of causality, but often the relationships are obscured by the complexity of the system. In studying these parts of the system, we can isolate them somewhat and derive some of their properties, we can discern how some of the inter-relationships work. But it is not simple. If we try thought experiments, or quantify thought experiments into a numerical simulation model, we usually cannot follow all the possible interactions on all time and space scales on which they operate.

6. Climatic Variability and Climatic Patterns: Structural and Statistical Considerations

We digress here to describe in some detail a laboratory experiment that illustrates some aspects of how the atmospheric circulation works in response to the forces driving it - the distribution of heat between the equator and poles and the rotation of the earth. In Fig. 9.2(a) the experimental set-up is depicted.[6] A flat pan is heated around its outer wall and a small cylinder that can be cooled is placed in its centre. The whole system is filled with water, and is rotated upon a turntable or other device. Dyes or particles in the water allow the motions to be discerned. This apparatus simulates some of the features of the dynamics and heating distribution of the earth-atmosphere system, as shown schematically in Fig. 9.2(b). The rotation of the pan introduces a rotating frame of reference for that of the fluid, as for that of the atmosphere with respect to the earth. The heat supplied through the outer wall is analogous to the heat supplied to the atmosphere from the sun, which falls mainly in the tropical regions. The cooling at the centre represents the net heat loss at the earth's poles. The real earth, of course, may radiate energy to space and therefore cool over its entire surface, and in fact it does so. But the heat gained from the sun is greater than this loss in the tropical regions, and thus there is a net heat gain there. The poles do receive some heat for part of the year from the sun, but the

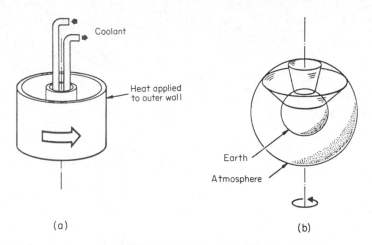

Fig.9.2. (a) schematic of experiment, showing rotating cylinder, cooled at centre, warmed at rim, filled with water; (b) schematic of earth-atmosphere (not to scale) showing analogy of rotating cylinder (after Greenspan, *Physics of Rotating Fluids*).

predominate energy flow is a loss to space. Somewhere in between the equator and the poles (at about 60° latitude) the heat gained is balanced by the heat loss, but we must also take into account that the system is dynamic. The atmosphere and the oceans can move. In fact, it is their motion that transports excess heat from the tropics to the poles to make up for the deficit there. Otherwise, the tropics would become ever hotter and hotter and the poles ever cooler and cooler. This does not happen. On the average, the earth maintains a stable equilibrium, at least for one régime of climate, between the energy input from the sun to its loss to space. The weather patterns, and hence the climate, can change somewhat because small amounts of energy, representing a small imbalance of the earth's heat budget, can be stored for various times within the climate system - for example, as large anomalies in the sea surface temperatures, growing or retracting ice sheets, changes in cloud cover and precipitation, etc.

In order to conduct our analogue experiment, we set the pan to rotate at a rate that is in conformity with the analogue to the earth's rotation, considering the fluid properties of water as compared with those of air. We then hold this rotational speed constant.

The experiment we describe consists of slowly increasing the temperature gradient in the fluid between the centre and the outer walls. At first, the fluid rotates with the inner and outer cylinders, in a smoother laminar type of flow, as depicted in Fig. 9.3(a). The flow régime here is adequate to transport the heat input as the outer wall to the heat sink at the inner wall.

As the temperature gradient is increased (usually by increased heating at the outer wall), the flow tends to concentrate. An annular jet stream is formed, Fig. 9.3(b), which has a high temperature gradient across it. We find such jets in the atmosphere and oceans.

With further increase in temperature gradient, waves form on the jet, since waves can introduce radial-type motion over a larger cross-section and hence increase the

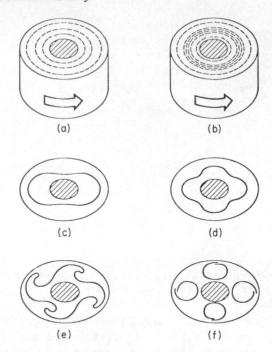

Fig.9.3. Flow régimes in rotating-cylinder experiment: (a) uniform flow at low-temperature difference between centre and rim; (b) formation of jet flow; (c) establishment of first wave régime; (d) increased number of waves to adjust to higher temperature gradient; (e) eventual wave distortion as temperature gradient becomes too high for wave régime to account for heat transport; (f) turbulent eddies form for even more efficient energy transport at high temperature gradient. (After R. Hide.)

transport of heat radially across the jet-stream region as we have depicted in Fig. 9.3(c). Such waves are found in atmospheric and oceanic flow. In Fig. 9.3(d) we see that additional waves are formed as the rim heating is increased; more and more heat must be transported to the centre to maintain equilibrium and thus the waves increase in number. Eventually, the number of waves cannot increase around the annular path, and the waves become distorted, Fig. 9.3(e). Finally at some critical temperature gradient, the waves break up into turbulence elements, Fig. 9.3(f). Thus we distinguish quite distinct flow régimes: laminar; concentrated but still laminar (with a jet); wave, distorted wave, turbulent. All of these régimes can be seen in our atmosphere.

If the experiments are repeated, and the physical system is large enough to observe small details carefully, it will be seen that these same régimes repeat themselves quite regularly, at least in terms of their characteristic kinds of flow. There will be, however, variation in exactly where the waves occur, or they may drift along the flow, or they may actually be unevenly spaced. Also, the waves could oscillate between flow conditions of, say, three waves or four around the annulus.

It is interesting to note that an even simpler experiment, in which there is no temperature gradient at all, will exhibit similar behaviour. Such an experiment consists of two concentric cylinders, each of which can be rotated independently. If they rotate at the same speed, a laminar flow régime will be established. If now, we speed up one of the cylinders, the fluid motion will progress through the same series of régimes described above.

If we number régimes A, B, C, D, E, etc., and number experimental runs 1,2,3, . . .n, then we will see that state B2 will be different from B7, and similarly for other distribution of states. We will have a statistical spread of the states that will depart from some mean behaviour.

While these rotating cylinder and pan experiments reproduce some of the features of the circulation of the atmosphere, and also ocean circulations, they are only rough analogies.

A close analogy can be obtained by using numerical models. Here, a set of equations are derived: the motion of fluid under specified forces, the heating and cooling and energy transformation through the change of state of water, the limiting boundary conditions. This set of related equations can be solved in an approximation (which is as accurate as we wish depending on the size of the computer) that allows us to simulate numerically both the atmospheric and oceanic circulations. Work on atmospheric models is far more advanced and we limit discussion to them. Note that a numerical model is not a theory or explanation. It is simply a convenient way of relating in very explicit mathematic terms the inter-relations of many physical processes that all work together to define how the fluid, in this case air, moves and transports heat. We can also make the model generate clouds and produce rain.

Models, of course, have limitations. An important one is that our available computers are still small; we cannot take into account all energy processes on all scales because we do not have an infinitely large computer. Moreover, as yet we may not have complete understanding of all the physical processes involved and especially of their inter-relationships.

Let us imagine a series of experiments with a modern, complex model. We specify the location of the continents, take into account the fact that the surface is not smooth (e.g. we specify mountains), we specify that the surface temperature has some climatic distribution, we let the earth rotate, we place the sun at the proper midday elevation for every point, with the proper day-night characteristic for the time of year, and we start with an atmosphere at a uniform temperature. As time goes on, motions evolve that gradually produce a temperature distribution that is very much like the real atmosphere, on the average, for the time of year and location. We now say that the model is a satisfactory simulation of the real atmosphere. We try it again at a different time of the year and the model produces a circulation that is different, but like the real circulation at that time of year. We now believe that the model reproduces the general characteristics of the seasons.

Many such model representations exist today. They are all somewhat different from each other, depending on the assumptions that each model-maker decides to use. Each group has to design their own model to meet their own requirements for study and their own interpretations as to which are the most realistic approximations.

If a good model, e.g. one that satisfactorily reproduces daily and seasonal variation, is now run for a year (that is, in computer time), it will reproduce the seasons. We can take seasonal means of temperature, cloudiness, precipitation, etc., as well as maxima and minima of temperature and precipitation. If the model is run for a second, third, fourth year, etc., and seasonal means are taken for each "year", we will find that each year will be different from the other, randomly, but in some statistical distribution around an average. If enough such runs are made, we will see a number of seasons, year to year, that will have a range much like that we actually observe in nature. The occasional rare event of an extreme year with means much larger or smaller than the average has not yet been reproduced randomly. However, we see that, with no change in conditions, as in the rotating-pan experiments, we find a number of possible solutions. There are so many ways of satisfying the condition that the average heat balance must be maintained that many possible solutions occur. It seems most probable that some random perturbations, or differences, at some point in the process determine which evolutionary path will be taken by the fluid motion in the rotating pans or by the numerical models.

We may call these random differences noise. In models, some noise is introduced by computer limitations, when we have to cut off calculations and round up or down. Or, we may have made approximations in our equations and how they are represented that introduce small errors. These errors can be random, and thus produce a series of statistically distributed results.

In nature, there are no errors as such. But, as a result of the complexity of the system, and the fact that not every part of the system responds to a perturbation in the same time, there is a certain amount of freedom in the way in which the various physical factors interact with each other. This is particularly true when the physical factors are all linked by complex chains of relationships.

The purpose of the preceding lengthy and disgressing discussion is to introduce the following concept. The climate system - comprising atmosphere, oceans, land, ice, man and biosphere - is one of the most complex natural systems, outside of life itself. As discussed in Chapter 5, such a system can have properties of a dissipative system, in the terminology of Prigogine. It has resilience, as demonstrated by the rare and severe events which occur essentially at random but which do not flip the system into a new régime. It also has endurance, since some régimes last for very long times. It can also have fragility, for sometimes it did flip from one state to another within a régime, but without changing the régime itself.

It may well be, as a result of the extreme complexity of the climate system itself, and the fact that it can respond in so many ways, that it can occupy with some probability a number of states within a given régime, moving from one state to another with no explicit physical cause.[7] The causes may well be simply the natural variability, or noise, of the constituent elements themselves. If such is the case, at least for some aspects of climatic variability, we cannot expect explicit predictive relationships to be successful for all types of variability.

Many other natural systems exhibit this probabilistic nature. It is one of the triumphs of modern particle physics that many properties of atoms and molecules can be "predicted" using statistical understanding of the non-explicit nature of the so-called elementary particles and their behaviour. We may be able to learn enough about the statistics and probabilities of the climate system to assign probabilities to states, changes, etc., useful for long-range planning.

7. Some Statistical Considerations of Climate Information

It is useful and important to man's activities and planning concepts to think of climate averages, but we must also be aware of pitfalls. There are many kinds of averages that can characterize climate. In some regions, for example, where rainfall occurs throughout the year, annual averages can be useful. For agricultural use, however, it is more important to know rainfall amounts at specific times of the growing season, length of growing season, time of last spring frosts and first autumn frosts and, for some crops, incidence of hail or winds. Thus it can be seen that the kinds of climatic information most useful for man's activities can be rather complex. The kinds of averages used should be tailored to their use. The amount of information and its detail will also to a considerable extent depend on the human structures in a given region - how well are societal segments prepared to make use of detailed information, what are limiting cultural conditions or practices, what are limiting political and/or economic factors?

A long-time series of information can be used to derive the needed specific averages. As we have seen, however, climate can be quite variable within a long-term stable régime. It seems to be the rule rather than the exception, looking at the recent climate record, that the normal state of climate is to be quite variable, with runs of good years, runs of bad years, punctuated by rarer and severe events. Many lands heavily used for agriculture tend to be in these kinds of climate régimes, and marginal lands, such as in the Sahel or North-east Brazil, are the most susceptible to the larger climatic fluctuations.

In long-time series of events that are more or less regularly spaced, e.g. where there is rain reasonably regularly throughout the year, we can derive useful statistical properties of the records. One useful statistical quantity is the standard deviation, which applies in principle only to a series of events each of which is independent of the others. If a rainfall record, for example, has a variability superimposed upon a trend, the trend must be removed before the standard deviation is calculated from the variabilities. Similarly, we must filter out cycles. If the events are reasonably distributed, most of the variability is within the limits of one standard deviation, which will include about 70% of the number of events or, in the case of evenly distributed rainfall monthly means, will account for the variability for about 70% of the time. The magnitude of the standard deviation will be a very good value for planning, say, the water-control systems needed for a place; a dam, for example, designed to contain the mean precipitation plus one standard deviation will fail 3 years out of 10, not an acceptable margin of safety to be sure, but this knowledge allows a reasonable additional margin to be designed. However, even two standard deviations (which will account for about 99% of the variability) will not tell anything about the infrequent but possibly very severe rare event, such as the so-called hundred-year flood. In most places the magnitude of the hundred-year flood, or any other similar or analogous event, is usually deduced from recent instrumental records and from recent historical accounts; an additional insight can be gained from geological evidence, such as the size of flood boundaries in a flood plain. However, figures derived from such information often are very imprecise as to actual probabilities of occurrence, or return times. Rare events do not occur on schedule, and the times of a few of them generally do not permit one to say much about their real spacing in time. A second "hundred-year" event can occur 10 years after the previous one, then not again for 150 years. In the long term, this is still a good measure of the mean return time (for some specific examples, see Maggiolo, Volume 3).

Regions with a strong wet/dry season characteristic (e.g. monsoonal) or even a double wet season feature, pose different kinds of problems for climate statistics. Of course, if the rainfall, temperature and sunshine could be specified in detail for specific months and the portions of the growing season, then the months for zero rainfall would not need to be considered. In these kinds of regions, annual rainfall figures are clearly meaningless, or at least subject to uncertainty. It does occasionally rain in the dry season, for example in East Africa during the time covered by this study. Such rain, however, is generally useless for agriculture, unless it is stored for the next season, although it could be helpful to some activities: direct use for humans and animals, and as a temporary impulse to otherwise dry pasture lands.

Some kinds of climate averages taken from a long period of observations, say 100 to 200 years, probably represent reasonably well the real climate statistical mean, or norm, and the smaller departures from norms. In some kinds of climate statistics, however, shorter periods are commonly used, for example rainfall averages are usually taken for 30-year periods as standards by which to judge percentage departures. After 10 years, a new 30-year average is taken. The climate record, however, shows trends of duration of this order when one 30-year average would not characterize at all well the rain expectations for an adjacent 30-year period, even with the 20-year overlap. Thus, longer-term averages should be used as a base to specify climate norms. In many areas, however, long-term records do not exist. They should be started as soon as possible, adding each year to the data base and calculating a new average, which will then, as the years progress, approach a good statistical characterization of the norm. In this process, occasional analysis will be needed to detect trends or cyclical behaviour so that they can be removed. The utility of 30-year means itself is open to question.

8. Optimal Climatic Periods

In this work so far, and throughout much of this report, and indeed in most similar studies, most of the attention is paid to negative departures from norms. But what of changes for the good? An occasional good year with a bumper crop is hardly a disaster. A few good years in a row might be a pleasant experience for many people. What of a more extended period, a decade or so? Human memories, unfortunately, tend to be short; after several years of good weather people can easily forget the longer-term norms, and be encouraged to "make hay while the sun shines". By ironic coincidence, some rather good years at the time of the implementation of the Green Revolution gave euphoristic optimism that at last the food solution was in hand. Nature, however, turned us a trick and then returned to normal. But we are capable of being more "intelligent", and make use of our understandings of climate mechanisms.

Climate studies and good understanding of climate statistics are an important factor in "intelligent" long-range planning. Here the word intelligent is meant as implying use of all information (intelligence) available. We need to have just as good information on optimal periods as we have on disastrous ones. In one way, Nature helps us a little. Optimal periods, low variability, reliable climate, seem to be much rarer in the climate record than periods of high variabilities. There may be no simple way to understand why.

In the past, there is evidence that many ancient peoples appreciated the limitations of nature and achieved a workable balance with Nature, that is, with the medium-term carrying capacity of the land. There is evidence that the occasional run of good years was not allowed to induce unlimited population expansion or expansion of agriculture into lands traditionally held to be normally marginal. There is even speculation that some of the early great organization efforts of ancient peoples, such as pyramid building and the construction of large-scale pictographs in the Peruvian desert,[8] may have had some impetus from desires to organize and structure society to keep the populations busy on public projects in good times when food stocks were ample. There is evidence, however, that while the Sahelian peoples did appreciate the "average" carrying capacity of the regions, other pressures were present to increase animal stocks, sometimes to the point of problems for bad years. In bad years, the limited animal and human populations could move freely, following the rains south, or west, or wherever there was water and forage and generally the people were able to cope. However, as shown by Bonte (Volume 3) occasional severe droughts served as a natural regulator to pull societies back to the average carrying capacities. Droughts were an essential occasional instability that helped produce a long-term stability to the Sahelian society, until other forces, as Bonte elaborates, appeared.

As a footnote, it is interesting to ponder why some peoples elect to live in very marginal places, where at best existence is hard, mortality high, and natural events such as climate shifts occur that make life even harder. Perhaps some people choose the Arctic, Tierra del Fuego, or the Sahel because the carrying capacity, while limited, is sufficient for existence provided that adequate social structures exist, and not so great that other peoples contest the ownership of the land. Thus some hardships are accepted for being left more or less in peace.

9. The Major Features of the 1972 Droughts

There has been much meteorological study of the regional and planetary situations in the late 1960s and early 1970s that led to the widespead climatic anomalies centred on the year 1972. There are detailed descriptions in the literature,[9] but we cannot regard anything that we have to read as an "explanation". Rather, one may find that one author will interpret as an explanation the movement of the rainfall zones away from the Sahel coherent in time with shifting patterns of atmospheric motions. Of course, if the motions of the atmosphere change, the climatic zones in some critical areas will also change. But what made the motions change? If we go back a step further, we may find, as some have done, that there were precurser motions elsewhere that influenced the changes, and prior to that the appearance of anomalies in the sea surface temperature in the Pacific Ocean. But why did they appear? And can we relate in a logical and supportable causal chain such events linked so tantalizingly in time? Are the precurser signals reliable predictors?

We shall review here very briefly some of the results of meteorological studies carried out as part of this project, and shall cite some other analyses to give some picture of the African situation, since it was concern over the 1972 drought that stimulated organization of this project.

First signs of rainfall deficiencies were noted in 1968 in West Africa, rising to a culmination in 1973, with some rains returning to Senegal in 1974. The drops in rainfall slowly moved westwards, and East Africa did not experience the full effects of

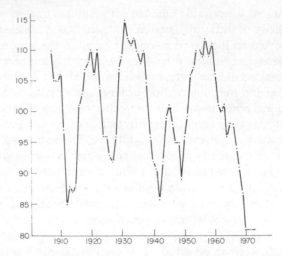

Fig.9.4. Five-year means of rainfall, West African marginal rainfall areas, percentages of long-term average. (See note 19.)

the droughts until the mid-1970s, 1973 and 1975 being the dryest years there.

With respect to West Africa, we show a graph in Fig. 9.4 of mean annual precipitation in the Sahel in this century.[10] A long-term trend is noted, against which the departures should be considered. It is seen that precipitation was at the lowest point in 1970 in this short record, in which four other drought periods are shown. As remarked in other sections of this Report (e.g. by P. Bonte, in Volume 3), the 1970-73 situation did represent a serious rainfall deficit, but only on a short-term basis of a few years. On a 5-year basis, he says that the drought in the second decade of the century was somewhat worse. Both droughts spread well into regions not normally affected by smaller departures, into the southernmost regions of the area, which are also the best agricultural lands. Also, it may be noticed that the 1972 period followed a rather extensive period of good rainfall, one which also coincided with great attempts to modernize agriculture in marginal regions and one in which there were great efforts to develop economies (e.g. produce exportable materials to pay for industrialization). Lands were pushed into production on the basis of the rainfall distribution during the good times. When the bad times came, the effect was severe. As an aside, the drought around 1930 produced an effect far more pronounced than inspection of Fig. 9.4 would lead one to suppose. The area had, like the rest of the world, been hit by severe economic disruption and the drought was a strong aggravating factor.

Based on analysis of Fig. 9.4, it is not possible to label the 1972 drought as much worse, if any, than the other bad drought of this century. Evidence of droughts even earlier are less quantitative, but other analyses indicate that the 1972 situation was by no means excessively severe in comparison with a long run of such occurrences in the history of the region.

A study by Ogallo[11] of rainfall as measured by a network of sixty-nine stations, showed absence of general trends, and no conclusions could be drawn. Perhaps there were insufficient data. Ogallo also found that the rainfall records tended to show an oscillatory nature of the annual means. He was able to find a number of frequency peaks in the rainfall figures, only two of which seemed to have importance, one of 2.0 to 2.5 years, a second of 2.7 to 3.3 years. The first of these may possibly be related to the quasi-biennial oscillation of the atmosphere, which seems to have a mean period of about 26 months, and which has thus far defied attempts at interpreting to the point of predicting its behaviour. The second peak might possibly be related to some other geophysical phenomenon, such as the wobble of the earth's axis of rotation with respect to a fixed direction in space. This wobble has been analysed extensively and a number of preferred frequencies have been found. Attempts have been made to correlate these with rainfall records. We find it difficult to relate these oscillations satisfactorily to other kinds of events, or to understand the 1972 rainfall deficiencies in terms of such oscillations such as to provide predictive capability. Perhaps the clues are hidden in the data, some day to be revealed.

One of the project studies for East Africa attempted to see if any understanding of the 1972 drought could be found in analysis of the atmospheric motion in the region. Kiangi[12]found that indeed the winds were different from the "normal" year of 1967, while the atmospheric structure itself was essentially the same. That is, there might have been about the same amount of water vapour in the atmosphere, but under a shift in the wind régime there was less dynamic inducement to cloud formation and rain. The understanding and explanation of these situations, and why 1972 was different from the control year, 1967, remain hidden.

In a different kind of analysis, Palutikoff[13] studied the kinds of rain distribution that produce drought: an annual deficit by itself will cause lower agricultural production; the normal annual rainfall may be spread over too many months, instead of being concentrated in the agricultural season; heavy rain may fall in the normally dry season when the land is unprepared and the people unable to use the rainfall. Thus the annual amount as well as its distribution are both important, especially in areas like East Africa with a strong wet-dry seasonality. Palutikoff's analysis shows that a serious aspect of the 1970s was that the drought persisted in many of the regions for 2 and 3 years, and thus overwhelmed any possible remedial action by the farmers. However, she did not find in the limited records, going back to the 1940s, any differences that one could use to label the 1972 situation as more of a disaster than some other similar periods. She ascribes the main impacts as having arisen from non-meteorological aspects of the situation, a thesis to which this entire report is directed.

A series of studies carried out in Mexico on local situations showed that in three different regions there were, to be sure, climatic effects in 1972. The physical effects were rather similar to each other. The social results, however, were far different, reinforcing our assertion that it is society that really structures the effects of physical perturbations.[14]

Much other evidence could be adduced, but we resist the temptation to look further. We find it difficult to come to any dramatic conclusion, except to agree with many others that the 1972 situation, while severe, was not significantly different in magnitude or character from many previous drought episodes, to which the Sahelian zone and East Africa is very prone, owing to their geographic situation. Such drought events, in our current climatic régime, are to be expected normally in these regions. Each one will be slightly different from the others, in physical terms. We have no working hypotheses about their predictability, other than statistically. We should not be surprised that extensive research efforts now underway, and likely to continue throughout the 1980s, will not provide in the future useful and explicit causal explanations. We may have to be satisfied with a refinement of the statistical understanding of these events, as physical phenomena. On the other hand, it may be even harder to forecast the evolution of human social and economic structures in the next interdrought period that will condition society to the occurrence of the next one, and determine as propounded in this Report the nature of the final impacts on humans.

However, we turn back to Fig. 9.4 for one last comment. The kinds of variability demonstrated by this figure have been, are, and will remain with us. The human structural organization of some regions successfully coped with such variabilities in the past. It seems that many modern human structures do not cope as well, as discussed in detail in this Report. It probably is true that industrial development and social evolution, and great elaboration of modern ways of life make it harder to include this factor in our social planning. But just because it is harder does not mean that we can more readily neglect the importance of the range of natural conditions. It seems axiomatic that future human structural organization must include the existence of these natural variabilities as important elements, as factors that must be accounted for in setting performance requirements for human structural systems. We may look forward, as discussed below in the next section, to better understandings, and even some kind of approaches to prediction but that will not make the natural variabilities disappear. They only become invisible when we forget that they are there and need to be accounted for in our plans. Many human systems, agricultural productive systems, for example, must allow for the range of variability illustrated in Fig. 9.4.

10. An Outlook Towards Further Understanding

The discussion in this chapter has not painted an altogether optimistic picture that we are on the verge of solving the climate problem. We are faced with a physical system that is bewilderingly complex, that operates on many time scales, that would require enormous efforts to observe in detail for a long period of time. It does exhibit some aspects of deterministic behaviour, but it does so in very complex ways with many non-linear feedbacks. It also exhibits features that appear to be indeterministic, at least from the strictly explicit mechanistic point of view.

Yet, the climate system is one of our most basic factors in shaping and limiting human society. It is often said by some that technology can conquer all of Nature's limitation. To those who say that "technology is the answer" we can make only a wistful response. "Yes, but what is the question?"[14] Some aspects of this Report have demonstrated that use of technology can be helpful for some situations, but can also create its own set of new problems, especially for human structures. For these kinds of problems, we can write no equations nor find explicit and elegant mathematical expressions.

Technology is making it possible to study natural systems and to observe natural processes deeply. Armed with technical tools, scientists are studying by themselves, in groups, and through some large-scale co-ordinated efforts the natural environment and climate. We have been remarkably successful in piecing together a useful picture of the past climate changes and fluctuations within states. This is of great help in understanding the nature of modern fluctuations and their probable limits.

Theoretical studies are proceeding, partly through the use of very complex mathematical models in which all of the important factors that we have identified enter in, explicitly where appropriate, or implicitly through fundamental functional relationships with other factors. Through such models we seek to understand the sensitivity of the climate system to changes in such things as solar input, amount of snow and ice, distribution of precipitation in one season, amount of carbon dioxide and other radiatively active gases in the atmosphere, and other aspects of man's activities.

As the building of even more complex models proceeds, and especially as we learn to build models that influence both atmosphere and oceans - their dynamics and inter-relationships - we may improve our ability to simulate the behaviour of the climate system, to study the evolution of trends, and reasons for their onsets and cessations or changes in sign.

As we investigate further the tantalizingly statistical relations that some researchers have found with sunspots or other solar activity, with wobbles of the earth's axis, with other quasi-periodic events in nature that may influence the state of climate, or the probability of occurrence of some kinds of weather, we make some further progress towards some useful predictability methods.

As we investigate further the relationships between large-scale elements of the climate systems, we may find suitably reliable and unequivocable precurser signals that will allow us to understand the sequence of events removed from each other in space and time (climatologists use the expression teleconnections). We may find some useful empirical relationships for better outlooks for seasonal or annual departures from the climatic norms.

Whatever progress we may make in these areas, designed to be able to make some useful predictions, we must also work on increasing the reliability of descriptions of the climatic variability, *per se*. It seems clear that good knowledge of climatic variability, place to place, and in particular with specific details as determined by the nature of human activity that is involved (e.g. agricultural production), must be included in considerations of how societies can cope with, not great disasters, but with the more common and normal kinds of variability. These variabilities enter into our ability to provide a productive society system within any cultural-physical framework, taking into account that there will be a range of natural conditions to be encountered. The swings up or down should not surpass the resilience of the human structures. The human structures should be designed to keep vulnerability down but productivity high. At least, this should be our aim.

Notes

1. We do not treat here the dark-light cycles at the poles, which amount to a 12-month "day". There the atmosphere cools only to some equilibrium temperature that is established between the heat lost to space, as described later, and the heat transported to the poles from the tropics by motions of the atmosphere and oceans.

2. See Charney, J. (1975), "Dynamics of deserts and drought in Sahel", *Q.J.R.M.Soc.* 101, 193-202.

3. For example, see Bryson, R. A. and Peterson, J. T. (1968), "The influence of atmospheric particles in the infrared radiation balance of Northern India", Department of Meteorology, University of Wisconsin, pp. 153-63.

4. Some interesting speculation has been discussed in the geological forces at play that culminated in the onset of modern glaciation cycles, which have been traced back now to about 2,000,000 B.P. Evidently Antarctica drifted into its present position, separately from Australia, about 25,000,000 B.P. Ice began to accumulate there. There is evidence that the north polar sea, and surrounding land, however, remained ice free (on an annual basis) until much later. Perhaps around 5,000,000 B.P. ice began to become permanent in the Arctic. For further details see, for example, Kennett, J.P. (1977), "Cenozoic evolution of antarctic glaciation, the circum-antarctic ocean, and their impact on global paleo-oceanography", *J. Geophys. Res.* 82, 3843-60.

5. GARP Publication Series No 16 (1975), *The Physical Basis of Climate and of Climate Modelling.* Published by WMO.

6. These experiments have been conducted by D. Fultz and R. Hide in the 1950s. A discussion of these experiments and their interpretation is given in *The Theory of Rotating Fluids,* H.P. Greenspan, Cambridge University Press, 1969.

7. Lorenz, E.N. (1971), "Climate change as a mathematical problem", in *Man's Impact on the Climate,* edited by Matheus, Kellogg and Robinson.

8. *Scientific American,* October 1978.

9. For example, see *Drought in Africa* (1973), International African Institute, London.

10. Jenkinson, A. F. (1975), "Some quasi-periodic changes in rainfall in Africa and Europe", *Proceedings of the WMO/IAMAP Symposium on Long-term Climatic Fluctuations,* WMO Publication No. 421, pp. 453-60.

11. Ogallo, Laban, *Rainfall in Africa.*

12. Kiangi, Peter, "Physical and windflow characteristics of the atmosphere over Eastern Africa during 1967 (normal year) and 1972 (drought stricken year)."

13. Palutikoff, Jan, "The early seventies drought in East Africa. Climatic reality or myth?"

14. Our colleague, M. Glantz, appears to be the originator of this formulation. Glantz has discussed "myths" of disaster in *The Politics of Natural Disaster,* Praeger, 1976. See also his *Value of a Reliable Long Range Climate Forecast for the Sahel: a Preliminary Assessment,* National Center for Atmospheric Research, Boulder, Co., USA, May 1976.

CHAPTER 10

Some Thoughts on Contemporary Global Climatic Variability

by Joseph Smagorinsky

I. Introductory Remarks

Climatic variations occur on many different time scales (Fig. 10.1). Variation is the rule rather than the exception. However, it is not the intention to dwell on ice ages or even on variations of climate from century to century. Instead we shall concentrate on the problem of variations from year to year. For example, why do we have large-scale warm or cold anomalies or drought from time to time; why may these anomalies persist for several months or recur again in the following year?

There are a few things that we know with some certainty: about the empirical nature of interannual variability, its regional characteristics and how it is related to the day-to-day weather variations. We shall try to mould this discussion around our theoretical understanding of the physical and dynamical processes that are operative. In many instances this understanding is reasonably firm, in others, it is more speculative.

It is not necessary to invoke extra-terrestrial influences such as sunspots, nor the influence of human activity such as the release of carbon dioxide or industrial heat. We have yet to fully understand to what extent the natural processes within the earth-atmosphere system can be held accountable for our presumed observational knowledge.

One should not rule out the possibility that climate predictability in the range of a few months to a few years may possibly be deterministic in some meaningful statistical-mechanical sense. However, this has yet to be established mainly because the physical processes primarily responsible for natural variability on this time scale have yet to be conclusively understood. We do know that the radiatively forced contemporary seasonal change is of the same magnitude as the climatic variations over the past million years.

Climatic variations in the range of a few months to a few years is, therefore, a problem of great scientific interest as well as of great potential practical impact.

But, we have yet to establish empirically the structure of this variability. It seems reasonably clear that even a full observational knowledge of the variability of meteorological parameters at the earth's surface, i.e. what is normally referred to as "climate" is, by itself, insufficient. A complete definition, in order to understand the mechanisms, must include the variation and structure of the general circulation of the atmosphere, and, at least to a limited extent, that of the oceans.

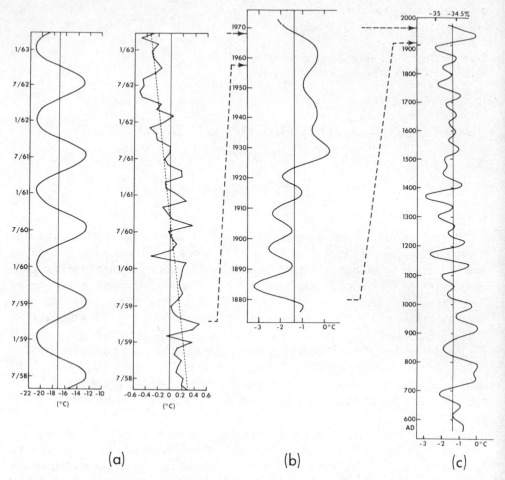

(a)   (b)   (c)

Fig.10.1 Some examples of typical variations of the actual climatic indices.
(a) A 5-year record of the monthly-mean temperature averaged over the entire Northern Hemisphere mass between the surface and 75 mb (about 18 km height) for the period May 1958 through April 1963 (after Star and Oort, 1973). Plotted are the raw values (*left*) and the values after the annual and semi-annual cycles were removed (*right*). The dashed line indicates the least-square linear trend in the data (-0.60°C/5 year).
(b) A 90-year record of observed Greenland temperatures smoothed to remove variability of 10 years or less (after Dansgaard *et al.,* 1975).
(c) A 1400-year record of the ^{18}O concentration in snow fallen at Crete, Central Greenland. The curves are smoothed to remove variability of 60 years of less. The curves are based on systematic, direct observations (after Dansgaard *et al.,* 1975).

And yet even the structure and variability of the surface climatology is not well known, mainly because of the large ocean expanses. This, of course, is primarily also the reason why the interhemispheric differences are not well determined empirically. The promise of more versatile remote sensing techniques will ultimately give us global coverage without regional bias.

Without such observational information, theoretical investigations are doomed to being conducted in the dark. There are numerous examples of sweeping incorrect conclusions being drawn from critically incomplete data sets. One finds instances where local or regional short-term variations are taken to be indicative of long-term hemispheric or even global events.

Much of the data I will discuss was provided for me by my colleague Dr. A. H. Oort, some as yet unpublished. It will ultimately be part of a 15-year study of aerological data from 1959 to 1973.

II. Some Observational "Facts"

A. EXISTING DATA SOURCES

The invention of the telegraph made it possible, about a century ago, to establish meteorological networks. This was the beginning of many of the present-day national weather services. The land-based observations at the earth's surface have provided us, in addition, with a good, but very limited, climatological observing system. It was not until the 1940s that aerological observations became sufficient in number to tell us something about the vertical structure and the general circulation of the atmosphere; but this also was confined overwhelmingly to land-based measures. In the 1960s we began to see the first global observations from satellites. Our ability to extract quantitative information is improving slowly. Under the Global Atmospheric Research Programme (GARP) a supreme effort will be made in 1979 to use a great variety of platforms: satellites, continents, islands, aircraft, ships, buoys and balloons, to obtain a unique global data set for one year, the First GARP Global Experiment (FGGE). For the decade to follow, a comprehensive global climate monitoring system is now being planned.

B. HEMISPHERIC AND GLOBAL CHANGES SINCE 1940

With these observational limitations in mind, what can be said about the hemispheric or global temperature changes over the past 30 or 40 years? Depending mainly on surface-based climatological data, Budyko and Vinnikov (1976) conclude that there has been a general warming since 1967. In this opinion they are supported by Broecker (1975). Both, incidentally, subscribe to the idea that increased atmospheric CO_2 is already operating to systematically warm the lower atmosphere. On the other hand, H. H. Lamb (1975) disagrees; he belongs to the "ice-age-is-coming" school.

Starr and Oort (1973) have made an analysis of the Northern Hemisphere aerological data for the periods 1959 to 1963 (Fig. 10.2). With the normal seasonal variation removed, a cooling trend of about 0.6°C/5 years was apparent. This seems to support the cooling assertion, but obviously extrapolation would have been misleading for the years 1969 to 1973. For the latter 5-year period, Oort (personal communication) also had marginally sufficient data to attempt a similar determination for the Southern Hemisphere (Fig. 10.3). Except for 1970, strong interhemispheric coupling is apparent. On the other hand, Damon and Kunen (1976), in an analysis of surface data for 1955 to 1974, judge that there was decoupling between the climates of the two hemispheres for the entire period, claiming a premature CO_2 greenhouse warming in the Southern Hemisphere.

Returning to the Northern Hemisphere, Dronia (1974) also calculated the mean temperature of the lower 6 km of the atmosphere for the period 1949 to 1973 for part of the Northern Hemisphere. He also found cooling in the 1959 to 1963 interval, but

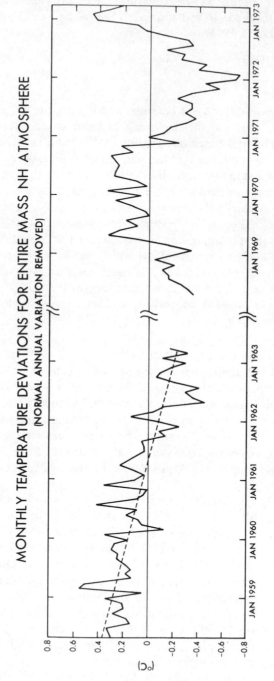

Fig.10.2. Monthly temperature deviations (°C) for entire mass of the Northern Hemisphere atmosphere - normal annual variation removed (1958-63: after Starr and Oort, 1973; 1968-73: after Oort, to be published).

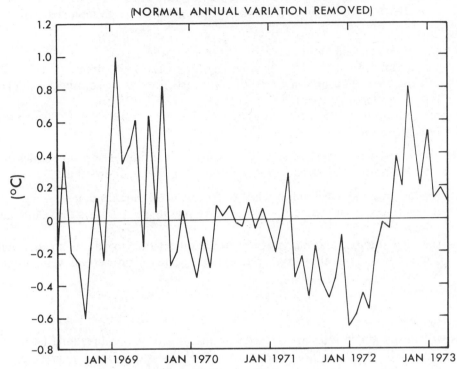

MONTHLY TEMPERATURE DEVIATIONS FOR
ENTIRE MASS SH ATMOSPHERE
(NORMAL ANNUAL VARIATION REMOVED)

Fig.10.3. Monthly temperature deviations (°C) for entire mass of the Southern
Hemisphere atmosphere - normal annual variation removed (after Oort, to be published).

unlike Oort sees the trend continuing in the following decade. However, a somewhat
more recent aerological study by Angell and Korshover (1975) indicates that the
Northern Hemispheric cooling between 1963 and 1973 was compensated by a similar
increase in the Southern Hemisphere.

A consensus study by Kukla *et al.* (1977) concludes that the oscillatory cooling
observed in the past 30 years in the Northern Hemisphere has not yet been reversed.
A comparative investigation by Harley (1978) of the lower tropospheric mean
temperature for the Northern Hemisphere between 25° and 85° latitude indicates a
rise in the latter 1950s, a fall until 1965, a small rise for the following decade and
then a sharp drop in 1975 and 1976.

This illustrates some of the disparities in defining the variability of very large-scale
integral properties of *recent* climate indices, even when a reasonably modern observ-
tional system is available!

There seems to be no clear evidence that the contemporary amplitude of climatic
variability is significantly different from the natural variability of the past century.
Nor can we discern whether present variability is appreciably the result of unnatural
influences.

C. LONGITUDINAL STRUCTURE

Now let us concentrate on some further analyses by Oort, keeping in mind how large the experimental error could be. Let us examine the vertically integrated temperature for the 45° to 55°N latitude zone for years 1958 to 1963 and for 1968 to 1973 (Fig. 10.4). Here the normal annual variation has not been removed. We note that:

—the largest annual amplitudes occur in winter;
—longitudinal wave no. 2-3 (the wavelength $\lambda \sim 120\text{-}180°$) dominates;
—minima tend to occur to the west of east coasts (i.e. on the continental side) of Asia and North America;
—maxima occur to the west of west coasts (i.e. on oceanic side) of Europe and North America.

The poleward heat flux by the atmospheric wave disturbances over time scales of 1 day to 1 month for this period at 45°N latitude (Fig. 10.5) shows that:

—the longitudinal wave number is 4 to 5 ($\lambda \sim 70\text{-}90°$ longitude);
—maxima occur at, or just west of, extrema in temperature (maxima and minima);
—the wave number and phase of longitudinal heat-flux variations are as would be expected from the wave relationships of temperature and wind in the winter-time mid-latitudes.

D. INTERANNUAL VARIABILITY

Now let us begin to look more closely at interannual variability. First let us examine the longitudinal profiles of heat flux at 60°N for each of the Januaries for the 1959-63 period (Fig. 10.6). We should note that:

—these include the contributions of all wave motions or eddies, both transient and stationary;
—the best aerological station network occurs at 60°N;
—the shaded area is the 5-year average.

We see that:

—the largest variability occurs at preferred longitudes, as was also evident in the previous figure;
—from year to year, there are both changes in amplitude as well as small phase shifts of $\sim \pm 1/8 \, \lambda$ (i.e. $\pm 15°$ longitude);
—variations in the zonal average are small but monotonically increasing from 1959 to 1963 (but this may all be experimental error).

It is significant to point out that the transient eddies, which because they have random longitudinal phase and a characteristic time scale of less than 1 month, for the most part only affect the zonal mean value of the heat flux but not the phase of the monthly mean. Hence, the small longitude phase shifts in the monthly mean mainly reflect changes in the quasi-stationary eddies. This is the crux of the matter.

Such fluctuations in the longitude of the semipermanent surface pressure features are also evident over much longer time scales (Fig. 10.7).

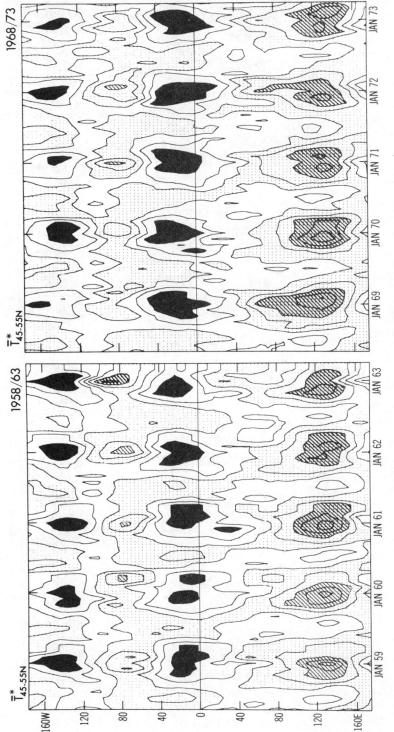

Fig.10.4. Vertically averaged temperature for the 45 - 55°N latitude zone, with the zonal average removed. Clear areas are positive and, where black, greater than + 4°C. Stippled areas are negative and, where cross-hatched, less than -4°C (after Oort, to be published).

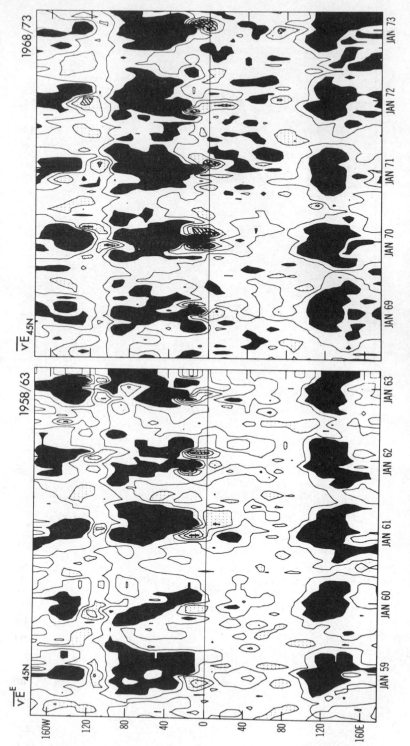

Fig.10.5 Vertically averaged poleward sensible plus latent heat flux due to transient and stationary eddies through 45°N latitude. Clear areas are positive and, where black, greater than +20 (°C m sec⁻¹). Stippled areas are negative and, where cross-hatched, less than -20 (°C m sec⁻¹) (after Oort, to be published).

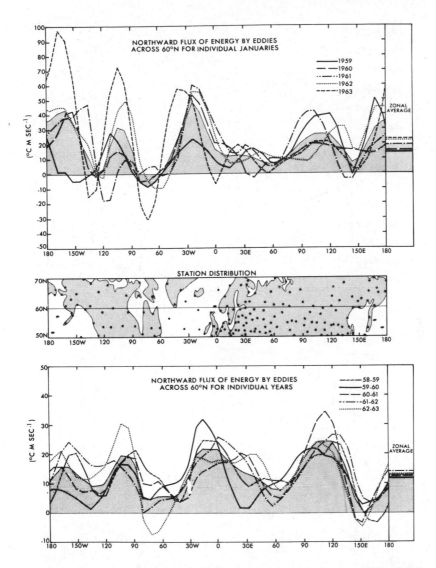

Fig.10.6. Poleward flux of energy across 60°N by transient plus standing eddies for individual January months (top) and for individual years (bottom). The shaded areas indicate the long-term mean contributions. Units are in °C m/sec (after Oort, 1974).

Now let us examine the longitudinal temperture profile in the 45-55°N zone, for 1958-63 and 1968-73 (Fig. 10.8), this time with seasonal variability removed. Here we note that:

—temperature anomalies are not necessarily longitudinally biased, but anomalies over the ocean may appear to be small because of observational bias;

—mainly wave no. 1-3 dominates, with some shorter modes present;

—there is evidence of occasional persistence of winter anomaly, e.g. 1969 and 1970;

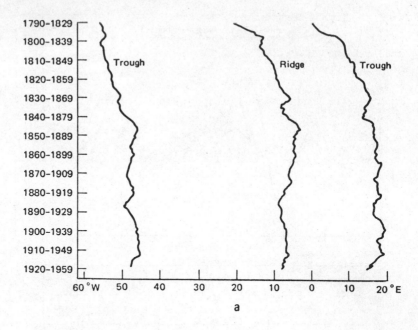

a

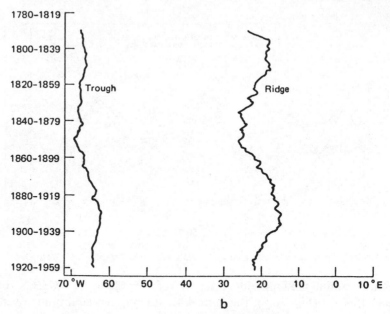

b

Fig.10.7. Forty-year running means of the longitudes of the semipermanent surface pressure troughs and ridges in the North Atlantic (after H.H. Lamb, 1969): (a) at 45°N in January; (b) at 55°N in July.

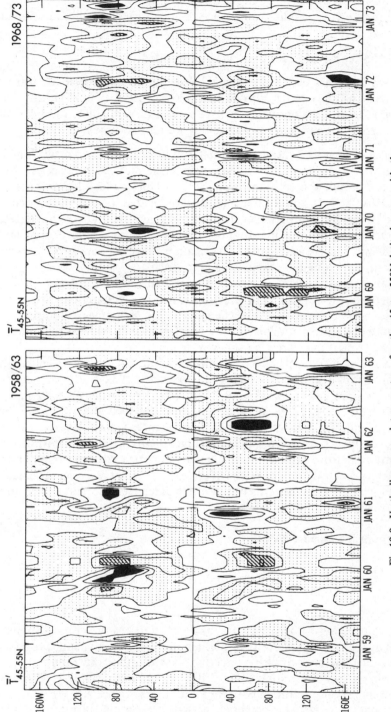

Fig.10.8. Vertically averaged temperature for the 45 to 55°N latitude zone with the seasonal variability removed. Clear areas are positive and, where black, greater than +2°C. Stippled areas are negative and, where cross-hatched, less than -2°C (after Oort, to be published).

—winter 1963 reflects extreme cold weather in January in North America and in western Europe (we shall return to this later);

—longitudinal coupling of surface temperature anomalies are not uncommon, e.g. 1960.

In this last connection, one should be reminded that:

—several years ago, there was a 3-year period of abnormally warm winters in eastern US, western Europe and western USSR ($\lambda \sim 60°$);

—and in the summer of 1976 there was abnormally large rainfall in the western USSR, but drought in central US, western Europe and Siberia.

It is of interest to mention in passing that this drought in central United States was the third in a sequence of droughts there, each about 20 years apart. Naturally the sunspots' proponents see significance in this. During these decades, the 1930s, 1950s and 1970s, the east coast of the United States tended to have more precipitation than usual. In the decades between, the mid-1940s and the mid-1960s, the situation was reversed. Excessive precipitation occurred in central United States, and extensive dryness was experienced in the East. Again we perceive small systematic phase shifts of about ±15° longitude from decade to decade.

As another example of extensive longitudinal coupling, there is a notable correlation between the Sahelian and North-west Indian precipitation anomalies during the extreme years between 1940 and the early 1970s. Examples of longitudinal coupling are quite common, but differ in how far they extend. More often it extends for less that 180° longitude, rarely all the way around.

One finds that the 1976-7 extreme winter in the Western Hemisphere shows many similarities, in degree and in character, to that of 1962-3. This can be seen by comparing the pressure anomalies at 3 km (the 700-mb level) in January 1963 and January 1977 (Fig. 10.9). We shall return to the 1963 and 1977 situations shortly.

On the other hand, there can be large differences from one year to another, for example the Januaries of 1961 and 1962 (Fig. 10.10). It is quite significant that the corresponding storm tracks over North America during these months were characteristically different, as one might expect. However, a superficial examination of the pressure-wave patterns of these two Januaries does not appear to show large differences.

III. Physical Considerations

A. RELATION OF WEATHER AND MONTHLY AVERAGES

1. Baroclinic instability

We shall refer to "baroclinicity" as a situation in which there is potential energy that is available for transformation to kinetic energy by dynamic processes. The major weather systems of the winter mid-latitudes are the result of an important dynamic process of the atmosphere called "baroclinic instability". This instability is excited in response to the radiatively induced pole to equator temperature gradient, the "zonal mean available potential energy" ($\overline{P}$). Baroclinic instability is the most efficient mechanism for transporting heat poleward and is accomplished in the form of five to eight eastward propagating wave disturbances distributed along a latitude circle (Fig. 10.11), especially in the winter-time when the radiative gradient is largest. The small phase difference between the waves of temperature and wind current is sufficient to transport heat poleward very efficiently, at the same time manifesting a transformation of zonal available potential energy ($\overline{P}$) to available potential energy (P') and kinetic energy (K') of the eddy or wave motion (Fig. 10.12).

A deducible consequence of the wave dynamics is that upward vertical motion must occur in the warm part of the wave train and downward motion in the cool part (Fig. 10.11); this is necessary to accomplish $\overline{P} \rightarrow P'$. Since water vapour is present, condensation and precipitation occurs on the rising adiabatically cooling warm air.

2. Life cycle of extratropical disturbances

Because these disturbances are super-efficient heat-transport mechanisms, as they grow to finite amplitude they reduce the zonal available potential energy (i.e. the pole-to-equator temperature difference) below the instability threshold faster than radiation can create it (Fig. 10.13), turning the growth off (day 23) but leaving finite amplitude disturbances that no longer transport heat because the temperature and wind are in phase. This is the "occlusion stage" which is well known from weather maps. At this point, the quasi-two-dimensional character of the flow requires that K' be transformed to kinetic energy of the zonal flow ($\overline{K}$), thereby intensifying the planetary jet steam. Meanwhile, as radiation prevails, the $\overline{P}$ is building up, and when the instability threshold is attained the flow becomes unstable again (day 28). As we shall see, the presence of an ocean below complicates the energy cycle.

3. Index cycle

This cyclic behaviour just described is highly over-simplified. The half-life of a single wave disturbance is from about 4 to 7 days (Fig. 10.14(a)). Other waves, forming a family of extratropical cyclones (Fig. 10.14(b)) may occur sequentially in time, each ultimately the size of about half of Europe. Especially in winter, several (five to eight) will co-exist at different longitudes but probably in a somewhat different time phase of development. If one were to calculate the eddy kinetic energy over the whole hemisphere, we would find an ensemble quasi-cyclic behaviour with a half-period of 10 to 30 days. This is the index cycle.

Viewed over a 6-month interval (Fig. 10.14(c)), the hemispheric K' would show many such index cycles, and the amplitude would be greatest in winter when the latitudinal radiative gradient is maximum. Running averages for a month would not quite filter out the longer index cycles. Two-or three-month averages would be less susceptible to aliasing distortion. An actual calculation of the energy components over a 5-year period using 10-day averages (a poor averaging interval) had been made by Kruger *et al.* (1965) (Fig. 10.15), note the differences from year to year.

B. INFLUENCE OF THE LOWER BOUNDARY IN GENERAL - MONSOONAL FORCING

The state of affairs just described was relatively simple, involving a self-excited instability, free oscillations and then a stability process, all driven by radiative heating and dissipated frictionally. It was unencumbered by the consideration of properties of the lower boundary.

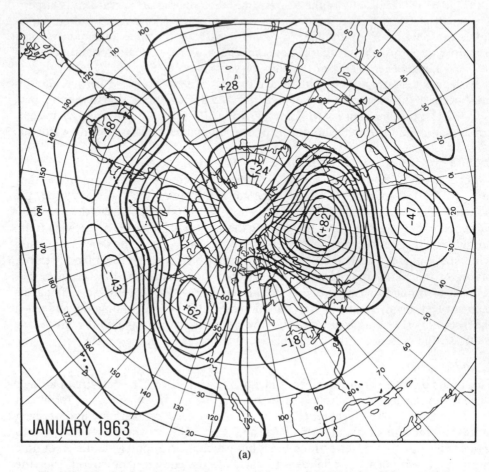

Fig.10.9. 700 mb height departures from normal (in tens of feet) (a) after O'Connor, 1963.

However, we already noted that in actuality there were substantial differences in $\bar{P}$ from year to year, even though presumably the interannual radiative differences cannot be large. One possible source of interannual difference is that the time phase of the index cycle relative to that of the seasonal cycle will vary randomly from year to year, reinforcing one year and compensating during another. We might refer to this as the "initial condition" influence. But is this all? Since the atmosphere does not have a large capacity to store heat, it can not easily in itself have much of a thermal memory. The only place we can find such a memory is in the lower boundary.

The main influence has to be in the irregular array of continents within the World Ocean and the varying topography. Consider the following hierarchy of hypothetical complications. Note that most of the sun's radiation passes through the atmosphere. That which is not reflected is absorbed by the lower boundary and the re-radiated in the infrared, which is readily absorbed by the atmosphere: in short, we have an atmospheric "greenhouse".

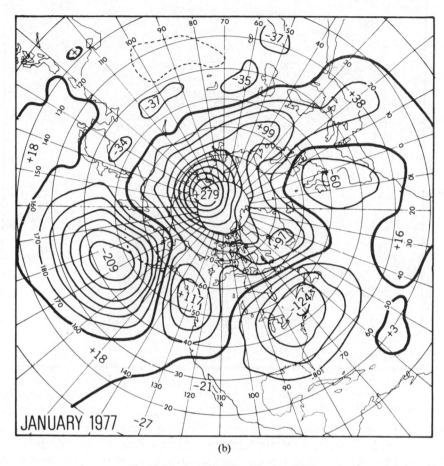

(b)

Fig.10.9 (*cont.*) (b) After Wagner, 1977.

1. *Uniform lower boundary—effectively the condition of our earlier discussion*

(a) *Uniform continental surface with no heat capacity*
 —The surface temperature adjusts instantaneously to satisfy the heat balance requirement at the continental surface.
 —The baroclinic instability growth rate is dynamically determined.
 —The longitudinal phase is random.
 —Time averages of a month or two would show no longitudinal differences, i.e. there would be circumpolar or zonal symmetry.

(b) *Earth completely covered by an ocean of large heat capacity*
 —In its asymptotic state, the surface temperature will be longitudinally uniform, but will have a latitudinal gradient that does not vary seasonally. This gradient drives the baroclinic instability and the index cycle.

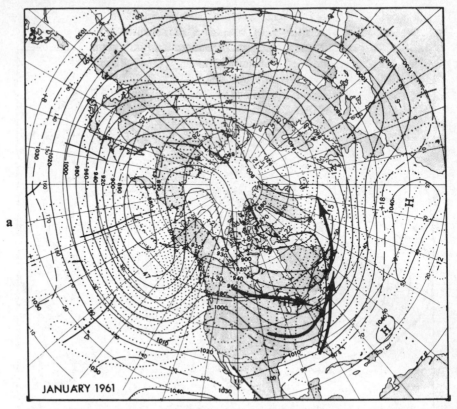

a

JANUARY 1961

Fig. 10.10. Mean 700-mb contours (solid) and height departures from normal (dotted), both in tens of feet. Heavy lines and arrows show prevailing storm tracks over North American region (*a,* after Green, 1961; *b,* Stark, 1962).

—The mobile ocean participates in the poleward heat transport, thus necessitating less intense baroclinic disturbances in the atmosphere.

—The surface temperature adjusts slowly and is capable of relatively small seasonal variation.

—The pole-to-equator temperature gradient in the oceans is established over a long succession of winters, and can drive the summer atmosphere (albeit more weakly) even in the absence of a summertime radiative gradient (cf. Fig. 10. 15).

2. *Ocean - continent distribution*

   (a) *Ocean with large heat capacity and some continents with no heat capacity*

   —The driving available potential energy is no longer symmetric with respect to the poles—but will have alignments influenced by the coasts of the continents (Fig. 10.16).

   —Baroclinic instability will more likely be initiated at some longitudes than at others, in particular along the east coasts.

   —Although the latitude of baroclinic instability is dynamically determined for a uniform lower boundary, east-west continental boundaries can force a latitudinal shift of the belt of maximum cyclogenesis (e.g. Antarctica and the Gulf coast of North America).

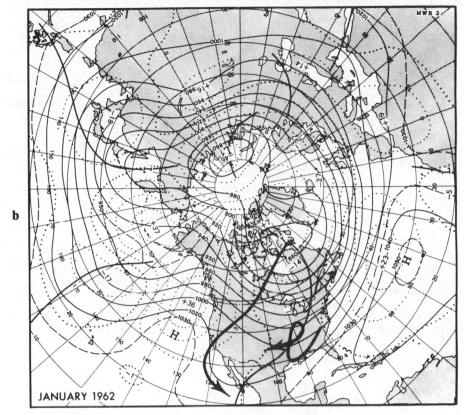

b

JANUARY 1962

Fig.10.10 (*continued*)

—Hence, averaging over many index cycles, say for 2 months or a season, would be expected to show a latitudinal and especially a longitudinal bias.

(b) *Ocean with large heat capacity and continents with small heat capacity*
—Year-to-year differences will not only be due to initial conditions but also a result of the slowly variable heat storage of the oceans.

(c) *Reality*
Added to the previous situation one now allows the continents to store moisture in the soil, which requires heat to evaporate it, and this heat can be transferred by the atmosphere in latent form, to be released in some other geographical location.

—The continents may also retain snow cover, which can alter the radiative reflectivity (or albedo) of the lower continental boundary and also requires heat to melt the snow and to evaporate it.
—Continental soil moisture and snow cover are therefore heat-storage mechanisms, in addition to that of the oceans, which can give rise to geographical and interannual asymmetries of weather and short-term climatic régimes.

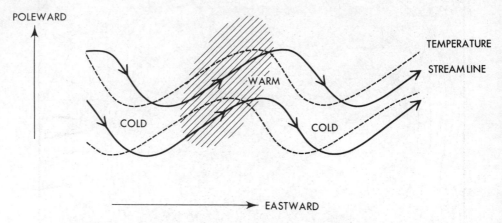

Fig.10.11. A typical baroclinic wave in mid-atmosphere travelling eastward along a mid-latitude circle - it is ultimately connected with extratropical cyclones at the earth's surface. The wavelength is 45 to 75° longitude. Hatched area shows typical location of precipitation. The fact that the temperature wave lags westward behind the streamline wave means that cold air is being transported equatorward and warm air poleward. Hence the zonally asymmetric eddies are responsible for a systematic poleward heat transfer.

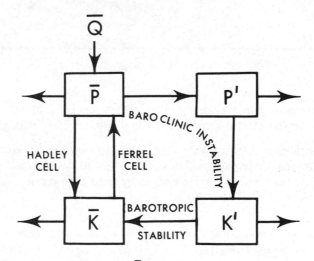

Fig.10.12. Schematic energy balance. $\bar{Q}$ is the external heating source of zonal mean available potential energy ($\bar{P}$), P' is the eddy available potential energy, $\bar{K}$ and K' are the zonal mean and eddy kinetic energies respectively. The unmarked arrows denote small-scale sinks of energy.

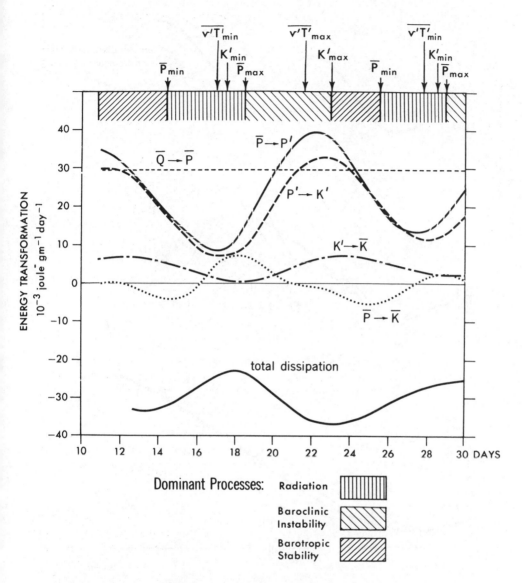

Fig.10.13. The time variation of contributing atmospheric energy sources, sinks, conversions and transformations during a typical life cycle of an extratropical cyclone (after Smagorinsky, 1963). A more-or-less constant radiative heat source over a 2-week period gives rise to cyclic variations in the energy exchanges and the energy components themselves. Note that $\overline{Q}$ is balanced by frictional dissipation when averaged over a complete life cycle of about 11 days.

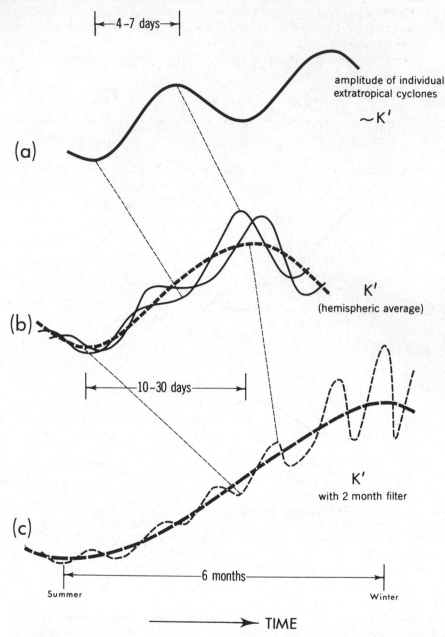

Fig.10.14. The schematic time variation of eddy kinetic energy (K′) in three of its primary modes:

(a) An individual extratropical cyclone of less-than-continental dimensions growing exponentially from a nascent disturbance to a finite size and then occluding and losing its energy to $\overline{K}$ (cf. Fig.10.13).

(b) An index cycle (dashed curve) consisting of several typical individual extratropical cyclones in different geographic regions. The minimum in K′ tends to coincide with a maximum in $\overline{K}$ ("high index") and vice versa ("low index") (cf. Fig. 10.13).

(c) A running average of index cycles over a season. This will differ somewhat from year to year (cf. Fig.10.15).

—Furthermore, the high relativity of the snow cover diminishes the radiative warming of the earth's surface and regionally leads to milder summers - a positive feedback mechanism.

—One must also mention the kinematic effects of the great mountain masses. Although the mountains do not change over the time scales we are discussing here, the disturbances and biases they create depend on the shape and intensity of the circumpolar currents.

—Hence, since the continents, oceans and mountains differ between the Northern and Southern Hemispheres, we should expect different regional climatic régimes and different year-to-year variations in the two hemispheres. But then again, since the two hemispheres can communicate, there may be significant coupling between them, as has occasionally been suggested.

In summary,

—There should be changes in effective continentality (or monsoonal forcing) from year to year because of the slowly variable heat-storage characteristics of the non-uniform lower boundary.

—These surface variations clearly are the result of the atmosphere itself - soil moisture, snow and especially the establishment of the sea-surface temperature distribution.

—The year-to-year climatic differences, averaged over a month or season, could be in amplitude changes (such as was mainly the case of the Western Hemisphere in 1977) or in small longitudinal phase shifts of the quasi-stationary temperature and precipitation régimes. In either case, significant local year-to-year anomalies could be expected.

—The anomalies of the monthly averaged conditions imply anomalies in the shorter-term weather events, such as the location of storm tracks.

C. CLASSIFICATION OF WAVE MODES

On theoretical grounds, it is possible to classify the wave modes that are self-excited (i.e. pure baroclinic instability) or forced; and then further according to their horizontal scale, their vertical thermal structure and whether they are freely propagating (i.e. transient) or geographically fixed (i.e. quasi-stationary).

Stone (1977) has collected these characteristics in a table (Fig. 10.17) and also has shown, from a large number of observational studies, their typical relative contribution to the mean to eddy potential energy conversion ($\overline{P} \rightarrow P'$) and the eddy kinetic energy (K'). First of all, we note that the synoptic scale transient eddies (1) have random longitudinal phase with periods of about a week. These are filtered out by averaging over, say 2 months. Hence, bi-monthly average anomalies from year to year may purely be the result of small phase shifts of the orographically-induced modes, that is (in Stone's table) the

2. planetary scale transient eddies,
3. non-baroclinic stationary eddies,
4. baroclinic stationary eddies.

Together these three classes of wave or eddy modes account for over half of the kinetic energy and of the $\overline{P} \rightarrow P'$ conversion. In summary, the planetary scale

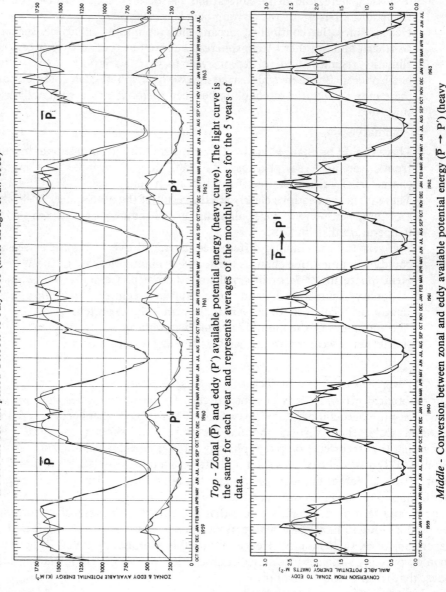

Fig.10.15 Variation of 10-day averages of the elements of the energy cycle for the layer 850-500 mb for the period October to July 1963 (after Kruger *et al.* 1965)

Top - Zonal ($\overline{P}$) and eddy (P') available potential energy (heavy curve). The light curve is the same for each year and represents averages of the monthly values for the 5 years of data.

Middle - Conversion between zonal and eddy available potential energy ($\overline{P} \rightarrow$ P') (heavy curve). The light curve is the same for each year.

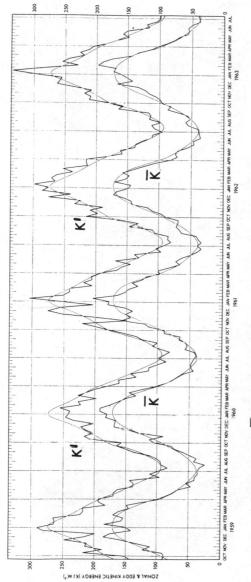

Bottom - Zonal ($\overline{K}$) and eddy (K') kinetic energy (heavy curve). The light curve is the same for each year.

Note that: P' lags $\overline{P}$ by about 5 weeks, the variation of $\overline{P}$ from year to year is not the result of radiation variations, but probably rather the result of anomalies of surface heat storage; $\overline{P}$ is positive in the summer because of long-term heat storage in the oceans even though the solar radiative gradient is virtually non-existent.

January   July

Fig.10.16. Normal sea-level pressure (solid lines) in millibars and temperature in degrees
Fahrenheit (dashed lines) (after Smagorinsky, 1974).
Note that the isotherms are not parallel to latitude circles, but are distorted by the ocean-
continent distribution. A 1-month normal consisting of many years is adequate to eliminate
aliasing, whereas an average over 1 month for a single year may not be adequate.

	EDDY TYPE	LONGITUDINAL WAVE-NUMBER	ENERGETICS*		SOURCE
			K'	$\overline{P} \to P'$	
(1)	Synoptic-Scale Transient Eddies	5-8	40%	35%	baroclinic instability
(2)	Planetary-Scale Transient Eddies	1-3	40%	35%	baroclinic instability initiated by external forcing? *mainly in winter*
(3)	Non-Baroclinic Stationary Eddies (no heat transport)	mainly planetary (1-3)	10%	0%	orographic forcing
(4)	Baroclinic Stationary Eddies (heat transport**)	mainly planetary (1-3)	10%	30%	baroclinic instability in favored locations? *mainly in winter*

*annual mean
**very efficient and very variable

Fig.10.17. Rough estimates of the percentages of the total amount of eddy kinetic energy (K') and of the total conversion of mean to eddy perturbed energy ($\overline{P} \to P'$) supplied by four eddy types in the Northern Hemisphere on an annual basis (after Stone, 1977).

transient eddies (2) and the baroclinic stationary eddies (4) can be altered by apparent changes in continentality due to long-term anomalies in sea-surface temperature, continental snow cover, and continental soil moisture. Even the non-baroclinic orographically-induced stationary eddies (3) can slightly shift in phase due to variations in the intensity of the zonal westerly winds.

We have postulated that fluctuations in the regional continentality are mainly the result of what is happening in the atmosphere itself. The nature of the reaction back upon the atmosphere itself in altering the position and amplitude of the long quasi-stationary modes ((3) and (4)) or in exciting planetary scale transient modes (2) will depend on the specific circumstances. There may be an amplifying positive feedback or there may be an attenuating negative feedback. Since these waves modes are of planetary dimensions, a regional feedback will give rise to a broad longitudinal response by the atmosphere. This in turn may set up further feedbacks, positive or negative, in far-removed regions. This seems to be the reason for extensive longitudinal coupling of the observed anomalies. The testing of this conjecture in specific instances cannot easily be done by waving one's hands or by simple calculation. We shall return to this shortly.

D. INFLUENCE OF LOWER BOUNDARY - SOME SPECIFIC POSSIBILITIES

Are there any observational or theoretical evidences to support some of my speculations? Let us touch on a few.

1. *The Ocean*
    (a) The winter of 1976-77

We have already noted that the extreme winters of 1962-3 and of 1976-7 are quite similar especially in the Western Hemisphere (cf. Fig. 10.9). The extraordinary cold in the eastern United States and the warm dry of the West were mainly associated with a large increase in the amplitude in the quasi-stationary flow. J. Namias, a pioneer in the role of atmosphere-surface inter-actions influencing seasonal and interannual climatic anomalies, has assembled the Northern Pacific Ocean sea-surface temperature records for the months of June 1976 through February 1977 (Namias, 1978). From Fig. 10.18 we see that most striking is the several season persistence of a warm anomaly (with respect to normal) in the normally very cool upwelling waters off the American West Coast. The anomaly in the central and western North Pacific Ocean, on the other hand, was of the same magnitude but cool and larger in scale. The specific role of these striking sea-surface temperature anomalies in this winter's climate, and how the atmosphere itself is responsible for ocean's state, is not specifically known although, as you can imagine, there is a variety of qualitative speculation. One should also mention that in a recent observational study, Namias (1976) showed a strong relationship over many years between the summertime sea-surface temperature anomaly in the North Pacific Ocean and the subsequent sea-level pressure anomaly over the Aleutian area.

    (b) Influence of the Somali Current on the Indian Monsoon

Simulation experiments with numerical general circulation models of the atmosphere (Shukla, 1975) show that a persistent 3°C cold anomaly of the Somali Current in the Western Arabian Sea can give rise to a reduction of the monsoonal rains over India by a factor of 2. Also, it is known that the Somali Current itself is

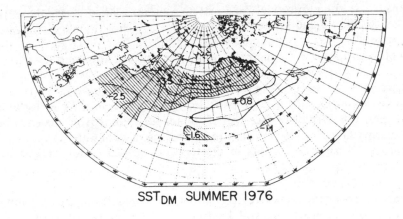

SST$_{DM}$ SUMMER 1976

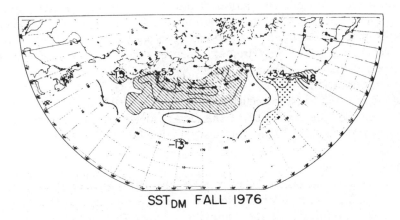

SST$_{DM}$ FALL 1976

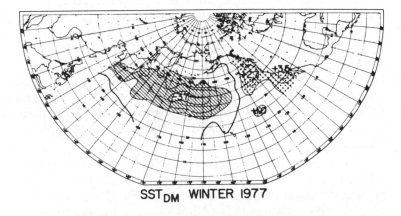

SST$_{DM}$ WINTER 1977

Fig.10.18 Sea-surface temperature anomalies, contours drawn for each °F, with core centres numbered. Hatched areas are in excess of 1°F. *Top* - Summer (June, July, August) 1976; *middle* - Autumn (September, October and November) 1976; *bottom* - Winter (December, January and February) 1976 (after Namias, 1978).

quite sensitive to the monsoonal wind system—a clear case of close interaction between the atmosphere and ocean.

(c) El Niño

As another example, the equatorial ocean currents are known in general to react relatively rapidly to surface wind changes; this is connected with the fact that the undercurrents lie relatively close to the sea surface. The equatorial current feeding the Somali Current is such a case, as is also the situation in the equatorial eastern Pacific. There the normal surface easterly winds (i.e. winds from the east) blowing from western South America result in the upwelling of cool water. Every so often a reduction of the easterlies results in the less cooling—El Niño—and an anchovy catastrophe occurs.

(d) Remote reactions

The late J. Bjerknes (1966) reasoned that large-scale sea-surface temperature anomalies in the eastern equatorial Pacific would have a remote and delayed influence on the mid-latitude circulation of the winter hemisphere. Rowntree (1972) performed several 30-day simulation experiments with such a 3.5°C anomaly and indeed found that the Aleutian low-pressure area shifted eastward and intensified about a week later. In fact, less dramatic changes occurred later on downstream in mid-latitudes to the east. This is an intriguing result, the significance of which may have major proportions.

It is of interest that El Niño occurred in the winter of 1976-7, but not in the winter of 1962-3. Hence, the similarity of the flow and temperature anomalies in the Januaries of 1963 and 1977 may not be wholly for the same reason.

2. *Continental snow*

We will cite only one study. Hahn and Shukla (1976) have found a distinct empirical relationship over a 10-year period between Eurasian snow cover and the monsoonal rainfall over India in the following summer (Fig. 10. 19). As suggested earlier, this could be primarily the result of large increases of reflectivity of the continent; or it could be that the radiative heat normally expended in increasing the continental surface temperature as winter yields to summer, is diverted to melting and evaporating the excessive snow cover thereby reducing the summer monsoonal continentality. Or it could be both.

The long-term climatic interaction of snow cover, particularly its albedo (or reflective) effect, has been postulated by Budyko (1968). His calculations, and others since with very simple climate models, indicate that a sufficient reduction of the solar constant, or a decrease in atmospheric CO_2, could result in a complete glaciation of the earth.

3. *Another intriguing idea*

The devastating persistent summer droughts in the Sahel of just a few years ago, and which broke in 1974, captured the attention of the world. A number of explanations were offered. Some insist it is within the expected natural variability. However, Bryson (1974) considers it part of inexorable and systematic climatic change as a result of dust and particulates. Charney (1975) thinks it may be the result of destablizing feedback resulting from poor agricultural practices altering the reflective character of the underlying crop lands. Very recently, P. J. Lamb (1978) found

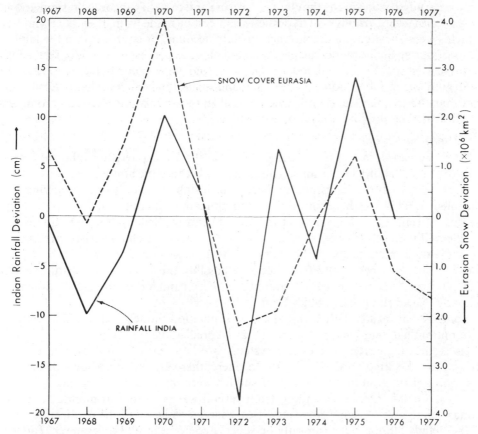

Fig.10.19. Graphs of year-to-year variation of winter snow cover departure over Eurasia south of 52°N, and the corresponding variation of summertime area mean rainfall departure for India (after Hahn and Shukla, 1976 and updated to 1977 by personal communication).

that the 1968-74 Sahclian drought when compared with a 60-year background reference shows that during the July-September rainy season there is a distinct correlation with the latitude of the North Atlantic sea surface temperature maximum. This would place the argument back under *The Ocean* (section D.1).

Since by drought we mean a significant reduction of precipitation where it normally occurs, a drought should also occasionally be expected over the oceans as well. Indeed, during the autumn of 1976, Hawaii suffered a drought: they had one-third the normally expected precipitation.

E.THE MODELLING PROBLEM

We have tried to relate the character and the structure of a large variety of climatic variations over the past several decades. We have also tried to expose a variety of possible explanations, but mainly those that are a consequence of intricacies of the natural climate system itself - the atmosphere, the oceans, the continental surfaces. Inevitably, complex interactions must be invoked, complexities for which intuitive causal lines of argument often fail, even qualitatively. A definitive data base is a necessary augmentation to stimulate conjecture and to verify theoretical simulation.

A precise testing of physical hypotheses can best be made by mathematical models which systematically take the interactions into account, of course within the limitations of our ability to model the participating physical processes. We have seen a few examples where this has already been done and have contributed to positively enlarging our insights, both qualitatively and quantitatively. As scientists, our object must be to understand and, where possible, to use this understanding to make predictions that may be useful to society.

1. *Deterministic limits*

Over the past decade it has become clear that the atmosphere has inherent deterministic predictability limitations. This is mainly because the atmosphere can sustain several types of dynamic instability (baroclinic instability is only one) rendering it a turbulent fluid in which viscous dissipation ultimately balances the radiative energy source. Specifically it appears that individual extra-tropical cyclones are limited in predictability to several weeks. Which means that since the characteristic lifetime of an individual freely propagating transient storm is several days, we can expect at most to account specifically for second-or possibly third-generation disturbances. The phase preferences forced by the continent-ocean and mountain distribution may actually extend the predictability limit.

Some recent results with comprehensive simulation models indicate that certain intermittent but long-lived phenomena may be predictable for longer periods. In this class is the stagnation of weather systems over the eastern mid-latitude oceans known as "blocking". Also in the stratosphere, there are the breakdown of the circumpolar circulation and the onset of sudden warming in certain regions.

Thus, for the interval extending from several weeks to several months, and we hope even to several years, some statistical characteristics might be predictable even if the details cannot. This can only be speculated upon now. For example, for the shorter interval, the position and intensity of storm tracks might be predictable rather than individual storms. In the seasonal range, characteristics of the index cycle and the regional bi-monthly anomalies of precipitation and temperature may be deterministically accessible. From year to year, the seasonal regional anomalies might be also deducible from physical considerations.

2. *Modelling hierarchy for the climatic spectrum*

As climatic time scale increases, one has to take slower-acting physical interactions into account. So far the time scale we have been concerned with here, the ocean below several hundred metres and the slow variations of sea-ice can be ignored. Even the effects of clouds on radiation can be related by simple empirical algorithms (i.e. parameterizations'') deduced from contemporary data. Over much longer periods, encompassing large swings of climatic régime as ice ages, such an empiricism might not be adequate.

These and other considerations suggest that the modelling problem for this time scale of interest is more simple and closer to our already existing modelling capability that for longer climatic periods. Also because we are dealing with relatively short intervals, say several years, we can apply present-day computers to solve a relatively rigorous and complete set of model equations without the simplifications which would be necessary to simulate climatic evolutions over centuries or longer.

IV. Conclusions

The problem of climate and general circulation variability from one month to several years is virtually untouched, observationally and theoretically.

Observationally we need a global surveillance system (probably space based) to document the regional, inter-regional, interhemispheric, interseasonal and interannual structure of the
—continental and oceanic surface temperature and precipitation,
—continental ground hydrology (snow cover and soil moisture),
—sea-ice,
—cloud cover,
—general circulation

Theoretically
—general circulation models seem most appropriate,
—ocean coupling is necessary, at least down to the seasonal thermocline,
—such models should then be used to perform controlled experiments to test the sensitivity of monthly or seasonal mean states to specific boundary conditions and to their interactive feedback mechanisms.

This seems to be the right time to begin to consider this class of problems seriously.

References

Angell, J. K. and J. Korshover (1975) "Estimate of the global change in tropospheric temperature between 1958 and 1973", *Monthly Weather Review,* 103 (11), 1007-12.

Bjerknes, J. (1966) "A possible response of the atmospheric Hadley Circulation to equatorial anomalies of ocean temperature", *Tellus,* 28, 820-9.

Broecker, W.S. (1975) "Climate change: are we on the brink of a pronounced global warming?", *Science,* 189 (4201), 460-3.

Bryson, R.A. (1974) "A perspective on cimatic change", *Science,* 184 (4138), 753-9.

Budyko, M.I. (1968) "On the origin of glacial epochs (in Russian), *Meteorology and Hydrology,* No. 11, 3-12.

Budyko, M.I. and K. Ya Vinnikov (1976) "Global Warming, *Meteorology and Hydrology,* 7, 16-26.

Charney, J.G. (1975) "Dynamics of deserts and drought in the Sahel", *Quarterly Journal of the Royal Meteorological Society,* 101, 193-202.

Damon, P.E. and S. M. Kunen (1976) "Global cooling?", *Science,* 193 (4252), 447-53.

Dansgaard, W., S. J. Johnsen, N. Reeh, N. Gundestrup, H. B. Clausen and C. U. Hammer (1975) "Climatic changes, Norsemen and Modern Man", *Nature,* 255, (5503), 24-28.

Dronia, H. (1974) "Über Temperaturänderungen der Freien Atmosphäre auf der Nordhalbkugel in den letzten 25 Jahren", *Meteor. Rund.* 27, 166-74.

Green, R.A. (1961) "The Weather and Circulation of January 1961". *Monthly Weather Review,* 89 (4), 137-43.

Hahn, D.G. and J. Shukla (1976) "An apparent relationship between Eurasian snow cover and Indian monsoon rainfall", *Journal of the Atmospheric Sciences,* 33 (12), 2461-2.

Harley, W.S. (1978) "Trends and variations of mean temperature in the lower troposphere", *Monthly Weather Review,* 106 (3), 413-16.

Kruger, A.F., J. S.Winston and D. A. Haines (1965) "Computations of atmospheric energy and its transformations for the Northern hemisphere for a recent five-year period", *Monthly Weather Review,* 95 (4), 227-38.

Kukla, G.J., J.K. Angell, J. Korshover, H. Dronia, M. Hoshiai, J. Namias, J. Rodewald, R. Yamamoto and T. Iwashima (1977) "New data on climatic trends", *Nature,* 270 (5638), 573-80.

Lamb, H.H. (1969) "Climatic fluctuations, world survey of climatology", 2, *General Climatology* (Ed. H. Flohn), Elsevier, New York, 173-249.

Lamb, H.H. (1975) "Remarks on the current climatic trend and its perspective", *Proceedings of the WMO/IAMAP Symposium on Long-Term Climatic Fluctuations,* WMO Rep. No. 421, 473-7.

Lamb, P.J. (1978) "Large-scale tropical Atlantic surface circulation patterns associated with subsaharan weather anomalies", *Tellus,* **30,** 240-51.

Namias, J. (1976) "Negative ocean-air feedback systems over the North Pacific in the transition from warm to cold seasons", International Conference on Simulation of Large-Scale Atmospheric Processes, Hamburg, Aug. 30 - Sept. 4, 1976, *Annalen der Meteorologie,* No. 11, 241-6.

Namias, J. (1978) "Multiple causes of the North American abnormal winter 1976-7", *Monthly Weather Review,* **106** (3), 279-295.

O'Connor, J.F. (1963) "The weather and circulation of January 1963", *Monthly Weather Review,* **91** (4), 209-17.

Oort, A.H. (1974) "Year-to-year variations in the energy balance of the Arctic atmosphere", *Journal of Geophysical Research,* **79** (9), 1253-60.

Rowntree, P.R. (1972) "The influence of tropical East Pacific Ocean temperatures on the atmosphere", *Quarterly Journal of the Royal Meteorological Society,* **XCVIII** (416), 290-321.

Shukla, J. (1965) "Effect of Arabian sea-surface temperature anomaly on Indian summer monsoon: A numerical experiment with the GFDL model", *Journal of the Atmospheric Sciences,* **XXXII** (3), 503-11.

Smagorinsky, J. (1963) "General circulation experiments with the primitive equations, I. The Basic experiment", *Monthly Weather Review,* **91** (3), 99-164.

Smagorinsky, J. (1974) "Global atmospheric modeling and the numerical simulation of climate", Weather and Climate Modification (Ed. W.N. Hess), Wiley, 633-86.

Stark, L.P. (1962) "The weather and circulation of January 1962", *Monthly Weather Review,* **90** (4), 167-74.

Starr, V.P. and A.H. Oort (1973) "Five year climatic trend for the Northern Hemisphere," *Nature,* 242 (5396), 310-13.

Stone, P.H. (1977) "Generation of atmospheric eddies", *Investigations of the Synoptic Variability of the Ocean,* Materials of the Joint Soviet-American Theoretical Institute POLYMODE (Yalta, 1976), Academy of Sciences of the Uk.SSR, Sevastopol, 400-21.

Wagner, A.J. (1977) "Weather and circulation of January 1977", *Monthly Weather Review,* **105** (4), 553-60.

Index